P9-DTX-354

Culture
&
Mental Illness

A Client-Centered Approach

Related titles in culture and mental illness

Casebook in Abnormal Psychology: An Integrative Approach
Timothy A. Brown and David H. Barlow
ISBN: 0-534-34247-7

Exploring Psychological Disorders (A CD-ROM for Macintosh and Windows)
Douglas L. Chute and Margaret Bliss
ISBN: 0-534-23179-9 (Macintosh); ISBN: 0-534-26688-6 (Windows)

Meanings of Madness: Readings on Culture and Mental Illness
Richard J. Castillo
ISBN: 0-534-34560-3

Seeing Both Sides: Classic Controversies in Abnormal Psychology
Scott O. Lilienfeld
ISBN: 0-534-25134-X

Related titles in culture

Culture and Psychology
David Matsumoto
ISBN: 0-534-23220-5

Cultural Influences on Research Methods and Statistics
David Matsumoto
ISBN: 0-534-23766-5

People: Psychology from a Cultural Perspective
David Matsumoto
ISBN: 0-534-19338-2

A World of Diversity: Videos with Student Workbook and Facilitator's Guide
David Matsumoto
ISBN: 0-534-23226-4 (two-volume video set)
ISBN: 0-534-23227-2 (student workbook)

Culture
&
Mental Illness

A Client-Centered Approach

Richard J. Castillo
University of Hawaii—West Oahu

Brooks/Cole Publishing Company

I**T**P® *An International Thomson Publishing Company*

Pacific Grove • Albany • Belmont • Bonn • Boston • Cincinnati • Detroit
Johannesburg • London • Madrid • Melbourne • Mexico City • New York • Paris
Singapore • Tokyo • Toronto • Washington

Sponsoring Editor: *Marianne Taflinger*
Marketing Team: *Lauren Harp, Deborah Petit*
Editorial Assistant: *Laura Donahue,*
   Scott Brearton
Production Editor: *Nancy L. Shammas*
Manuscript Editor: *Kay Mikel*

Permissions Editor: *Cathleen S. Collins*
Cover and Interior Design: *Lisa Thompson*
Art Editor: *Kathy Joneson*
Indexer: *Do Mi Stauber*
Typesetting: *Bookends Typesetting*
Printing and Binding: *Edwards Brothers, Inc.*

Copyright © 1997 by Brooks/Cole Publishing Company
A Division of International Thomson Publishing Inc.
I(T)P The ITP logo is a registered trademark under license.

For more information, contact:

BROOKS/COLE PUBLISHING COMPANY
511 Forest Lodge Road
Pacific Grove, CA 93950
USA

International Thomson Publishing Europe
Berkshire House 168-173
High Holborn
London WC1V 7AA
England

Thomas Nelson Australia
102 Dodds Street
South Melbourne, 3205
Victoria, Australia

Nelson Canada
1120 Birchmount Road
Scarborough, Ontario
Canada M1K 5G4

International Thomson Editores
Seneca 53
Col. Polanco
México, D.F., México
C.P. 11560

International Thomson Publishing GmbH
Königswinterer Strasse 418
53227 Bonn
Germany

International Thomson Publishing Asia
221 Henderson Road
#05-10 Henderson Building
Singapore 0315

International Thomson Publishing Japan
Hirakawacho Kyowa Building, 3F
2-2-1 Hirakawacho
Chiyoda-ku, Tokyo 102
Japan

All rights reserved. No part of this work may be reproduced, stored in a retrieval system, or transcribed, in any form or by any means—electronic, mechanical, photocopying, recording, or otherwise—without the prior written permission of the publisher, Brooks/Cole Publishing Company, Pacific Grove, California 93950

Printed in the United States of America

10   9   8   7   6   5   4

Library of Congress Cataloging-in-Publication Data

Castillo, Richard J., [date]
   Culture & mental illness : a client-centered approach / Richard J.
Castillo.
      p. cm.
   Includes bibliographical references and index.
   ISBN 0-534-34558-1 (pbk.)
   1. Cultural psychiatry.   2. Psychology, Pathological.   I. Title.
II. Title: Culture and mental illness.
RC455.4.E8C38   1996
616.89—DC20
                            96-41263
                               CIP

About the Author

Richard J. Castillo is a medical anthropologist specializing in the cross-cultural study of psychopathology and psychotherapy. He received his B.A. *(magna cum laude*, Phi Beta Kappa) in Philosophy (1983) and his M.A. in Asian Religions (1985) from the University of Hawaii—Manoa. He received his M.A. (1989) and Ph.D. (1991) in Medical and Psychiatric Anthropolgy from Harvard University. Dr. Castillo is a Professor of Psychology at the University of Hawaii—West Oahu, and Clinical Professor of Psychiatry at the University of Hawaii School of Medicine.

Dr. Castillo is a Fellow of the American Anthropological Association and a member of the National Institute of Mental Health Group on Culture and Diagnosis who served as cultural advisors on the composition of DSM-IV. His principal research interests are in cultural factors affecting dissociative disorders and the relationship of dissociative symptoms to schizophrenia and other psychotic disorders. His other works include *Meanings of Madness* (1998, Brooks/Cole). He resides in Honolulu, where he enjoys Hawaii's multicultural environment.

Contents

Part I
Introduction & Theoretical Issues   *1*

Chapter One
Why Culture?   *3*
Anthropology and the Study of Mental Illness   5
    Illness and Disease   7
DSM-IV Historical Background   7
    DSM-I: The Biopsychosocial Model   7
    DSM-II: Beginnings of a Paradigm Shift   8
    DSM-III: Disease-Centered Psychiatry   8
    DSM-IV: Beginnings of a Paradigm Shift   10
    Validity   11
Paradigms   12
    Disease-Centered Psychiatry   13
    Paradigm Shifts   16
Phenomenology   16
    Intentionality   17
    Reifications   19
Cultural Meaning Systems   20
    Four Functions of Cultural Meaning Systems   20

Chapter Two

Culture & Clinical Reality

25

Case Study in Depression 25
Clinical Reality 27
    Five Ways Culture Affects Clinical Reality 27
Healing and Curing 31
Four Ways Mental Illness Has Meaning 33
    Symptom as Symptom 33
    Cultural Significance 34
    Personal and Social Meanings 34
    Explanatory Models 35
Evolution of Clinical Reality 36

Chapter Three

Culture and Personality

39

Sociocentrism versus Egocentrism 39
Dominance Hierarchies versus Egalitarianism 40
Modern versus Premodern Meaning Systems 44
    Postmodernism 45
Adolescence and Personality Development 46
A Cross-Cultural Look at Personality Development 49
    Culture and Personality in India 49
    Culture and Personality among the Senoi Temiar 50
    Culture and Personality among the Swat Pukhtun 51
    Culture and Personality in Japan 52
    Culture and Personality in the United States 52

Chapter Four

Cultural Assessment

55

Culture and Emotion 55
    A Cognitive Model of Emotion 56
    Cultural Assessment of Emotions 58
    Amok as Cultural Emotion 60
DSM-IV Outline for Cultural Formulation 62
    Cultural Identity of the Individual 63
    Cultural Explanations of Mental Illness 64
    Cultural and Psychosocial Environment 67

Culture and Clinician-Client Relationship   69
Overall Cultural Assessment   71
Use of Diagnostic Interview Schedules   73
The Meaning of Hearing Voices   74

Chapter Five
Client-Centered Treatment   **77**

Therapeutic Use of Hope   77
Coherence in Healing   78
Symbolic Healing   82
South Asian Shamanism as Symbolic Healing   83
Symbolic Healing of "Spirit Loss" in Nepal   86
Symbolic Healing of Alcoholism among Native Americans   87
Symbolic Healing among Charismatic Christians   87
Effects of Treatment   89
Suggested Clinical Guidelines   90

Part II
Culture & DSM-IV Diagnoses   *93*

Chapter Six
Personality Disorders   *95*

The Personality Disorders   97
Cluster A Personality Disorders   98
Cluster B Personality Disorders   102
Cluster C Personality Disorders   106
Suggested Clinical Guidelines   109

Chapter Seven
Sexual and Gender Identity Disorders   *113*

Culture and Sexual Behavior   114
Male Dominance and Female Sexuality   114
Human Cultural Variations   120
The Paraphilias   124

Exhibitionism   125
Fetishism   127
Frotteurism   128
Pedophilia   128
Sexual Masochism   130
Sexual Sadism   131
Transvestic Fetishism   132
Voyeurism   132
Paraphilia Not Otherwise Specified   133
Gender Identity Disorder   134
Gender Identity and Status   135
The Sexual Dysfunctions   138
Hypoactive Sexual Desire Disorder   138
Sexual Aversion Disorder   140
Female Sexual Arousal Disorder   141
Female Orgasmic Disorder   142
Vaginismus and Dyspareunia   143
Male Erectile Disorder   143
Male Orgasmic Disorder   144
Premature Ejaculation   144
Suggested Clinical Guidelines   145

Chapter Eight

Eating Disorders

149

Anorexia Nervosa   150
Relation to Body Dysmorphic Disorder   150
Bulimia Nervosa   151
Culture and Eating Disorders   151
Nonwestern Anorexia Nervosa   152
Gender Differences   153
Ethnic Differences   153
Suggested Clinical Guidelines   154

Chapter Nine

Substance-Related Disorders

157

Four Major Diagnostic Groups   157
The American Disease Model   158
Genetic Studies   159
Culture and Substance-Related Disorders   161

Personality and Substance-Related Disorders   165
Suggested Clinical Guidelines   168

Chapter Ten
Anxiety Disorders   *171*

Anxiety   174
    Panic Attacks and Agoraphobia   175
    Panic Disorder   176
    Phobias   177
    Generalized Anxiety Disorder   178
    Obsessive-Compulsive Disorder   179
    Posttraumatic Stress Disorder   181
    Acute Stress Disorder   182
Nonwestern Syndromes   183
    Nervios   183
    Susto   184
    Koro   184
    Taijin Kyofusho   185
    Hwa-byung   185
Suggested Clinical Guidelines   186

Chapter Eleven
Somatoform Disorders   *189*

Somatization Disorder   190
Undifferentiated Somatoform Disorder   191
    Neurasthenia in China   191
Conversion Disorder   192
    Hysteria in India   193
Pain Disorder   195
Hypochondriasis   196
Body Dysmorphic Disorder   197
Suggested Clinical Guidelines   198

Chapter Twelve
Mood Disorders   *201*

Mood Episodes   202
    Major Depressive Episode   202
    Manic Episode   208

Mixed Episode   209
Hypomanic Episode   210
Depressive Disorders   211
Major Depressive Disorder   211
Dysthymic Disorder   215
Bipolar Disorders   215
Bipolar I Disorder   215
Bipolar II Disorder   216
Cyclothymic Disorder   216
Suggested Clinical Guidelines   217

Chapter Thirteen
Dissociative Disorders   *219*

Dissociation   219
Trance as Adaptation   219
Trance as Focused Attention   221
The Dissociative Disorders   224
Dissociative Amnesia   224
Dissociative Fugue   224
Dissociative Identity Disorder   225
Depersonalization Disorder   226
Cross-Cultural Differences   226
Dissociative Trance Disorder   228
Dissociative Disorder Not Otherwise Specified   233
Dissociative Hallucinations and Delusions   235
Dissociative Trance Disorder versus
Dissociative Identity Disorder   237
Other Nonwestern Syndromes   237
Suggested Clinical Guidelines   238

Chapter Fourteen
Psychotic Disorders   *241*

Schizophrenia   242
Culture and Psychosis   242
Culture and Delusions   244
Culture and Negative Symptoms   245
Schizophrenia and Dissociation   246
Culture, Course, and Outcome   248

Schizoaffective Disorder   251
    Cross-Cultural Case Study   251
Brief Psychotic and Schizophreniform Disorders   253
    Cross-Cultural Case Studies   253
Delusional Disorder   256
    Cross-Cultural Case Study   256
Shared Psychotic Disorder   256
Suggested Clinical Guidelines   257

Chapter Fifteen
Toward a Client-Centered Paradigm: A Holistic Synthesis   261

Culture-Based Stress and Emotional Trauma   262
    Social Stress for Females   263
    Psychological Trauma   264
Individual Sensitivity to Stress and Emotional Trauma   267
Brain Plasticity and Individual Experience   268
    Culture and the Mind-Brain   268
    Neural Network Plasticity   269
    Tuning the Central Nervous System   270
Boundary Between Mental Health and Mental Illness   272
Factors That Affect Duration of Illness   273
Culture-Based Clinical Realities   275
    Culture-Bound Dissociative Syndromes   275
    Effects of Culture-Based Clinical Realities   276
Culture-Based Treatments   277
    Exorcism as Culture-Based Treatment   278
    Neuroleptics as Culture-Based Treatment   279
Culture-Based Outcomes   280
Summary   280

Glossary   283
References   297
Name Index   325
Subject Index   331

Rigorous biological determinism has long been the cultural fashion in general medical practice. However, a holistic view of pathology and treatment is now becoming more widely accepted. This same trend can be found in the treatment of mental disorders. The traditional biomedical paradigm is being replaced by a more holistic view that includes social and cultural factors in both diagnosis and treatment of mental illness. The focus has shifted from treating the *disease* to treating the *patient*.

Sociocultural forces play a significant role in the etiology, structure, and treatment of mental disorders. Recent advances have made it clear that behavior, both normal and abnormal, is a product of a continuous interaction among biology, individual thought processes, and the sociocultural environment. With the publication of the *Diagnostic and Statistical Manual of Mental Disorders-IV* (DSM-IV) and its emphasis on cultural information, the biomedical paradigm can no longer be recognized as a sufficient explanation for mental illness, nor as an adequate theoretical basis for treatment.

This book presents a client-centered model of assessment and diagnosis based on a holistic paradigm that integrates known biological, psychological, social, and cultural factors. Cross-cultural studies and their implications for the assessment and diagnosis of mental illness provide the basis for understanding this new direction in clinical practice.

This book is intended for advanced undergraduate and graduate level courses in anthropology, psychology, psychiatry, nursing, and social work programs. It can be used as a primary text in courses on culture and mental illness or as a supplementary text in abnormal psychology courses. Written for a global audience, examples and case studies are drawn from a worldwide variety of cultural and ethnic groups.

The text is divided into two parts. Part One consists of five chapters that outline the theoretical issues underlying the psychological, social, and cultural factors in the etiology, structure, and treatment of mental illness. Chapter 1 provides a history of the evolution of thought through the classification system used in the *Diagnostic and Statistical Manual of Mental Disorders* from its inception through the current DSM-IV edition. Chapter 2 focuses on culture and clinical reality, drawing examples from culture-based diagnosis and treatment programs and highlighting the various meanings of mental illness cross-culturally. Chapter 3 addresses culture and personality studies, employing specific examples for comparison and contrast. Chapter 4 explores cultural assessment, including assessment of emotion, assessment of the cultural and psychosocial environment, and the use and limits of diagnostic interview schedules across cultures. The final chapter in Part One, Chapter 5, outlines a client-centered treatment model that takes into account the value of traditional folk healers and the symbolic healing processes used in many cultures.

Part Two reviews the major DSM-IV diagnostic categories from a client-centered perspective, highlighting important cultural factors in assessment and diagnosis. Chapters 6 through 14 each deal with a single diagnosis category—personality disorders, sexual and gender disorders, eating disorders, substance-related disorders, anxiety disorders, somatoform disorders, mood disorders, dissociative disorders, and psychotic disorders. In each chapter, the diagnostic categories are explored with an emphasis on what is universal and what is culture specific with regard to assessment, presenting symptoms, possible treatment strategies, and successful outcomes. Recent cross-cultural research is presented that questions assumptions of western science about the very nature of mental illness and the universality of the mind. Finally, Chapter 15 provides a client-centered model for the assessment and treatment of mental illness that will help clinicians provide the best possible outcome taking into account cultural differences that they may encounter in their clients and between their clients and themselves.

The book also contains a glossary to help the reader understand the new terminology presented here. In addition, to augment this text, I have compiled a companion reader, *Meanings of Madness: Readings on Culture and Mental Illness.*

Acknowledgments

Special thanks go to my mentor at Harvard University, Arthur Kleinman, for his inspiration and guidance. His teachings have led the way toward a new client-centered psychiatry. I am also deeply indebted to my colleagues in the National Institute of Mental Health Group on Culture, Diagnosis, and Care who served as cultural advisers on DSM-IV: Juan E. Mezzich, Arthur Kleinman, Horacio Fabrega, Jr., Delores Parron, Byron J. Good, Gloria Johnson-Powell, Keh-Ming Lin, Spero Manson, Roberto Lewis-Fernández, Carlos A. Gonzalez, Ezra E. H. Griffith, Roland Littlewood, Laurence J. Kirmayer, Mitchell Weiss, Marvin Karno, Janis H. Jenkins, Peter J. Guarnaccia, Dona L. Davis, Gilbert Herdt, Renato D. Alarcon, Edward F. Foulks, Charles C. Hughes, Ronald C. Simons, Ronald M. Wintrob, Joseph Westermeyer, Glorisa Canino, Ian Canino, William Arroyo, Cheryl Ritenbaugh, Catherine Shisslak, Nicolette

Teufel, Tina K. Leonard-Green, Raymond Prince, Armando R. Favazza, Victor R. Adebimpe, Candace Fleming, Atwood Gaines, James Gibbs, David J. Hufford, J. David Kinzie, Francis Lu, Enrique Madrigal, Theresa O'Nell, Wen-Shing Tseng, and William H. Sack. Their extremely valuable work in promoting cultural awareness in the study, diagnosis, and treatment of mental illness has made this book possible.

I am also indebted to my colleagues on the Cultural Psychiatry Task Force in the Department of Psychiatry at the University of Hawaii School of Medicine for their many valuable insights on various aspects of culture and mental illness, including Wen-Shing Tseng, Jon Streltzer, Iqbal Ahmed, Danilo Ponce, Dykes Young, Junji Takeshita, David Bernstein, Alan Buffenstein, Patricia Harrison, Gary Cohen, Steve Chaplin, R. Andrew Schulz-Ross, Barry Carlton, and Leslie Matsukawa.

I am also extremely grateful to the reviewers of this book for their many thoughtful and constructive criticisms on various drafts of the manuscript: Dona Davis, University of South Dakota; Juris G. Draguns, Pennsylvania State University; Edward Foulks, Tulane University; Carlos Gonzalez, Griffin Hospital; Lorraine Gutierrez, University of Michigan, Ann Arbor; Steven Lopez, University of California, Los Angeles; and Richard Watts, East Texas State University.

Finally, I would like to thank the book team at Brooks/Cole for their encouragement, enthusiasm, hard work, and dedication to the project, including senior acquisitions editor Marianne Taflinger, production editor Nancy Shammas, design coordinator Kelly Shoemaker, permissions editor Cat Collins, art editor Kathy Joneson, and freelance copy editor Kay Mikel. It has been a great pleasure to work with such a talented team.

Richard J. Castillo

Culture
&
Mental Illness

A Client-Centered Approach

Part One

Introduction
&
Theoretical Issues

Chapter One

Why Culture?

Mental disorders are easily described but not easily defined. Scientists have come to realize that a mental disorder encompasses a highly complex construction of experience and biology involving many factors, with no clear boundary between mental illness and mental health. The introduction to the *Diagnostic and Statistical Manual of Mental Disorders* (DSM-IV) characterizes mental disorders this way:

> Whatever its original cause, it must currently be considered a manifestation of a behavioral, psychological, or biological dysfunction in the individual. . . . In DSM-IV, there is no assumption that each category of mental disorder is a completely discrete entity with absolute boundaries dividing it from other mental disorders or from no mental disorder. (American Psychiatric Association [APA], 1994, pp. xxi–xxii)

Thus, in DSM-IV, mental disorders are not conceptualized as discrete disease entities.

However, from the 1960s to the mid-1980s, many researchers believed that mental disorders were caused primarily by "chemical imbalances" in the brain stemming from genetic abnormalities. This conception arose primarily because of the limited success obtained from treating mental disorders with psychotropic medications. In this biomedical paradigm, mental disorders were conceptualized as brain diseases, and treatment was aimed at treating the disease. This approach is referred to in this book as **disease-centered psychiatry.**

Presently, however, it has been found that attributing mental disorders primarily to diseases in the brain is too simplistic an explanation to accommodate recent research findings or to serve as a basis for consistently successful treatment. It is now known that the psychotropic medications currently in use treat *symptoms,* not *diseases* (Guttmacher, 1994). An emphasis on treating a disease rather than treating the individual can result in dehumanization of the client in psychiatric practice (Brody, 1995; Fleck, 1995).

Some of the information that has been found to be most significant in spurring a move beyond the boundaries of disease-centered psychiatry has come from cross-cultural studies of mental illness. For example, the finding that in nonindustrial societies the duration of schizophrenia is shorter, the course is more benign, and the outcome is better than in industrialized societies has caused many researchers to reassess their conceptions of schizophrenia (Jablensky & Sartorius, 1988; Jablensky et al., 1992; Jilek & Jilek-Aall, 1970; Karno & Jenkins, 1993; Leff et al., 1992; Rin & Lin, 1962; Sartorius, Jablensky, & Shapiro, 1977; Sartorius et al., 1986; Waxler, 1974, 1979; WHO, 1973, 1979). These cross-cultural findings on schizophrenia are contrary to expectations if the problem is conceptualized as a genetically based, incurable brain disease. The conclusion drawn by researchers who worked on DSM-IV is that culture must play an important role in the duration, course, and outcome of schizophrenia, the extent of which is still unknown. However, the data from cross-cultural studies have been convincing enough for psychiatric anthropologists and other cross-cultural researchers to be involved for the first time in the composition of the DSM (DSM-IV).

The treatment of mental disorders with psychotropic medications on the assumption that this reversed the effects of a genetically based brain disease led to conclusions in assessment and diagnosis that were unwarranted. For example, this disease-centered view of mental illness promoted the conclusion that complete recovery from schizophrenia was unlikely if not impossible. We now know that this is not necessarily true. Complete recoveries from schizophrenia are not unknown in industrialized countries (Angst, 1988; Harding et al., 1987; McGlashan, 1988), but they are significantly more common in nonindustrialized societies. These cross-cultural findings indicate that a complete recovery from schizophrenia is possible, and that schizophrenia needs to be conceptualized in a more complex, holistic fashion.

Thus, the realization has slowly dawned that the etiology, structure, course, and outcome of mental disorders are far more integrated than previously imagined. It is now becoming clear to most researchers that mental disorders need to be defined in a holistic manner that includes the interactions of the sociocultural environment and the effects of diagnosis and treatment on a human brain with plastic (modifiable) neural networks. All of these factors combine and interact to produce an actual illness experience in a given person (Castillo, 1991a, 1994c, 1995; Desjarlais, Eisenberg, Good, & Kleinman, 1995; Fabrega, 1989a, b, 1992, 1993a, b, 1994a, b; Fleck, 1995; Gaines, 1992a, b; Gaw, 1993; Good, 1992; Hinton & Kleinman, 1993; Kleinman, 1986, 1988b, 1992; Kleinman & Good, 1985; Lidz, 1994; Littlewood, 1991; Lu, Lim, & Mezzich, 1995; Marsella, 1989; Mezzich, 1995; Mezzich et al., 1992, 1994; Mezzich, Honda, & Kastrup, 1994; Mezzich, Kleinman, & Fabrega et al., 1996).

The traditional biomedical paradigm in psychiatry is now being expanded to include the *neurobiology of adaptation and learning*. This theoretical expansion includes the effects of neuronal changes in the brain resulting from psychotropic medications and psychotherapy as well as the neurobiological effects of individual and cultural learning.

For example, it is now understood that neuroleptic medications can affect neuronal structures. Neuroleptic medications administered over a long term cause the brain to adapt to the neuroleptics by **upregulation** of the dopamine system. This means that the brain increases the number of dopamine receptors as well as increases the avidity with which receptors seek the dopamine (Guttmacher, 1994). Although blocking dopamine receptors with neuroleptics does reduce psychotic symptoms in a majority of people, leading to short-term improvement, over the long term, an upregulated dopamine system has the potential of escalating and prolonging the illness. For example, Birley and Brown (1970) found that individuals with schizophrenia who reduced or discontinued the use of neuroleptics were more likely to relapse without the involvement of stressful life events than those who had taken no neuroleptics for at least 12 months. In addition, upregulated dopamine receptors in the motor cortex caused by prolonged neuroleptic dopamine blockage cause various kinds of movement disorders such as *tardive dyskinesia*, characterized by abnormal, involuntary movements. These movement disorders can be viewed by the client as well as by untrained observers as part of the disease. The effects of treatment can become part of the illness experience of the client as well as affect the course of the disease and the structure of the brain (APA, 1994).

It has also been discovered that individual learning and memory storage change the neuronal structure of the brain (Kandel & Hawkins, 1992). Because culture determines many aspects of learning, **cultural learning** also has a biological basis in the brain and, therefore, in mental disorders. Thus, it is possible to conceptualize a biological basis for cultural differences in mental disorders.

The likelihood of culture-based differences in the brain argues for an essentially anthropological viewpoint of mental illness, utilizing anthropology's deliberately holistic perspective and methodology, combining neurobiological, psychological, social, and cultural theories and data. This book specifically attempts to embrace a cross-cultural, client-centered approach to assessment and diagnosis. In **client-centered psychiatry,** rather than diagnosis and treatment of a *disease*, diagnosis and treatment are centered around a *client's* thoughts, emotions, social context, and cultural identity.

Anthropology and the Study of Mental Illness

Anthropologists have been interested in mental illness since the early days of the discipline (Marsella, 1993). However, anthropology had little direct impact on psychiatric theory until the 1980s, due to the widely held assumption of the **psychic unity of humankind.** That is, it was assumed that all people have the same basic brain structure and, therefore, universally have the same basic mental processes. Even if all people do not think the same thoughts, it was assumed that they think in the same basic way.

However, recent findings in the neurobiology of learning, memory, and cognition clearly indicate that this is not true. For example, the way males and females think is different, probably because of the influence of sex hormones on the brain during fetal development (Gur et al., 1995; Kimura, 1992). Also, there are clear findings on the neurobiological differences of learning and memory on the cellular and molecular levels of the brain, constituting to a great extent the biological basis of individuality of consciousness (Kandel & Hawkins, 1992). It follows that the same neurobiological processes operating in learning to create individual differences in the psychobiology of the brain and mind also operate at the collective level to create biological differences in the brain across cultures. Thus, the psychic unity of humankind can no longer be assumed on the basis of biological sameness. This has profound implications for the study of mental disorders.

In the disease-centered paradigm, because of the assumption that the normal brain is the same in structure and functions in all people, any differences in brain structure or functioning could be assumed to represent brain disease. Until the discovery of neuronal adaptability in the brain, there was little need to include brain plasticity in conceptions of mental illness. However, we now know that neural structures in the brain are altered in adaptations to emotional stress and trauma, medications, psychotherapy, personal experience, and cultural learning. All of these can affect the neural networks of the brain and consequently the etiology, structure, and outcome of mental disorders.

The assumption of the psychic unity of humankind was made, sometimes even in anthropology, up until the late 1970s. The cognitive revolution of the 1970s in the behavioral sciences changed that assumption. The discovery was made that learned **cognitive schemas** of an individual actually construct his or her subjective experience of the world (Neisser, 1976). Cognitive schemas are learned structures of cognition used by an individual to make sense of and construct, to some extent, his or her experience of the world. Furthermore, the subjective construction of experience can be dramatically different in the same situation among different individuals. The discovery was also made that cognitive schemas are dependent to a very large extent on cultural learning (D'Andrade, 1984). This meant that **cultural schemas** are formed within the mind-brains of cultural groups. These cultural schemas can cognitively construct a particular behavior as an episode of mental illness, whereas a different set of cultural schemas can cognitively construct a similar behavior as something normal and normative. These differences in cognitive construction result from cultural learning, which is stored in plastic neuronal structures.

Researchers realized that mental patients could cognitively construct an experience of mental illness one way, while the doctor or folk healer could cognitively construct it in a different way, based on their own set of cultural schemas. The patient could experience the illness as one particular kind of problem, while the clinician could diagnose it as something entirely different. This is the distinction made by medical anthropologists between *illness* and *disease*.

Illness and Disease

Psychiatrist and anthropologist Arthur Kleinman introduced the distinction between illness and disease. The term **illness** refers to the subjective experience of the patient. It is the subjective experience of being sick, including the experience of symptoms, suffering, help seeking, side effects of treatment, social stigma, explanations of causes, diagnosis, prognosis, as well as personal consequences in family life and occupation (Kleinman, 1988a).

In contrast, the term **disease** refers to the diagnosis of the doctor or folk healer. It is the clinician's definition of the patient's problem, always taken from the paradigm of disease in which the clinician was trained. For example, a disease-centered psychiatrist is trained to diagnose brain diseases, a psychoanalyst is trained to diagnose psychodynamic problems, and a nonwestern folk healer might be trained to diagnose spirit possession or sorcery. In each case, the clinician's diagnosis is the "disease."

In psychiatric anthropology there is no assumption that only disease-centered psychiatrists can diagnose "real diseases." In psychiatric anthropology, the clinician's diagnosis as well as the patient's personal illness experience are cognitive constructions based on cultural schemas.

DSM-IV Historical Background

The modern study of mental illness is not culture-free. The scientific study of mental illness is a product of a particular culture-based intellectual tradition. This can be seen by examining the cultural evolution of psychiatry in the United States. This cultural evolution is readily discernible in definitions of mental disorders in the official manuals of the American Psychiatric Association (APA, 1952, 1968, 1980, 1987, 1994).

DSM-IV is the fourth edition of the APA's official manual, the *Diagnostic and Statistical Manual of Mental Disorders* (1994). The original reason for developing a nomenclature for mental disorders was the need to collect statistical information for census purposes. The early systems of classification developed in the late 19th and early 20th centuries had the compilation of census data on people with mental illness as their primary aim. A broader nomenclature was developed by the U.S. Army and Veterans Administration during and after World War II for U.S. servicemen and veterans. Subsequently, the World Health Organization (WHO) published the sixth edition of the *International Classification of Diseases (ICD-6)* (WHO, 1948), that included a section on mental disorders heavily influenced by the Veterans Administration nomenclature. ICD-6 included 26 categories of mental illness.

DSM-I: The Biopsychosocial Model

The American Psychiatric Association developed a variant of ICD-6 that was published in 1952. This was DSM-I, the first official manual designed with clinical uses in mind, although its historical background as a statistical manual was evident. DSM-I was based largely on Adolf Meyer's **biopsychosocial paradigm** of mental illness. The text used the term *reaction* throughout, reflecting the dominant view at the time that mental disorders were reactions of the personality to biological, psychological, and social factors. Thus, the classification system in DSM-I was *etiological* in structure rather than *descriptive*. That is, diagnostic categories were generally defined based on the assumed causes of the disorders rather than on their symptoms.

The basic assumptions of the biopsychosocial paradigm have been summarized by Mitchell Wilson (1993):

> 1) that the boundary between the mentally well and the mentally ill is fluid because normal persons can become ill if exposed to severe-enough trauma, 2) that mental illness is conceived along a continuum of severity—from neurosis to borderline conditions to psychosis, 3) that the untoward mixture of noxious environment and psychic conflict causes mental illness, and 4) that the mechanisms by which mental illness emerges in the individual are psychologically mediated (known as the principle of psychogenesis). (p. 400)

In the biopsychosocial paradigm of DSM-I, mental disorders were not discrete but were seen as the same general psychopathological process manifested along a *quantitative spectrum* from mild to severe. Treatment based on this paradigm was psychodynamic in nature rather than biomedical. Therapy was designed to understand and undo the *psychogenic causes* of the disorders rather than to treat symptoms directly through the use of medications or other biomedical treatment.

DSM-II: Beginnings of a Paradigm Shift

DSM-II, published in 1968, was very similar to DSM-I but eliminated the term *reaction*. This was the result of a shift in emphasis from psychological and social etiological factors to the biomedical paradigm that occurred after the introduction of lithium and neuroleptic medications during the 1950s and 1960s. Biologically oriented psychiatrists were advocating a move toward the disease model, and the paradigm shift to disease-centered psychiatry that occurred in the 1970s is first signaled in the changes in DSM-II.

DSM-III: Disease-Centered Psychiatry

DSM-III, published in 1980, was completely different from its predecessors and represented the culmination of a paradigm shift in psychiatry to the disease-centered perspective. DSM-III instituted a descriptive approach to the classification of mental disorders rather than the etiological approach presented in DSM-I and DSM-II. By 1980 the assumption that mental disorders were based in brain diseases had become the dominant paradigm in modern psychiatry. Indeed, according to Robert Spitzer, chairman of the DSM-III Task Force, DSM-III was intended to be a "defense of the medical model as applied to psychiatric problems" (Wilson, 1993). With acceptance of the disease-centered perspective, the earlier etiological classification system found in DSM-I and DSM-II, which was based on a psychodynamic paradigm that included psychological and social factors, was largely abandoned (Fleck, 1995).

In the disease-centered paradigm there was no assumption of brain plasticity that could be implicated in brain abnormalities resulting from psychological trauma or other forms of adaptation to the environment. There was also no assumption that psychological treatment could affect the structure of the brain. Therefore, training in psychiatry during the 1970s and early 1980s was almost exclusively centered around the use of psychotropic medications and electroconvulsive therapy as the primary treatments.

Because the brain was viewed as essentially static with any brain abnormality considered a disease, it was believed necessary to discover the precise brain pathology assumed to underlie each separate disorder. Therefore each disorder had to be accurately and narrowly defined so researchers could study the brain physiology and anatomy of afflicted persons to uncover the disease responsible for the disorder and, in turn, help define proper biomedical treatment. However, the first step in this process was accurate classification of mental disorders. In DSM-III it was decided that disorders should be classified by descriptive patterns of symptoms rather than by etiology. DSM-III was the first attempt to classify mental disorders along these lines.

In contrast, the client-centered approach presented in this book tends to view mental disorders as psychobiological adaptations to emotional stress and trauma rather than as brain diseases. In this view, mental disorders occur in a brain that is adaptable and plastic in its structure and mental processes. Thus, brain abnormalities can result from the way in which the brain is habitually used or from emotional trauma (Chapter 15).

Reliability

The emphasis in the composition of DSM-III was on **reliability**. Reliability refers to the ability of separate clinicians or researchers to consistently diagnose the same disorder after observing the same pattern of symptoms in patients. If clinicians and researchers can use the same diagnostic instrument, observe similar patients, and arrive at similar diagnoses, then the diagnostic instrument is said to be *reliable*. Because the underlying goal of DSM-III was to provide accurate classifications of mental disorders for laboratory researchers looking for discrete brain diseases, mental illness in DSM-III was divided into hundreds of separate disorders, each with its own descriptive pattern of symptoms.

However, in the late 1970s there was no existing proof that each of the hundreds of disorders defined in DSM-III was based in a separate brain disease. It was simply assumed in the disease-centered paradigm that each of the disorders could first be defined along descriptive parameters (Fabrega, 1994a). The classification system came first. Then laboratory research could provide the empirical evidence to conclusively define the precise brain diseases involved.

The disease-centered paradigm in DSM-III was continued in DSM-III-R. DSM-III-R, published in 1987, was a minor revision of DSM-III designed to eliminate inconsistencies in the diagnostic system and to further clarify diagnostic criteria. In DSM-III-R, the same basic classification system was retained from DSM-III, along with the same disease-centered paradigm.

DSM-IV: Beginnings of a Paradigm Shift

DSM-IV, published in 1994, is analogous to DSM-II in that it retains the disease-centered paradigm of its predecessor but shows enough change in underlying theory to signal a future paradigm shift.

Among the reasons for change in underlying theory is that after thousands of studies and many millions of dollars spent on research, the laboratory confirmation of specific brain diseases as the underlying causes of the hundreds of mental disorders in DSM-IV has not arrived as expected. Of course, numerous brain abnormalities have been found to be correlated with various mental disorders, but none of these have been confirmed as *causing* the mental disorders.

Because we now know of the plasticity of the brain, abnormalities that have been discovered could just as easily be the *effects* of mental disorders as the *causes*. As a result, this statement is included in DSM-IV in almost all of the major psychiatric categories, under the heading of *associated laboratory findings*: "No laboratory findings that are diagnostic of [specific disorder] have been identified." This is true even of the major disorders such as schizophrenia and major depression that had been widely publicized as genetically based brain diseases.

In the case of schizophrenia, laboratory findings have found abnormalities in brain anatomy and biochemistry in some individuals with schizophrenia. These abnormalities include enlargement of the ventricular system and indications of excessive activity in the dopamine system. However, no specific brain disease has been found to be the cause of these abnormalities or of schizophrenic symptoms (Chua & McKenna, 1995). For example, it is possible to have enlarged ventricles without schizophrenic symptoms and to have schizophrenic symptoms without enlarged ventricles. Many people with schizophrenia do not have enlarged ventricles, and this abnormality is not required for the manifestation of schizophrenic symptoms. Also, this abnormality is modest, and there is a large overlap with the normal population. Moreover, no brain abnormality is necessary for making a diagnosis of schizophrenia. A diagnosis of schizophrenia in DSM-IV is made based on the presence of purely psychological symptoms.

Similarly, in the case of major depression, studies have found abnormalities in neurotransmitters associated with depression, but the relationships involve several neurotransmitters in complex interactions that are not yet fully understood. As a result, researchers now generally agree that no single neurotransmitter system is involved in a specific and isolated manner with major depression. And again, these abnormalities could be the effects of depression and not the cause. As DSM-IV states, "It appears that the same laboratory abnormalities are associated with a Major Depressive Episode regardless of whether the episode is part of a Major Depressive, Bipolar I, or Bipolar II Disorder" (APA, 1994, pp. 323–324). In other words, the same alterations in biochemistry are associated with major depression, bipolar I (manic-depression), and bipolar II (hypomanic-depression). This is contrary to the notion of discrete mental disorders being based in discrete brain diseases.

Furthermore, DSM-IV goes on to state, "Most laboratory abnormalities are state dependent (i.e., affected by the presence or absence of depressive symptoms), but some findings may precede the onset of the episode or persist after its remission" (APA, 1994, p. 324). Thus, according to DSM-IV, most alterations in brain biochemistry associated with depression are **state dependent,** that is, dependent on the presence or absence of a depressed mood. Because it is well known that brain biochemistry normally alters with changing moods, including a depressed mood (Pardo, Pardo, & Raichle, 1993), alterations in brain biochemistry occurring with depression can hardly be considered the effects of a brain disease. It is a chicken and egg question. Does the alteration in brain biochemistry cause the depressed mood? Or, does the depressed mood cause the alteration in brain biochemistry? Based on current knowledge, there is not justification to conclude that there is an identifiable brain disease. Therefore, as of now, no specific brain disease has been identified to be the cause of major depression.

As discussed in Chapter 15, because of brain plasticity, it is possible that a chronically depressed mood can cause an abnormality in brain biochemistry. The uncertainty caused by the discovery of brain plasticity and adaptation, as well as alterations in brain biochemistry resulting from changes in mood, have prompted many researchers to look beyond biology for answers to the question: What is a mental disorder? The expansion of DSM-IV to include social and cultural factors is a manifestation of this expanded search on the part of scientists.

If, indeed, DSM-IV is analogous to DSM-II in signaling the beginning of a paradigm shift, then the future DSM-V should be analogous to DSM-III in establishing a new paradigm within the official diagnostic system. The paradigm that will be at the basis of DSM-V is still unclear at this point, but the postmodernism that has swept through the social sciences in recent years is likely to influence any new paradigm in the study of mental illness. That influence is most likely to come from psychiatric anthropology. Although anthropological studies and theory had only a minor impact on the composition of DSM-IV (APA, 1994), it was enough to signal a change in direction from disease-centered psychiatry to a client-centered approach. As this book testifies, that influence is likely to increase in the future.

Validity

In contrast to the disease-centered paradigm of psychopathology, exemplified by DSM-III, with its great emphasis on reliability, the study of mental illness within psychiatric anthropology has been concerned primarily with the **validity** of categories. Whereas reliability refers to consistency of diagnoses, validity refers to the reality of the diagnostic categories themselves. In other words, is the diagnostic category (for example, schizophrenia) a real entity independent of our diagnosis, and is the diagnostic category an appropriate means of naming that entity?

Neurasthenia, a diagnostic category referring to "tired nerves" and including symptoms of fatigue, anxiety, and various somatic complaints, originated in the United States but is no longer part of the DSM classification system. Yet neurasthenia is a very common diagnosis in China (Kleinman 1986, 1988a, b). The question of whether individuals in China really have neurasthenia is a question of validity. Is neurasthenia a valid diagnosis? It may be reliably diagnosed by all of the clinicians in China, but that in itself does not make the diagnosis valid. Likewise, schizophrenia can be reliably diagnosed using DSM-IV diagnostic criteria, but is the category itself a valid one? The answer to that question depends to a great extent on the paradigm held by the person doing the asking.

Paradigms

Psychiatric anthropology, like all of the social sciences, has been greatly influenced by the work of Thomas Kuhn. Kuhn's book, *The Structure of Scientific Revolutions* (1970), describes how paradigms control scientific research. **Paradigms** are the highest, most general level in a hierarchy of scientific intellectual structures. A paradigm is a generally accepted view of the nature of a scientific discipline; the paradigm defines the discipline in question and sets limits on inquiry. All researchers within a discipline with an accepted paradigm assume that the paradigm is an accurate description of the field of study, and they do not question its basic premises. They seek only to refine problems and answer unanswered questions. These activities are called **normal science** (Kuhn, 1970).

A paradigm not only defines what kinds of things a scientific discipline contains, but it also defines what kinds of things it does not contain. For example, in the Middle Ages the discipline of astronomy contained a universe with Earth in the center, and the Sun, planets, and stars revolving around Earth. It did not contain Earth revolving around the Sun. Therefore, all astronomical observations of that time were attempts to accurately track the movements of the Sun and planets around Earth.

A paradigm provides the foundation and limits for the practice of a scientific discipline. Any science that is working within a paradigm is a normal science. The paradigm itself defines what problems are relevant, what methods can be used, what counts as the solution of a problem, and what problems can be assumed to have solutions. These are the only problems that the scientific community working within a paradigm will admit as being scientific within their discipline. In a geocentric paradigm, the question of how long it takes Earth to go around the Sun would never be asked. It would be considered an inappropriate and unscientific question if it was even considered.

The formal study of a particular paradigm is what prepares a person for membership in a scientific community. That person learns the rules of the paradigm and also what constitutes deviance. From within the boundaries of the paradigm, any deviance is thought to be caused by ignorance (incompetence), moral depravity, or mental illness.

Disease-Centered Psychiatry

Disease-centered psychiatry is one example of a paradigm. In this paradigm, mental disorders were thought to be caused primarily by specific brain diseases. Nancy Andreasen summarized the paradigm of disease-centered psychiatry when this perspective was at the height of its influence in her book *The Broken Brain: The Biological Revolution in Psychiatry* (1984):

> *The major psychiatric illnesses are diseases.* They should be considered medical illnesses just as diabetes, heart disease, and cancer are. . . . *These diseases are caused principally by biological factors, and most of these factors reside in the brain.* . . . *As a scientific discipline, psychiatry seeks to identify the biological factors that cause mental illness.* This model assumes that each different type of illness has a different specific cause. . . . The *treatment of these diseases emphasizes the use of "somatic therapies".* . . . The somatic therapies used most frequently are medications and electroconvulsive therapy (ECT). Because these diseases are considered to be biological in origin, the therapy is seen as correcting an underlying biological imbalance. (pp. 29–31, emphasis in original)

The paradigm of disease-centered psychiatry outlined above proclaimed itself as *"a scientific discipline"* that *"seeks to identify the biological factors that cause mental illness."* As such, mental disorders were conceptualized as specific biological diseases in the brain with the same ontological status as diabetes or cancer. According to this paradigm, these diseases should be the same in all societies, regardless of cultural differences.

Within a paradigm, in descending order are lower level intellectual structures called **models, theories,** and **hypotheses.** Models are general theories that explain a large part of the field of inquiry within the scientific discipline. Theories are more specific explanations for particular unanswered problems. Hypotheses are the lowest level, the most specific testable explanations for an unanswered problem. Within an established paradigm, all the lower levels must be logically consistent with the higher levels. Therefore, the paradigm controls what questions will be asked, what methods will be used, and what counts as an acceptable answer. Box 1.1 gives an example of a hierarchy of scientific intellectual structures.

Anomalies

In normal science the goal is to add to the scope and the precision with which the paradigm can be applied. No one doing normal science is trying to overthrow or undermine the paradigm. No one is looking for anything outside the

---

Box 1.1

Hierarchy of Scientific Intellectual Structures

1. *Paradigm*: Disease-Centered Psychiatry (mental disorders are caused by specific brain diseases)
2. *Model*: Psychotic Disorders (disorders caused by specific chemical imbalances)—with complementary models
3. *Theory*: Schizophrenia (caused by excess activity in dopamine system)
4. *Hypothesis*: (schizophrenia is the same disease in all societies)—testable

---

paradigm (new phenomena or concepts). However, in the course of the routine practice of normal science, new and completely unexpected events or data emerge from the work in completely accidental ways. The researchers will be expecting one thing, based on the paradigm, and something else happens that cannot be explained according to the existing theory, model, or paradigm. This is called an **anomaly.**

An anomaly is a deviation from the usual or normal—something that is not supposed to happen. An example of an anomaly is the discovery that individuals in nonindustrialized societies generally have a shorter, more benign course and a better outcome for schizophrenia than individuals in industrialized societies. According to the paradigm of disease-centered psychiatry, schizophrenia is seen as an incurable brain disease so this should not happen. Moreover, in wealthy industrialized societies where patients have access to the greatest number of and most sophisticated health care facilities and treatments, clients should have the best outcome for their mental disorders; yet this is not the case. The discovery of this fact was unexpected and was not predicted by the disease-centered paradigm. The existence of this finding, which has been replicated several times, is an anomaly. Similarly, the repeated inability to identify a specific brain disease as the cause of schizophrenia is also a serious anomaly.

However, discovery begins with the awareness of anomalies and continues with their exploration. Anomalies have to be accommodated in the existing paradigm or the paradigm itself is threatened. However, paradigms are very resilient and not easily replaced. A paradigm can usually be adjusted to accommodate new knowledge. Alternatively, new research methods may replace old methods in response to anomalies. Similarly, anomalies may open new areas of research outside of the discipline in which they were discovered. Box 1.2 provides a summary of the steps in accommodation of anomalies.

Novelty emerges only with difficulty. There is tremendous inertia built up within a paradigm, especially within one that has been successful in the past. Therefore, even an awareness of an anomaly can take time. Expectations defined by the paradigm form scientific schemas that control cognition so that researchers are much more likely to see what they expect to see. Thus, an anomaly is sometimes difficult to recognize.

When an anomaly is recognized, its accommodation within the paradigm requires conceptual changes that can threaten established positions; there is

---

| **Box 1.2** |

Steps in Accommodation of Anomalies

1. Awareness of anomaly
2. Observational and conceptual recognition
3. Consequent change in paradigm categories or methods (often resistance)
4. Begin new discipline (if necessary)

---

always considerable resistance to change within a paradigm. As a result, science can become increasingly rigid. However, paradigms are necessary and good for science because anomalies can appear only against the background of a paradigm.

Paradigm Crisis

When anomalies last a long time and penetrate deeply into a paradigm, the scientific discipline affected by the anomaly can be said to be in a state of **paradigm crisis.** When an anomaly is serious and cannot be resolved or somehow accommodated within the existing paradigm, it, in effect, demands the large-scale alteration of the paradigm and major shifts in the problems and methods of normal science.

Science is always trying to bring theory and observed facts into closer agreement as validation of accepted theory. Of course, normal scientists are trying to validate theory and the existing paradigm. The object is to solve a problem, the solving of which is essential to the validity of the paradigm. One or two failures to solve such an essential problem only discredits the scientists involved and not the paradigm. However, repeated failure, time after time, by the best scientists in a field demands alteration in the paradigm.

The only time a paradigm is significantly altered is after a crisis in normal science. A crisis occurs when a problem that was considered to be all but solved, like pinning down schizophrenia as a specific brain disease, turns out not to be solved. At this point, more and more attention and energy are devoted to the problem, and the most eminent scientists in the field become involved in trying to resolve it. However, when the problem still is not solved—and it does not look as if it will be solved anytime soon—paradigm crisis ensues. At this point, formerly standard methods and expectations are called into question, and researchers begin looking outside the paradigm for answers.

This is a transition from normal science to what Kuhn calls **extraordinary science.** Psychiatry went through a period of extraordinary science during the paradigm shift that occurred between DSM-II (APA, 1968) and DSM-III (APA, 1980). It appears that psychiatry has now entered another period of extraordinary science. The period of extraordinary science is an exciting time for scientists because of the possibility of applying new ideas and methods to the most difficult problems in the discipline.

However, even during a period of extraordinary science, scientists still want to have an operating paradigm. Even if the existing paradigm needs to change, it will not simply be abandoned. Researchers will maintain their faith in the parts of the existing paradigm that still work and still provide reasonable answers. They will cautiously move beyond that to address problems that could not be solved within the boundaries of the old paradigm, as is presently occurring in psychiatry.

Paradigm Shifts

A new paradigm is at least a partial reconstruction of a scientific discipline and can include alterations in basic theoretical generalizations and methods of research. A great overlap will usually exist in the problems that can be solved between new and old paradigms, but the means of solution to problems can be very different. When the transition is complete, the field will exhibit changes in theoretical construction, in methods, and sometimes even in goals, as illustrated by the paradigm shift that occurred in psychiatry between the publication of DSM-II and DSM-III. DSM-II heralded the beginning of a **paradigm shift** toward the disease-centered paradigm. With the publication of DSM-III, the shift was complete. Psychiatry had redefined itself. Rather than the biopsychosocial paradigm that preceded it, the disease-centered study of mental illness was now almost exclusively a biological science, akin to neurology. Its methods of research were now almost exclusively biological, and its research goals were to discover and successfully treat the specific biological causes of mental disorders.

  The changes in DSM-IV (APA, 1994), especially the introduction of cultural factors, are an expansion beyond the traditional boundaries of disease-centered psychiatry. However, the underlying structure in the diagnostic system has been retained from DSM-III. The cultural information in DSM-IV is, in effect, "tacked on" to the preexisting classification structure based on the disease-centered paradigm. This is due to the inherent conservatism of science and the undesirability of abandoning structures and methods that have proven to be valuable. The classification system in DSM-III was instrumental in allowing researchers to compare data on similar patterns of symptomatology, which was a great advance in the scientific study of mental illness. A major challenge for future researchers will be to move beyond this classification system with its emphasis on reliability and to devise a system that emphasizes greater validity.

Phenomenology

When paradigms change, the disciplines defined by the paradigms also change. All of a sudden, familiar objects in the discipline look different. Of course, the objects themselves have not changed. Only the cognitive schemas representing those objects have changed. Phenomenologists and cognitive psychologists have demonstrated that objects are cognized within cognitive

Figure 1.1
Faces and Vase

schemas. There are no *things-in-themselves* in the construction of cognition. The three figures shown here are well-known multistable phenomena. Figure 1.1 can be seen as a vase or faces. The necker cube in Figure 1.2 can be seen in different positions, and Figure 1.3 can be seen as a flat-topped pyramid or a hallway. The objects themselves remain the same, only the cognitive schemas change, and with them, the experiences of the objects. Thus, natural objects are to a certain extent "in the eye of the beholder."

Intentionality

The German philosopher Edmund Husserl (1962) is generally credited as being the founder of **phenomenology.** Phenomenology is concerned with the study of *phenomena,* that is, the mental construction of cognition out of raw sensory data. A *phenomenon* is an experience of an object by a subject. In phenomenology, it is the *experience* of the object that is the phenomenon, not the object itself. A subject does not know the object itself, only the experience of the object. This is because of what phenomenologists call **intentionality.**

Intentionality is the processing that goes on in the brain between perception and cognition. In phenomenology, *perception* is distinguished from

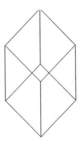

Figure 1.2
Necker Cube

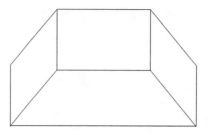

Figure 1.3
Pyramid/Hallway

cognition. Perception is the intake of raw sensory data through sensory mechanisms. Cognition is the end product of brain processing, that is, knowledge of an object. The mental processing of sensory data (intentionality)—turning sensory data into cognition—is the primary object of study of phenomenology.

Phenomenology rejects the naive realism inherent in some empirical methods of the natural sciences, including disease-centered psychiatry, because the empiricism employed in these methods ignores the effects of intentionality. Phenomenologists realize that the subject knows only the experience of the object and not the object itself. Thus, the subject and what is known are not separate. The subject constructs to varying degrees the experience of the object and, therefore, the knowledge of the object.

Phenomenologists conceptualize a phenomenon in what can be called a **noetic pole.** This can be visualized metaphorically as a physical pole with two ends—the *noesis* (cognizer) and the *noema* (cognized). Husserl used the Greek terms *noesis* and *noema* deliberately to avoid using the terms *subject* and *object*. Using the terms *subject* and *object* implies two separate entities. The noetic pole is a single thing, an experience with two ends. Figure 1.4 illustrates this concept.

Because of intentionality, cognition is partially structured by past experience. The cognizer automatically and precognitively *intends* what he or she will experience, based on knowledge that is already stored in long-term memory. The concept of intentionality recognizes the assimilation and influence of values, attitudes, and knowledge that people acquire and carry with them. This collection of knowledge that people carry in the neural networks in their brains structures a continuous use of cognitive schemas in the construction of experiences. These cognitive schemas impose form, content, and meaning onto raw sensory data, turning those data into a cognition—that is, knowledge of the world.

Because the cognitive schemas are largely based on cultural patterns of thinking and personal experience—and, in the case of scientists, on professional training—what a person experiences is a construction based on the factors that influence intentionality. Thus, the **object-in-itself** may remain unknown.

Noesis (cognizer)   Noema (cognized)

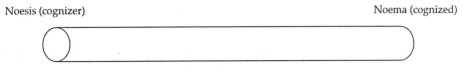

Noetic Pole (an experience)

Figure 1.4
Noetic Pole Concept

Reifications

Because intentionality is an automatic process that requires no effort on the part of the cognizer, the result of the process—the cognition—appears to be completely natural and real. The object invariably appears in cognition as a completely separate entity with its own qualities independent of the cognizer, even though the cognizer has been an active participant in the construction of the experience by shaping the form, content, and meaning of the object cognized. The person grasps the experience as true and real. This can occur even if the object cognized is something wholly created by the person. For example, a hallucination can be experienced as something true, real, and separate from the cognizer.

Furthermore, if a group of people similarly cognize something, even if it is something they have completely created by their own group mode of thinking, they can collectively validate its existence as something true and real by comparing and confirming the similarity of their experiences (reliability). For instance, the reality of tribal gods is regularly confirmed by the consistency and similarity of experiences of the tribespeople. This does not mean that the tribal gods actually exist outside the collective intentionality of the tribespeople (validity). However, the gods are as real as any other object in the natural world for the tribespeople. This collective cognitive process of treating a human-made product as if it was something possessing its own independent reality in nature is called **reification.**

The term *reification* comes from the verb "to reify" (to make real). It occurs when people are collectively projecting onto an object a level of reality the object does not actually possess. Yet the people themselves are not aware that it is their own collective cognitive process that is accomplishing this. They believe in the things they experience. In this way, they are good empiricists and naive realists. The problem is, intentionality is highly variable. As a result of the variability of intentionality arising from brain plasticity, objects unique to certain cultures, such as tribal gods, can be created and experienced as absolutely real. Also, natural objects can be collectively reified into a variety of different experiences in different cultures, each contradicting the other, yet each of them will appear completely true and real to the people in that culture.

Natural Attitude

Societies always possess a wide range of reifications that identify them as a unique cultural group. Collectively they experience the world in their own special way. A society's own unique cultural way of experiencing the world is known in phenomenology as their **natural attitude.** The term *natural attitude* refers to the way someone "naturally" experiences the world. "Naturally" is put in quotes because the way the person is experiencing the world is actually not natural at all, but cultural. Because of brain plasticity, collective intentionality, and the creation of reifications, what appears to be a "natural" experience is actually a cultural construct unique to that group of people. Nevertheless, to the individual the experience is completely "natural." Therefore, the natural attitude is the cognitive style, based in plastic neural networks and cultural learning, that individuals and groups use to create and maintain their own unique experience of the natural world.

Cultural Meaning Systems

A **culture** is the sum total of knowledge passed on from generation to generation within any given society. This body of knowledge includes language, forms of art and expression, religion, social and political structures, economic systems, legal systems, norms of behavior, ideas about illness and healing, and so on. This body of knowledge is always organized in a systematic fashion so that it can be easily passed on and is internally logical. These systems are referred to in anthropology as **cultural meaning systems** (D'Andrade, 1984). Cultural meaning systems are analogous to scientific paradigms, but much larger. A cultural meaning system generally structures cognitive reality for an entire society.

Categories of experience are embedded in cultural meaning systems. These meaning systems vary among societies. Therefore, universal categories of experience may be valid in some instances, but not all, and all those supposedly universal categories are suspect. Cultural anthropologists prefer **emic** (indigenous) categories of experience rather than **etic** (nonindigenous) ones. This is because etic categories (for western scientists) are based on western cultural schemas (for example, DSM categories of mental disorders) and may be inappropriate for use in nonwestern societies.

Four Functions of Cultural Meaning Systems

Four functions of cultural meaning systems occur in all societies, and they can be conceptualized as occurring in a particular sequence. They will be discussed sequentially in the following sections.

Representational Function

Cultural meaning systems enable individuals within a cultural group to represent the world *symbolically* to themselves and to others. Every cultural meaning system must fulfill this function for the persons in a group to operate as a social organization. It allows them to communicate information. Without this ability, individuals would be unable to function as a group. This is the **representational function** of cultural meaning systems.

Nonhuman societies also have systems of communication, but human societies are unique in the extensive elaboration of communication through symbols. The word *symbol* is used here as a technical term coming from **semiotics,** the study of *signs* (Peirce, 1962). Signs are objects that represent something else. In semiotics, there are three kinds of signs: (1) **icons,** (2) **indexes,** and (3) **symbols.**

The first type, an icon, is a sign that actually looks like the thing it represents. An example would be a photograph, a drawing, or a statue of a person. Icons are familiar to anyone who uses a personal computer employing a graphic user interface.

The second type of sign, the index, is slightly different. An index does not look like the thing it represents, but it has a direct connection to it. In many cases, an index may be something that was physically connected to the represented object at some time. An example is a cross for Christians. The cross represents Jesus, because there was a direct physical connection at one time. However, a crucifix (a cross with a crucified Jesus on it) is an icon, something that resembles what it represents. A plain cross is an index, something that has a direct connection to the thing it represents.

The third type of sign, the symbol, is completely different. A symbol has no logical connection whatsoever to the thing it represents. A symbol is an arbitrary sign. It is used simply out of convention, and its use results primarily out of historical accident. Examples of symbols are the words you are reading at this moment. These words have meaning only because you know how to read English. Languages are almost exclusively systems of symbols. Without knowledge of the symbols on this page (words and letters) and the rules for putting them together, all you would cognize are black marks on a white page.

All of the objects that you see on this page are arbitrary signs. Different arbitrary signs could have been used in their place and would have worked just as well as long as you understood the system. For example, the letters of the English alphabet are replaceable by other symbols, which could work just as well as long as everyone knows and agrees on what they mean. The same can be said about words. The word *tree* is used in the English language to represent the object "tree." However, there is no logical connection between the word *tree* and the object that it represents. We could have used the word *automobile* to represent a tree, and it would have worked just as well. The word *automobile* is not required to mean "self moving." That is a meaning attributed to it by a symbolic system called a language, which is actually a historical convention developed by accident and consensus over many centuries.

However, for the person brought up within a particular symbolic system, the information contained in that system seems completely natural, true, and self-evident, when, in fact, most of it is arbitrary. The logic and meaning of symbolic systems are mostly contained within the boundaries of the system. Outside the system, the meanings and associations between objects will be different. What makes this distinction important is the fact that most of the information that exists in human cultures is encoded in symbolic systems. Thus, the information is largely arbitrary in its arrangement and meaning and makes sense only if you know the cultural meaning system.

Constructive Function

As a result of representing the world to themselves and to each other by means of systems of symbols—that is, communicating to each other—people create **cultural entities.** A cultural entity is something created by the social agreement that something counts as that entity. By telling stories and making up explanations of the world, people create the subjective and intersubjective world they inhabit. This is the **constructive function** of cultural meaning systems. Cultural meaning systems construct things—things that would not exist without the meaning system that created them (for example, tribal gods).

Certain behaviors that people go through count as "getting married." If you think about what people do at a wedding ceremony, you will recognize it as a culture-based ritual; that is, it is a scripted pattern of behavior that has the power to construct something. In this ritual there is a set of *constitutive rules,* which if followed have the power to bestow reality. In our culture, the couple stands before an official who says the proper words (symbols). There is the exchange of rings (symbols). And, as if by magic, the two who were a moment ago not married are now married. As long as we all agree to it, we make it real. The couple behave toward each other and society as if they are married. The society behaves toward the couple as if they are married. And by our collective actions and intentionality, we create the "marriage." To create "divorce," we essentially do the same thing—in reverse. As long as we all agree that something counts as a particular object, we can, with our collective intentionality, create the object. Some of the things that cultural meaning systems have created include private property, deviance, prestige, nationality—and even family and racial categories.

Now, let's consider the diagnostic classification system in DSM-IV as an example. This is essentially the same system of classification as that devised for DSM-III. Many of the criteria for DSM-III disorders were derived by committee consensus; that is, a group of experts communicated with each other and collectively decided on what constituted the presence of a particular disorder (Spitzer, 1991). For example, in DSM-IV, the diagnosis of "schizophrenia" requires the presence of schizophrenic symptoms for at least six months' duration. Prior to six months, DSM-IV specifies "schizophreniform disorder" as the proper diagnosis, and prior to one month, "brief psychotic disorder." Why is it six months instead of four months, or twelve months? Is six months somehow based on scientifically significant data? Unfortunately, no. Six months is more than simply a convenient number, but it represents only a committee's best guess at what constitutes the serious mental disorder known as schizophrenia. However, thousands of clinicians all over the world use these diagnostic criteria in a way that can reify the concept into an entity possessing a higher level reality than it actually deserves. Thus, DSM-IV is operating as a set of constitutive rules that have the power to create cultural entities. Many of the diagnostic categories in DSM-IV are potentially cultural entities, that is, objects created by the social agreement that something counts as that entity. The objects-in-themselves may be something quite different without the supporting cultural meaning system, its set of constitutive rules, and the collective intentionality used to experience and collectively validate them.

For example, it is interesting to note that no adequate descriptions of schizophrenia appear before about the year 1800. When examining historical records and ancient literature, no mention of anything that resembles the current conception of schizophrenia appears (Barlow & Durand, 1995). Of course, "madness" or serious mental illness existed before that time, but the symptomatology and course of illness characterized as schizophrenia appears to be associated with the advent of a modern cultural meaning system. The fact that the least modernized societies—those most removed economically and culturally from western culture—have on average the shortest course and best outcome for schizophrenia may be related to the apparent absence of schizophrenia in premodern western culture. It is possible that a modern cultural meaning system is related not only to the diagnosis of schizophrenia but also to the presence of schizophrenia.

Directive Function

People create cultural entities, and those entities then become part of the cultural environment, having an impact on people's lives and directing their behavior. This is the **directive function** of cultural meaning systems.

For example, in India people have created the *caste system*. The caste system is a cultural construction that directs persons in their behavior. In India, if a person is born into a high caste family, he or she is obligated to behave according to the rules governing that particular caste, for example, not eating meat.

Similarly, cultural entities such as diagnostic categories can also direct behavior. For example, being diagnosed with a particular disease may require a patient to seek out a particular form of treatment or therapy. Likewise, a diagnostic entity may be conceptualized in the cultural meaning system to direct society to behave toward a patient in a particular way, perhaps to help, stigmatize, or to avoid the patient (for example, someone with AIDS). Thus, the cultural meaning system is directing the behavior of the patient, clinicians, and others in the social environment.

Evocative Function

Because cultural meaning systems create cultural entities, which in turn direct behavior, they also evoke certain emotions. This is the **evocative function** of cultural meaning systems.

For example, having your property stolen may make you angry, graduating from college may make you happy, and a death in the family may make you grieve. The cultural meaning system provides rules for how to feel, because it defines what a particular situation means. Depending on the cultural meaning system, a death in the family may indicate that grief is appropriate for some specified period of time or that no grief is indicated or even that celebration is indicated.

Cultural meaning systems may also provide the most emotionally meaningful moments in a person's life. People do not usually realize it, but many of the things that are most emotionally meaningful in life—things that evoke the greatest passion, happiness, and sadness—are cultural entities created by cultural meaning systems.

Let's use a fictional story as an example. Pretend you are a married female college student and your dream is to go to medical school. However, to get high grades you spent so much time studying that you neglected your husband, and he started secretly seeing another woman. Eventually, you found out about it and at first got angry. Then you got depressed. As a result of your depression, you did poorly in your schoolwork and were not accepted to medical school. This made you even more depressed. As a result of the depression, your husband decided you were no longer fun to be around, and he left you for his new girlfriend. This made you even more depressed. The situation got so bad that you felt suicidal. It got so bad that you had to go to a psychiatrist who told you that you were suffering from a brain disease, a genetically caused chemical imbalance in the brain. He gave you medication to take to control your brain disease, and you ended up being labeled mentally ill, which made getting into medical school even more difficult.

What do you think about this woman's situation? If you analyze it carefully, you will see that this woman was a victim of her own cultural meaning system. Everything that happened to her, from the marriage to the brain disease, as well as her passionate emotions, resulted from her cognitive and emotional involvement with cultural entities—things created by a social agreement that something counts as that entity. What is significant is that everyone inside that cultural meaning system believes it is all absolutely real.

Chapter Two

Culture & Clinical Reality

The previous chapter ended with a fictional story of a woman who was depressed. If you think stories like that do not happen in real life, here is a real story based on the case history of an actual client.

Case Study in Depression*

Bill, a successful pediatrician, committed suicide at the age of 45. He had been a *magna cum laude* graduate of Harvard and an honors graduate from medical school. However, during Bill's fourth year of medical school, his father (also a physician) died. Bill had been very close to his father and became depressed after his death. The depression lasted about four months. During that time, he was busy completing his medical training in the hospital wards, but he was obviously in emotional distress. One of the residents suggested that Bill see a psychiatrist. He saw the psychiatrist and was placed on antidepressant medication. Because of his problem with mental illness, the Promotions Committee of the medical school decided Bill should not be permitted to graduate. He would be required to repeat his fourth year of medical school and if he was symptom-free for that year, he would be allowed to graduate.

Bill repeated his fourth year and graduated from medical school with honors. However, he had some difficulty getting accepted into internship and residency programs because hospitals were reluctant to accept doctors with a history of mental illness.

During his residency, Bill got married, and after completion of his residency he went into private practice. Bill and his wife had two daughters. Things remained relatively stable until Bill was 35. At that time his wife developed terminal cancer of the liver. She hung on for a year, and Bill watched her

*Based on Nancy Andreasen's *The Broken Brain* (1984, pp. 2–7).

slowly decline. His daughters were then ages two and four. Bill wondered how he could cope without her, managing his practice and trying to raise two small daughters on his own at the same time. Facing this prospect, two months before his wife's death Bill became depressed once more and was hospitalized in a psychiatric facility for a month.

After his wife's death, Bill immersed himself in his work and did not date for about a year. He eventually married a nurse, a divorced woman ten years younger than himself. She was very different from his first wife—unintellectual and interested primarily in sports events and barhopping. Nevertheless, the marriage went well for a few years. When Bill was in his mid-forties and his second wife was in her mid-thirties, she expressed dissatisfaction with the marriage. She was tired of monogamy and wanted to have an open marriage. She was getting older, and she felt that she didn't want to have her thirties spoiled by a husband and two daughters. So they agreed she could go out three nights a week with no questions asked. Thus, she began to go out with other men on a regular basis. Bill made a half-hearted attempt to have an affair with another woman, but he was not really interested and ended up staying home with the children. It was at this time that Bill began to feel depressed once again.

Bill told his wife that he still loved her, but an open marriage was not working for him. He wanted to return to monogamy. Instead, she decided to divorce him. Making things worse, after the divorce Bill's ex-wife continued to live in the same town, and Bill repeatedly ran into her with her various boyfriends. Feeling humiliated after seeing her one night at a local restaurant with her newest boyfriend, Bill got drunk, drove to her apartment, and pounded on the door demanding to speak with her. She called the police. He was arrested for public intoxication, which made the headlines in the local newspaper.

After this public humiliation, Bill went to pieces. He was hospitalized for six weeks in a psychiatric facility and treated with medications and ECT. When he returned home he learned that the state medical examiners had decided to temporarily suspend his license because of his mental illness. Bill had to appeal his case at the state capitol. The story was picked up by the local newspaper and television. His medical license was reinstated, but two weeks later he committed suicide.

Bill had substantial life insurance, which provided for his two daughters. It is possible he may have felt that his medical career was ruined and he was better off dead.

In her comments about Bill's case, Nancy Andreasen assumes the correctness of the disease-centered paradigm, stating, "People who suffer from mental illness suffer from a sick or broken brain. . . . As the public grows to understand its implications better . . . they could relate to the mentally ill with greater compassion, understanding, and patience" (1984, pp. 8–9).

Box 2.1

Five Ways Culture Affects Clinical Reality

1. Culture-based subjective experience
2. Culture-based idioms of distress
3. Culture-based diagnoses
4. Culture-based treatments
5. Culture-based outcomes

SOURCE: Based on Kleinman, 1980.

Clinical Reality

This chapter is about culture and **clinical reality.** Clinical reality refers to the cognitive construction of reality in the clinical setting. Clinical reality is created within a clinical context by the clinician and the client employing their learned cultural schemas. The case summarized here is an example of how one person's mental illness was cognitively constructed in a particular cultural context. In her comments on this case, Andreasen concludes that the paradigm of disease-centered psychiatry allows those suffering mental illness "greater compassion, understanding, and patience." Yet, it was the paradigm of disease-centered psychiatry that was defining the clinical reality of Bill's case.

Five Ways Culture Affects Clinical Reality

Culture affects the clinical reality of mental illness in five ways. These are listed in Box 2.1.

The case of Bill the pediatrician can be analyzed in the context of the five ways that culture affects the clinical reality of mental illness. Here was a man who suffered severe emotional shocks in his life. First, his father died, then his first wife died of cancer. Later, his second wife divorced him in a humiliating fashion. Each time one of these severe emotional shocks occurred in his life, he became depressed for a matter of months and recovered. Yet, when assessed using the approach of disease-centered psychiatry, this man can be diagnosed as suffering from a brain disease. I suggest it was this culture-based clinical reality that denied him the compassion, understanding, and patience he needed to recover from his emotional distress.

Culture-Based Subjective Experience

The first way that culture affects the clinical reality of mental illness is through **culture-based subjective experience.** Bill was a physician and the son of a physician. He was brought up and professionally trained to think about illness in biological terms. For him, illness was probably synonymous with biological disease. When he became ill himself, it was likely that he would subjectively experience his mental illness as a biological problem. Of course, as is stated in DSM-IV, "No laboratory findings that are diagnostic of a Major Depressive Episode have been identified" (APA, 1994, p. 323). That is, no specific brain disease causing a major depressive episode has been identified. Nevertheless, because of his culture, Bill probably conceptualized himself as having such a biological problem. Bill's culture, and particularly the biomedical paradigm he was raised and trained in, defined and constructed his illness in this fashion.

Dhat syndrome.   To provide cultural contrast, it is necessary to look at another experience that would be considered major depression in the paradigm of biomedical psychiatry—but one that occurs in a different cultural context. The example is **dhat syndrome** in India. The term *dhat syndrome* comes from the Sanskrit *dhatu*, which means "essential element." The Sanskrit literature describes seven types of *dhatus* or essential elements that make up the physical body. Of the seven *dhatus*, semen is considered to be the most important *dhatu*. In Indian culture it is thought that the *dhatus* determine the body's immunity or susceptibility to disease. It is commonly believed that 40 drops of butter (a religiously pure substance) produce one drop of blood, and 40 drops of blood produce one drop of semen. Thus, the loss of semen leads to physical and mental weakness and susceptibility to disease (Singh, 1985). Excessive masturbation or sexual intercourse are thought to produce mental and physical illness. The most common symptoms of *dhat* syndrome are fatigue, weakness, body aches, severe headaches, depression, anxiety, loss of appetite, insomnia, heart palpitations, and suicidal feelings. Among western trained psychiatrists in India practicing disease-centered psychiatry, the standard diagnosis for this syndrome is major depression (Behere & Natraj, 1984; Singh, 1985).

While doing fieldwork in north India in 1986, I observed a case of *dhat* syndrome that fit this South Asian cultural pattern. The client was a 45-year-old clothing merchant, Mr. B. N. Sinha (pseudonym), who was married and had four children. I visited him and his family at his home where I stayed for several days. Mr. Sinha was convinced that his illness was caused by loss of semen. His illness began in adolescence when he began to masturbate regularly. Because in Indian culture the cognitive schema for ejaculating semen is one of losing an essential element of the body necessary for maintaining good health and well-being, this was his subjective experience. Because he was masturbating every day, he was sure that he was "losing" too much semen, which the Indian culture identifies as a cause of illness. Before long Mr. Sinha began to feel the symptoms of *dhat* syndrome. His illness continued on and off into middle age. If he had sexual intercourse too often with his wife, the symptoms would return. He told me:

> This has got direct relation with my mental condition. I am very much vexed with too much sexuality in my life. I indulge in that, and I would hate it. I indulge because I am in the habit. I try to observe chastity, but I don't succeed

very much. Due to my bad habits during my childhood, you may say, during my adolescence.

Now, I can tell you one thing, during my high school days I was—well—I will put all the facts very open before you. I was in the acute habit of masturbation. And this habit of masturbation had made me very weak and feeble. Because, all the time I used to be indulged in sexual feelings—thinking about that. Always, you can say, daydreaming. So I used to be lost in daydreaming—doing masturbation. *Extremely.* So all this made me very weak, much more weak mentally than physically. And I connect the causes of the mental illness with that.

In Mr. Sinha's culture, excessive "semen loss" causes illness characteristic of major depression in western cultures. Thus, we can see the effects of Indian culture on subjective experience.

Culture-Based Idioms of Distress

The second way that culture affects the clinical reality of mental illness is through **culture-based idioms of distress.** Idioms of distress are the ways people behave to express that they are ill. This can include physical actions, including seeking out clinical care, and also mannerisms, figures of speech, and cognitive emphasis on certain symptoms while ignoring others. In the case of Bill the pediatrician, because he probably cognized his illness as a biological problem, he sought out the clinician he thought would be most appropriate, that is, a disease-centered psychiatrist.

In the case of Mr. Sinha, his cognitive and verbal construction of the illness as a case of semen loss was an obvious culture-based idiom of distress. He still had sex with his wife, but he felt guilty about it. He tried to refrain from having sex as much as possible, but he did not succeed as much as he would like. To treat his ailment, he sought out a folk healer, an Indian guru. These behaviors are culture-based idioms of his distress.

Culture-Based Diagnosis

The third way that culture affects the clinical reality of mental illness is through **culture-based diagnosis**—that is, the way that indigenous clinicians assess and diagnose the problem consistent with the local culture. For Bill, the indigenous clinicians were his psychiatrists. The culture-based diagnosis was, of course, major depression, which was culturally schematized as a brain disease.

For Mr. Sinha, the culture-based diagnosis was *dhat* syndrome, which in Indian culture is schematized as a physical illness caused by the loss of too much semen. Mr. Sinha's indigenous clinician, a Hindu guru, confirmed the diagnosis of *dhat* syndrome.

If the client and the clinician are from the same culture, they will usually agree on the nature of the illness and its cause. In this way, cultural meaning systems can construct "diseases" that are experienced subjectively by clients and confirmed objectively by clinicians.

Culture-Based Treatment

The fourth way that culture affects the clinical reality of mental illness is through **culture-based treatment.** This refers to the appropriate treatment for an illness as defined by the cultural meaning system or clinical paradigm. In Bill's case, the appropriate treatment as defined by his clinical reality was anti-depressant medications and electroconvulsive therapy. Because his illness was defined as a brain disease, only somatic treatments were deemed effective.

In Mr. Sinha's case, his clinician prescribed sexual abstinence and regular meditation. The clinical reality also defined the illness as a biological problem, in this case, the excessive loss of semen. In Hindu culture, the traditional remedy for *dhat* syndrome is complete abstinence from sexual activity to "retain" the semen and thus store up energy, power, and, therefore, health.

Ideas concerning the virtues of sexual abstinence are pervasive in Hindu culture. In the mythology of the god Shiva, the god stores up spiritual power and energy by remaining celibate for thousands of years at a time (O'Flaherty, 1973). Likewise, Mahatma Gandhi remained celibate for many years even though he was married. This was thought to be a source of his spiritual and political power (Willner, 1984). Similarly, if Mr. Sinha remains sexually absti-nent for two weeks, his symptoms remit. If he begins to have sex too often, the symptoms return. He told me:

> I will be the happiest man when both of us—I mean myself and my wife—will treat one another like brother and sister. That would be the most successful day in my life. And I would be the happiest man. Because, the ultimate suc-cess of spiritual life is to forget the difference between male and female—to identify one another as the soul, not as the body. The difference between male and female exist only to the extent you are conscious about the body. So the moment you forget that you are a body, or the person before you is a body, both of you are as soul—I think that is the perfect state of spirituality. This we have been taught by our teacher [guru]. This is the real goal of spiritual life. Thus, I tell you I find a very close relation between this chastity and the con-dition of the mind. It has got a very close relation.

It is clear from these examples that in the minds of the client and the clin-ician the appropriate treatment is determined by schemas in the culture-based clinical reality.

Culture-Based Outcome

The fifth way that culture affects the clinical reality of mental illness is in the **culture-based outcome.** This refers to the outcome that occurs because an ill-ness has been cognitively constructed and treated in a particular cultural fash-ion. Unfortunately, in the case of Bill, the outcome of his illness was suicide. This is not the usual outcome in western culture for major depression, but sui-cide is a potential outcome for some individuals. The majority of people treated for depression in the United States recover from their illness.

However, Bill was not a typical case; he was a medical student and physician and, therefore, he inhabited the subculture of American medicine. Within this subculture there is very little compassion, understanding, or patience for medical students or doctors suffering from mental illness. For example, it was the Promotions Committee that held Bill back for an extra year of medical school. Also, it was the hospital administrators who were reluctant to accept him for internship and residency training. It was the board of medical examiners who suspended his medical license. All of this occurred because of Bill's problem with depression. Rather than looking at his life and recognizing that Bill was going through painful grieving processes following the deaths of his father and his first wife, and the very painful divorce from his second wife, members of this medical subculture constructed the clinical reality that Bill was suffering from a serious and chronic brain disease. The notion of depression as a serious brain disease defines the problem as internal to the client (in his brain), stable (chronic), and general (affecting many areas of his life). This type of cognitive construction can promote a sense of hopelessness and helplessness, potentially aggravating the problem (Chapter 5).

Grieving over a death or a shattered marriage is no reason to ruin a promising medical career, but a serious and chronic brain disease is. It was the paradigm of disease-centered psychiatry that decontextualized and dehumanized Bill's emotional processes, completely ignoring the traumatic events in his life and reducing his personal and emotional problems to an imbalance in his brain biochemistry. Kleinman, Eisenberg, and Good (1978) have referred to this dehumanization of clients' emotional lives as a *veterinary* style of clinical practice. The mental patient is reduced to nothing more than a "broken brain," without regard to environmental circumstances, emotional trauma, or shattered relationships (Fleck, 1995). In this clinical reality, if the client commits suicide, it is attributable to his "brain disease."

In the case of Mr. Sinha, he has recurring episodes of symptoms if he engages in sex too often with his wife. However, his symptoms remit if he maintains sexual abstinence for two weeks at a time. This is an example of a Hindu culture-based outcome of mental illness.

Healing and Curing

Special problems in constructing a clinical reality occur if the client and the clinician come from differing cultural backgrounds. If their cultures are different, the "illness" experienced by the client is not likely to be the same as the "disease" diagnosed by the clinician. Because clinicians are trained to treat the "diseases" defined by their own cultural reality or professional paradigm, the prescribed treatments must match the "diseases." For example, the "disease" major depression is treated in disease-centered psychiatry by medications and ECT, because the "disease" is a chemical imbalance in the brain as defined by the paradigm. Likewise, *dhat* syndrome in India is treated by sexual

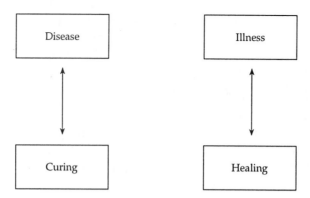

Figure 2.1
Treating Disease and Illness

abstinence, because the "disease" is defined in the cultural paradigm as a loss of too much semen.*

Treating "disease" in this way has been described by Kleinman (1988a) as **curing.** In contrast, the treatment of "illness"—that is, the client's subjective experience of being sick—is described by Kleinman as **healing.** Disease and curing go together, as do illness and healing (see Figure 2.1). This distinction and the problems that can arise from it are apparent when the client and the clinician come from differing cultural backgrounds.

Imagine what would happen if a western client with major depression was treated by a Hindu folk clinician like Mr. Sinha's guru. Upon hearing about the symptoms the client was experiencing, the Hindu clinician might inquire about the client's sex life, suspecting *dhat* syndrome. If the client was having sex more than a few times a week, the diagnosis might be the "disease" *dhat* syndrome. The "curing" might consist of a ritual in which the guru imparts a special mantra that the client repeats to take his mind off sex, and the prescription of sexual abstinence. In this situation, the western client is not likely to believe in the diagnosis of *dhat* syndrome and will probably be unwilling to comply with the "cure." The outcome in this case is likely to be poor because of the cultural differences. The "illness" of the client is major depression, but the guru is "curing" *dhat* syndrome.

The opposite case, in which an Indian client with the "illness" *dhat* syndrome goes to a disease-centered psychiatrist who diagnoses the "disease" major depression, is likely to have just as poor an outcome, as was confirmed by actual cases reported by Singh (1985).

> Follow up of these patients is very poor, majority (64 percent) did not come again after the first visit and hence the response to anti-depressant treatment could not be assessed. It is probable that these patients were not satisfied with our explanation that seminal loss was not harmful but that their symptoms

*Women can also get *dhat* syndrome; they are also thought to possess semen in this cultural meaning system.

Box 2.2

Four Ways Mental Illness Has Meaning

1. Symptom as symptom
2. Cultural significance
3. Personal and social meanings
4. Explanatory models

SOURCE: Based on Kleinman, 1988a.

---

were due to their excessive worrying about this for which we would prescribe them the treatment. On the contrary, it seems extremely naive to believe that after telling a patient that he is not suffering from the illness for which he has come, we should expect him to take our treatment for an illness which he does not believe even exists. (p. 122)

Curing is thus likely to have a poor outcome if the disease that is diagnosed is not simultaneously the illness that has brought the client in for treatment. Clinicians need to be aware of both illness and disease so that they can administer both healing and curing.

Four Ways Mental Illness Has Meaning

Treating the subjective experience of mental illness—that is, healing—is important because in many ways a mental disorder itself is a complex system of *meanings*. As was discussed in the previous chapter, cultural meaning systems create cultural entities—that is, objects that exist solely because of the collective social agreement that something counts as that entity. Among the cultural entities created by various cultures are mental disorders. Kleinman (1988a) described four ways in which illnesses have meaning; these are listed in Box 2.2.

Symptom as Symptom

The first way that mental illnesses have meaning is by identifying **a symptom as a symptom.** A symptom is an indicator of illness. A particular experience—a sensation, thought, emotion, or behavior—becomes a symptom (an indication of illness) only when it is cognized as such. Cognizing something as a symptom is an interpretation. The interpretation or cognitive construction of the event takes place within a cultural meaning system. A particular event is experienced as a symptom because the cultural meaning system defines it as an indicator of illness. This is important because the construction of an experience as a symptom can, in itself, cause further suffering.

For example, in the case of Bill, his symptom of grief for four months following the death of his father was assessed as a symptom of mental illness because the cultural schemas had already defined that particular emotional experience as an indicator of the disease major depression.

Grieving for four months after the death of a family member is not necessarily a symptom of mental illness. Assessing grief as a symptom of mental illness is an interpretation. Thus, grief as a symptom of mental illness is a cultural entity, not a natural one. Kramer (1993) notes, for instance, that it is normative for widows in Greece to grieve for five years after their husbands' death. The appropriate grieving period is prescribed by the cultural schemas. In the Greek cultural context, grieving for only four months might be considered an indicator of deviance. Yet, in Bill's cultural context, four months was too long. This period of grief was assessed as a symptom of a chronic brain disease, a cultural construction that in itself can cause further worry, fear, anxiety, sadness, stigmatization, and other forms of suffering.

Because different societies have divergent meaning systems, cultural differences exist in what is identified as a symptom and what the symptom signifies. Nevertheless, because the cultural schemas prescribe what kind of symptoms will occur, and those symptoms are consequently experienced, the symptoms are considered to be completely natural and independent of human intentionality. The symptoms become reified and are observed to be natural entities happening on their own.

Cultural Significance

The second way that mental illnesses have meaning is through **cultural significance**—that is, the meanings projected onto the mentally ill person by the surrounding society, which then structure the person's experience of suffering. These meanings include what the society thinks about the ill person, about his or her particular mental disorder, and about mental illness in general. These meanings and their consequences become part of the lived illness experience of the individual. This is especially true in societies where mental illness is seen as particularly stigmatizing. The individual is forced to live with the meanings imposed by the culture.

For example, Bill was forced to deal with the stigma of mental illness imposed by the meaning system of biomedicine. In this meaning system, Bill was seen as a person with an internal, chronic disease in his brain that would affect many areas of his life. This was a meaning imposed upon Bill by his society, yet it was probably accepted by him, structuring his own subjective experience of suffering as well as his illness behavior.

Personal and Social Meanings

The third way that mental illnesses have meaning are through **personal and social meanings.** This refers to the interpersonal relations and social life of the mentally ill person. Interpersonal relationships, particularly family relations, possess meanings that can add to or shape the suffering associated with mental illness.

For example, Mr. Sinha tries as much as possible to refrain from having sex with his wife. It is something he struggles with on a daily basis. He ideally wants his relationship with his wife to be "like brother and sister." Yet he continues to have sex with his wife and he suffers emotionally as a result of the meanings that this behavior has in his culture.

In the case of Bill, his social life, especially his professional life, was severely disrupted by his mental illness. First, he was forced to repeat his final year of medical school, and later he had his medical license suspended. Thus, his professional identity and competence as a medical student and physician were compromised and ultimately spoiled because of the meanings of his illness. The loss of self-esteem and the threat to his ability to make a living as a pediatrician and support his children no doubt added tremendous pressure and emotional suffering to his illness, ultimately ending in his suicide.

Explanatory Models

The fourth way that mental illnesses have meaning is through the **explanatory model**. This model refers to the way a set of cultural schemas explains the cause of mental illness—why the onset occurred when it did, the effects of the illness, what course the illness will take, and what treatments are appropriate. These meanings dramatically affect the lived experiences of people with mental illnesses, in many ways structuring the subjective illness experiences.

For example, Mr. Sinha experiences his symptoms after "excessive semen loss." This is the indigenous explanation for the cause of his illness. It is highly unlikely that a westerner would experience a similar illness. Yet this syndrome is very common in South Asia, and it occurs after persons engage in what they consider to be excessive sexual activity or loss of semen during sleep or urination. The semen loss is cognitively schematized as draining the body of a vital element necessary for health and well-being. The cultural schemas specify that the course of this illness is directly related to the amount and frequency of semen loss. If sexual activity is reduced and semen is "stored up," then health and well-being will automatically return. If sexual activity is not curtailed and semen continues to be "lost" in excessive amounts, then the illness will continue indefinitely. The appropriate treatment in this explanatory model is sexual abstinence, which is usually possible only by keeping the mind off sexual things. Abstinence is thought to require a spiritual discipline such as meditation and yoga to control the mind and keep it on spiritual thoughts instead of sex. This is the preexisting explanatory model of *dhat* syndrome in South Asia. The explanatory model gives meaning to the life experiences of persons, structuring their experiences and their illnesses. It is a culture-based explanatory model, yet South Asians experience it as existing independently of their own intentionality, as a completely natural and biological process.

The same is also true of westerners who accept the paradigm of disease-centered psychiatry. In this explanatory model, Bill's illness was caused by a chronic disease in the brain. According to the model, the onset and course of the disorder are determined by mostly biological factors, and the appropriate treatment must therefore be biological: medications or electroconvulsive therapy (ECT). This is the preexisting explanatory model of major depression that gives meaning to the life experiences of many persons in western culture and elsewhere, structuring their experiences and their illnesses. This is also a culture-based explanatory model, yet like *dhat* syndrome in India, many westerners experience major depression as a completely natural and biological problem, existing independently of their own intentionality and cultural schemas.

Evolution of Clinical Reality

The same general process in which preexisting cultural meaning systems construct culture-specific mental disorders occurs across cultures in both space and time. Looking at mental disorders during earlier times in western culture, the cultural meaning systems that existed in those times gave meaning to the symptoms and life experiences of the people in those eras, and thus structured their illnesses.

For example, in medieval Europe the cultural schemas of that time structured mental illnesses around the central concepts of demonic possession and witchcraft. In medieval society, war, famine, and plagues were recurring events. Life was generally hard and short. The Christian church provided society's view of nature, and life in the world was seen as a constant struggle between the forces of God and Satan. The mentally ill were culturally schematized as either demonically possessed or the victims of witchcraft. This was the culture-based clinical reality of mental illness in medieval Europe.

However, this clinical reality was not merely a belief system. The cultural meaning system of that time (like all others) had the power to construct cultural entities, including God, Satan, witches, angels, and demons. These cultural entities were part of the daily lived experiences of people in this time and place. Demons and witches were real to them in their time. Because of cultural learning structured in the neural networks of the brain, God, Satan, witches, angels, and demons were not merely believed in but were encountered and personally experienced on an everyday basis. Thus, in subjective experience—idioms of distress, culture-based diagnoses, treatments, and outcomes—individuals of those times *were* possessed by demons and victimized by witchcraft.

In our modern times, scientists tend to look back on the medieval period in western culture and view the people as almost hopelessly ignorant, living in "darkness." The usual disease-centered view of mental illness during the medieval period is that the people were suffering from brain diseases such as schizophrenia, but because of their superstitious ignorance, they misinterpreted the illnesses as demonic possession. Thus, because the real problem was a brain disease, the treatments employed by healers of that time, such as exorcism, were just another manifestation of their ignorance and were completely useless in treating the actual problem.

This disease-centered view of the medieval period further assumes that it has only been with the rise of science that the true biological nature of mental illness has been realized. Thus, only now, with our scientific knowledge of mental illness, can effective treatments be provided. This is the view that most college students have been taught concerning the history of mental illness in western culture. Disease-centered clinicians have been portrayed as enlightened saviors of the mentally ill, freeing them from the ravages of superstition and occult practices.

The change from a religious to a scientific view of mental illness in western culture should be viewed as the evolution of clinical reality based on an evolution of the general cultural meaning system. The scientific and political revolutions occurring in the 17th and 18th centuries altered overall European culture. Because the cultural meaning system changed, the mentally ill were no longer culturally schematized as being possessed. Moreover, the individuals themselves generally no longer experienced themselves as being possessed. That is, the subjective experience of mental illness had changed as well as the diagnoses. Most of the sick no longer experienced themselves as being "possessed" but were now "psychotic." This was the evolution of the possessed into the schizophrenic. It was an evolution of clinical reality based on an evolution of cultural schemas.

In medieval times, individuals actually did experience themselves as being possessed. Moreover, the entities "possessing" them actually experienced themselves as being demons. They were subjectively demons, spoke as demons, behaved as demons, and were seen as demons by observers. In the medieval world, these demons were a lived reality. This medieval reality has its counterparts in many contemporary nonindustrialized societies where demons, gods, witches, and other supernatural entities still commonly exist. In numerous nonindustrialized societies, people are still commonly possessed by various types of gods, demons, and ghosts or are the victims of witchcraft.

Anthropologists have been studying mental illnesses in these nonindustrialized societies for several decades. Generally, it has been found that the mental illnesses existing in these societies are structured by the indigenous set of cultural schemas. Some of the mental illnesses are in fact cultural entities. They exist in particular cultural contexts and are responses to certain precipitants in the indigenous meaning system. These mental illnesses have been labeled **culture-bound syndromes** (Levine & Gaw, 1995). Some of these culture-bound syndromes are included in the appendix of DSM-IV.

Contrary to the disease-centered view, traditional cultural treatments for these nonwestern forms of mental illness are sometimes effective. It is not necessary to diagnose a "possessed" nonwestern patient with schizophrenia or some other scientific diagnostic category and provide biomedical treatment to obtain a good outcome. Numerous reports have demonstrated that so-called witchdoctors, shamans, religious healers, and so on are capable of getting good clinical results (see Chapter 5).

The reason these folk healers sometimes get good clinical results is because they are treating an "illness," that is, the subjective experience of the patient, rather than only a "disease," the diagnosed disorder of the clinician. The ill-nesses in many of these cases are some form of spirit possession. To treat the subjective experience of the patient, it is necessary to treat the patient for pos-session. This is what a folk healer does, usually through some form of ritual healing. The result is sometimes the complete recovery of the patient. Treating the same possessed patient exclusively for a biological disease can result in a poor outcome.

Judging from the effectiveness of folk healers in today's nonwestern soci-eties, it appears that the view of medieval folk healers as being ineffective char-latans immersed in worthless occultism is culturally biased. Of course, the scientific evaluation of the effectiveness of folk healers is limited by the prob-lems associated with research in the field. Therefore, assessments of the effec-tiveness of folk healing are largely based on ethnographic observations rather than on rigorously controlled treatment outcome studies. However, the general consensus is that traditional folk healers have much to offer in the clinical set-ting in cooperation with modern clinicians.

Chapter Three

Culture &
Personality

Every human experience, including every thought, has its biological basis in the neural networks of the brain. The gross structure of those neural networks is defined by genetic inheritance, but dendritic structure, receptor properties, and the connections between individual neurons and patterns of neurons are developed over time through experience of the physical and social environment. Thus, the neural networks of the brain that control cognition, emotion, and behavior are structured through the brain's interaction with its environment, including internalization of cultural schemas.

An individual learns a language, a belief system, social roles, and appropriate behavior to function successfully in a particular society. A person cannot develop into a functioning individual without internalizing cultural schemas in the neural networks of the brain. To assess mental disorders without appreciation of this basic fact of human development results in a skewed view. Culture, mental illness, and personality development are intimately related.

The study of culture and personality development has been a central endeavor in cultural anthropology since the early decades of the 20th century. There is a vast anthropological literature on this topic. It is not my intention to provide a history of culture and personality studies in anthropology (see Piker, 1994, for an excellent review). Rather, the goal here is to review recent theoretical advances that are specifically relevant to the study of mental illness.

Sociocentrism versus Egocentrism

One of the most useful concepts for the study of mental illness coming from the anthropological study of personality is the distinction between **sociocentric** and **egocentric** personality structures (Shweder & Bourne, 1984). In cross-cultural psychology, this distinction is usually referred to as *collectivism* versus *individualism* (for example, Triandis, 1995). A sociocentric personality is, as the name implies, a personality with an identity centered in the group or society. This individual derives his or her primary identity from membership in a social group, usually the extended family. The family is typically seen as an immortal structure in which the individual constitutes only a temporary, subordinate part (Lewis-Fernández & Kleinman, 1994). There are variations in sociocentrism across cultures, but what all sociocentric cultures have in common is that individual interests are subordinated to the good of the collectivity.

A sociocentric society has strict rules of interdependence. Social obligations are of paramount importance, and proper behavior is determined by the individual's position in the social structure. Individuals are not perceived as possessing a fully formed identity outside of group membership. In many ways, group membership provides personal identity. There is little or no attempt to distinguish the individual from the social position he or she occupies. The group is seen as a kind of organic whole, and the individual is a living cell within this organism. Life outside the group is usually not attempted, but if it is contemplated, it is seen as a kind of exile and loss of identity.

Western concepts of personal freedom and individual human rights are foreign to sociocentric societies and have very little if any meaning. Rather than individual freedom, emphasis is placed on duties and social obligations. Thus, in sociocentric societies individuals are deeply dependent on others in their group for their own sense of self and personal well-being.

In contrast to sociocentric personalities, egocentric personalities have their personal identity centered in the self. They perceive themselves as autonomous individuals with personal choices, desires, and rights, and they see dependence as being an undesirable trait. In an egocentric society, the "self" becomes the primary object of interest, and personal freedom and power are supreme values.

In an egocentric society, social relationships are viewed as voluntary associations arising out of consent by the individuals involved. Individuals are free to terminate associations if they so choose. In this type of society, individuals are perceived to be autonomous agents with the freedom to pursue their own personal goals, in some cases, even to the detriment or harm of others.

Egocentrism and sociocentrism play important roles in personality development by focusing thought on the welfare either of the self or the group. However, these two factors will influence personality development differently depending on whether a society is egalitarian or has a dominance hierarchy.

Dominance Hierarchies versus Egalitarianism

The presence or absence of **dominance hierarchies** in a society's social structure has a powerful influence on personality development. Of course, this is the central insight of Marxist theory—that persons always act as *social* individuals. Individuals are not actually autonomous, regardless of how independent they believe they are. Individual behavior is influenced to a large extent by social position (Bock, 1994).

Table 3.1
Violent Crime Rates in Modern Nations (1987)

	Crime rate per 100,000 inhabitants		
	Homicide	*Forcible rape*	*Robbery*
United States	8.3	37.4	212.7
Germany (FRD)	4.3	8.6	46.0
France	4.1	5.8	86.9
United Kingdom	5.5	11.1	65.4
Japan	1.3	1.5	1.5

SOURCE: From "Law and Order in Contemporary Japan: Commitment, Sanctions, and the Quality of Life," by C. R. Fenwick. In Charles B. Fields and Richter H. Moore (Eds.), *Comparative Criminal Justice*, p.101. Copyright © 1996 Waveland Press. Reprinted with permission.

In large-scale societies, there can be gender, class, age, race, and ethnic dominance hierarchies. Industrialized societies invariably have class hierarchies. This is especially true in capitalist societies because of the unequal distribution of goods and services inherent in a free market economy. In a capitalist society, there will always be economic winners and losers. This economic inequality can be mitigated somewhat by systems of government redistribution or control (such as a progressive tax system), but some level of class hierarchy is unavoidable in a capitalist system.

The presence of a class hierarchy inevitably leads to class conflict as each class attempts to either maintain or improve their living conditions in relation to the other classes. However, some industrialized societies have managed to achieve a high level of class egalitarianism, even while being part of the world capitalist system. In societies such as Germany or Japan, indicators of class conflict such as violent crime are far lower than they are in an industrialized society such as the United States, which has great disparities in class structure. The differences in violent crime rates among industrialized societies can be seen in Table 3.1.

Racial and ethnic dominance hierarchies are common in societies that are racially or ethnically heterogeneous. These societies are often characterized by high levels of aggression and conflict because force or the threat of force is usually needed to maintain dominance and privileged status. For example, in a society such as the United States, which is racially and ethnically diverse, individuals are very concerned with racial and ethnic status and are aware that certain racial or ethnic groups rank higher or lower than others. In the United States, both governmental and private aggression and intimidation have been used against blacks with the intention of "keeping blacks in their place." In contrast, a large-scale society that is relatively homogeneous in its racial and ethnic makeup has a much easier time achieving internal racial and ethnic egalitarianism.

In general, the presence of dominance hierarchies based on gender, class, race, age, ethnicity, or any combination of these characteristics has a direct influence on the development of an individual's **primary role identification**

(Rohrer & Edmonson, 1960). That is, elements of individual personality development are structured in relation to positions in the dominance hierarchy. Thus, an individual identifies with a particular primary role and the correlated behavior assigned to that role based on his or her position in the dominance hierarchy of that society.

In an extremely hierarchical society such as India, an individual's primary role identification may be minutely delimited by such factors as caste, gender, age, language, region, village, and family. In this case, a particular role carries with it norms of behavior and patterns of thought that are appropriate for that particular primary role and only for the person occupying that social position.

The presence of dominance hierarchies allows for systems of discrimination that reify social distinctions, thus legitimizing the status and privileges of the ruling groups. This is far different from an egalitarian society that classifies people as a single group, with similar status, role expectations, norms of behavior and similar patterns of thought for everyone.

In a society with dominance hierarchies, individual at the low end of the social scale have a stigma or impaired identity imposed upon them by dominant groups. The **moral career** of these stigmatized individuals is compromised in interpersonal relations. The term *moral career* refers simultaneously to the *moral status* and the *morale* of the individual. The moral status of individuals is an indication of their perceived value in society—that is, whether they are "good" or "bad" persons as judged by the cultural definitions of morality within the context of the social dominance hierarchy. Thus, someone in a stigmatized social group (for example, blacks in the United States) can be judged to be a "bad" person by definition of the cultural meaning system. When moral status is compromised in this fashion, the individual's morale or sense of self-esteem can also be negatively affected (Goffman, 1963).

There are a number of ways that a person with a stigmatized moral career can adapt to the social environment, thus structuring personality development. For example, stigmatized persons can accept their status and "act accordingly," that is, passively accept their low status. These persons will likely have low self-esteem. They accept society's definition of them as being inferior, flawed, incapable, unworthy, inadequate, unacceptable, and so on. They internalize this stigmatized view of themselves, literally structuring it into the neural networks of their brains. These neural networks then structure their cognition of the world.

For these low self-esteem, stigmatized individuals, the social environment can be a very hostile, frightening, and painful place. They typically attempt to adapt by acting submissively, accepting domination, and avoiding situations that might expose them to rejection, humiliation, or hostility. The symptoms of avoidant or dependent personality disorders may be more likely to develop in such cases (see Chapter 6).

Alternatively, a person with a stigmatized moral career can attempt to hide the stigma, to "pass" as a "good" person. For example, in Japan it has been common in the past for persons of Korean ancestry to take Japanese names and attempt to "pass" as Japanese to avoid the social consequences of being labeled and treated as "inferior." Similarly, in the United States, persons of mixed ancestry have in the past attempt to hide their nonwhite background to "pass" as "good" white people. Using this type of adaptation, individuals live in constant fear of having their stigmatized moral career discovered, thus greatly increasing life stress.

If stigmatized persons cannot hide their low status, they may try to copy the dominant group down to the minutest detail of behavior. This kind of adaptation was common in colonial situations. For example, in colonial India there was a stratum of Indian society made up of elitist Indians who copied English behavior in such detail that they almost became better Englishmen than the English. People with this type of psychosocial adaptation to stigma are likely to be overly concerned with order, rules, details, rigid morality, and deference to authority. Persons with this type of adaptation may be more likely to develop the symptoms of obsessive-compulsive personality disorder (see Chapter 6).

Another way a stigmatized person can try to overcome negative status is through some kind of superlative effort—that is, be better than the average stigmatized person. They avoid the stigma of their group to some extent by proving themselves to be superior in some special area of achievement. Examples of this are successful African American athletes who, by virtue of their wealth and celebrity, avoid some forms of discrimination imposed on less fortunate African American males. However, if they are not able to perform at some extraordinary level, they may make-believe or pretend that they are superior. In some cases, they may even come to believe it themselves. Persons with this type of adaptation may develop the symptoms of narcissistic personality disorder (see Chapter 6).

Another alternative adaptation to a stigmatized moral career is violent resistance to the social system. These people feel unfairly stigmatized, perceiving that there is no fairness in the system. They feel that they have been unfairly harmed, victimized, exploited, and so on. They view this victimization as being built into the system, and thus normal and expectable. Their adaptation is to victimize others before allowing themselves to be further victimized. This type of adaptation is more likely to develop into the symptoms of anti-social personality disorder (see Chapter 6).

Another alternative adaptation to a stigmatized moral career is violence against the self. These people are likely to have very low self-esteem. They try to force the acceptance, affection, and caring they seek and are not receiving from others by harming themselves. They may make numerous suicide threats or attempts. Persons with this type of adaptation may develop the symptoms of borderline personality disorder (see Chapter 6).

The presence of dominance hierarchies also affects personality development in the members of dominant groups. For individuals in dominant groups, the presence of a social hierarchy can be accepted as "natural" and lead to feelings of inborn superiority, lack of empathy for individuals in the dominated groups, and a sense of unquestionable entitlement. For example, in the United States, white supremacist groups such as the Ku Klux Klan and others are manifestations of the effect the preexisting racial dominance hierarchy has on some of the personalities being raised in the dominant white group.

Similarly, in India, high caste Hindus are taught as children that the caste hierarchy is the result of "natural law," thus influencing them to view low caste persons as inherently inferior. Likewise, in societies with high levels of male dominance, young males may be raised to believe that females are inherently inferior and that males are either "naturally" superior or were "created" superior by God.

Societies can be egalitarian or hierarchical and egocentric or sociocentric in different combinations. Another important factor is whether societies possess *premodern, modern,* or *postmodern* meaning systems.

Modern versus Premodern Meaning Systems

Most social scientists today view societies from a *postmodern* perspective, which is critical of earlier social scientists who viewed societies as either premodern or modern (for example, Levy, 1967; So, 1990; Vago, 1989). A **modern society** was defined as one with a relatively high level of technology, great specialization in social and economic organization, large-scale interdependency in the flow of goods and services throughout the society, a permanent bureaucracy controlling many aspects of social life, a dependence on rationality and scientific reasoning for solving problems, and an attitude of expecting material progress in life (Levy, 1967).

Normal personality development within a modern society was expected to be dependent on at least a minimum level of education in modern standards of literacy, science, technology, history, and politics and a general acceptance of the scientific view of the world. An individual with a normal **modern personality** was further expected to possess a sense of personal efficacy in controlling and being responsible for his or her own life and was expected to be independent and autonomous of traditional (particularly religious or parental) sources of authority and able to make rational individual choices about life goals. Also, a person was expected to be cognitively flexible and able to accommodate new experiences and ideas and be ready for the changes that are inevitable in a society dedicated to progress and change (Inkeles & Smith, 1974).

In contrast to a modern society, a **premodern society** was defined as one in which the level of technology was relatively low. There was little specialization in social or economic organization. There was a subsistence economy with the flow of goods and services occurring on a relatively small scale. Social organization was based primarily on kinship systems. There was a great reliance on traditional religious-familial authorities. There was an assumption of supernatural causation for life events consistent with the local religious tradition. Also, there was a belief that life conditions changed very little over time (Levy, 1967). This type of society was called "premodern" in the belief that modernization would eventually spread throughout the world and turn premodern societies into modern ones, and premodern personalities into modern personalities.

Personality development within a premodern society was described as producing individuals who were fatalistic, accepting their place in life without any expectation of improving their condition. Characteristics of a **premodern personality** include a lack of a sense of personal efficacy to change conditions, an acceptance of traditional (religious and familial) sources of authority, and reliance on divine intervention for any change in an individual's life. Causes of illness and healing were generally accepted as coming from supernatural sources. Individuals with premodern personalities were also thought to lack the cognitive flexibility to adapt successfully to rapid social change because they lacked the expectation of change (Vago, 1989).

Postmodernism

In general, modernist theorists have posited that modernization is the process by which agrarian societies become industrialized societies. This was thought to be accomplished by a transplantation of western technologies, social organizations, belief systems, and patterns of personality development to premodern, nonwestern countries (Vago, 1989). Western forms of thinking, social organization, and personality development were thought to be so inherently superior that it was assumed by modernist theorists that modernization (essentially westernization) was a type of universal social solvent that would transform all societies in contacted into something resembling a modern western society (So, 1990).

This assumption of the modernist theorists has been challenged in recent years. In the movement within the social sciences known as **postmodernism,** the assumptions of **modernism** have been criticized as being ethnocentric and tied to intellectual and economic colonialism (Wallerstein, 1987). Numerous studies have shown that social well-being is not necessarily dependent on wholesale adoption of western values, economic practices, social organizations, ways of thinking, or personality development (So, 1990).

Modernism is generally an ethnocentric perspective that views western culture, values, ways of thinking, and personality development as being obviously superior to nonwestern or premodern forms. This type of ethnocentric thinking has also pervaded western psychiatry. As a result, the personality disorders listed in DSM-IV are still largely based on western conceptions of normative *modern* personality development.

This textbook is written from a postmodern perspective that does not accept the ethnocentrism of modernist theory or modernism in general. However, the descriptive categories of *premodern* and *modern* can still be used from a postmodern perspective. Persons and societies with the characteristics described as premodern do exist, and the term *premodern* can be used to identify them as long as it is not assumed that they are deviant from, inferior to, or

Table 3.2
Premodern versus Modern Societies and Individuals

	Premodern	*Modern*
Societies	Religious political authority	Secular democracy
	Low technology	High technology
	Agrarian economy	Capitalist economy
	Focused on tradition	Focused on progress
Individuals		
	Focused on tradition	Open to change
	Religious/familial authority	Personal freedom
	Belief in supernatural	Belief in science
	Fatalistic orientation	Personal efficacy

SOURCE: Based on So, 1990.

somehow at a lower level of evolution or development than modern persons and societies.

Likewise, persons and societies with the characteristics described as modern do exist, and the term *modern* can be used to describe them as long as it is not assumed that they are naturally normal, superior, or at a higher level of development than those described as premodern. The characteristics of premodern and modern societies and individuals as identified by modernist theorists are summarized in Table 3.2.

Adolescence and Personality Development

One aspect of modern societies related to personality development is the concept of **adolescence.** In all societies adolescence is the period between the onset of puberty and the attainment of adulthood. This period of development seems very much like a "natural" state directly related to human biological development and, therefore, a universal stage present in all societies. However, cultural factors play an important role in defining adolescence, particularly in the behavior expected of the adolescent and in the length of time spent in this period. Thus, adolescence probably is as much cultural as it is natural.

In modern societies adolescence is commonly defined as the period between the onset of puberty and an individual's 18th birthday, the usual definition of adulthood. During this period, the adolescent is expected to learn the basic knowledge and skills considered necessary to function as an adult in that society. In the United States, this is the period of intermediate and high school education. However, in premodern societies, which is where humans have spent the vast majority of their evolutionary history, this period is spent learning advanced survival skills associated with foraging or subsistence agriculture and learning religious customs. Moreover, the length of time spent in adolescence is quite different.

In modern societies such as the United States, the onset of puberty frequently occurs sooner than it does in premodern societies. In the United States puberty commonly occurs around age 10 or 12, whereas in premodern societies it is more common for puberty to occur later, around age 13 to 15. Thus, in the United States adolescence covers a period of six to eight years. However, in premodern societies the period is much shorter, usually lasting only several days, weeks, or months. In premodern societies, individuals enter adulthood shortly after the onset of puberty.

This is because the definition of adulthood varies by culture. In premodern societies, individuals normally already know most of the survival skills they will need as adults by the time they reach puberty. What is necessary for them to become adults is a culturally defined transition period characterized by training in religious customs and ending in an initiation ceremony marking the death of the individual's existence as a child and the birth of his or her life as an adult. After this initiation, they are socially classified as adults and have adult roles and behavior available to them, such as marriage and raising children.

The transition period from childhood and adulthood is a period of **liminality.** Liminality refers to the period "betwixt and between" two social categories and states of being (Turner, 1962). In premodern societies, once a child has reached sexual maturity, that individual ceases to be socially recognized as a child but is not yet an adult until formally initiated into adulthood. That period in between is the premodern society's equivalent of modern adolescence.

However, unlike premodern societies where this period of liminality is usually quite short, modern societies have an extended period of liminality for individuals making the transition from child to adult. This has relevance to the discussion of mental illness, because any period of liminality is a difficult time for the individual. The period of liminality involves the death of one personal identity and social status and the birth of a new personal identity and social status. This period of transition can be accompanied by mourning over the death of the child self, confusion about personal identity, emotional upheaval, and apprehension about adult responsibilities.

Making this transition smoothly requires help from the community through their collective intentionality and through behavioral support in reifying the individual's new social status and personal identity. Without help from the community in the form of ritual initiation and formal recognition and support of the new status, the individual can struggle on his or her own, keeping alive the child self and not fully integrating into the adult role and self identity. This is why initiation ceremonies marking entry into adulthood in premodern societies frequently make use of altered states of consciousness induced through fasting, drugs, or pain—making a clear break with the old child personality and imprinting a new self-identity into consciousness. This new self is also frequently marked with physical symbols such as bodily mutilation, which serve as public signs that this individual is now an adult and should be treated as an adult. The old child self is internally and externally eliminated, and the new adult self is subjectively and publicly created.

In modern societies, this clear break with the child identity and the public creation of the adult self does not usually occur. Rather than a brief period of liminality between childhood and adulthood, ending with a definite creation of an adult self, modern societies have the long period of liminality we call adolescence. This period is in effect a culturally mandated extension of childhood; individuals are still considered "boys" and "girls" and denied adult roles, even though they are sexually mature. This cultural practice keeps alive the child self and behavior well past the onset of biological adulthood, and keeps the individuals psychologically and socially immature.

During this long period of liminality, individuals are expected to *gradually* mature from children into adults in a more or less biological process, because adolescence is viewed as a biological stage of development in western culture. Modern adolescence is generally not viewed as a cultural construct, even though that is what it appears to be from an anthropological perspective.

This cultural extension of childhood for several years into the period of biological maturity can create confusion in self-identity in that the person is biologically mature yet is socially defined as immature and is denied access to adult roles and behaviors. This has an impact on self-identity in that the individual may be forming an adult self-identity but is given conflicting messages by society.

Moreover, the denial of adult roles and behavior can be frustrating to adolescents, particularly in the area of sexuality. Unlike many premodern societies, which allow sexual intercourse and marriage shortly after initiation (Chapter 7), some modern individuals are expected to maintain childlike, sexually immature behavior even though they are sexually mature. For example, in the United States, adolescent females are often admonished to abstain from sexual intercourse until they reach the age of 18. Thus, a female may be expected—by both her parents and society—to refrain from adult forms of sexual behavior for several years after reaching reproductive maturity. This expectation is reinforced through the use of social sanctions and punishments, and by teaching her that she is "too young," "still a child," and so on. Because she is biologically mature, she may surreptitiously engage in sexual intercourse— simultaneously enjoying it and feeling guilty about it. The need to hide this activity from parents and others, and the need to reconcile this adult activity with an immature self-identify can lead to anxiety, identity confusion, sexual frustration, rebellion against parental authority, and depression.

It has been suggested that the symptoms of borderline personality disorder (see Chapter 6) are far more common in adolescents and young adults of modern societies than in premodern ones (Paris, 1991). This may be related to the long period of liminality between childhood and adulthood that is forced on individuals in modern societies. Peters (1994) hypothesizes that the absence in modern societies of initiation ceremonies that mark the transition from childhood to adulthood and help solidify the new self identity has led to disruptions in personality development that are associated with borderline personality disorder. Individuals in modern societies, especially in the highly egocentric United States, are left to more or less form their own adult self-identity with little help or support from the community—and several years after the individual reaches biological maturity.

A Cross-Cultural Look at Personality Development

Societies can be more or less hierarchical or egalitarian, egocentric or sociocentric, and modern or premodern. There is a spectrum for each of these social factors. Every society can be placed somewhere on each spectrum. Also, different combinations of these factors can be present to varying degrees in every society. Although there is still much individual variation in personality development due to variations in personal experience, these macro level social factors influence personality development to a great extent in individuals everywhere as they adapt to their social environment. A look at how these three factors combine in different societies will help to illustrate these concepts.

Culture and Personality in India

India is clearly a sociocentric society. An Indian derives his or her primary identity from membership in a family and caste. That person's individual interests are generally subordinated to the good of the family. Moreover, Indians perceive themselves as being interdependent, both as individuals within the family and as castes within the society. Duty to his or her social group is of primary importance, and proper behavior is determined by caste, gender, and age. Different castes have different roles to play, as do different genders. Thus, an Indian's personal identity is provided by his or her social position. There is little or no attempt to distinguish the value of a person from the value of the social status he or she occupies (Dumont, 1980; Mandelbaum, 1970).

In India, modern western concepts such as individual human rights are part of the Indian Constitution, and some effort is made by the government to upgrade the status of the lower, so-called scheduled castes and women. However, the vast majority of people in India find the concept of individual rights to be foreign and contrary to "natural law," which places persons and groups in various positions in the social hierarchy. The caste hierarchy itself (*varnashrama dharma*) is seen as something that is structured in nature and not a cultural artifact (Shweder, Mahapatra, & Miller, 1990).

India is a sociocentric society with an elaborate system of overlapping dominance hierarchies. The fact that India is a sociocentric society makes the dominance hierarchies especially oppressive for certain individuals (women and low caste persons) because individual desires are subjugated to the will of the group. Group obligations and social pressure amplify the effects of the dominance hierarchies.

India is also largely a premodern society. Although there has been a great deal of economic development in recent years with a burgeoning westernized middle class, the majority of people still live in rural villages where the level of technology is relatively low. In addition, the Hindu belief in *karma* makes the people essentially fatalistic, accepting their place in life without any expectation of improving their condition. The rural Indian does not possess a sense of personal efficacy to change his or her life other than to rely on prayer, ritual, submission to God, or some other religious method of gaining control over the events of life.

Therefore, in India there are oppressive dominance hierarchies structured in a sociocentric society that is largely premodern in its attitudes. This social situation promotes exploitation of individuals and groups as well as communal violence in which caste and religious groups fight each other for improved position in the dominance hierarchies. It also promotes violence against individuals who are low in the hierarchical system (low caste persons and females).

The social stress generated by these conditions affects everyone in the society and influences personality development. All of the DSM-IV personality disorders can be identified in India, although they may not be perceived as personality disorders within the indigenous cultural meaning system.

Culture and Personality among the Senoi Temiar

The Senoi Temiar are a tribal society who live in the rain forest of Malaysia (Roseman, 1990). In contrast to the situation in India where the society is extremely hierarchical, sociocentric, and mostly premodern, the Senoi Temiar are highly egalitarian, sociocentric, and highly premodern. These differences, primarily the presence of egalitarianism rather than dominance hierarchies, create a social environment that contrasts greatly with that of India. The absence of dominance hierarchies among the Temiar, combined with sociocentrism, allows the society to be extremely peaceful, without the exploitation and violence seen in societies with clear dominance hierarchies.

The Senoi Temiar have only informal leaders who attempt to lead by influence and persuasion. If there is a dispute, the Temiar resort to four methods for resolving the problem: (1) mediation, (2) group discussion moving toward consensus, (3) harangue, and (4) fission.

Physical violence of any form is not used within Temiar society. Nor is anger expressed in face-to-face interactions. Rather, anger is expressed in an indirect form Roseman (1990) refers to as "harangue." In a harangue, the angry person waits until the middle of the night and then addresses the person with whom he or she has a dispute, but always from a separate room or separate building, and often in the third person. The person is addressed as "he" or "she," rather than "you" to further distance the confrontation. Even then, this indirect form of address is considered a hyperdirect and aggressive form of interaction among the Temiar.

If disputes cannot be resolved using peaceful methods, the group will fission into two groups with one group moving to a new location. Thus, in Temiar society the cultural meaning system structuring a society that is egalitarian, sociocentric, and premodern influences individual personalities to be peaceful. It is unclear whether all the personality disorders listed in DSM-IV are present in Senoi Temiar society. It is possible that some, such as antisocial personality disorder or narcissistic personality disorder, may be missing.

Culture and Personality among the Swat Pukhtun

The Swat Pukhtun are a tribal people who live in the mountains of northern Pakistan (Lindholm, 1997). Their society is very hierarchical, highly egocentric, and premodern. The dominance hierarchies in this society, based primarily on gender and wealth, create a social environment in which there is much aggression and violence. The fact that this society is also egocentric means that the aggression and violence occur mostly between individuals, although alliances of individuals can quickly form for purposes of conflict.

The Pukhtun social environment is harsh and competitive. The combination of dominance hierarchies and extreme egocentrism influences individuals to strive for personal power and prestige. In this society, there are only two types of people—the weak and the strong. The strong take from the weak, dominate them, and thereby gain prestige. The weak are controlled, exploited, and dominated by the strong. The weak are then stigmatized because of their weakness.

Pukhtun individuals are completely ruthless in the pursuit of personal power and wealth, and these values are taught to children at a young age. Children are taught to fight, steal, lie, cheat, and be completely self-seeking. The primary values of this society are aggression, egotism, pride, fearlessness, and treachery. No one dares to trust anyone else (Lindholm, 1997).

Because of the extreme egocentrism in this society, there is a great deal of violence within families. Husbands regularly beat their wives, and wives fight back. Pukhtun women display the scars incurred during fights with their husbands as signs of honor. Children are also regularly beaten by their parents, and this preoccupation with violence manifests in the behavior of the children. Children constantly fight among themselves for dominance or over personal possessions, and they are frequently cruel to animals.

Pukhtun individuals experience no guilt for their many forms of exploitation and violence against others. Guilt or remorse appears to be an emotion that is missing from this society. However, they do experience shame when they are caught attempting to victimize someone and are prevented from completing the act. They are ashamed because they were not successful.

Thus, among the Swat Pukhtun, the social environment emphasizing hierarchic egocentrism influences individual personality development in the direction of violence, aggression, treachery, egotism, and cruelty. In this social environment, the symptoms of antisocial personality disorder and narcissistic personality disorder appear to be the norm rather than the exception. Therefore, the indigenous cultural meaning system would probably not recognize these as pathological categories.

Culture and Personality in Japan

In comparison to India and the Swat Pukhtun, society in Japan can be described as moderately hierarchical, sociocentric, and modern (Doi, 1981; Roland, 1988). Japan has an oppressive gender dominance hierarchy, a moderate class hierarchy, and racial and ethnic hierarchies.

The Japanese have traditionally looked down on Koreans or other ethnic minorities within their society. The same holds true for persons of different race in Japan. However, racial and ethnic minorities are extremely small in Japan compared to other industrialized nations. Overall, Japan is a highly homogeneous society. Moreover, because the Japanese believe that they as a group are superior to other peoples, every Japanese deserves to be treated with at least a minimum level of respect. Furthermore, the class hierarchy is restricted in range by a wage system that lacks the great discrepancies in pay between managers and workers that is present in the United States. Also, the sociocentrism of Japanese society puts tremendous pressure on individuals to conform with the group. Mostly, people in Japan want to be like everyone else. There is little incentive for standing out. This, combined with the homogeneity of Japanese society, moderates the negative effects of the class hierarchy. Thus, the effects of dominance hierarchies in creating social conflict is less in Japan than in other large societies such as the United States. This is illustrated by the extremely low crime rate in Japan compared to that in the United States (Fenwick, 1996).

The social environment in Japan, which can be characterized as moderately hierarchical, sociocentric, and modern, influences individual personalities to be relatively peaceful, focused on social obligations, open to change, yet aware of social status and wealth. This social environment likely produces persons with all of the DSM-IV personality disorders, but perhaps with a greater percentage of persons with the symptoms of avoidant, dependent, and obsessive-compulsive personality disorders and a much lesser percentage of persons with the symptoms of antisocial and narcissistic personality disorders.

Culture and Personality in the United States

The United States can be described as a society that is hierarchical, egocentric, and modern. The usual class hierarchy in capitalist societies is present in the United States. However, because the United States has a particularly free market style of capitalism that is missing the usual safeguards protecting the poor found in most industrialized societies (for example, guaranteed health care and housing), there is a wider range in the class dominance hierarchy in the United States. Thus, there are higher percentages of wealthy and poor people in the United States, and a greater gap between them, than in many other modern industrialized societies. This tends to increase class conflict. This is one of the reasons there is such an extremely high violent crime rate in the United States compared to that of other modern nations (see Table 3.1 for specific crime rates).

In addition to a well-developed class hierarchy, there are also gender, ethnic, and racial hierarchies in the United States. In recent decades, the gender dominance hierarchy has been slowly crumbling. This is illustrated by the ever increasing employment opportunities for women in the United States, especially in occupations that were previously reserved for men. However, the gender dominance hierarchy still exists and influences personality development and interpersonal relations. Domestic violence is still a major problem in the United States that stems directly from the traditional gender dominance hierarchy.

Because American society is extremely heterogeneous in its racial and ethnic composition compared to other industrialized nations, the racial and ethnic dominance hierarchies have been especially great sources of conflict. The exploitation and violence experienced by racial and ethnic minorities in the United States have been truly monumental. Ranging from the genocide of the Native Americans and the slavery of African Americans to more recent forms of economic exploitation and discrimination of these and other ethnic and racial minorities, the manifestations of racial and ethnic dominance hierarchies have created physical and emotional scars that are passed on from generation to generation. These dominance hierarchies are sources of continuing conflict and emotional pain that influence personality development in the United States for both the dominant and the dominated.

In addition to being hierarchical, American society is also egocentric. The people of the United States value "rugged individualism," self-reliance, and personal freedom—including an extraordinarily free access to guns—more than any society among the modern industrialized nations. This high level of egocentrism produces individuals who are primarily interested in the self. Social obligations and the welfare of others come second to personal gain and profit. Like the Swat Pukhtun, egocentrism in a hierarchical society influences individuals to be aggressive, selfish, prideful, and violent. This combination is, in effect, criminogenic. The United States is the most violently criminal society among modern industrialized nations. Because the personality disorders in DSM-IV are primarily based on concepts of pathological personality development occurring in the United States, all of these personality disorders are present in American society.

Macro level social forces play an important role in shaping personality development, both normal and abnormal. The dramatic differences between the Swat Pukhtun and the Senoi Temiar or between the Japanese and Americans illustrate the fact that cultural meaning systems have a significant impact on individual personality. Therefore, social structures that are socio-centric or egocentric, hierarchical or egalitarian, and premodern or modern cultural meaning systems should be evaluated in any cultural assessment of psychopathology. This is addressed in more detail in Chapter 4.

Chapter Four

Cultural Assessment

Cultural assessment is essential in a client-centered psychiatry because of the impact culture has in structuring clinical reality. Clinicians need to understand such things as why auditory hallucinations are not necessarily a symptom of a psychotic disorder. Also, they need to understand why clients may need emotional healing or cognitive restructuring of life events as well as biomedical treatment to achieve the best outcome.

Mental disorders are far more complex in their origins and structures than what most people have previously imagined. Mental illnesses can be constructed, maintained, exacerbated, and treated on several different levels simultaneously. For mental disorders to be treated most efficiently and effectively, all of the different levels and their interactions need to be assessed in a holistic fashion.

Clinicians cannot assume that all clients should be treated in the same way. The "psychic unity of humankind" that was assumed in disease-centered psychiatry does not exist. Taking a universal approach to assessment, diagnosis, and treatment is inappropriate. People are more than biological organisms. They have thoughts, feelings, emotions, social relationships, and above all, they have culture. Cultural schemas structure their individual and collectively experienced realities. A mentally ill person is more than just a "broken brain." Assessing and treating mental patients as if they were nothing more than dysfunctioning biological machines reduces psychiatry to the level of a veterinary science.

Culture and Emotion

So much of mental illness is related to human emotion that it is necessary first to discuss the assessment of culture and emotion before we get to the discussion of overall cultural assessment. The assessment of mental illness should be based on an understanding of the cultural nature of human emotions.

Generally, anthropologists adhere to a **cultural constructionist** view of human emotion (Good & Kleinman, 1985; Jenkins, Kleinman, & Good, 1990; Levy, 1984; Lutz, 1985, 1988; Ratner, 1989; Rosaldo, 1984; Shweder, 1985; Solomon, 1984). This refers to the idea that adult human emotions depend on cultural concepts. That is, cultural schemas mediate between sensory stimuli and emotional reactions. Because cultural schemas provide the cognitive structure for the appraisal of sensory stimuli, the meaning of events and norms of behavioral responses for adult human emotions are not uniform across cultures.

For example, consider a simple event in human interpersonal relations and its impact on emotion. Imagine you are a single, adult North American woman. Further, imagine that a man walks up to you in a private location and kisses you passionately on the mouth. What kind of emotion does this event evoke in you?

You are not sure? The reason you are not sure is because you do not have enough information about who the man is and his relationship to you. The identity of the man and his relationship to you will determine the *meaning* of the situation and, therefore, the proper emotion as defined by the cultural schemas regarding kissing.

For example, imagine that the passionate man is your new lover. What quality of emotion does this situation evoke in you now? This situation probably evokes some kind of pleasant emotional response, perhaps romantic feelings or sexual arousal.

For a second example, imagine that the man kissing you passionately on the mouth is your father. What quality of emotion does this different situation evoke in you? Your emotional response is probably quite different from the first example. Why? Because the *meaning* of the situation is now different. Cultural schemas about incest taboos, and the emotions that go along with them as defined by your meaning system, will probably be experienced.

As a third example, imagine that the man kissing you passionately on the mouth is your employer. What quality of emotion does this situation evoke in you, and why? Your cultural schemas will probably structure this event in your consciousness as an occurrence of sexual harassment. The feelings you experience may be anger, and your behavioral response may be to call your lawyer.

In each of the above cases, the actual physical events are the same—an adult man kisses an adult woman passionately on the mouth in a private location. Yet in each case, the meaning of the event is different, and the emotions evoked are different. Understanding the influence of cultural schemas on emotion is essential to a client-centered assessment of disordered human emotions.

A Cognitive Model of Emotion

Robert Levy (1984, following Ekman, 1980) has proposed a three-stage cognitive model for understanding human emotion. Levy defines emotion as all three of these stages combined. Box 4.1 summarizes Levy's stages of emotion.

Box 4.1

Three-Stage Cognitive Model of Emotion

1. Initial appraisal
2. Emotional feeling
3. Culture-based behavioral response

SOURCE: Based on Levy, 1984.

Initial appraisal. In Levy's three-stage model, the first stage, *initial appraisal*, is the stage of cognitive assessment. The meanings of events are assessed in this stage, drawing on cultural definitions of the status of the persons as well as cultural schemas prescribing norms of behavior. The status of the persons involved—female self, new lover, father, employer—and the proper roles or norms of behavior associated with these social statuses are structured in cultural schemas. These may seem to you to be natural categories, but in fact they are created by collective human intentionality (Chapter 1).

For example, a person need not have a female body to have a female status in society (see Chapter 7). Likewise, the cultural schema of a lover, a father, or an employer is dependent on people collectively agreeing on who counts as that person. These statuses and roles are cultural constructs (Schneider, 1980). For example, does a stepfather count as a father? What about an adoptive father, or a father-in-law? In some societies, the identity of a woman's biological father is not usually known. If a woman does not know it is her biological father kissing her, does it make a difference?

In this first stage, appraisal, the meaning of the event is determined by a cognitive assessment, based on cultural schemas. The woman being kissed in the three examples feels pleasure when being kissed by her new lover, anxiety when being kissed by her father, and anger when being kissed by her employer because the cultural schemas have predefined the meanings of these events.

Emotional feeling. The first stage of appraisal leads into the second stage, which Levy calls *emotional feeling*. Emotional feeling refers to the bodily sensations that are felt as a result of cognitive appraisal. For example, consider the emotion *anxiety*. What kind of bodily sensations are present when you get anxious? You may experience rapid breathing, tightness in the stomach, blood rushing to the head, headache, or other similar bodily sensations. These sensations result from an event that you have cognitively constructed in a way that justifies anxiety, for example, fear of some future consequences of events. It is the cognitive construction of the event that gives rise to the bodily sensations.

As another example, consider the bodily sensations occurring as result of being passionately kissed by your new lover. These bodily sensations may be those of *sexual arousal* if you cognitively construct your lover's kiss as an invitation for lovemaking.

In both cases, the bodily sensations and underlying physiological changes occur as a response to a cognitive appraisal of the situation. Thus, the mind and the body are not separate. Cognition and emotion are not separate. The content of cognition has immediate and dramatic effects in overall physiology and biochemistry. In each of these examples, it is the content of cognition that determines the physiological response, and it is the cultural schema that determines the content of cognition. Therefore, accurate assessment of emotional states without reference to cultural schemas is not possible.

Culture-based behavioral response.   The third stage of emotion in Levy's cognitive model is the *culture-based behavioral response*—that is, the observable action carried out by the individual in response to the first two stages.

In the examples above, the woman being kissed by her lover may become sexually aroused and kiss him back. The woman kissed by her father may pull away in a state of anxiety. In both cases, the proper behavior is determined by the cultural schemas and is preprogrammed into the individual through cultural learning.

The culture-based behavioral response is usually automatic and instantaneous because it has been previously structured in the neural networks of the brain. The brain automatically cognizes the events in a particular way consistent with cultural schemas because of cultural learning and prior individual experience. Emotion seems so "natural" and "biological" because emotions are structured in the nervous system. Thus, cultural schemas play a central role in the construction of emotions through the cognitive construction of meanings with resulting physiological changes and behavioral actions.

Cultural Assessment of Emotions

Cultural psychologist Richard Shweder (1985) has devised a six-aspect procedure for the cultural assessment of emotions; this procedure is summarized in Box 4.2.

When an anthropologist goes to a different culture to study the emotions of the people there, he or she first asks the question: What type of emotions does a particular cultural group experience? This is what Shweder (1985) refers to as the *taxonomic question*. The reason this is necessary is because some emotions that are found in western culture may not be present in the culture being studied, and other emotions not found in the West may be present. For example, guilt seems to be an emotion that is not found among the Swat Pukhtun (see Chapter 3). In contrast, Micronesians have a number of different emotions related to what westerners would call depression or sadness, all centered around the quality or loss of close personal relationships (see Chapter 12). Thus, we cannot assume that all cultural groups experience the same exact set of emotions.

The next question that needs to be asked is: Which emotions are elicited by which situations? This is what Shweder (1985) calls the *ecological question*. For the highly sociocentric Micronesians, loss of a close personal relationship such

---

Box 4.2

Aspects of Cultural Assessment of Emotion

1. *Taxonomic question:* What types of emotions does a particular cultural group experience?
2. *Ecological question:* Which emotions are elicited by which situations?
3. *Semantic question:* What do the emotions mean to indigenous observers?
4. *Communication question:* What are the vehicles or means of expression for the communication of an emotion?
5. *Social regulation question:* What emotions are proper or improper for a person of a particular social status?
6. *Management question:* How are unexpressed emotions handled?

SOURCE: Based on Shweder, 1985, pp. 184–191.

---

as a parent is highly meaningful and can elicit a number of negative emotions. In contrast, for the Swat Pukhtun, loss of a parent (especially a father) could be seen as a positive event because of the possibility of inheritance. The same situation cannot be presumed to elicit the same emotion across cultures.

The next question that needs to be asked is: What do the emotions mean to indigenous observers? This is what Shweder (1985) calls the *semantic question*. This is a crucial question when assessing pathological emotions. For example, Bill the pediatrician (see Chapter 2) experienced depression after the loss of loved ones. In his biomedically oriented culture, this meant that he was suffering from a serious brain disease. For the sociocentric and premodern Micronesians, the same emotional response would mean something entirely different. The meaning of emotions differs across cultures.

The next question that needs to be asked is: What are the vehicles or means of expression for communication of an emotion? This is what Shweder (1985) refers to as the *communication question*. This is extremely important when assessing pathological emotions, because emotional distress can have varying cultural idioms of expression. These are known in medical anthropology as *idioms of distress* (see Chapter 2). This refers to the fact that cultural groups have their own unique ways of expressing emotional distress. For example, a Malaysian man experiencing loss of honor may "run *amok*" (see example in next section), whereas a Senoi Temiar man experiencing loss of honor is likely to express his emotional distress in a midnight "harangue" (see Chapter 3). It is very important to understand differing cultural idioms of distress when assessing emotions.

The next question that needs to be asked is: What emotions are proper or improper for a person of a particular social status? This is what Shweder (1985) refers to as the *social regulation question*. This is also very important when assessing emotional pathology because of the effects of dominance hierarchies on personality development (see Chapter 3). Social structures define the status of people in different ways with differing sets of emotions and behaviors that are considered proper or improper according to social rank (gender, race, ethnicity, and so on). For example, sexual aggressiveness and the open expression of lust by a woman are considered deviant and even pathological in some cultures, whereas the same behavior and expression of emotion may be considered normal in a man. In other cultures women are allowed the freedom to express their sexual desires (see Chapters 6 and 7). Thus, the effects of dominance hierarchies in a particular culture need to be considered when assessing an individual's emotions.

The next question that needs to be asked is: How are unexpressed emotions handled? This is what Shweder (1985) refers to as the *management question*. This is also very important when assessing emotional pathology. For many people, especially those in subservient positions, the open expression of emotional distress may be socially or politically difficult, as this could imply dissatisfaction with the status quo (Kleinman, 1986). For these people, some alternative means of expression must be found that does not reflect on them in a social or political way. One common avenue of expression is *somatization*— that is, expression of emotional distress in somatic (bodily) symptoms (see Chapters 10 and 11). Another possibility is *dissociation*, in which the person takes on an alternate identity from the cultural repertoire (for example, through spirit possession) and expresses those negative emotions in a way that does not reflect on the person because he or she is considered to be possessed by a demon or spirit (see Chapter 13). One example of the expression of emotional distress through dissociation is the culture-bound syndrome of *amok* in Malaysia.

Amok as Cultural Emotion

The cultural constructionist view is important in assessing how culture affects emotions, and therefore in developing a client-centered perspective on mental disorders. Taking **amok** as an example, it is possible to assess the emotional qualities of this syndrome within its cultural context using Levy's and Shweder's models.

Amok, a Southeast Asian trance syndrome, is usually characterized by a short-lived (a few minutes to several hours) sudden outburst of unrestrained violence, usually of a homicidal nature, preceded by a period of brooding, and ending with exhaustion. There is typically dissociative amnesia (see Chapter 13) for the episodes. The cause of *amok* is indigenously attributed to interpersonal conflict, personal abuse, intolerable embarrassment, shame, and loss of honor (Burton-Bradley, 1968; Carr, 1985; Carr & Tan 1976).

The origins of *amok* are probably found in ancient India. Ancient Indian Hindu warriors entered a trance state before a battle and would fight with indiscriminate abandon—having no fear, feeling no pain—and would slaughter the enemy without stopping until they were either killed or collapsed in exhaustion. They believed they were possessed by warrior gods and would have no memory of the battle afterward. In effect, it was the warrior god "possessing" them who did the fighting.

This aspect of Indian culture was transferred to the Malay Archipelago during Indian colonization of the area during the fourth and fifth centuries. Malay warriors adopted the tactic. In a trance they would charge the enemy en masse screaming "*Amok! Amok!*" (probably from the Sanskrit *amuc*, "no freedom"), indicating to the opponents that no prisoners would be taken and that they would be killed to the last man.

The evolution of military *amok* into personal *amok* is unclear. However, it was almost always a man who would be sitting quietly with friends and then suddenly grab a knife or sword and indiscriminately attack anyone within reach. The attack could go on for hours and lasted until the person was either killed, subdued, or collapsed in exhaustion. The *amok* person would then go into a deep sleep for several days, followed by complete amnesia for the event (Carr, 1985).

To assess *amok* in its cultural context, it is necessary to know that Malays are highly sensitive to loss of honor or respect. This is a hierarchical society (Chapter 3), and social interactions are highly controlled. Everyone must use the correct behavior and language appropriate to the rank and status of the persons involved. Failure to do so is a serious breach of etiquette and an insult, especially to a man's honor. An insult to a Malay man's honor is a dangerous act. Thus, a Malay man should be treated with fear and respect. He should be treated this way because he is potentially extremely violent; he can run *amok* if his honor is slighted.

In the *amok* man, there is an intense sense of grievance and loss of self-esteem because he feels he has been treated with disrespect (Carr, 1985; Gullick, 1958). Running *amok* is a way for him to achieve revenge or restitution for a perceived loss of honor. Because slights to his honor may have been received from many people, it is not illogical for his violence to be indiscriminate. However, the *amok* man is not considered to be responsible for his actions because he is possessed by a spirit, and because he has no memory of the events.

If we assess *amok* as a cultural emotion using Levy's three-stage model, we clearly see all three stages. The *initial appraisal* stage is the cognized loss of honor in some social situation as constructed by the Malay cultural schemas. The *emotional feeling* stage is comprised in the intense physical feelings in the body of anger, incoherent rage, grievance, and loss. The third stage of *culture-based behavior* is going into a trance and the unrestrained homicidal violence. All of these things are cultural entities, predefined within the Malay cultural meaning system and learned through cultural schemas.

Amok can also be culturally assessed using Shweder's model. First is the *taxonomic question*: What types of emotions exist in Malay culture? Obviously, *amok* is a predefined category of emotion and behavior specific to this culture. It is a cultural entity that has been constructed in cultural schemas.

Second is the *ecological question*: What situations evoke *amok*? In this cultural context, it is a series of insults to a man's honor in social situations. The social situations, as well as appropriate and inappropriate behavior, are predefined and structured in Malay cultural schemas.

Third is the *semantic question*: What does *amok* mean to Malay observers? Here it is seen that *amok* signifies to observers that the person has been possessed by a spirit who controls his body and causes him to commit indiscriminate violence and homicide. They also recognize that this occurred because the man was insulted or treated inappropriately. These are obvious cultural entities constructed by the indigenous meaning system.

Fourth is the *communication question*: What are the behavioral vehicles for the expression of *amok*? The trance state, the indiscriminate homicidal violence, and the dissociative amnesia are the behavioral vehicles for the expression of *amok*. These are cultural entities borrowed from a military context and used in Malay social situations.

Fifth is the *social regulation question*: What emotions are proper or improper for a person of a particular social status? In this case, we see that men are primarily the ones who run *amok*. The evolution of military *amok* into personal *amok* probably has its origins in the notion that all Malay men should be seen as warriors and are therefore dangerous. Thus, Malay men should be treated with fear and respect in social interactions because they are potentially homicidal if treated with disrespect. In this way, *amok* serves a social regulation function by helping to define and maintain the dominance hierarchy.

Sixth is the *management of emotions question*: How are unexpressed emotions handled? In the case of *amok*, it is seen that anger, grievance, and loss of honor are not expressed by the person directly but by a "spirit" possessing the person. The person himself is not considered to be responsible and has no memory of the event. The trance state and spirit possession of *amok* allow the person to express emotions that he cannot express in his ordinary state of consciousness.

It is clear that without understanding the cultural schemas of the Malay people it is not possible to assess *amok* as a cultural syndrome. It is necessary to understand the dominance hierarchies and situations that are constructed, the meanings of those situations, and the emotional responses that are evoked as a result.

Reducing *amok* to a simplistic "brain disease" would dehumanize the people involved, trivialize the complexity of the situation, and lead to a reductionistic style of treatment. For this reason, the cultural schemas structuring the client's emotions must be assessed by the clinician for optimal care to be realized. This is the essence of a client-centered assessment of emotional distress. Assessing and understanding the cultural schemas and personal cognitive patterns underlying emotional distress is crucial for placing those emotions within a larger context and understanding the sources of distress and identifying possible avenues of emotional healing.

DSM-IV Outline for Cultural Formulation

DSM-IV includes an **Outline for Cultural Formulation.** This cultural outline is the first attempt in the DSM to alert clinicians that assessment of a mental disorder should be made within the cultural context of the client and to judge the

---

Box 4.3

DSM-IV Outline for Cultural Formulation

1. Cultural identity of the individual
2. Cultural explanations of the individual's illness
3. Cultural factors related to psychosocial environment and levels of functioning
4. Cultural elements of the relationship between the individual and the clinician
5. Overall cultural assessment for diagnosis and care

SOURCE: From American Psychiatric Association, 1994, pp. 843–844.

---

implications that has for clinical treatment. Box 4.3 summarizes the DSM-IV Outline for Cultural Formulation.

DSM-IV suggests that the clinician making an assessment of a client provide a narrative summary for each of the categories in the Outline for Cultural Formulation. This is in essence a **brief clinical ethnography** (Kleinman, 1988a). Each of these five aspects of assessment will be discussed in detail in the next sections.

Cultural Identity of the Individual

The first category in the cultural outline is the cultural identity of the individual. This refers to the collective mass of cognitive schemas of an individual's cultural or ethnic reference groups. As you have seen, mental disorders vary by culture. Thus, there will be typical forms of mental illness in each culture. What is typical in one culture may be exotic in another. How this behavior is understood depends on the cognitive schemas of the observer. For example, the behavior of a Malaysian man who runs *amok* is understood differently with knowledge of his cultural schemas than it would be without this knowledge.

Subcultural groups also have differing forms of mental illness. Immigrants in North America may have varying degrees of involvement with the culture of their country of origin and the Anglo American culture in the United States. Therefore, they will behave with varying degrees of consistency to cultural norms of mental illness. For example, a Malay immigrant to the United States may or may not have the potential to run *amok*. The same type of situation is also true for ethnic minorities.

Conversely, in nonwestern societies, a westernized minority segment of the society with individuals possessing a more western cultural identity may present with westernized forms of mental illness. Therefore, in a client-centered psychiatry it is vital that the cultural identity of each patient be assessed individually.

Differences in cultural identity may involve differences in language, religion, educational level, class, social status, and gender status. Because cultural identity is variable across individuals within any immigrant or minority group, stereotypes of ethnic groups should be avoided. For example, assuming that a client is a Roman Catholic because she is Mexican American is a stereotype (Galanti, 1991). Mexican Americans do tend to be Catholic, and clinicians should be aware of that generalization and any implications it might have for clinical treatment. But not all Mexican Americans are Catholic. To prevent stereotyping, generalizations about ethnic groups should be used only as a background to the assessment of a particular individual (Lu, Lim, & Mezzich, 1995). Each client needs to be assessed as an individual and should not be stereotyped (Lewis-Fernández & Kleinman, 1994).

To understand the cultural identity of the patient, the clinician must assess the individual's cultural schemas. This involves clinicians studying the cultures of the persons they are likely to see in their region's clinics and hospitals. Prior knowledge of the individual's culture will allow clinicians to know what factors to look for. However, knowing whether a particular client fits a cultural generalization comes only from asking. Because cultural schemas vary by individual, each client should be treated as a unique case. Each individual should be asked about cultural identity in an open-ended fashion, allowing the person to elaborate on his or her cultural schemas.

As you have seen, a cultural meaning system defines reality for an individual. Meanings about how the world works, the status of the people in it, what emotions to feel, and what behavior is appropriate in certain situations are all structured in cultural schemas. Assessment of mental disorders without reference to the client's cultural identity is therefore inappropriate and may lead to less than optimal care.

Cultural Explanations of Mental Illness

One of the core concepts of client-centered psychiatry is the distinction between illness and disease. The second aspect of the DSM-IV cultural outline is the assessment of cultural explanations of an individual's illness. This is where the distinction between *illness* or the client's subjective experience of being sick, and *disease*, the clinician's diagnosis, becomes crucial. If the clinician is not treating illness but only disease, the course and outcome of the case is likely to be detrimentally affected. But if the clinician can simultaneously treat illness as well as disease, the course and outcome of the case are more likely to be benefited.

Mental illness in Bali. An example of treating both illness and disease comes from a psychiatrist treating mental illness in Bali. Denny Thong (1993) relates his experience as an Indonesian doctor trained in western psychiatry who was the director of the only state mental hospital on the island of Bali for nearly two decades.

Thong (1993) describes his transformation from a disease-centered psychiatrist adhering to a strictly biomedical model of mental illness to a client-centered practitioner utilizing a holistic model of mental illness and treatment. This transformation was brought about by his studies of Balinese culture, including trance states and their relationship to Balinese forms of mental illness, and the use of traditional folk healers and folk methods in the treatment of his patients.

As Thong quickly discovered, religion is all-pervasive in Balinese culture. Deities and spirits are encountered everywhere by the Balinese people and are collectively constructed and maintained by Balinese cultural schemas. In this culture, all of these cognitively created supernatural entities are capable of possessing a person and causing various illnesses. Likewise, Balinese sorcerers can cause illness by manipulating various minor spirits and, through the technique of "object intrusion," are believed to cause illness by magically implanting a harmful object in a victim. Furthermore, the Balinese are highly aware of geographical orientation in relation to the holy mountain at the center of the island. Without constant awareness of this geographical direction, Balinese will become *paling*, a disoriented, confused state in which they are unable to function.

Mental illness is called *buduh* in Bali and has as its indigenous symptoms: *inguh, pusing, paling*, and *lengeh*, being dizzy, confused, or disoriented; *ngamuk*, running *amok*; *bengong* and *samun*, being apathetic or dazed; *ngumikmik*, raving, being incoherent, or talking to oneself; *nyeh*, being anxious, frightened, or excessively timid; *malumbar*, running away and resisting restraint; and *ngumbang*, wandering aimlessly. The causes of these symptoms are indigenously attributed to inherited factors, possession by spirits and gods, ancestral or divine curses, and sorcery (Connor, 1979, cited in Thong, 1993).

It was into this cultural context of mental illness that Thong was placed in 1968, armed with his medical knowledge and the latest psychotropic medications. He discovered that adhering to a strictly disease-centered model of mental illness and treatment did not produce the best possible results for his patients. Taking a more pragmatic and client-centered approach in clinical assessment and treatment, he developed a culturally appropriate Balinese system of mental health care. His clinical results were impressive.

First, he organized his hospital and staff into a *banjar*. The *banjar* is the smallest and most basic unit of social organization in Bali next to the family. It consists of 500 to 1,500 people and confers a highly important social identity and spiritual connection on its members. Each *banjar* has its own temple, which serves as a seat for the *banjar*'s god and a location for religious festivals. To organize a *banjar*, Dr. Thong and his staff had to build a temple on the hospital grounds and perform religious rituals there. This temple became the seat of Djero Gede, a powerful Balinese god with the power to heal the sick. This spiritual power became an important part of Thong's symbolic arsenal for dealing with mental disorders. Emotional distress was relieved by the symbolic power of the god and the temple. Some patients felt better just by walking onto the grounds of the hospital.

Next, Dr. Thong looked at the architecture of the hospital. He discovered that because hospitals had been designed by Dutch colonials many years earlier none of them took into consideration the sacred geography of Bali. Balinese are forbidden to sleep with their heads in certain directions. If this rule is disobeyed, it can cause anxiety and confusion. Yet hospitals in Bali built on a western model of a large hall with two rows of beds on either side took no notice of this aspect of Balinese culture. Beds pointed in the wrong direction were likely to evoke anxiety in the patients, worsening their mental disorders.

To avoid the culturally inappropriate architecture of the hospital, Thong built what he called the Family Ward. This was a complex of four compounds built in traditional Balinese style capable of housing one patient and his or her family. In the Family Ward, patients received the usual psychiatric medications, but the families were allowed to stay with the patients. Also, the hospital staff spent much more time with the patients and families than in the usual hospital setting, involving them in therapy and discussing their personal and family problems.

In addition, if the patient or family requested it, a traditional Balinese folk healer (*balian*) was brought in to treat the patient. Thong even went so far as to make a *balian* a regular part of the staff. He found the *balian* to be very competent in treating *bebainan* (illness caused by sorcery), spirit possession, psychotic episodes, family disputes, and "bad luck," as well as muscular problems, bone fractures, and mild fevers.

Dr. Thong and the folk healers treated the *illnesses* of their Balinese patients as well as their *diseases*. This was vital to the quickest recovery for each patient. As Thong states, "The Balinese patient will not rest until he or she has seen a healer who will agree to treat the supernatural cause that brought about the ailment" (1993, p. 114). Thus, Thong found that without treating the illness experience as constructed by the patient's cultural schemas the outcome was poor.

During the one year that the Family Ward was in operation, 14 patients were treated there. Nine were diagnosed with a chronic mental illness (7 schizophrenia, 1 endogenous depression, 1 substance disorder). Of the 9 chronic patients, 7 recovered and 2 were still hospitalized. The 7 who recovered spent an average of 40 days in the Family Ward and were released. Dr. Thong attributes the high rate of recovery to the fact that they were treated in the Family Ward in a more traditional Balinese fashion. Thus, the treatment was client-centered rather than disease-centered.

Similar experiences of successfully treating Balinese patients with traditional Balinese healing methods have also been reported by Suryani and Jensen (1993). Clinicians all over the world can learn from these clinicians' client-centered approach, cultural sensitivity, and therapeutic applications of cultural knowledge.

Eliciting an explanatory model.   Arthur Kleinman (1988a, pp. 43–44) has defined what a clinician needs to do in assessing cultural schemas regarding an individual's illness. The clinician needs to *ask the client* what he or she thinks is the nature of the problem. The clinician needs to ask:

1. Why has the problem affected you?
2. Why has the illness had its onset now, and what course do you think the illness will follow?

3. How does the illness affect you?
4. What treatment do you think is appropriate, and what treatment do you want?
5. What do you fear most about the illness and its treatment?

Disease-centered psychiatrists are not typically willing to give this much control to the individual in defining the nature of the problem and its treatment. Training programs in psychiatry usually teach clinicians to assess and diagnose on the basis of symptoms observed by the clinician, followed by appropriate treatment as defined by the disease-centered paradigm (for example, medications).

However, this disease-centered approach does not assess the illness experience of the patient. If this is ignored, the patient may not receive the treatment that will be most effective in alleviating the illness, and may even exacerbate or complicate the patient's condition, as in the Balinese cases.

Cultural and Psychosocial Environment

The third aspect of the DSM-IV cultural outline is assessing how culture is related to the psychosocial environment and levels of functioning. This refers to culture-based sources of social and environmental stress on the individual as well as to the impact of social supports on functioning, impairment, recovery, and relapse. In client-centered psychiatry, clinicians need to assess the client and his or her mental disorder within the total sociocultural context. This includes looking for unusual or severe stressors on the client in the social environment as well as how resulting emotional distress manifests in the cultural context and illness experience of the client.

A "ghost" in North India.   A case of possession by a "ghost" in India reported by Freed and Freed (1964) is an instructive example of a sociocultural environment constructing both a highly stressful situation and a person's illness response to it.

The ill person was Daya, a newlywed 15-year-old girl of the Chamar caste (leatherworkers and laborers ranking close to the bottom of the caste hierarchy). During her possession behavior she became "Chand Kor," a "ghost" possessing Daya. The "ghost" Chand Kor knew of Daya's activities, but Daya had no knowledge or memory of the periods when Chand Kor possessed the body.

Villagers in north India believe that the soul of a dead person may become a ghost for three reasons: (1) dying before the time allotted a soul to live; (2) dying tortured; and (3) dying after actions contrary to village customs (Freed & Freed, 1990). The death of Chand Kor fit these circumstances. In real life, Chand Kor had been a childhood friend of Daya's and was as close to her as a sister. Chand Kor has been forced by her natal family to commit suicide because of a premarital pregnancy. A girl of approximately the same age as Daya, she had been having an affair with a man in her home village prior to being married to a man in another village.

Girls in rural India are well aware of the risks they run by having premarital affairs. Daya knew that Chand Kor was having sexual relations with a man and warned her that she would not be allowed to live if her father or new husband found out. However, Chand Kor was already pregnant when she went to live with her new husband's family and was therefore rejected and returned to her parents. She begged for forgiveness but was told by her father, "I won't keep you. Go jump in a well." Her parents continued to verbally abuse her for several days, telling her to go jump into a well—the traditional way for women to commit suicide in rural India. One day while playing with a group of girlfriends, she excused herself and ran and jumped into a well.

Daya told the Freeds that she was terrified of having sex with her husband. Her spirit possession experiences began during the third visit with her husband's family. In this region of India (Uttar Pradesh) villages are exogamous, and marriages are patrilocal. However, the movement of the bride to the husband's village takes place in stages. The first visit to the husband's village occurs at the time of the wedding ceremony and lasts for a few days. No sexual intercourse takes place during the first visit. The second visit is also brief, and the first mating will occur during this period. The third visit is usually an extended stay, and it is expected that the new couple will have regular sexual intercourse.

When Daya went to her husband's village, she slept with her husband for three or four nights and had regular sex. It was at this point that her spirit possession episodes began, after which she did not sleep with her husband for two weeks. After two weeks her husband began sleeping with her again, but they did not have sexual intercourse, as Daya felt ill even when the "ghost" did not have control of the body.

The Indian cultural meaning system and its construction of a dominance hierarchy with young females at the bottom places females in a vulnerable and potentially highly stressful situation, possibly prompting mental illness. Furthermore, the cultural schemas have predetermined what the typical form of her mental illness should be, that is, spirit possession. The cultural schemas further determine what kind of treatment she should receive if she is to recover, that is, an exorcism of the "ghost" that is possessing her that also simultaneously alters the family dynamics, relieving the individual of significant stress in the family (Lewis, 1989). Thus, cultural schemas determine both sources of illness and of healing. This relationship between correlated sociocultural sources of illness and healing should not be overlooked by clinicians when assessing clients. In assessing the cultural and psychosocial environment, clinicians need to inquire about social relationships including dominance hierarchies within the family structure that may be sources of extreme stress.

Immigrants may also have severe emotional stress or trauma in their personal histories. For example, refugees may have endured tremendous hardships including possible torture, beatings, starvation, rape, and imprisonment. Clients may have also lost family members, homes, financial resources, careers, and so on. Clinicians need to assess possible traumatic experiences and losses in refugees (Lu, Lim, & Mezzich, 1995).

Culture and Clinician-Client Relationship

The fourth aspect of the DSM-IV cultural outline is the effect of culture on the clinician-client relationship. This refers to differences in the construction of clinical reality caused by differing cultural schemas in the clinician and the client. This can manifest as something simple like a misunderstanding of the clinician's instructions based on class or language differences, or something more serious like a misdiagnosis based on widely differing cultural backgrounds. For example, a western trained clinician might diagnose a spirit possession type illness based strictly on disease-centered conceptions of mental illness. This is likely to contribute to misdiagnosis and less than optimal treatment and outcome.

Diagnostic ethnocentrism.   Clinicians need to be aware that it is not just the client who has cultural schemas. The clinician also has cultural schemas, and **diagnostic ethnocentrism** can lead to many problems in assessment and diagnosis. Typically, clinicians understand a client's problem according to the way they have been professionally trained. Thus, clinicians need to critically assess the effects of their own cultural schemas in relation to individual clinical cases (Hinton & Kleinman, 1993).

The earlier example of an Indian folk healer diagnosing *dhat* syndrome in a western patient with the symptoms of major depression illustrates this problem. To avoid diagnostic ethnocentrism, clinicians need to reflexively assess their own conceptions of a client's illness and attempt to see the situation from the client's perspective as much as possible. This client-centered approach is essentially an ethnographic technique. Anthropologists in the field attempt to understand as clearly as possible the subjective experience of the people being studied, to "get things right" from the native's point of view. In the clinical situation, the "native" is the client. This is the person with firsthand experience of the illness. Understanding his or her subjective illness experience is central to making an assessment of the differences between the clinician's and client's conceptions of the problem. This can allow the clinician to critically assess what disease concepts are being appropriately or inappropriately projected onto the client and allow for assessment of diagnostic ethnocentrism.

Use of interpreters.   Language barriers can complicate communication in a psychiatric assessment. These barriers can be overcome through the use of interpreters, but this method has its own problems. Frequently, the most convenient interpreter is a bilingual member of the client's family. However, a family member may or may not want to reveal information about the client and the family that could be clinically important. For example, information about the client or family that could be embarrassing or shameful might be withheld. This could result in a distorted explanation of the client's problem.

Conversely, information given to the client by the clinician may be filtered by the family member in response to some family dynamic or cultural restriction that distorts the message. For example, clinicians' instructions regarding anything related to sexuality could be withheld or altered by the interpreter because of cultural taboos on discussion of sexual matters between certain family members. Therefore, if a family member is used, clinicians should be aware of the possibility of communication problems arising from family dominance hierarchies and ideas of proper gender role behavior including sexuality, religious beliefs, family honor, and shame (Galanti, 1991).

For these reasons, ideally, a clinician who speaks the client's primary language should assess the client. If that is not possible, a neutral interpreter with some clinical training (preferably of the same gender as the client) is the next best option. However, even a neutral interpreter might have difficulty because of cultural taboos regarding speaking to someone of the opposite gender, or the interpreter might withhold or alter information that could be seen as embarrassing to the ethnic group as a whole.

Interviewing techniques.   Clinicians should recognize that the same interviewing techniques may have different effects on individuals with differing sociocultural backgrounds. For example, among middle class persons in the United States, it is normal to have rather direct eye contact while conversing. This is an indication of polite interest. However, among some cultural or ethnic groups, direct eye contact has different meanings (Galanti, 1991; Ivey, 1994). Many Asians consider it disrespectful to look someone of superior status directly in the eye. Similarly, among some Native Americans, eye contact by the young is a sign of disrespect. And among many Middle Easterners, direct eye contact between persons of the opposite gender is a sign of sexual invitation. Clinicians should be aware of these differing customs and be able to adjust to the norms of the client.

The amount of personal space required for comfort in conversation also differs by culture. For instance, among North Americans slightly more than an arm's length is required for a comfort zone between people. The British prefer even greater distance. Hispanics generally prefer less distance, and Middle Easterners usually converse face to face. Not following these customs may create discomfort in the client.

Also, in some cultures individuals may normally speak more quickly and appear more animated, or speak more slowly and appear more reserved than is the norm among Anglo Americans. These cultural differences need to be accounted for in assessment of clients from different cultural backgrounds. Clinicians should be flexible enough to adjust their interviewing styles to match the cultural identity of the client. This will provide a better opportunity for creating a sense of comfort and rapport in the clinician-client relationship.

Box 4.4

Steps in Overall Cultural Assessment

1. Assessment of cultural identity
2. Use of reference sources to understand the pertinent ethnic or cultural groups relevant to the client
3. Assessment of cultural meaning of key symptoms, idioms of distress, and culture-bound syndromes
4. Assessment of client and family explanatory models of illness
5. Assessment of effects of family, work, and community settings on client's illness
6. Assessment of socially significant forms of stigma or other social responses to illness
7. Self-reflexive assessment of ethnocentric biases by clinician
8. Negotiation of clinical reality and treatment plan between client, family, and clinician

SOURCE: Based on Kleinman, 1992, p. 26.

Overall Cultural Assessment

The fifth aspect of the DSM-IV cultural outline is overall cultural assessment. This step is essentially a *negotiation of clinical reality* between the clinician, the client and, ideally, the client's family. A plan of treatment should be drawn up that is the result of a negotiated consensus of the problem and the appropriate treatment. In this way, all the parties concerned will be operating on the same set of assumptions and will understand and willingly agree to follow the course of treatment. This provides the best opportunity for creating a therapeutic alliance and obtaining optimal care and outcome.

Steps in overall cultural assessment.   Overall cultural assessment is actually a summary of the aspects already mentioned. An overall assessment should include the following steps as listed in Box 4.4.

Step 1 in Box 4.4 is the assessment of cultural identity as outlined previously. Step 2 refers to the clinical use of ethnographic or other sources of cultural expertise to understand the cultural meaning system of a client. Step 3 refers to the assessment of cultural meanings associated with symptoms such as in the *amok* example. These symptoms have a specific meaning in the indigenous culture. Understanding these meanings will help the clinician understand the client's illness. Step 4 refers to the assessment of an explanatory model as outlined previously. This should be done for both the client and the family. This assessment could uncover clinically useful information regarding client-family relations.

Step 5 refers to the effects of the social environment on the client's illness. The social environment can be very important in structuring course and outcome. Wolf (1990) describes the case study of a mentally ill woman in a Taiwanese village. The woman was hallucinating, and people in the village thought she was either being called by a god to speak for him (thus become a shaman) or was going crazy. Because she was woman in a highly male-dominated society and her family was new to the community, her status in the village was low. Her low status disallowed formal training in shamanistic techniques that would have been required for her to become a successful shaman and thus possibly avoid being labeled crazy. If this woman had possessed a higher status, she might have avoided serious mental illness. In the end, the woman was not allowed to become a shaman, was labeled crazy, and took on the social role of a seriously mentally ill person. Thus, the effects of the social and cultural environment need to be assessed.

Step 6 refers to assessment of the culturally significant meanings of illness imposed on the individual by the society, especially stigma. For example, Scheper-Hughes (1987) describes the various cultural meanings of psychosis in a white, working class neighborhood of South Boston. The outpatients with severe mental illness were in many ways disenfranchised of their usual status and roles in the community because of the stigma of their illnesses. The author concludes that although these individuals are seriously mentally ill, they are still sensitive to the cultural meanings and social responses to their illness found in their social environment. Thus, although psychosis disenfranchises an individual, it does not deculturate the person. Therefore, a client's psychosis is still affected by the social and cultural environment. Consequently, assessment of those cultural meanings may help the clinician understand the client's illness experience.

Step 7 refers to the self-reflexive assessment of diagnostic ethnocentrism by the clinician as well as various problems in communication that can plague the clinician-client relationship. Clinicians can have preconceived notions about various ethnic and racial groups or genders. These biases can affect clinical judgment in assessment and diagnosis. For example, bias and stereotyping in the diagnosis of schizophrenia in Afro-Caribbean patients in England have been reported (Lewis, Croft-Jeffries, & Anthony, 1990), as well as in the diagnosis of schizophrenia and bipolar disorder in African American patients in the United States (Jones & Gray, 1986). Conversely, mistakenly interpreting psychopathologic symptoms as being culturally normative due to limited cultural familiarity is also possible (Chandrasena, 1983).

Gender can also affect the clinician-client interaction. Various cultures have different rules concerning interaction between men and women. Women in many cultures may be reluctant to display positive affect to an unrelated male interviewer. This could lead to an inaccurate diagnosis of flat affect on the part of the clinician (Bayes, 1981; Broverman et al., 1981). Thus, emotions as well as other aspects of mental health should be assessed in relation to gender and cultural identity.

Step 8 refers to the negotiation of a clinical reality as outlined previously. The steps outlined in Box 4.4 are basic requirements, allowing clinicians to go beyond cultural sensitivity and apply cultural knowledge for client-centered assessment, diagnosis, and treatment. Each step should be followed in order with every client, including nonminority western clients.

Every client is a unique individual with his or her own personal history. A thorough cultural assessment will provide useful information on psychological, social, and cultural patterns that can be extremely helpful in obtaining an accurate diagnosis as well as optimal treatment and outcome.

Use of Diagnostic Interview Schedules

A research and clinical methodology that is currently popular is the use of **structured diagnostic interview schedules.** These are diagnostic questionnaires with set lists of questions inquiring about the presence of specific symptoms. The use of one of these diagnostic questionnaires with clients from a different culture from that in which the interview schedule was developed is highly problematic. It is not enough merely to translate the questions into a different language, because the illness concepts in the diagnostic interview are taken from a particular set of cultural schemas. Thus, those illness concepts may not even exist in another culture. If they do exist, they may have a different meaning or cultural significance (Marsella, 1989; Patel & Winston, 1994). For example, hearing voices is not necessarily a symptom of psychosis.

Unfortunately, cross-cultural psychiatric epidemiology has frequently used standardized diagnostic interviews based on western conceptions of psychopathology. Especially in the 1970s and 1980s there was a positivist bias among epidemiologists based on the disease-centered paradigm (Guarnaccia, Good, & Kleinman, 1990; Kleinman, 1988b; Patel & Winston, 1994). Certain mental disorders were assumed to be present and the same across cultures, and many studies in cross-cultural psychiatric epidemiology were designed to prove this point. This is what Arthur Kleinman calls the **category fallacy.** The category fallacy is the "reification of one culture's diagnostic categories and their projection onto patients in another culture, where those categories lack coherence and their validity has not been established" (1988b, p. 14).

This reification and projection of western diagnostic categories onto non-westerners has occurred in the study of depressive disorders. For example, in some societies such as China (Kleinman, 1982), Kenya (Ndetei & Muhangi, 1979), and India (Rao, 1973), persons do not readily report being depressed and do not consider themselves to be depressed. However, they may report other symptoms that are associated with major depression in the West, such as somatic symptoms. Some researchers have tended to count these as cases of "masked" depression (Patel & Winston, 1994). To count these as cases of depression equivalent to western depression is a category fallacy. For epidemiology to gain in validity, it should be preceded by ethnographic research so that indigenous conceptions of mental disorder are incorporated into the epidemiological research instruments (Marsella, Sartorius, Jablensky, & Fenton, 1985).

The Meaning of Hearing Voices

Many nonwestern cultures maintain communication with dead ancestors by going into trances and conversing with the "spirits" of the ancestors. If these societies have ancestor cults, the spirits of the dead ancestors are mostly beneficial to the surviving relatives. Thus, the ancestors are consulted regularly on any important decision of the family, and they maintain a constant connection to the living relatives. Death itself has a different meaning in these societies. Death does not remove someone from the family either physically or spiritually. Because the spirits of the dead ancestors are not to be feared as ghosts but are still active members of the family, their dead bodies are usually not removed from the living relatives to some special place reserved for the dead. Rather, they are typically buried nearby or under the floor of the family's house or hut, as they are still part of the family and need to be kept close so they can be consulted on a regular basis. The dead ancestors are thus interacting with the living relatives on a regular basis and are not considered frightening.

In these societies, there is regular communication between the living and the dead. The living can hear the voices of their dead ancestors, who advise them and help them in all kinds of worldly affairs. In these societies, it is normal to hear the voices of dead ancestors, and indeed, the people would feel abandoned and anxious without the help and guidance of their ancestral spirits (Bradbury, 1966; Lehmann & Myers, 1993; Malefijt, 1968; Mbiti, 1970; Swanson, 1964).

In contrast, in societies in which the spirits of the dead are considered to be frightening and are not supposed to interact in the daily affairs of the living, their dead bodies are usually burned or buried in a place away from the living specifically reserved for the dead, such as cemeteries. In these societies, hearing the voices of dead ancestors is usually considered an attack by malevolent "ghosts" or possession by evil spirits. This cultural appraisal of the situation typically produces tremendous anxiety in the individuals and their families. And, of course, in western societies this same situation would be considered an episode of mental illness.

If one was to take a structured diagnostic interview schedule designed to diagnose mental disorders among Anglo Americans to these nonwestern societies and use it for epidemiological purposes, any questions regarding hearing voices would mean something completely different to those people. In societies in which people regularly hear the voices of their dead ancestors, hearing voices is a normal and normative experience. In contrast, in those societies that conceptualize hearing voices as the attack of evil spirits, they will understand the interview questions in those terms. Yet the typical western diagnostic interview schedule conceptualizes hearing voices as a symptom of psychosis.

Therefore, structured diagnostic interview schedules need to be based on concepts from the indigenous cultural schemas. This usually requires a thorough translation and backtranslation process, as well as ethnographic research to discover indigenous illness categories and symptoms unrelated to the western model. In this way, a clear understanding of illness phenomena within the nonwestern cultural context is obtained.

However, because resulting interview schedules will be based on differing cultural schemas, the data obtained may not be easily comparable across cultures. Nevertheless, comparisons can be made, and some human universals structured differently across cultural contexts may be observable. For example, the process of trance appears to be a human universal that is variously structured in different cultures. However, the use of any diagnostic interview schedule that universally assumes only one meaning for a particular human experience across all cultures should be abandoned.

Chapter Five

Client-Centered Treatment

The focus of this book is on assessment and diagnosis, however, a few comments can be made about client-centered treatment. Because an individual's subjective experiences of mental illness are structured by cultural schemas, the treatment of mental disorders should be appropriate to the cultural identity and explanatory model of that person to obtain optimal outcome. Symbols from the client's cultural background can be applied to psychotherapy to make the treatment more meaningful and symbolically powerful.

For example, if a Chinese man is feeling downcast because of some misfortune, then quoting the Chinese proverb about an old man whose fate changed for the better after he lost his horse could be therapeutic (Tseng, Qiu-Yun, & Yin, 1995). Similarly, the use of Jewish healing symbols may be therapeutic for an Orthodox Israeli man. Witztum and van der Hart (1993) described how an Israeli client complaining of possession and persecution by a demon was successfully treated by employing symbolic forms from the client's own meaning system in conjunction with hypnotherapy. In addition, Thong (1993), and Maclachlan, Nyirenda, and Nyando (1995) recommend the use of qualified folk healers in collaboration with clinicians in treatment of psychiatric patients in Indonesia and Africa. These are examples of the application of cultural knowledge to psychotherapy.

Therapeutic Use of Hope

As discussed in Chapter 1, the distinction between *illness* and *disease* is an important one, because much of what constitutes a mental disorder is made up of the cognitive construction of emotions. That is, constructed meanings, especially related to anxiety, hopelessness, and helplessness, interacting on several levels simultaneously can create, perpetuate, exacerbate, alleviate, or cure a mental disorder. There will, of course, be corresponding neuronal and biochemical processes in the brain supporting the illness experience.

In the recent past, disease-centered psychiatry has tended to perceive mental disorders primarily as "genetically based incurable brain diseases." In the new client-centered psychiatry now emerging, this is no longer the case. Nevertheless, the disease-centered approach is still followed by many practitioners. Clinicians should be aware of the effect that this kind of theoretical construction can have on the cognition of the client. By defining a client's mental disorder as a "genetically based incurable brain disease," the clinician is promoting the idea that the problem is internal to the client (brain disease), stable (chronic), and general (affecting many aspects of life). Constructing a clinical reality according to these principles has the possibility of creating hopelessness and helplessness, thus exacerbating or perpetuating emotional distress and mental disorder. This is one of the most unfortunate aspects of the disease-centered approach.

This aspect of disease-centered psychiatry may help to explain why clients (especially those with schizophrenia) who believe in the disease paradigm and its treatment methods may do poorly in terms of clinical outcome. If the treatment paradigm is itself promoting the idea of incurability, this can result in the client taking on a long-term patient role, viewing him- or herself as incurably sick. In this case, the client may become medication dependent, with the client's brain adapting to the presence of the medication. For example, it is now understood that long-term use of neuroleptics results in upregulating the dopamine system in the brain.

The cognitive construction of emotions as it relates to mental illness highlights the need for the **therapeutic use of hope.** Because mental illnesses are so intimately connected to emotions, and therefore to cognition, it is imperative for clinicians to combat hopelessness and helplessness in all clients regardless of their diagnoses. By providing hope to clients, the clinician is creating a therapeutic effect on the clients' emotions and, therefore, on their mental disorders.

Some clinicians who still believe in the concept of serious mental disorders as "incurable brain diseases" may view giving hope to all clients regardless of their diagnoses as providing "false hope." However, there is no such thing as "false hope." Hope is not in itself a guarantee of good outcome or a cure. *Hope* is merely cognizing a situation as something other than *hopeless*. When it is recognized that the only alternative to hope is hopelessness, which is in itself harmful to the patient, it is clear that providing hope to mental patients should not be optional for the clinician.

Coherence in Healing

Aaron Antonovsky (1979) formulated the concept of **coherence** in healing. With coherence, a client has the cognition that his or her internal and external environments are predictable and reasonably under control. By gaining coherence, the ill person gains hope and thereby avoids hopelessness. There are three components to the concept of coherence: *comprehensibility, manageability,* and *meaningfulness.*

Comprehensibility refers to a sense of order. It means that the ill person can understand the source of the illness, the mechanism of illness, and its effects on the body and on his or her life. The illness is no longer unknown; it is known and understood. This is very important as few things are more frightening than the unknown. The unknown can be anything and take on any proportions or catastrophic dimensions in the cognition of the client. This kind of cognition can produce highly distressful emotions, exacerbating any preexisting emotional or mental disturbance. This is why it is so important to provide comprehensibility to the client. By providing comprehensibility, the client's emotions are therapeutically altered, and he or she gains a sense of order in the world and is not faced with the unknown.

Some clinicians might view providing comprehensibility to clients as an impossible task, especially in cases where the clinician does not know the source or mechanism of the illness. However, providing comprehensibility is still possible. It is not necessary for the understanding of the source or mechanism of the illness to be true or correct; it is only necessary for the client to accept it for the therapeutic alteration of emotions to occur. This is easiest to accomplish by supporting the client's own understanding of the illness, as long as this includes the possibility of reasonable treatment and possible cure.

If providing comprehensibility on the basis of incorrect information seems inappropriate, it should be pointed out that clients are commonly told that they are suffering from incurable brain diseases, even though the cause of their illness is actually unknown by the clinician. Thus, information that the clinician does not know to be true is given to clients regarding their illnesses. This practice in disease-centered psychiatry is less than optimal because it promotes the idea of incurability. However, even this notion of the incurable brain disease is better than the unknown. The explanatory model of brain disease does provide a measure of comprehensibility, and therefore it can be therapeutic for the right patient.

Providing comprehensibility is probably one of the main reasons traditional folk healers in nonwestern societies sometimes get good clinical results in their treatment of mentally ill patients. It would be very unusual for a folk healer to tell an individual that the source and mechanism of his or her illness were unknown. Folk healers know that they need to provide *healing*—that is, treatment of the individual's subjective experience of illness, especially the individual's emotions. The explanations given to clients may vary considerably and can include such things as soul loss, soul theft, spirit attack, spirit possession, breach of taboo, neglect of ancestral spirits, sin, object intrusion, sorcery, witchcraft, and biological disease. It is not necessary for these explanations to be true in any absolute sense. They are still capable of providing comprehensibility to the right client, thereby altering the client's emotions in a therapeutic fashion.

Providing comprehensibility is one of the key factors in healing mental illnesses in nonwestern societies. Of course, the cultural schemas of the individual will usually determine what the assumed source and mechanism of the illness will be. This is where knowledge of the cultural identity and explanatory model of the client becomes central to treatment. The most powerful source of comprehensibility will likely come from the client's own explanatory model. This is why eliciting an explanatory model can be so important in applying cultural knowledge to treatment.

For example, in Bali, Dr. Thong (Chapter 4) prescribed the usual psychiatric medications for his patients, while simultaneously utilizing the patients' own explanatory models to provide comprehensibility for their illnesses. It is not necessary to educate and convert everyone to a western scientific model of thinking to provide comprehensibility. Scientific explanations are not necessarily more comprehensible to any given individual. Indeed, it is much easier and quicker to use the explanatory model that the client brings to the clinical situation.

The second component of coherence in healing is **manageability.** This refers to a cognition of control or competence to meet the demands of the illness. Just knowing that the situation is not out of control is itself therapeutic. An illness out of control can be extremely distressing, evoking emotions of anxiety and possibly hopelessness and helplessness. By providing manageability, the clinician provides the client with the sense that the illness can be handled— that there is a treatment for it, and perhaps even a cure. Thus, the situation is not hopeless, and the client has powerful allies in the clinician and his or her treatments. Just by having a sense of manageability, the client can feel better. Manageability is very important in *healing* mental illnesses. Manageability provides powerful symbolic value in the therapeutic alteration of emotions.

The treatment methods used to provide manageability may vary from the ritual healing ceremonies of folk healers to the biomedical treatments of modern psychiatry, but all are capable of providing manageability to the right person. The type of treatment that will be most effective in providing the symbolic power of manageability, of course, depends on the cultural identity and explanatory model of the client.

One example of providing manageability in disease-centered psychiatry is the explanation of mania as a lithium deficiency. The view of mania (Chapter 12) as a chemical imbalance in the brain undoubtedly stems from the discovery that lithium is effective in treating manic episodes and in preventing recurrent episodes. In fact, this discovery was instrumental in heightening interest in the use of psychoactive medications for the treatment of mental illness in the 1950s and promoted the development of the disease-centered paradigm.

Lithium is a naturally occurring substance in the human body. Therefore, an extremely simplistic view of mania as a lithium deficiency in the brain was promoted in disease-centered psychiatry and became popular among the general public. It is an erroneous idea that still continues. A lithium deficiency state has never been experimentally produced in humans, and the amount of lithium that is therapeutically effective in the treatment of mania is 600 to 800 times the amount naturally occurring in the human body (Jefferson & Greist, 1989). In fact, at therapeutic dosages, lithium can have serious neurological side effects including tremor, fatigue, and slowed cognitive processing. Also, therapeutic dosages are dangerously close to levels causing neurotoxicity, therefore, blood serum levels must be periodically checked to prevent over- dose. Overdose can cause seizures, irreversible neurological damage, coma, and death.

Lithium treatment for mania does not normalize brain chemistry but takes it far out of the normal range. Despite this, I have spoken to people being treated with lithium for bipolar I disorder (manic depression) who believe they have a lithium deficiency. This explanatory model is based on the disease-cen- tered paradigm: nevertheless, it can be effective in providing comprehensibil- ity and manageability for the right clients. However, clinicians who use this lithium deficiency explanatory model should be aware that they are construct- ing a clinical reality that is not actually true.

Lithium treatment can have both psychopharmacological and symbolic value to the client. It does not matter that the explanatory model is actually false if the client believes it. The client will gain comprehensibility and man- ageability and will experience a therapeutic alteration in emotions. This is cen- tral to *healing* mental illness. However, in every case, it is easiest for clinicians to utilize information from the explanatory model of the client when providing comprehensibility and manageability. A foreign explanatory model with little symbolic power should not be imposed on the client. This is a key component of client-centered treatment.

The third component of coherence in healing is **meaningfulness.** This refers to providing a sense of *purpose* to the illness experience. Meaningfulness is commonly found in various forms of religious healing of mental illness. Religion is capable of providing a *moral* reason for illness, or a religious *value* in the illness. Examples would be a mental illness resulting from a breach of taboo or from commission of a sin.

Simultaneously, meaningfulness also provides a possible mechanism for symbolic healing. For example, by reversing the breach of taboo or atoning for the sin, the reason for the symptoms of illness can be alleviated. Similarly, by giving the experience of suffering associated with the illness some beneficial religious value, the emotions associated with the illness can be therapeutically altered, thus relieving emotional distress and perhaps curing the illness. Providing meaningfulness in healing mental illness is found throughout pre- modern or nonbiomedical methods of treatment. Folk healers specialize in pro- viding meaningfulness in their healing rituals in a process referred to by anthropologists as *symbolic healing.*

Unfortunately, the disease-centered approach does not easily permit the therapeutic use of providing meaningfulness in healing mental illness. The dis- ease-centered approach itself precludes the use of providing meaningfulness. In this paradigm, mental disorders do not possess meaning in any moral sense, or in a way that provides positive value to the individual. This paradigm for- feits the use of altering emotions in this fashion. This is an unfortunate limita- tion of possible treatment, and inappropriate in the treatment of clients who possess a cultural identity and explanatory model that may not only permit but require the therapeutic use of providing meaningfulness for optimal clinical outcome (for example, mental illness in Bali, see Chapter 4). This is where the client-centered approach can expand beyond the boundaries of disease-centered psychiatry.

The effectiveness of culturally appropriate psychotherapy or symbolic healing in the treatment of nonwestern mental illness has been attested to in many studies (Asuni, 1979; Awanbor, 1982; Baddeley, 1985; Boyer, 1964; Cheetham & Cheetham, 1976; Corin & Bibeau, 1980; Edgerton, 1971; El Islam, 1982; Harding, 1975: Harvey, 1976; Heinze, 1988; Hooper, 1985; Jilek, 1993, 1994; Ketter, 1983; Kinzie, Teoh, & Tan, 1976; Kleinman, 1980; Kortmann, 1987; Lebra, 1982; Obeyesekere, 1977; Pattison, 1977; Peters, 1978; Salan & Maretski, 1983; Sanua, 1979; Thong, 1993). However, because these studies were done in the field, they generally were not rigorously controlled. Nevertheless, there is enough evidence to conclude that culturally appropriate folk healing practices can be effective in the treatment of many mental disorders. This is to be expected as these traditional healing methods can be considered premodern, culture-based forms of psychotherapy.

Because of human brain plasticity, there is the possibility of effectively treating mental disorders with modern and premodern psychotherapies. Psychotherapy is capable of producing changes in cognitive patterns, thereby producing therapeutic changes in the construction of emotions. Also, psychotherapeutic treatments are capable of altering brain structures and biochemical processes (Kandel, 1989; Schwartz et al., 1996). This suggests that using both biomedical treatment and culturally appropriate psychotherapy in a client-centered combination are preferred to obtain optimal recovery for the client.

Symbolic Healing

The folk treatment of mental disorders in premodern societies consists primarily of altering the cognitive construction of meaning in the individual, thereby therapeutically altering emotional experience (that is, providing *meaningfulness*). This process of providing meaningfulness is referred to in medical anthropology as **symbolic healing.** Symbolic healing refers to the use of transformational symbols in healing rituals for the purpose of therapeutically altering the meaning of life events, emotional experience, and mental disorders. This therapeutic process can be analyzed according to a model of symbolic healing reformulated from earlier sources by Dow (1986). Box 5.1 summarizes the four steps of symbolic healing.

Through a negotiated diagnosis and prognosis, the clinician engaged in symbolic healing isolates part of the client's set of cultural schemas relevant to the illness and interprets the problem in terms of this negotiated clinical reality. In the therapeutic process, transformational symbols are formed that become intellectually and emotionally charged for the client.

Transformational symbols can be any ideas, objects, or actions performed by the healer that facilitate the individual's transformation of emotions and

---

Box 5.1

Four Steps of Symbolic Healing

1. The experiences of clinicians and clients are structured in terms of specific symbols from a set of cultural schemas.
2. A suffering individual comes to a clinician, who negotiates the construction of a clinical reality with the client using symbols from the cultural schemas.
3. The clinician attaches the client's intellect and emotions to transformational symbols particularized from the cultural schemas.
4. The healer manipulates the transformational symbols to help the client therapeutically restructure his or her cognitive appraisal of events and emotions.

SOURCE: Based on Dow, 1986, p. 56.

---

subjectively experienced reality. Examples of transformational symbols include medications, herbs, massage, prayer, rituals of reconciliation, penance for sin, various "holy" objects, sacred words, incantations, proverbs, scriptures, and so on. If the client accepts the healer's explanation as a valid model of his or her illness, then by skillful manipulation of the transformational symbols, the client's cognitive construction of emotions and lived experience of the illness can be therapeutically altered. Dow (1986), following Ehrenwald, refers to this alteration as the *existential shift*—that is, a change in the individual's experienced reality creating new opportunities for psychological adaptation.

In the therapeutic process of symbolic healing, the clinician and the client do not need to share the same set of cultural schemas. For example, a clinician may provide a placebo treatment that can have a highly therapeutic effect on the client based on the symbolic value of the placebo in the mind of the client. However, the manipulation of symbols and placebos is greatly facilitated if both clinician and client understand the meaning of symbolic objects based on the same set of cultural schemas.

South Asian Shamanism as Symbolic Healing

In South Asian cultural schemas, particularly in the rural areas, it is generally accepted that ghosts and demons may possess persons and cause illness and antisocial behavior. It is also generally accepted that gods and goddesses may possess persons. In the latter case, the possession is a spiritual gift and an expression of the power of the deity. It is also generally accepted that gods have power over ghosts and demons. Gods may punish ghosts and demons and order them to depart. Sometimes elaborate rituals are necessary in which the shaman is possessed by a succession of increasingly powerful gods with very high status in the spiritual hierarchy to banish a particularly difficult demon (for example, Freed & Freed, 1964; Gold, 1988, Harper, 1963; Kakar, 1982; McDaniel, 1989; Obeyesekere, 1970, 1977, 1981; Opler, 1958; Wadley 1976).

In the treatment of demonic possession by symbolic healing, the shaman usually induces a state of trance in the patient if he or she is not already in an active state of possession. This is done so that the shaman can converse directly with the possessing demon, determine its identity, the reasons it is possessing the victim, and what it wants in exchange for its departure. Negotiations between the shaman and the demon are then begun. Frequently, the demon refuses to leave, and the shaman must threaten the demon with supernatural harm from his or her own spiritual powers. Usually the shaman will have one or more gods that he or she can call on in a state of trance to possess the shaman (take control of his or her body) and do battle with the demons possessing the client. The healing rituals are primarily aimed at establishing, negotiating, and manipulating the symbolic relations between the shaman's god and the individual's demon.

In the traditional shamanic treatment of demonic possession in South Asia, the healer and patient share a common set of cultural schemas (Dow's Step 1). The South Asian shaman then negotiates a clinical reality between himself and the possessed person, which is taken from the cultural schemas (Step 2). This defines the nature of the participants for the ensuing rituals and the relative status of the parties. That is, the shaman, in conjunction with the patient, diagnoses a particular type of demonic possession requiring a particular type of healing ritual.

The shaman then involves the patient's intellect and emotions with transformational symbols (Step 3). In South Asia, the symbols taken from the cultural schemas are typically recited sacred verses (mantras) or the presence of a particular deity who possesses the shaman (highlighted by appropriate costuming and props) and who is acknowledged within the meaning system to have the power to banish demons. Other ritual objects may also be used, such as amulets or charmed strings tied around the patient's wrist or neck. Also, a cutting of the patient's hair may be ritually consigned to some sort of sacred container (a cloth or clay pot) and removed from the premises or ritually burned, symbolizing removal of the spirit. Various offerings and gifts to the spirit may also serve the purpose of transformational symbols.

By skillful manipulation of these symbolic objects, the shaman transforms the meaning of the demon's existential status, thus altering the subjective experience of the patient (Step 4). It must be noted that the patient is usually in a trance and thus may be highly susceptible to hypnotic suggestion. The shaman uses this heightened suggestibility to persuade, cajole, and threaten the demon into leaving, thus healing the patient.

A South Asian case study.   Obeyesekere's (1977) account of a healing ritual is an excellent example of the use of symbolic healing in the shamanic treatment of demonic possession in South Asia. Obeyesekere describes how the shaman, his assistant, and the patient, named Somavati, all go into trance, take on alternate supernatural identities, and negotiate the departure of the demons possessing Somavati. This healing ritual is analyzed at some length to illustrate the use of symbolic healing for the treatment of mental illness in a nonwestern context.

The ritual begins with drumming performed by assistants and chanting by the shaman. By narrowly focusing their attention on these rhythmic stimuli, both the shaman and Somavati enter into a trance. The shaman dances and becomes possessed by the god Skanda, while at the same time the demons possessing Somavati emerge. The shaman, in the guise of the Skanda, converses with the spirits. In this way, the shaman establishes the relevance of the cultural schemas and the superior status of his identity (Skanda) in relation to the demons.

The demons (the patient) cooperate as instructed by the shaman. The drums beat faster, and the body of Somavati, taken over by the demons, dances briskly, imitating the movements of the shaman. The action takes place according to the cultural schemas. Thus, the powerful god Skanda establishes his authority over the demons. Skanda (the shaman) grabs the patient by the hair and pulls her into the center of the arena. The demons are forced to identify themselves and the circumstances in which they possessed Somavati. This validates for the audience the diagnosis of demonic possession and further serves to define the problem and cure taken from the cultural schemas. Somavati is possessed by the demons Kalu Yaka, Riri Yaka, and Mahasona, and by three ghosts. Complex negotiations now ensue in an effort to obtain the demons' agreement to depart.

However, the demons possessing Somavati are difficult. They do not show the proper respect for Skanda, and it is necessary for Skanda to summon the lesser god Dadimunda, who is known in the Sinhalese meaning system as Skanda's minister and the punisher of demons. Although Dadimunda is lower in the hierarchy of gods than Skanda, this is actually an escalation in symbolic weaponry on the part of the shaman. This is because Dadimunda's job is the punishment of demons, and he is only called in to handle particularly tough cases.

The part of Dadimunda is played by the shaman's assistant, named David. He enters the arena dressed in the appropriate costume (the shaman was also dressed as Skanda) and is possessed by the god Dadimunda. His treatment of the demons is markedly different from Skanda. He is rough, brusque, and coarse. He asks the demons why they did not surrender to Skanda, and he threatens them with punishment. However, the demons still refuse to depart.

The shaman reenters the arena, now costumed as the goddess Kali. The presence of Kali is the ultimate escalation in symbolic weaponry. Kali is the most fearsome deity in the pantheon, and her status in the hierarchy is equal to that of her husband Shiva, the highest of the gods. In this set of cultural schemas, no demon can possibly disobey Kali. Confronted by the powerful gods Kali and Dadimunda, the demons possessing Somavati eventually depart.

The healing ritual lasts all night, and I have eliminated much detail for the sake of brevity. This is certainly not conventional psychotherapy, but it can be effective within this cultural context. The healing ritual alters consciousness. Old cognitive patterns are being altered, and the messages of the ritual are being implanted in the client's neural networks. The symbolic healing process has proceeded through the mechanisms of trance, hypnotic suggestion, and manipulation of culture-based healing symbols.

The immediate effect of Somavati's symbolic healing was the eradication of all symptoms, both somatic and psychological. Her symptoms included headaches, body aches, nausea, fatigue, as well as the usual signs of possession by demons, such as extreme agitation and assaultive behavior in the guise of a demon. Somavati had complete amnesia for the events of the ritual. "Somavati"—that is, the patient's primary personality—was unconscious for the entire length of the ritual. Only her possessing "demons" were conscious during the ceremony. This is consistent with the South Asian cultural schema that the behaviors of the individual during the ritual are actions performed by demons having an identity and existence separate from that of the client.

Symbols, in this case manifested as "gods," were manipulated to therapeutically alter the experienced reality of the client. Because the "demons" possessing Somavati subjectively experienced themselves as demons, they recognized the power of the "gods" to banish them. This was healing through the use of symbols. All of it was accomplished on the level of cognition, facilitated by trance and hypnotic suggestion.

Symbolic Healing of "Spirit Loss" in Nepal

One of the most common forms of illness among the Yolmo Sherpa people of Nepal is a malady that can be translated as "spirit loss." The Yolmo believe that one's spirit can be caused to leave the body by a sudden fright. The spirit then wanders around the countryside, prey to ghosts, demons, and witches. When this happens, the individual experiences extreme fatigue, lacks the will for activity, and does not care to eat, talk, work, or socialize. There may also be insomnia and other symptoms (Desjarlais et al., 1995). In many ways "spirit loss" among the Yolmo is similar to the Latin American illness *susto* (see Chapter 10). From the perspective of modern psychiatry, the patient appears to be suffering from major depressive disorder (Chapter 12).

When a Yolmo suffers from spirit loss, a shaman is brought in to perform an all-night healing ritual in which the shaman recites sacred chants, is possessed by deities who inform about the causes of the patient's illness, and manipulates other symbolic objects. Toward the end of the healing ritual, the shaman performs a "spirit-hooking" ceremony in which his or her own spirit flies out like a bird to search for the patient's lost spirit. Upon locating the lost spirit, the shaman "hooks" it and returns with it to the patient's house where the spirit is deposited into several foods set before the patient. By eating from each of these foods, the patient recovers his or her spirit and is healed (Desjarlais et al., 1995).

Symbolic Healing
of Alcoholism among Native Americans

Western type Alcoholics Anonymous groups have not generally been success-ful among Native American populations (Heath, 1983). This is to be expected, because the cultural schemas underlying the AA healing ceremonies are not consistent with Native American culture. Healing systems consistent with Native American culture will have more symbolic healing power. Therefore, in recent decades, many Native American groups have revived the Sweat Lodge ceremony for healing alcoholism (Hall, 1986).

In the Sweat Lodge, hot rocks are placed in the center of the lodge and are sprinkled with water to release steam. In the small enclosed space, this pro-duces profuse sweating in the small group who sit in a circle facing the center. Beyond the direct therapeutic effects of the sweating, the ceremony utilizes symbolic objects manipulated by a spiritual leader to alter the cognitions and emotions of the participants. The ceremony itself and the objects used within it are symbols of the revival of Native American culture and the removal of the harmful effects of the dominant "white" culture. The ceremony is experienced as a purification from the pollution of white culture and the effects of alcohol, which are seen as a manifestation of white cultural pollution. The ceremonies are designed to help individuals strengthen their Indian personal and group identity; relieve depression related to cultural alienation, relative deprivation, and ethnic identity confusion; and create a new healthy way of life for the indi-vidual and the group (Jilek, 1994).

This transformation is achieved in a ritualized symbolic death of the old polluted self and the rebirth of a new, strong, purified Indian self. The socio-centric bonds of traditional Native American culture are renewed and strengthened in the ceremony, and the individuals receive the emotional sup-port of group identity and escape the alienation of the egocentric white culture. This creates new social networks, alters negative social relationships, and allows healed individuals to take on new social roles. The sick role of the alco-holic is exchanged for the prestigious role of the supernaturally purified tradi-tional Native American identity (Jilek, 1994).

This use of culturally validated symbolic healing and group reinforcement of the new healthy identity is more effective in this sociocultural context for the treatment of alcoholism than the typical western type Alcoholic Anonymous healing method. For optimal outcome, treatment for alcohol and drug depen-dence should always be conducted in a way that is consistent with the cultural identity of the individual.

Symbolic Healing among Charismatic Christians

Thomas Csordas (1983) and Meredith McGuire (1988) describe three types of symbolic healing used by some Charismatic Christians in the United States. These are *spiritual healing, healing of memories,* and *deliverance.* Spiritual healing is conceptualized by Charismatic Christians as God healing a soul that has been injured by sin. Healing of memories is treatment for traumatic memories that may be troubling a person even after that person has received the Holy Spirit. Deliverance is treatment characterized by freeing a person from the adverse effects of demons or evil spirits. In this case, a distinction is made between *oppression*, in which the effect of a demon is experienced in some limited aspect of a person's life, and *possession*, in which a demon takes over complete control of a person. Oppression by a demon usually takes the form of sinful behavior, such as lust, masturbation, adultery, and so on. Possession by a demon is essentially the Charismatic Christian equivalent of the spirit possession illnesses previously described in South Asia and elsewhere. Deliverance can be described as the Charismatic Christian version of exorcism. The exorcism ritual is very similar to the ceremony described in the South Asian case of Somavati. The offending demon is contacted, addressed by name, and commanded to depart in the name of Jesus Christ.

The *healing of memories* ritual is somewhat different from deliverance and clearly illustrates the structure of symbolic healing. In healing of memories, the individual's entire life is prayed for in chronological stages from conception to the present. Special attention is paid to any events or relationships that caused the individual emotional pain or trauma. The individual is usually asked to visualize the painful incident but to alter the original memory by visualizing Jesus there at the person's side, more or less guiding the person through that painful event. The meaning of the event is thus altered. The individual now has the understanding that Jesus was there all the time and wanted the person to go through that difficult time to bring the person closer to Himself. Therefore, the event was actually a good thing, because it brought the individual closer to God. Thus, the *meaning* of the event is altered. This allows the negative emotions surrounding the painful incident to be released and replaced with feelings of gratitude toward Jesus. Simultaneously, any lingering effects of the stress or trauma will also be reduced. This process is done for all stressful events, in effect, "walking Jesus through" the person's life, thus altering the meaning of all those events and, therefore, the emotions associated with them (that is, providing *meaningfulness*).

The alteration of meaning is the central mechanism of symbolic healing. This is important in the treatment of mental illness because so much of mental illness is focused in negative emotions. As discussed in Chapter 4, emotion is essentially a three-stage cognitive process: (1) initial appraisal, (2) emotional feeling, and (3) culture-based behavioral program. By changing cognition, emotion can be regulated, altered, and therapeutically manipulated.

The key is to change the initial appraisal stage of the emotional process. By changing the initial appraisal (that is, the meaning of an event or incident), the next two stages—emotional feeling, and culture-based behavioral program—can also be altered. This is exactly what the Charismatic Christian healing of memories accomplishes. By placing Jesus in those traumatic or stressful events, the events are given a beneficial meaning and a purpose they did not previously possess. Therefore, the feelings of sadness, shame, guilt, horror, anger, resentment, fear, helplessness, and so on that were previously associated with those memories are no longer applicable and can be replaced by feelings of love, gratitude, and happiness. This can have immediate and significant healing effects on an individual. Again, it is not necessary for any of this to be true in any absolute sense; it is only necessary for it to be symbolically powerful for the individual.

Cognitive processes are central to understanding emotional distress and, therefore, mental illness. Many mental disorders can be directly traced to patterns of cognition structured by cultural schemas. Cultural schemas carry within them sources of both emotional distress and emotional healing. It is the job of the clinician to discover what these sources are for each client and to use them to provide *coherence* in therapy. That is why it is so important to carefully assess all individuals, including their cultural schemas and explanatory models, and to use that information in treatment.

Effects of Treatment

In client-centered psychiatry, the effects of treatment on the client's subjective experience of mental illness must be taken into consideration. It is very important that treatment not make the *illness* (individual's subjective experience) worse in the course of treating the *disease* (clinician's diagnosis). For example, in disease-centered psychiatry, the long-term use of neuroleptics for the treatment of schizophrenia has been normative for the past few decades. However, neuroleptic medications have well-known side effects of slowed thinking, slowed speech, akathisia, and other types of dystonias, which are frequently seen by both the client and untrained observers as symptoms of the disease (APA, 1994, p. 742). Thus, distressing side effects of the treatment can become part of the client's subjective illness experience.

Therefore, client-centered psychiatry should take into account the psychological and neurological side effects of treatments, because these can become part of the overall illness experience, possibly distressing and even harming the client.

For example, it is now understood that neuroleptic medications can affect neuronal structures. Neuroleptic medications administered over a long term cause the neuronal structures to adapt to the neuroleptics by *upregulating* the dopamine system. This means that the brain increases the number of dopamine receptors as well as increasing the avidity with which receptors seek dopamine (Guttmacher, 1994). If psychotic symptoms are associated with increased activity in the dopamine system, then an upregulated dopamine system has the potential of escalating and prolonging the symptoms and making a relapse more likely if the medication is suddenly withdrawn.

Moreover, upregulated dopamine receptors in the motor cortex caused by prolonged neuroleptic dopamine blockage cause various kinds of movement disorders such as tardive dyskinesia (Guttmacher, 1994). Significantly, the move toward a client-centered approach has resulted in inclusion of listings for medication-induced movement disorders in the appendix of DSM-IV (APA, 1994, pp. 735–751). The disorders listed are: neuroleptic-induced parkinsonism, neuroleptic malignant syndrome, neuroleptic-induced acute dystonia, neuroleptic-induced acute akathisia, neuroleptic-induced tardive dyskinesia, and medication-induced postural tremor. This is the first time that a discussion of the impairments caused by psychiatric medications has been included in the official manual.

Client-centered psychiatry should take into account both the psychological and neurological effects of medication treatment. The human brain is a complex system of neural networks that adapt to external and internal environments. Brain plasticity allows the brain to alter its structure in response to the presence of medications, primarily in synaptic receptors. Long-term neuroleptic treatment causes the brain to upregulate the dopamine system, thus causing possible neurological damage. Significantly, successful treatment of acute psychosis without neuroleptic treatment in a small, homelike social environment has been shown to be as effective as neuroleptic treatment in a hospital ward setting (Mosher, Vallone, & Menn, 1995). This argues for the judicious use of neuroleptics.

When using psychotropic medications, the client's brain plasticity should be taken into account. It may even be possible to utilize brain plasticity in the treatment of mental disorders with medications. For example, successful treatment of psychotic symptoms might be accomplished through successful *downregulation* of the dopamine system by flooding the brain for one or two weeks with a dopamine agonist combined with a sedative to control for an increase in symptoms. This is just the opposite of traditional neuroleptic treatment, which creates a functional dopamine deficiency. After one or two weeks, the dopamine agonist would be withdrawn, leaving the client with a downregulated dopamine system and possibly alleviation of symptoms.

 Suggested Clinical Guidelines

1. Assess the Cultural Identity of the Individual

In all cases, client-centered treatment should be consistent with the client's cultural identity and explanatory model of illness and healing. If the client subjectively experiences an evil spirit taking control of his or her body, then an appropriate religious ritual by a qualified folk healer in collaboration with the clinician could be an important part of successful psychotherapy. Likewise, if sin is weighing heavily on the client's mind, then facilitating penance and atonement is probably appropriate. If traumatic events have left chronic emotional scars, then therapeutically altering the meaning of those traumatic events through symbolic healing should be attempted as part of psychotherapy. The healing symbols should be taken from the client's own cultural background. These will possess the most symbolic power for that particular individual.

2. *Negotiate Clinical Reality*

In all cases, the therapist should identify and use the cultural schemas the client brings to the clinical situation and not try to impose a modern scientific clinical reality on the client if that is not already present. Especially for individuals from premodern societies, a modern disease category for a psychiatric problem may have very little meaning and, thus, be less than effective in providing coherence in healing and an optimal treatment outcome. However, a premodern or religious explanatory model should never be imposed on a client possessing a modern set of cultural schemas. These clients will have their own objects such as medications that can be used as healing symbols in the process of symbolic healing.

In all cases, treatment should proceed based on careful cultural assessment. Investigating the client's cultural identity and explanatory model are basic steps to negotiating a shared clinical reality, creating a therapeutic alliance, and a client-centered treatment plan. The treatment plan should include the therapeutic use of hope, the creation of coherence in healing, and fulfill all four steps of symbolic healing. This approach will help provide optimal care and the best treatment outcome.

3. *Aim for Complete Recovery*

In the case of individuals possessing a disease-centered explanatory model of mental illness, negotiating a biomedical clinical reality and treatment plan is most appropriate, with the caveat that the notion of the "incurable brain disease" should be avoided if at all possible. This kind of cognitive appraisal can promote incurability and long-term illness. The goal of treatment should always be the complete recovery of the client. This means that the client is healthy and lives a normal life without the need for medications. The goal of treatment should not be to "manage" or maintain clients on psychotropic medications for many years. This approach risks creating permanently brain damaged individuals.

Instead of viewing clients as permanently ill, a client-centered perspective allows for the possibility of a complete recovery. The client-centered approach is optimistic in its view of mental illness and treatment. From this perspective, human brain plasticity allows for the possibility that both illness and disease can be therapeutically altered through an effective combination of biomedical and psychotherapeutic treatment. Successful psychotherapy can alter the mind-brain (Schwartz et al., 1996). Viewing the mind-brain as plastic instead of static allows for altering neurotransmitter systems and neural networks through reregulating and reconditioning the mind-brain with medications and psychotherapy, thus alleviating symptoms and allowing for complete recovery.

Culture
&
DSM-IV Diagnoses

Chapter Six

Personality Disorders

Part Two of this book begins with personality disorders because many of the factors influencing personality development, including pathological development, are also common to the other mental disorders in DSM-IV. However, this notion is not reflected in the organizational system of DSM-IV.

DSM-IV places the **personality disorders** on Axis II in the multiaxial system of assessment. The other mental disorders are placed on Axis I. This is because the personality disorders are viewed as being enduring patterns of subjective experience and behavior based in personality development rather than as some specific disease entity. Unlike Axis I disorders, the personality disorders generally do not have periods of significant remission, change in severity of symptoms, or improvement over time.

However, DSM-IV does recognize a spectrum relationship between some personality disorders and some Axis I disorders. Of course, a spectrum concept is not new. As discussed in Chapter 1 in the biopsychosocial paradigm that was at the basis of DSM-I (APA, 1952) and DSM-II (APA, 1968) the boundary between mental health and mental illness was thought to be fluid. The biopsychosocial paradigm accepted the psychodynamic principle that healthy people can become ill if they are exposed to severe-enough trauma. Along with this psychodynamic principle was the assumption that mental illnesses existed on a continuum or spectrum ranging from normality, to mild mental illness, to severe mental illness. Toward the mild end of mental illness were disorders collectively known as **neuroses.** At the severe end were disorders collectively known as **psychoses.** In the middle were borderline cases.

In the biopsychosocial paradigm, mental illnesses were not seen as discrete entities but rather as the same basic pathogenic process manifesting in various degrees of severity. Thus, neuroses were in a spectrum relationship with psychoses. The psychoses were seen as more severe forms of the same basic illness manifesting in neuroses but were characterized by a loss of **reality testing.**

With a loss of reality testing, the person misinterprets his or her relationship with the external physical and social environment. The presence of hallucinations or delusions is usually viewed as a loss of reality testing. In the disorders known as neuroses, reality testing remained intact. However, neuroses were thought to be prodromal or residual to psychoses. That is, the neuroses could be the early stages of psychoses or leftover forms of mental illness after recovery from a psychosis.

With the shift to the disease-centered paradigm in DSM-III (APA, 1980), the spectrum approach to mental illness was mostly abandoned. Mental disorders were now viewed as discrete entities with their own biological causes. The term *neurosis*, identified as it was with psychodynamic theory and a spectrum approach to mental illness, began to be replaced with specific categories of mental disorders with narrowly defined symptomatic descriptions. Those disorders thought to have a specific pathology independent of personality development, which included all the psychoses and the "hysterical" neuroses, were placed on Axis I. Those neuroses that were assumed to be related to personality development were placed on Axis II. Thus, in DSM-III there was a clear break with the spectrum approach, and many of the disorders that were previously labeled neuroses were now placed in a different diagnostic section of the manual.

With DSM-III (APA, 1980), the use of the term *neurosis* began to be discontinued because it no longer had the same meaning it carried in DSM-I and DSM-II. With the publication of DSM-IV (APA, 1994), the use of the term *neurosis* has been completely eliminated from the official diagnostic manual. However, the personality disorders in DSM-IV are direct descendants of earlier conceptions of neuroses, and one of them, *borderline personality disorder*, still bears the name of an illness on the *borderline* between a neurosis and a psychosis.

The client-centered model outlined in Chapter 15 that forms the conclusion of this book is a direct descendant from the **biopsychosocial paradigm.** Included in the client-centered model is the assumption that the boundary between mental health and mental illness is fluid. Also, the paradigm accepts the psychodynamic principle that mentally healthy people can become ill if they are exposed to severe-enough trauma. Combined with this psychodynamic principle is the assumption that mental illnesses exist on a continuum or spectrum from normality, to mild mental illness, to severe mental illness. Specific syndromes can be identified on this spectrum, but individuals over time may move on the spectrum from one syndrome or disorder to another. Also included in the client-centered model is the assumption that personality development and mental functioning have their psychobiological correlates in the neural organization of the brain. Thus, abnormalities in personality and mental functioning will always have some psychobiological basis.

All of the above assumptions come directly from the earlier biopsychosocial paradigm. What makes the client-centered paradigm in this book somewhat different is a more explicit and detailed appreciation and analysis of the effects of culture on the etiology, structure, and treatment of mental illness. This is also combined with a more sophisticated view of the brain plasticity associated with psychological trauma, adaptation, and cultural learning, and how those affect mental disorders (see Chapter 15).

The Personality Disorders

The personality disorders listed in DSM-IV are grouped into three clusters based on descriptive similarities. Cluster A is the "odd or eccentric" cluster and includes paranoid, schizoid, and schizotypal personality disorders. Cluster B is the "dramatic, emotional or erratic" cluster and includes antisocial, borderline, histrionic, and narcissistic personality disorders. Cluster C is the "anxious or fearful" cluster and includes aviodant, dependent, and obsessive-compulsive personality disorders.

Obviously, ideas about what constitutes a normal personality are intimately related to cultural values that differ by time and place, and the definition of personality disorder in DSM-IV explicitly includes cultural variability:

> A Personality Disorder is an enduring pattern of inner experience and behavior that deviates from the expectations of the individual's culture, is pervasive and inflexible, has an onset in adolescence or early adulthood, is stable over time, and leads to distress or impairment. (APA, 1994, p. 629)

The inclusion of a deviation from an individual's cultural norms in the definition of personality disorder assumes that individuals will have different cultural backgrounds and expectations of normal inner experience and behavior. This inclusion of cultural factors in the assessment of personality disorders is new in DSM-IV and demonstrates a partial move toward a client-centered perspective.

However, DSM-IV relies mostly on western concepts of normative modern personality development (Fabrega, 1994b). This means that there is an unstated assumption in DSM-IV that a "normal" personality is a modern (essentially western) personality as defined in modernization theory (Chapter 3). This is understandable because the underlying diagnostic system in DSM-IV (APA, 1994) has been retained from DSM-III (APA, 1980), which was highly ethno-centric and modern in its theoretical foundations. DSM-IV makes an attempt to be less ethnocentric and more postmodern by including cultural factors in diagnosis; nevertheless, it largely fails because of the modern theoretical structure of the underlying classification system.

Although the symptoms of personality disorders may be found in most cultures, the disorders themselves should not be considered absolute categories of illness universally diagnosable without regard to cultural norms and values. A cultural assessment should be standard practice for all clients presenting with symptoms of personality disorders.

It is clear that social and cultural factors play such a comprehensive role in personality development through primary socialization and enculturation that pathologizing personality traits belonging to a cultural group because they vary from western cultural expectations would be the height of scientific ethnocentrism and cultural arrogance. Even within western culture, personality disorders have the lowest levels of diagnostic validity and reliability of all mental disorders (Millon, 1981).

If an individual has personality traits that are normative in his or her culture of origin but are considered symptoms of a personality disorder in DSM-IV, those symptoms *do not constitute a personality disorder*. The DSM-IV definition of personality disorder is essentially functional in that it requires clinically significant impairment or distress for a diagnosis to be made. Clinically significant impairment or distress will frequently be culturally specific.

Cluster A Personality Disorders

DSM-IV recognizes that some personality disorders have a spectrum relationship with certain Axis I disorders. This includes the three disorders that constitute Cluster A: paranoid personality disorder, schizoid personality disorder, and schizotypal personality disorder. These three disorders are thought to have a spectrum relationship with schizophrenia and the other psychotic disorders. This means they can be premorbid or residual to a psychotic disorder. This is a holdover from earlier theoretical conceptions and indicates that the spectrum model of mental illness has not been completely abandoned in DSM-IV.

Paranoid Personality Disorder

The key feature of **paranoid personality disorder** is a pervasive distrust of other people such that others are virtually always perceived as threatening or hostile (APA, 1994). Persons with this pattern of personality development consistently assume that others will attempt to harm, exploit, or deceive them. They typically believe they have been injured or severely hurt in the past by other people, and therefore they trust no one. Even in situations in which there is no evidence that a particular person is dangerous, they assume the worst and are on constant guard, scrutinizing every action for hostile intent.

People with this disorder anger quickly, may be pathologically jealous, and typically assume that a spouse or sexual partner is unfaithful. They are people who want to maintain tight control over their surroundings and the people around them. Because they lack trust in others, people with this disorder feel a great need for self-sufficiency and autonomy. They will feel extremely uncomfortable in a dependent position, as this leaves them vulnerable to harm.

People with this disorder are keenly aware of dominance hierarchies and are very concerned with the importance of power and rank. They are very likely to be disdainful of any persons or groups of lower rank than themselves. Because of these tendencies, they may join fanatical groups that perceive themselves to be in a struggle for dominance, such as the Ku Klux Klan, Nazi Party, or other fringe political, militia, or religious groups. Stockpiling weapons can be seen as a logical activity by persons with paranoid personality disorder.

Persons with this type of personality development are more likely to be seen in societies that are hierarchical and egocentric, for example, the Swat Pukhtun and the United States (Chapter 3). In these societies, individuals pursue their own personal goals, sometimes to the harm or detriment of others. For example, all men in Swat Pukhtun society carry guns. They trust no one and are constantly vigilant in protecting their honor and their own personal interests. Pukhtun men distrust the sexual loyalty of all women to the extent of keeping them confined in their homes as much as possible. In Pukhtun society, the symptoms of paranoid personality disorder generally constitute normative personality development. The people of Pukhtun society are genuinely dangerous to each other. To not be constantly on guard and suspicious of everyone in Pukhtun society would be foolish. Paranoid personality disorder would not be an appropriate diagnosis among the Swat Pukhtun: this type of personality development is completely consistent with their cultural customs and values.

In the United States, members of minority groups or immigrants may be behaving in accordance with subcultural values or the customs of their country of origin, which may resemble the symptoms of paranoid personality disorder. Cultural assessment of each individual is crucial for proper diagnosis.

Also, the possibility of actual physical or emotional trauma in the personal histories of clients needs to be considered in possible cases of paranoid personality disorder. If an individual has a personal history of documented trauma, such as severe child abuse, physical assault, war trauma, or sexual assault, the effects on personality development may resemble the symptoms of paranoid personality disorder or other personality disorders. In this case, DSM-IV recommends a diagnosis of *posttraumatic stress disorder* (PTSD) be considered as an alternative (APA, 1994, p. 632). Some of the symptoms of PTSD (see Chapter 10) can closely resemble the symptoms of paranoid personality disorder.

Also, the symptoms of paranoid personality disorder can develop in situations in which there is very real persecution, discrimination, abuse, or humiliation for certain stigmatized individuals in the social or family environment. This may be especially true in societies with highly developed dominance hierarchies (Chapter 3). Clinicians should always view clients within their sociocultural contexts.

Schizoid Personality Disorder

The key features of **schizoid personality disorder** are a pervasive detachment from social relationships and a restricted range of emotions (APA, 1994). These people appear to be self-absorbed and not really connected to their social or physical environment. They appear not to feel strong emotions in relation to events in their lives. They feel neither happiness nor sadness. Events that would make most people feel strong emotions appear not to touch them. Thus, they appear to lack the emotional motivation for engaging in activities that most people find highly stimulating and meaningful, for example, work, family relations, romance, or sexual relationships. People with schizoid personality disorder are typically loners, with no desire to develop close personal relationships. They rarely date and usually do not marry. They typically have no close friends, and they appear to be awkward in social interactions.

Because of the significant detachment from the environment displayed by these people, I suspect that chronic mild depersonalization is occurring in this type of personality development. As mentioned in Chapter 13, Hindu yogis experience long-term depersonalization. Their depersonalization is similar to some of the symptoms of schizoid personality disorder. The yogis develop this type of personality voluntarily through intensive meditation practice over many years. Thus, the psychological mechanism operating in cases of schizoid personality disorder may be the self-absorption of narrowly focused, inwardly directed attention. In the case of the yogis, they pursue this method of adaptation to their environment usually because they are depressed. The depersonalization frees them from the emotional pain of depression. I suggest that in the case of schizoid personality disorder, these persons have adapted to a painful social environment by focusing attention inwardly, thus inducing mild depersonalization. They essentially detach themselves from their environment through this method of self-absorption.

However, when making a diagnosis of schizoid personality disorder, the cultural identity of the individual needs to be assessed. For example, in the case of Hindu yogis, their mental condition and personality development are directly related to their cultural values and customs. They become detached voluntarily. To be detached and unmoved by good or bad events is considered to be saintly in Hindu culture. A person with this type of personality is highly respected and even revered. This type of personality development would not be considered pathological in Hindu society. Schizoid personality disorder (or any other mental disorder) would be an inappropriate diagnosis for Hindu yogis. Thus, cultural values and norms of behavior need to be assessed before making a diagnosis of this or any other personality disorder. Individuals need to be placed in their sociocultural context before they can be judged pathological.

The symptoms of schizoid personality disorder may be more common in persons with a stigmatized moral career (Chapter 3). Having a stigmatized moral career could cause individuals to withdraw from social interaction. The symptoms of schizoid personality disorder are probably more likely to develop in hierarchical societies where stigmatization is more common.

Schizotypal Personality Disorder

The key features of **schizotypal personality disorder** are anxiety in social relationships accompanied by eccentricities of behavior characterized by superstitiousness, preoccupation with paranormal phenomena, magical thinking, or use of rituals in everyday situations (APA, 1994).

Because of the reliance on supernatural explanations in premodern societies (see Chapter 3), it is likely that the symptoms of schizotypal personality disorder may be more commonly observed in persons from premodern societies or subcultures. Because DSM-IV is based primarily on a modern view of what constitutes a normal personality—that is, someone who is rational, literate, and educated in modern scientific concepts of causality—persons who believe in supernatural powers, magic, metaphysical causation, and so on are viewed in DSM-IV as eccentric or odd.

However, the majority of humans on the planet live in societies that could be described as at least marginally premodern. This means that magical thinking, acceptance of metaphysical causation, and belief in supernatural powers are commonplace and normative in many parts of the world. Although many of these people might fit the diagnostic criteria of schizotypal personality disorder, to use this standard of modern personality development as a judgment of normality in a premodern society is ethnocentric. This diagnostic category is most appropriately used in modern societies where superstitiousness and magical thinking are not consistent with the prevailing cultural schemas.

It is clear from the description of this disorder in DSM-IV that a "normal" person is someone with a modern education and the social skills of a competent working- or middle-class individual. For example, DSM-IV states that a person with this disorder may use idiosyncratic or unusual phrasing in his or her speech. However, this symptom can result from inadequate education. DSM-IV also states that the person may be "unable to join in the give-and-take banter of coworkers," and further that the person may appear dressed inappropriately and stiff or constricted in manner (APA, 1994, p. 642). This description suggests that in modern societies such as the United States, persons with schizotypal personality disorder are likely to be poorly educated in the knowledge base expected of a modern personality and inadequately socialized in the interpersonal skills that are expected of a modern, working- or middle-class individual.

According to DSM-IV, persons with this disorder feel anxious in social situations. They feel that they do not "fit in." They may feel comfortable only with first-degree relatives. They also rely on their religious beliefs, including ritual behavior, to make decisions, comfort their fears, and give meaning to difficult or adverse conditions. However, this pattern of behavior is consistent with persons who are relatively premodern and sociocentric in their thinking, living within a larger society that is predominantly modern and egocentric. Persons who are relatively premodern and sociocentric will have a preoccupation with religious beliefs, be centered in their families, and feel uncomfortable outside of their group. Persons like this would not "fit in" in a larger society that is modern and egocentric (Chapter 3).

These subcultural differences may be the basis of some cases of schizotypal personality disorder. Situations like this are very likely to occur among ethnic minority or immigrant groups in the United States or in economically impoverished segments of society. Thus, careful assessment of an individual's cultural identity should be made in every possible case of schizotypal personality disorder. An individual's personality development should not be pathologized because he or she has a premodern cultural identity.

Cluster B Personality Disorders

Cluster B is the "dramatic, emotional, or erratic" group of personality disorders. This cluster includes antisocial, borderline, histrionic, and narcissistic personality disorders.

Antisocial Personality Disorder

The key feature of **antisocial personality disorder** is a persistent pattern of victimizing others. This disorder has in the past also been referred to as sociopathy or psychopathy. Persons with this disorder repeatedly victimize others through theft or destruction of property, physical assault (including spouse or child abuse), or deceit to gain personal profit or pleasure (APA, 1994).

Moreover, these persons feel little or no remorse for their actions. They may blame their victims for being foolish, naive, weak, or helpless. They seem to assume that "everyone is out for number one," and thus they feel they are acting appropriately. They may feel ashamed to have been caught in their victimization activities, but generally they feel arrogantly superior to their victims and lack any empathy with them.

The symptoms of antisocial personality disorder appear to be more likely to develop in societies that are conspicuously hierarchical and comprehensively egocentric. As mentioned earlier (Chapter 3), this combination of sociocultural factors could be considered criminogenic in its effect on personality development. The Swat Pukhtun are an excellent example of this effect (Lindholm, 1997). However, the sociocultural conditions in many inner cities in the United States also qualify as possible examples. In these kinds of conditions, the symptoms of antisocial personality disorder can become normative personality development.

It is tempting to view antisocial personality disorder as one form of personality development that should be considered universally pathological. However, it is possible to sustain a society in which this pattern of behavior is accepted as normal and even superior to other less aggressive and less violent alternatives. The Swat Pukhtun are proof of this. In societies that value aggression, power, prestige, self-aggrandizement, and personal autonomy, while at the same time abhorring weakness, passivity, dependence, and concern for others, individuals are more likely to develop a personality consistent with the symptoms of antisocial personality disorder. However, if the person's behavior is consistent with the values and customs of the dominant culture, then this diagnosis may not be appropriate in that cultural context. This point is debatable, but by employing DSM-IV standards we run the risk of defining a whole culture as antisocial. This could be an ethnocentric perspective.

Borderline Personality Disorder

The key feature of **borderline personality disorder** is a persistent instability in social relationships, self-image, and emotions. Central to this instability is fear of abandonment and rejection. Persons with this disorder are extremely sensitive to their social environment. They appear to have an intense unmet need for affection and personal closeness (APA, 1994).

It is common for persons with this disorder to have a personal history of physical, emotional, or sexual abuse in childhood; parental neglect; family conflict; or abandonment-separation from parents. These individuals typically have very low self-esteem and are hypersensitive to social reflection. They may have viewed their parents' neglect, abuse, or separation from them as rejection because of some fault of their own.

Their intense need for affection and fear of abandonment can lead to an intolerance of being alone. Because of this intolerance, they typically engage in frantic and impulsive behavior in an attempt to gain and hold the attention and affection of someone. This causes them to appear desperate and unstable. They can appear excited, desolate, passionate, angry, and suicidal, sometimes in rapid succession. This kind of instability can cause others to feel uncomfortable and may cause them to move away emotionally and physically. This only exacerbates the problem.

Transient dissociative symptoms are also common in persons with this disorder. Depersonalization, derealization (Chapter 13), and brief hallucinations may occur. There is some evidence that borderline personality disorder may have a spectrum relationship with dissociative identity disorder (formerly multiple personality disorder), as well as with Briquet's syndrome (hysteria). In studies of Minnesota Multiphasic Personality Inventory (MMPI) profiles, it was found that the MMPI profile for borderline personality disorder differs in degree but not in shape from the MMPI profiles associated with these other disorders (North, Ryall, Ricci, & Wetzel, 1993). Figure 6.1 illustrates the average MMPI profile, weighted by sample size, in several studies for each of three diagnostic groups (borderline personality disorder, multiple personality disorder, and Briquet's syndrome).

It is evident in Figure 6.1 that the three syndromes show similar psychopathology across the entire MMPI profile. The main differences are higher scores across the profile for dissociative identity disorder (multiple personality disorder), indicating greater pathology. This is suggestive of a spectrum relationship between borderline personality disorder and dissociative identity disorder. This relationship is also suggested by the fact that both borderline personality disorder and dissociative identity disorder occur in individuals who typically have experienced emotional trauma in childhood (Goldman, D'Angelo, DeMaso, & Mezzacappa, 1992; Ogata et al., 1990; Wagner & Linehan, 1994).

The syndrome of borderline personality disorder appears to occur in many societies (Loranger et al., 1994; Moriya et al., 1993). However, it has been suggested that this syndrome is far more common in the adolescents and young

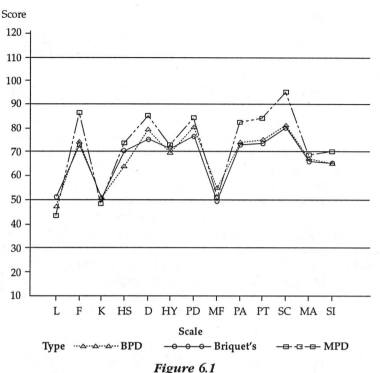

Figure 6.1
Average MMPI Profiles for Borderline Personality Disorder,
Briquet's Syndrome, and Multiple Personality Disorder

SOURCE: From *Mulitple Personalities, Multiple Disorders: Psychiatric Classification and Media Influence*, by Carol S. North, Jo-Ellyn M. Ryall, Daniel A. Ricci, and Richard D. Wetzel. Copyright © 1993 by Carol S. North, Jo-Ellyn M. Ryall, Daniel A. Ricci, and Richard D. Wetzel. Reprinted by permission of Oxford University Press, Inc.

adults of modern societies than in premodern ones (Paris, 1991, 1996). As mentioned in Chapter 3, this may be related to the long difficult period of liminality between childhood and adulthood that is forced on individuals in modern societies. Peters (1994) also hypothesizes that the absence in modern societies of initiation ceremonies that mark the transition from childhood to adulthood has left individuals to form their own adult self-identity with little help and support from the community, several years after the individual reaches biological maturity.

Because of differences in cultural meaning systems, the subjective experience, idioms of distress, culture-based diagnoses, treatments, and outcomes for the symptoms of borderline personality disorder may be variable. For example, similar symptoms may be seen in trance or spirit possession syndromes in many parts of the world. These culture-bound syndromes are frequently treated by culture-based forms of symbolic healing, including initiation ceremonies that alter the personal identity of the individual, the family social dynamics, and the social status of the individual (see Chapters 3, 5, and 13).

When treating clients from nonwestern cultures with similar symptoms, a careful assessment of cultural identity should be made, including the family and social structure and cultural schemas regarding personality development.

Histrionic Personality Disorder

The key features of **histrionic personality disorder** are excessive emotionality and attention-seeking behavior (APA, 1994). Of course, what constitutes "excessive" emotionality or attention-seeking behavior can vary widely by culture. This particular syndrome is probably the disorder that is most clearly based on modern, western ideas and values concerning personality development.

This personality disorder refers to a particular "style" of personal presentation that is considered to be pathological in DSM-IV. According to DSM-IV, persons with this disorder are overly dramatic, enthusiastic, and flirtatious. They persistently attempt to be the center of attention. They pay great heed to their personal appearance and may be expensively dressed. Also, they are overly sexual in their manner and dress in social situations. Their flirtatiousness and apparent seductiveness is usually not meant seriously but is done to attract attention. However, sometimes they cause interpersonal problems with friends by excessive flirting with others' spouses or romantic partners.

In the case of males with this disorder, DSM-IV states that a histrionic man may dress and behave in a "macho" style (APA, 1994, p. 656). This conception of pathological personality development is obviously ethnocentric. For example, in Latin cultures, both in Europe and in Latin America, the "macho" male is not considered inappropriate, and certainly not pathological. However, most persons diagnosed with this disorder are females. The fact that this pattern of flirtatious sexual behavior is considered pathological in DSM-IV says something about the type of behavior that is considered normal for females in Anglo American society. Apparently, normal females are expected to be passive and demure in their sexual relations and interpersonal interactions. A sexually aggressive female is seen as inappropriate and possibly pathological. This standard of female social behavior is certainly not common to all cultures. Some cultures allow females to be relatively aggressive in sexual relations (see Chapter 7). In its definition of histrionic personality disorder, DSM-IV takes a very Anglo American and gender-biased view of normal personality development. Therefore, any individuals with the symptoms of this disorder need to be assessed within particular sociocultural context before a diagnosis is made.

Narcissistic Personality Disorder

The key features of **narcissistic personality disorder** are an obsession with grandiosity, an intense need for admiration, and a lack of empathy. Persons with this disorder are pretentious and boastful while at the same time devaluing others. They are intensely aware of dominance hierarchies, and they believe they are superior (APA, 1994).

Underlying this intense need for admiration is a hidden fragility in self-esteem. Persons with this disorder may have some hidden flaw, which if revealed could disqualify them from membership in a dominant or elite group to which they believe they naturally belong. Thus, their moral career may be internally stigmatized (Chapter 3). To compensate for this flawed self-esteem, they may feel compelled to associate with only the "best" or "top" people, social groups, institutions, and so on. Therefore, they become overbearing elitists.

The symptoms of narcissistic personality disorder appear to be more likely to occur in societies that are hierarchical and egocentric, for example, the United States. Most persons diagnosed with this disorder are men. This gender difference should be expected because male dominance is the norm in the United States. It is likely that persons with this disorder will belong to one or more dominant groups in social hierarchies. Societies that are egalitarian and sociocentric, for example the Senoi Temiar (Chapter 3), are unlikely to produce individuals with this type of personality development. However, societies that are thoroughly hierarchical and egocentric, such as the Swat Pukhtun, may have social values that make the symptoms of narcissistic personality disorder very common. These symptoms could be seen as adaptive in this type of social environment. Thus, the symptoms of this disorder should be assessed within the sociocultural context of the individual.

Cluster C Personality Disorders

Cluster C is the "anxious or fearful" group of personality disorders. This cluster includes avoidant, dependent, and obsessive-compulsive personality disorders.

Avoidant Personality Disorder

The key features of **avoidant personality disorder** are social anxiety, low self-esteem, and hypersensitivity to criticism. A stigmatized moral career is likely to be present (Chapter 3). Persons with this disorder are so fearful of social interaction that they purposely avoid interpersonal contact that may result in rejection, humiliation, or criticism. They assume that others will find them inadequate, flawed, or somehow unacceptable. They believe in their own inferiority, and to avoid painful rejection they shy away from contact (APA, 1994). As a result of their social avoidance, persons with this disorder can become socially isolated and lonely. Thus, they may lack an adequate social support network to help them during times of personal crisis. Some persons with this disorder may also qualify for a diagnosis of *social phobia* (Chapter 10).

The symptoms of avoidant personality disorder appear to be more likely to develop in hierarchical societies. It is in this social context that persons are more likely to be labeled as inferior, inadequate, unacceptable, or some other form of stigmatization. These socially imposed labels can have significant negative effects on personality development. Persons who have internalized a stigmatized moral career may adapt to the situation by avoidance of interpersonal contact.

Special care should be taken when assessing persons from nonwestern societies. In many societies, extreme deference to superiors is normative behavior for all those in a socially inferior position. Thus, whenever this diagnosis is being considered, it is necessary to assess the individual in his or her sociocultural context. Consider how social aviodance fits in with the social expectations of a person with the client's social status. For example, in some highly patriarchal societies like India, females (especially young females) are expected to act very submissively and to avoid social contact with all men who are not close relatives. For a female to act otherwise would be socially deviant. Thus, persons from nonwestern societies should not be judged by the standards of modern egocentric societies that value independence and assertiveness as normative personality traits. Also, persons from nonwestern societies may view clinicians as high status individuals and therefore act very submissively during a clinical interview. This cultural trait should not be mistaken for the symptoms of avoidant personality disorder.

Dependent Personality Disorder

The key features of **dependent personality disorder** are an excessive need to be taken care of associated with submissive, clinging behavior, and fear of independence (APA, 1994). Persons with this disorder are passive and indecisive concerning their own lives. Decisions are made for them by a dominant individual or group. They do not feel capable of operating independently of others. Thus, their personal wishes are subjugated to the will of a dominant partner or group. Even if their personal interests are negatively affected, they will not express anger to the dominant parties for fear of separation. Thus, they are self-sacrificing. This leaves them vulnerable to exploitation and abuse.

According to DSM-IV, dependent personality is the most commonly diagnosed personality disorder. It is diagnosed more often in females. This should be expected, because females are dominated by males in most societies.

Great care should be taken in cultural assessment when symptoms of dependent personality disorder are present. Many societies differ from egocentric western society in the degree of independence or dependence that is expected of persons of various ages, social status, or gender. For example, sociocentric societies in general teach their children to be dependent, usually on family and work groups. Japan is an excellent example of this. Japanese individuals are taught to work in groups and not to take personal initiative. In Japan, mothers teach their children that "the nail that stands out gets hammered down." Thus, Japanese individuals generally value and practice dependent behavior.

However, just the opposite is expected in the egocentric United States, where individualism and personal autonomy are highly valued. For example, in its description of pathological dependence, DSM-IV states that adolescents with dependent personality disorder "may allow their parent(s) to decide what they should wear, with whom they should associate, how they should spend their free time, and what school or college they should attend" (APA, 1994, p. 665). This description of pathologically dependent behavior assumes that normal adolescents should make these decisions for themselves. This is obviously based on an assumption that independent, egocentric behavior in adolescents is "normal." This is certainly an ethnocentric assumption based on the model of egocentric personality development that is normative in Anglo American society. Anglo American adolescents are raised to value independence and personal autonomy.

However, most other cultural groups in the world do not follow this model. In many societies, it would be unthinkable for an adolescent to make important life decisions for him- or herself. Thus, great care needs to be taken to avoid pathologizing the behavior of other cultures simply because it differs from Anglo American values and customs. Only if a person's dependent behavior greatly exceeds his or her own cultural norms, thus causing social or occupational impairment or clinically significant distress, should this diagnosis be made.

Obsessive-Compulsive Personality Disorder

The key feature of **obsessive-compulsive personality disorder** is a persistent preoccupation with order, perfection, attention to detail, rules, and control. Persons with this disorder will sacrifice efficiency to guarantee that something is done according to established principles and rules. These people "go by the book" and pay minute attention to the "letter of the law." They can be ritualistic in their behavior, excessively repeating certain actions to make sure something is done perfectly (APA, 1994).

Persons with this disorder generally take life very seriously. In matters of morality, they tend to be extremely rigid and inflexible. They believe there is only one right way to do things, and they are willing to force themselves and others to follow these moral principles, even if this causes problems. This might be viewed by a clinician as causing social or occupational impairment.

However, this type of behavior can be common and perhaps seen as virtuous in some premodern societies or subcultural groups. For example, behaviors that might be considered symptoms of obsessive-compulsive personality disorder can be observed in persons who practice a particularly fundamentalistic style of religion. These people generally believe that their religious scriptures offer an absolutely correct description of reality and a set of behavioral rules that must be followed down to the smallest detail.

This type of behavior is seen in Galanti's (1991) description of a highly orthodox Jewish American man who brought his pregnant wife in active labor to the hospital during the Sabbath. Because it was the Sabbath, he was prohibited from doing any work. This prohibition included driving a car, using a telephone, handling money, or even pushing an elevator button. The only reason he was able to drive his wife to the hospital is because the Torah makes an exception when a life is at risk. However, after the delivery of the baby, a life was no longer threatened and the rules had to be followed. Therefore, he was unable to drive home after his wife's delivery or telephone someone to pick him up or even to go downstairs to the hospital cafeteria to buy his own meals. He had to stay in his wife's room and eat extra food brought by the nurses and charged to his wife's hospital bill.

This disorder is diagnosed twice as often in males as in females. This is to be expected because of the institution of male dominance in most societies. A well-structured dominance hierarchy would seem to be a likely prerequisite for this disorder. Also, a sociocentric society would appear to be more likely to produce this type of behavior, because in this context the interests of the group come before the interests of the individual. This can require strict discipline. Also, a premodern society is probably more likely to produce this type of personality development because of the heavy emphasis on traditional (particularly religious and familial) sources of authority.

Careful cultural assessment must be made when considering a diagnosis of obsessive-compulsive personality disorder. Persons from a cultural background that is hierarchical, sociocentric, and premodern, for example, highly orthodox Jewish Americans, should not have their behavior pathologized simply because it differs from the modern, egocentric culture of Anglo American society.

 Suggested Clinical Guidelines

1. Assess the Cultural Identity of the Individual

Different cultures have different ways of socializing their young; therefore, the norms of behavior from the individual's own culture should be the standard for judging personality development. This can be accomplished only if the client's cultural identity is carefully assessed.

2. Assess Cultural Schemas Regarding Behavior

The diagnostic categories of the personality disorders in DSM-IV generally assume that a "normal" personality is one that is consistent with the modern and egocentric personality that is the ideal of the dominant culture of the United States. These diagnostic categories should not be considered absolute natural entities. They are, for the most part, cultural entities describing personality development that is considered deviant or pathological by modern, egocentric Anglo American society. Clinicians should explore the cultural schemas of the client to uncover why the individual is motivated to act in a particular fashion.

3. Assess the Cultural and Psychosocial Environment

Clinicians need to see the individual and his or her personality development within the total sociocultural context. This refers to culture-based sources of social and environmental stress or trauma as well as social supports having an impact on functioning and impairment. Assessment of family, gender, age, race, or ethnic dominance hierarchies may be especially important in understanding a client's emotions or behavior. Emotions or behavior that would be seen as socially or occupationally impairing in Anglo American society may be normative or even required in social interactions in other cultural or subcultural groups.

Also, clients from premodern societies or possessing a fundamentalistic religious background may appear to be preoccupied with spiritual phenomena, magical thinking, or use of rituals. A premodern cultural identity should not be viewed as pathological personality development.

4. Assess Cultural Aspects of the Clinician-Client Relationship

Clinicians should critically assess their own conceptions of normal personality development and reflexively determine how these conceptions may be projected onto the client. A clinician trained in modern psychiatry might diagnose a personality disorder based strictly on modern, egocentric conceptions of normal personality development rather than allowing for the influence of premodern or sociocentric concepts of normative personality. Also, behavior of clients toward clinicians may be based on cultural schemas regarding status in dominance hierarchies. Some individuals may act very submissively toward clinicians who are viewed as high status persons.

5. Negotiate Clinical Reality

Personality disorders should not be viewed as absolute disease categories that can be imposed on an individual. The goal of clinical treatment should be optimal functioning within a particular sociocultural context. If the client belongs to an immigrant or ethnic minority group and the individual is experiencing significant emotional distress or social impairment resulting from cultural discrepancies in ideas of normative behavior or personality development, there should be a voluntary choice made by the individual to adapt to the behavioral norms of the host society. The host culture's values or behavioral norms should not be imposed on clients unless their symptoms result in gross impairment or severe social consequences. Therapeutic change in values and behavior is possible because human brain plasticity allows for substantial resocialization, including changes in worldview, religion, and personal values, especially during adolescence.

It should also be pointed out that immigrant parents from premodern or sociocentric societies may consider their adolescent children to be deviant or mentally ill if the children adopt Anglo American values and behavior, including egocentrism and independence from parental authority. Therefore, negotiation of clinical reality should be made between the clinician, the client and, ideally, the client's family. A plan of treatment should be drawn up that is the result of a negotiated consensus of the problem and the appropriate treatment. In this way, all parties concerned will be operating on the same set of assumptions and will understand and willingly agree to the course of treatment. This provides the best cognitive environment for optimal care outcome.

Chapter Seven

Sexual & Gender Identity Disorders

The sexual and gender identity disorders in DSM-IV contain three general categories: sexual dysfunctions, paraphilias, and gender identity disorder. The **sexual dysfunctions** are characterized by psychophysiological problems that have an impact on an individual's ability to have satisfying sexual relations, causing marked emotional distress and interpersonal difficulties. The sexual dysfunctions include: *hypoactive sexual desire disorder, sexual aversion disorder, female sexual arousal disorder, male erectile disorder, female orgasmic disorder, male orgasmic disorder, premature ejaculation, dyspareunia,* and *vaginismus.*

The **paraphilias** are characterized by recurrent sexual fantasies and behaviors involving objects, persons, or situations that are considered to be deviant in the prevailing set of cultural schemas, causing significant emotional distress or social impairment. The paraphilias in DSM-IV include: *exhibitionism, fetishism, frotteurism, pedophilia, sexual masochism, sexual sadism, transvestic fetishism,* and *voyeurism.*

Gender identity disorder is characterized by an intense and persistent sense of identity as someone of the opposite gender, causing significant emotional distress and social or occupational impairment.

The sexual and gender identity disorders are among the most culturally sensitive of all the disorders in DSM-IV. This is true of the sexual dysfunctions as well as the paraphilias and gender identity disorder. Cultural factors play a central role in that many of these disorders are, in fact, cultural entities; that is, the disorders exist because of the collective intentionality of a cultural group, in this case, primarily western culture. Because of the thoroughly cultural nature of sexual disorders, it is necessary to first present a discussion of the effects of culture on sexual behavior to put the sexual disorders within a proper social and cultural context.

Culture and Sexual Behavior

DSM-IV states that in making clinical judgments about a sexual disorder a client's cultural and religious background should be taken into consideration. It states, "For example, in some societies, sexual desires on the part of the female are given less relevance" (APA, 1994, p. 495). This is a great understatement, but nonetheless highlights the central problem when considering culture and sexual behavior. This central problem is the expression and control of female sexuality. All human societies have elaborate rules concerning sexual behavior, especially concerning the sexual behavior of women and postpubescent females.

Male Dominance and Female Sexuality

Female sexuality is highly controlled in most human societies. This high degree of control is illustrated by comparing human societies with other primate societies. Generally speaking, the higher the degree of male dominance existing in a primate society, the more complete will be the control over female sexuality. Conversely, the more freedom females have from male dominance, the less will be the control over female sexuality.

Male dominance is here defined by a social condition in which the lives of females are by and large controlled by males. In contrast, **female dominance** is here defined by a social condition in which the lives of males are by and large controlled by females.

This relationship between dominance hierarchies and sexual behavior is illustrated by categorizing the social organization of primate societies into five general types listed in Box 7.1.

Competitive Male Dominance

The five types of social organization listed in Box 7.1 are ideal types intended for heuristic purposes. In reality, there is much more variation as well as considerable overlap between categories. However, the categories are useful for illustrating differences in social organization and sexual behavior.

The first type of primate social organization listed is **competitive male dominance**. It is typified among primates by gorillas (Stewart & Harcourt, 1987; Watts, 1991). This social organization is characterized by males competing with each other through combat or other means for the exclusive sexual rights to a group of females. One dominant male controls a harem of females.

This is an extreme form of male dominance because the social group is small, usually only several individuals, and all of them are controlled by the physical force and threats of the alpha (dominant) male. Females are generally limited to sexual relations with the alpha male with only a few exceptions.

Box 7.1

Types of Primate Social Organization

1. Competitive male dominance
2. Semicooperative male dominance
3. Cooperative male dominance
4. Cooperative female dominance
5. Cooperative egalitarianism

Semicooperative Male Dominance

Chimpanzees exhibit somewhat more cooperation between males than do gorillas. They form larger social groups, and more sharing of sexual partners is found. This type of social organization can be categorized as **semicooperative male dominance.** Because of male dominance, chimpanzee females also tend to have relatively few sexual partners, and sexual behavior is associated with competition, aggression, and violence among the males and toward the females.

Cooperative Male Dominance

In contrast, **cooperative male dominance** is characterized by high levels of cooperation among males to dominate females and control female sexuality. Competition between males is typically controlled through elaborate systems of rules and rituals, and sharing the sexuality of females is generally compulsory.

Only one primate species has highly developed cooperative male dominance, and that is *H. sapiens sapiens.* By cooperating with each other, males assure their control over females and their access to female sexuality by sharing the females in social systems designed to provide exclusive sexual access—usually one female for every one male. This is the system of controlling sexual behavior known as *marriage.*

Almost all known human societies have some form of cooperative male dominance. Some are more extreme in their level of dominance, in which case they tend to look somewhat like competitive or semicooperative male dominant societies in which one male can control a small harem of females in the practice of polygyny. Other human societies have a lower level of male dominance, in which case they tend to look more like a cooperative egalitarian society, in which females have control over their own sexuality. However, almost all human societies have some degree of cooperative male dominance, and female sexuality is placed under at least nominal male control.

The systems of rules and rituals established by males in cooperative male dominant societies are known as religions and systems of laws. Females have largely been excluded from the governing bodies creating the rules that control sexuality in cooperative male dominant societies. For example, in almost all human societies, organizations of religious leaders, political leaders, police forces, military forces, secret clubs, and so on exclude females to some degree depending on the level of male dominance in that society. These powerful male organizations control female sexuality through either political force or religious belief, or some combination of both.

Some Islamic African societies are extremely male dominant and attempt to control female sexuality through required surgical removal of the clitoris (clitorectomy), or removal of the entire outer female genitalia and sewing up the inner labia (infibulation) during childhood. The woman's opening to her vagina is cut open slightly after marriage to allow for sexual intercourse, and later to allow childbirth, but she is stitched up again after giving birth. The surgery is thought to lessen her sexual desire by removing the sensitive outer parts of her genitalia (Ebomayi, 1987; Lightfoot-Klein, 1989).

In these Islamic societies, a man will not marry a woman who has not had the surgery as she is considered to be a "bad" woman with uncontrolled sexual desires. She would be a threat to the honor of her husband and his family because she might commit adultery. Because the females are socialized with this set of cultural schemas, they also largely believe and accept the practice, with the older females themselves performing the surgery on the young girls.

In the United States, control of female sexuality is attempted through a combination of religious beliefs and political force. Christianity has been the most important religious influence in American society. Christianity is, for the most part, antisex. The Fathers of the Church who formed the theology of Christianity between the 2nd and 6th centuries were mostly monastics dedicated to asceticism and celibacy. For instance, the Church Father St. Augustine considered human sexuality to be a result of the "Fall" in the Garden of Eden. According to him, even sex in marriage was sinful. Thus, all infants were born in a state of "original sin" because they were born as a result of lust, one of Catholicism's traditional sins. Therefore, in traditional Christian theology, sex should be used only for procreation—and even then it is sinful and should never be done for pleasure. For the traditional Christian, all types of sexuality engaged in strictly for pleasure—premarital sex, adultery, incest, masturbation, and homosexuality—are evil and sinful and should be prohibited with all the political force available.

In the last several decades, more liberal forms of Christianity in the United States as well as secularized segments of the population have supported more freedom in sexual behavior for women and men. However, for millions of people this fundamentalist Christian view of sexuality is still their cultural reality.

The theology of fundamentalist Christianity, like fundamentalist Islam, is an expression of cooperative male dominance. Cooperative male dominance was developed by men to facilitate control of female sexuality and to provide structures for large-scale male cooperation such as armies, police forces, priesthoods, legislative bodies, trading and economic systems, military and political alliances, and so on.

However, unlike the cultural schemas of Islam, which construct women as sexually insatiable and dangerous, fundamentalist Christian schemas construct women as uninterested in sexual pleasure, only submitting to sexual relations as part of their marital "duty" or for the sake of having children. This is especially seen in 19th century Victorian views of women, who were thought to have no sexual desires (Jacob, 1981).

Fundamentalist Christian (as opposed to Islamic) cultural schemas of female sexuality have even found their way into the scientific study of sexuality in the late 20th century. For example, sociobiology (Symons, 1979, 1987; Wilson, 1975) views females as naturally reluctant to have sex. In sociobiology, it is presumed that all individuals want to maximize their chances of successfully passing on their genetic material. Supposedly, this makes females choosy about sex partners because they have only a few eggs. The reasoning is that if these eggs are fertilized and develop, the females face a long period of childrearing. Thus, females are thought to be reluctant about sex, postponing sexual intercourse until they are sure they have the best possible partner. The best partner is defined in sociobiology as the one with the best genes, or the one best able to help with childrearing. Sex for the female, therefore, is thought to be controlled primarily by factors affecting procreation and childrearing. Thus, it is thought that women are not as interested in sexual pleasure as are men.

Men, in contrast, are thought to be naturally promiscuous. Because men produce millions of sperm, they can increase the chances of their genetic material being passed on by "spreading" their sperm to as many females as possible.

These ideas in sociobiology fit very well with fundamentalist Christian ideas about female sexuality and therefore seem like common sense to many Americans. However, the evolutionary theory in sociobiology concerning sexual behavior was devised without actually looking at the sexual behavior of most primate species, our closest animal relatives. It was simply assumed that because most human females traditionally have only one sexual partner (the husband) this was the natural pattern of sexual behavior for female primates. Thus, it was assumed that female primates are very choosy, generally having sex only with the father of their offspring.

It was also known that many mammals had a harem type social structure with one dominant male having won out in competition with other males. This also fit well with the ideas of sociobiology in that the females were viewed as "choosing" the successful male as the one with the best genes. These findings, compared with the marriage system seen in human societies, made the sociobiological view seem only natural.

However, during the past two decades many more studies of primate behavior covering more species have been done. The findings do not support the view of sociobiology. Most primate species do not have male dominance, either competitive like gorillas, semicooperative like chimpanzees, or fully cooperative like humans. Most primate species have cooperative female dominance or are egalitarian. As a result of not having male dominance, the female sexual behavior in these societies is radically different (de Waal, 1995; Small, 1993).

Cooperative Female Dominance

The relationship between sexuality and gender dominance is demonstrated by looking at primate societies that have **cooperative female dominance**. In these societies, females cooperate to control the lives of males. For example, Rhesus macaque societies are formed around large female family groups. A female macaque is born into a particular family group and stays in that particular group for her entire life, focusing on intense relationships with her close female relatives (Page, 1990; Rawlins & Kessler, 1986; Small, 1993).

Males are forced out of the family group at adolescence and must attempt to join another family group by behaving subserviently and by attracting the sexual attentions of one or more females in the new group. Thus, males move in and out of family groups by being accepted and rejected by the females. Males stay in groups only temporarily until the females no longer find them sexually attractive. Therefore, males are forced to move from group to group if they are going to have any chance for sexual relations. Thus, the lives of the males are controlled by the females (Small, 1993).

In macaque society, it is the females who are sexually aggressive, in many cases pursuing males and initiating copulation. There are also clearly defined dominance hierarchies within the female family groups. Physical aggression is mostly between groups of females, who fight to maintain family group dominance hierarchies and access to territory and food. Higher ranking females get both more sex and more food (Page, 1990; Small, 1993).

Macaque females have sex only during their estrus cycles, but during this time they have sex with as many males as possible. Also, macaque females have sex only when they want to, and only with males they have selected. No male macaque can force a female to have sex. Rape does not occur in primate societies without male dominance.

Most primate species have social organizations and patterns of sexual behavior similar to those of the Rhesus macaques (Small, 1993). When looking at sexual behavior across primate species, it is clear that in the majority of species females are not subject to male dominance. Contrary to the thinking of sociobiologists, in those societies where females control their own sexuality, they are highly "promiscuous"; that is, they are highly orgasmic, enjoy sex with a great many different male partners, and are not at all "choosy" or reluctant to have sex. However, in the few primate societies that have male dominance (for example, chimpanzees, gorillas, humans), females are allowed only a minimal number of sexual partners consistent with male dominance, and female orgasm may be less common or absent. Thus, we see that it is not "natural" but "cultural" for primate females to mate with only a limited number of male sexual partners. When primate females are allowed to express their sexual desires free from male dominance, they have many sexual partners (male and female) and are highly orgasmic.

Cooperative Egalitarianism

In **cooperative egalitarianism,** the two genders are roughly equal, and there is no gender dominance hierarchy. As a result, female sexuality is not controlled by male dominance or by a female dominance hierarchy. Bonobos (or "pygmy chimps") typify a primate cooperative egalitarian society (de Waal, 1987, 1995; Small, 1992, 1993).

The social organization and sexual behavior of bonobos is radically different from that of chimps and humans. In bonobo society, females band together to form close lifelong friendship bonds with other females. These female *homosexual* relationships form the primary social bonds and family structure of bonobo society. However, bonobos are not homosexual per se. They are *pansexual,* meaning that they have sexual relations with all of the other members of their social group, including females, males, and juveniles.

Small (1993) calls bonobos "the most sexual animals on earth" (p. 175). This is because both genders and all ages have sex every day, several times a day. Moreover, most of the time, bonobo sex has nothing to do with procreation. Bonobos appear to have sex mostly for the purposes of creating and maintaining close friendship bonds, to defuse disputes, and for sheer pleasure (de Waal, 1995). Unlike chimpanzee females who have sex only during their estrus cycles, bonobo females have sex every day. And as far as reproduction goes, bonobo females are not at all choosy about their male sex partners, unless you could call "choosing" every male she meets being choosy (Small, 1993).

In the bonobo egalitarian society, individuals have sex more often and in more variations than in any human society. Males have sex with males. Females have sex with females. Even juveniles participate by rubbing their genitals against those of adults, although adult males never actually insert their penises into juvenile females (de Waal, 1995; Small, 1993).

Juvenile males are also very fond of performing oral sex on each other. Bonobos also love to kiss, including inserting their tongues into each other's mouths like humans. Also interesting is that bonobos frequently have sexual intercourse face-to-face like humans, which is rare for chimps or gorillas. This is probably also related to the absence of male dominance in that the face-to-face position seems to be preferred by females as it allows more direct clitoral stimulation (de Waal, 1995).

Female bonobos have sex with each other by rubbing their genitals together and kissing and embracing. Female bonobos have large clitorises and are highly orgasmic. Group sex is also very common for bonobos. When two individuals initiate sex, others are free to join in by sticking their fingers into the genital area, or they may wait in line for copulation (Small, 1993).

Human Cultural Variations

When we examine the relationship of social organization to sexuality in human societies, it is seen that male dominance is created and maintained not only by political force, as it is in other primate societies, but also by complex symbolic systems relfecting humans' larger brains and greater cognitive ability. Nevertheless, the net effect of male dominance is the same—it limits females to a minimum number of male sexual partners.

Almost all human societies have some degree of cooperative male dominance, but there is much variation. Females can attain more freedom in some societies. In those societies with less male dominance and control on female sexuality, women typically have more sexual partners and are more likely to be orgasmic. In contrast, in human societies with greater male dominance and control on female sexuality, females have fewer sexual partners and are less likely to be orgasmic.

The contrast in sexual behavior resulting from social organization can be illustrated by looking at different human societies. It is not the intention here to give a comprehensive review of cultural variations of human sexuality (see Gregerson, 1983, and Suggs & Miracle, 1993, for excellent reviews) but only to demonstrate some of the extremes in the range of culturally normative sexual behavior.

Sexuality in Inis Beag

Inis Beag is a small island off the coast of Ireland studied by Messenger (1993) in the 1950s and 1960s. The society is a peasant community of devout Roman Catholics. When studied by Messenger, it was thought that the Catholicism of the islanders embodied a religious ideal unmatched in Ireland. It was a particularly ascetic style of religion with strong influences of Irish Catholic monasticism, Augustinianism, Jansenism, and some probable English Puritan influences.

In this society of the 1950s and 1960s, sexual renunciation was identified with moral and religious virtue. Moreover, male solidarity was idealized in the form of the "loveless Irishman" whose loyalty is directed toward his comrades. Women were relegated to serfdom. In this society, a "good" woman was one who did not like sex, and a "bad" woman was one who enjoyed sex. "Bad" women were thought to disrupt social relations between a man and his male comrades, distracting him from his purpose in life. Likewise, men were supposed to be socially active in the community, but women were restricted to visiting other women and attending church-related activities. Some women left their homes only to attend mass, wakes, and funerals.

In this society, virtually anything related to sex was highly controlled and socially suppressed. Courtship was almost nonexistent, and late marriage and celibacy were prevalent. After marriage, however, contraception was prohibited, and the women were under pressure from the local priests to produce as many offspring as possible. The women resented this because they felt it increased their work, restricted their freedom, and perpetuated their poverty. Moreover, they were resentful of the social freedom held by men.

Ignorance of sexual practices was profound in this society, along with a lack of sexual variation found in other societies. Sexuality was almost never openly discussed, and mothers rarely gave advice to daughters about sex, assuming that "after marriage nature takes its course." As a result, French kissing, kissing breasts, female hand stimulation of the male genitals, cunnilingus, fellatio, anal intercourse, premarital sex, extramarital sex, open homosexuality, and sadomasochism were either unknown, not performed, or so highly suppressed they were not discussable. However, masturbation was the primary sexual activity of single men; therefore, secret fetishisms were probable.

In Inis Beag, men were believed to be more interested in sex than women were. Like other highly traditional Christians, the islanders believed that sex is a "duty" that a wife must "endure." Therefore, the husband reached orgasm as quickly as possible, not wanting to make his wife "endure" intercourse any longer than necessary. Sexual foreplay was limited to kissing and rough fondling of the buttocks. The man on top was viewed as the only proper position to be used in coitus, and underclothes were worn during sex. The husband fell asleep immediately after orgasm, and female orgasm was either unknown, doubted to exist, or at least considered deviant.

Sexuality in Mangaia

In contrast to Inis Beag, the island of Mangaia in the South Pacific is a society in which females have achieved a great degree of sexual freedom. This traditional Polynesian society was studied by Marshall (1993) during the 1950s and 1960s.

The Mangaians of that time lived in single room huts housing 5 to 15 family members. From puberty on, all family members including daughters were free to copulate at night in this same room, with the rest of the family sleeping. Postpubescent daughters especially could receive and make love to varied suitors nightly. For the Mangaians, sex for pleasure was a major concern of their culture.

Mangaian boys began to masturbate at about age 7 or 8. Around age 13 or 14, boys underwent an initiation ceremony marking their transition to adulthood. The ceremony involved superincision of the penis—"beautifying" the organ—marking them as adult males and suitable sexual partners. After this, boys no longer masturbated but began regular sexual intercourse with postpubescent females.

The man who performed the superincision also served as an instructor in sex, educating the young initiate in how to please a woman. The young male was taught how to perform cunnilingus, how to kiss and fondle breasts, and how to stimulate a woman to multiple orgasms before his own climax. Also, about two weeks after the initiation, the young man received formal "hands on" training from an older, experienced woman who taught him various sexual positions and techniques in giving pleasure to a woman.

After this, the initiated Mangaian male would have sexual intercourse every night with various young females. A young male could have ten or more female sex partners. Multiple partners were preferred because the Mangaians believed that avoiding sex with the same partner prevented pregnancy.

The young Mangaian male developed a good reputation with the postpubescent females of the community if he proved he could continue the vigorous in-and-out motion of coitus for extended periods of time. By the age of 18, the average Mangaian male had three orgasms per night, seven nights per week.

Mangaian girls also began to masturbate early by pressing their thighs together, or by sitting on the ground with their right heel pressed against the clitoris and rocking back and forth. Mangaian girls were even known to masturbate in public using this method. Childhood sex play was also common and was not prohibited.

After their first menstruation, females began regular sexual intercourse with the initiated males of the community. The average postpubescent female could have three or four regular sexual partners. The Mangaians believed that a female learned to be orgasmic by sexual experience with a "good" man. The females learned to be orgasmic almost immediately after beginning regular coitus. Apparently, all females in Mangaia had orgasms every time they had sex, with most having multiple orgasms.

In Mangaia, females were also sexually aggressive. If they perceived that a man was not copulating often enough, they would tell him insultingly that he was lazy, letting his penis go to waste, and letting it "get rusty." They often made sexual remarks to men that in Anglo American society would be considered sexual harassment. Moreover, coitus was the only possible end of any sexual encounter. There was no equivalent of "dating" or "necking" in the American sense. Phrases such as "I love you" were understood as invitations to copulate.

Sexual intercourse was not achieved after demonstrating personal affection as it is in western societies. Rather, sexual intimacy was used to create and maintain bonds of personal affection. Also, adult women frequently performed fellatio on small boys in the family.

After marriage, Mangaians maintained sexual exclusivity with their spouses. They had sex most nights of the week, declining to about two or three times per week by age 48.

Sexuality among the Sambia

The relationship between the degree of male dominance and sexual behavior is also demonstrated by a society with such extreme male dominance that the cultural schemas defined sex with females as "polluting." It has been theorized that the highest incidence of male homosexuality occurs in extremely male dominant societies with great rigidity of gender roles (Reiss, 1986). This is illustrated by Gilbert Herdt's (1980, 1981, 1990) studies of New Guinean culture where gender segregation was practiced to ward off "female pollution."*

Before pacification in 1965, the men of the Sambia tribe in New Guinea were engaging in almost continuous intervillage warfare. There was a tremendous need for tough, aggressive fighters to replenish the ranks of warriors. Thus, the Sambia men created social institutions designed to produce the desired "warrior personality" within all the boys growing up in the tribe. The desired personality was one who would kill without hesitation, be unafraid of pain, be familiar with the sight of blood, and be completely bound to his male comrades.

The desired warrior personalities were produced by physically separating boys from their mothers and all other females around age 7 to 10 and collectively training the boys to become warriors over a 10-year period in which the boys were completely separated from females.

The Sambian cultural schemas constructed male gender identity (equivalent with being a warrior) as something that must be achieved. Training as a warrior, punctuated by initiation ceremonies at key stages of development, was considered necessary for the development of biological manhood. Without the training and rituals, it was believed that the boys would not grow into men. The training and rituals consisted of ridding the boys of polluting femininity and instilling masculinity in the boys. It was believed that the boys had been polluted by physical proximity to their mothers. This pollution was removed by bleeding the boys in a particularly traumatic and painful fashion.

Boys aged 7 to 10 went through their first initiation as a group. There were purificatory rites, collective male dancing, fasting, beating rites, enforced sleeplessness over several days, and ritual bleeding. The bleeding was a violent surprise assault on the boys in which sharp cane grasses were thrust into the mucus membranes of the boys' noses until profuse bleeding was produced. The boys were told that this was done to remove the mothers' female pollution. They were told to be strong and to be unafraid of the blood and pain.

The mothers' female pollution was not the only thing blocking male development in the boys. It was also believed that the boys must have semen to develop into men. However, they believed that males do not manufacture semen, only store it and pass it on. Therefore, to develop into men, the boys must obtain semen from their elders. This was done during the initiation ceremonies in which all the boys ingested the semen of their elders through ritual fellatio.

After the initiation, the young boys were completely cut off from female contact and so formed homosexual relationships with postpubescent males, ingesting the semen of the older males. After the young boys achieved puberty,

*Adapted from "Sambia Nosebleeding Rites and Male Proximity to Women," by G. Herdt. In J. W. Stigler, R. A. Shweder, and G. Herdt (Eds.), *Cultural Psychology*, pp. 366–400. Copyright © 1990 and adapted with the permission of Cambridge University Press.

they formed homosexual relationships with younger boys, "inseminating" them to aid in their male development. It was believed that this insemination was the only way the biological changes could occur that would turn a boy into a man.

After ten years of training and isolation from females, the Sambia male had become a warrior. He was then allowed to marry a woman and produce offspring. However, because females were seen as polluting and dangerous to his biological masculinity, each married man was required to periodically nosebleed himself to remove the polluting effects of physical contact with a woman. Female pollution was especially thought to enter through the nose. Thus, whenever a man engaged in coitus with his wife he plugged his nose to avoid the harmfully foul and polluting vaginal smell.

The Sambian cultural schemas provided religious legitimacy for male dominance. Females were construed as inherently polluting. Therefore, polluting females were responsible for the need to separate males from females and for the male pain from the nosebleeding rites. Moreover, the women were required to respect the men for the tremendous pain and discipline they had endured to become fully masculine. The men never let the women forget this, demonstrating their dominance and power over the women by regularly beating them.

In general, the initiations and training of young males were successful in creating fearless, extremely violent men, completely bonded to their male comrades. The extreme cooperative male dominance in Sambian society created and maintained a pattern of sexual development in which 100 percent of the males were homosexual until well into adulthood, after which they became bisexual, and eventually heterosexual. This illustrates the profound effects of social organization on sexual development and practices.

Sexual practices vary widely around the globe. The societies discussed here represent only a small fraction of the possible variations in social organization and sexual behavior. In all cases, however, the prevailing cultural schemas create and maintain patterns of behavior that profoundly affect individual sexual development and practices.

The Paraphilias

DSM-IV defines the paraphilias as "recurrent, intense sexually arousing fantasies, sexual urges, or behaviors generally involving (1) nonhuman objects, (2) the suffering or humiliation of oneself or one's partner, or (3) children or other nonconsenting persons" (APA, 1994, pp. 522–523). In some instances, the paraphilia may become the main sexual activity in the person's life.

Many people with these disorders experience no distress, claiming that their only problem is the response from society to their sexual behavior. However, many other people do experience significant emotional distress as a result of their paraphilia, which can be manifest as symptoms of anxiety and depression.

Most of the paraphilias are more prevalent in males. This is frequently explained by using the sociobiological theory that because males are trying to "spread" their genetic material as widely as possible they have a stronger sex drive than females. Thus, it is thought that males are more likely to engage in all types of sexual behavior more often than females, including abnormal sexual behavior. However, sociobiological views of human sexuality are seriously flawed, not taking into account social organization and social forces and their effects on sexual behavior.

In male-dominated societies, restricting sexuality is primarily aimed at young females, "protecting" them from sex and preserving their virginity for marriage. Females typically begin masturbating later than males in these societies because of restrictions on female sexuality. Thus, females learn to be sexual at a later age. Also, because males have external genitals, they are more aware of their genitals as a sexual organ at an earlier age than are females. Moreover, in male dominated societies, there are almost always fewer restrictions on male sexuality than on female sexuality. Thus, rudimentary knowledge about sexual arousal and orgasm, particularly in the form of masturbation, is available to males earlier than it is to females. As a result, most females learn masturbation at a later age than males do in these societies, in some cases not until adulthood (Hyde, 1994).

Restricting sexuality in young females also requires restricting young males. If sexual fulfillment is not available with females, then other forms of sexual behavior will be substituted. In some cases, this involves development of paraphilias linked with masturbation. This is probably one of the main reasons certain paraphilias are more prevalent in males.

Cultural factors in the paraphilias are both obvious and subtle. Obviously, certain activities that are considered deviant in one culture may be normal in another. More subtle may be paraphilias that are a behavioral response to some aspects of a particular set of cultural schemas.

Exhibitionism

Exhibitionism is an excellent example of a culture-bound syndrome. Exhibitionism involves the exposure of one's genitals to a stranger. Obviously, this definition has meaning only in societies where the genitals are normally covered in public. In many tribal societies in tropical areas, no clothing is traditionally worn. For example, the Mehinaku tribe of the Amazon region of South America wear only a thin shell belt around the waist. The genital areas of both men and women remain totally exposed. When the Mehinaku want to "get naked" they remove their belts (Gregor, 1990).

In western society, the genitals are almost always kept covered in public (nude beaches and nudist camps being the main exceptions). Exposure of the genitals to someone of the opposite gender is almost always associated with sexuality in western society. Therefore, in western society, exposure of the genitals to a stranger of the opposite sex is almost always considered to be a sexual act.

People who engage in exhibitionism do so because they derive sexual excitement from exposing themselves. The typical case is a young man exposing his erect penis to unsuspecting females. Sometimes he masturbates as he does so, or sometimes he masturbates to orgasm later while fantasizing a sexual relationship with the female he exposed himself to. His behavior usually evokes a strong emotional response in the female, typically one of surprise and shock.

The exposure of sexually aroused genitals to the opposite sex has a long evolutionary history among primates, in both males and females. Indeed, among nonhuman primates, one of the most common invitations for copulation is presentation of genitals swollen from sexual arousal to a particular member of the opposite sex (Haanstra, 1991; Small, 1993).

For example, a female chimpanzee in estrus will present her swollen genital area to a male by bending over in front of him, inviting him to copulate. Similarly, a male chimpanzee will do a kind of dance, waving his erect penis at a particular female as an invitation for coitus. Thus, it is probable that exposure of genitals swollen by the vasocongestion of sexual arousal can evoke a strong emotional response in the viewer because of an evolutionary "hard wiring" in the neural networks of the primate brain.

The question is: Why do some males use this primitive form of sexual expression? The answer is, of course, cultural. In western culture, exhibitionism usually develops in adolescence when boys begin masturbating. Exhibitionism can be an accidentally conditioned behavior, as when a boy is discovered masturbating or with an exposed erection by a female and receives an emotional response from the female. The emotional response evoked in the female may make the boy even more aroused, resulting in orgasm either spontaneously or through masturbation.

Thus, an association between exposing his erect penis to an unsuspecting female and orgasm may develop. If this happens repeatedly, the boy becomes conditioned to this type of sexual behavior. If no more mature forms of sexual expression develop, exhibitionism can become his primary sexual activity, and he may even be uninterested or unable to achieve sexual arousal and orgasm by other means.

This type of situation likely occurs in some societies because of the restrictions on coitus placed on adolescents. Adolescent boys are prohibited from having sexual intercourse in some societies and are thus limited to masturbation as a form of sexual expression. Masturbation is a nonspecific form of sexual stimulus in that the sexual object is usually provided by the imagination in sexual fantasies (frequently aided by some kind of object, for example, fetishes). Therefore, the sexual pleasure of masturbation can become associated with virtually anything, including all types of inanimate objects or interpersonal situations. Exhibitionism as a habitual behavior is probably caused by **masturbatory conditioning** in which the male becomes conditioned to experience sexual pleasure in this way through repeated occurrences (Bancroft, 1974; Barlow & Durand, 1995; Rachman & Hodgson, 1968).

However, in a society like Mangaia, where postpubescent males and females are allowed to have free access to the opposite gender for coitus, masturbation among young males becomes nonexistent (Marshall, 1993). Nonspecific masturbatory conditioning appears to be unlikely in such a society because young males are conditioned to express their sexuality through heterosexual copulation.

Fetishism

Fetishism involves the use of inanimate objects (the fetish) for sexual arousal. This is usually a male disorder. Commonly used fetishes are objects associated with females, for example, women's undergarments, stockings, shoes, or other articles of clothing (APA, 1994).

In fetishism, the presence of the fetish is always preferred and may be required for the individual to become sexually aroused. Again, this probably occurs because of masturbatory conditioning, usually commencing in early adolescence, although sometimes before.

Because adolescents are not allowed to copulate in many societies, they masturbate. Some inanimate object can accidentally become associated with sexual pleasure by being present at a time of sexual arousal and masturbation. A very common occurrence is for boys to become sexually aroused by females in their family and to associate that arousal with the panties or bras of their mothers or older sisters. The adolescent boys secretly obtain these objects and masturbate while holding or smelling the objects, or ejaculate into them. If this occurs repeatedly, the boy becomes conditioned to be sexually aroused by the fetish. If he does not grow out of this pattern of sexual behavior by developing more mature forms of sexual expression with women, he may be limited to masturbating with the fetish as his only expression of sexuality.

A historically important case was reported by Von Krafft-Ebing in his book *Psychopathia Sexualis* (1886/1965, case 114). The patient was a 24-year-old man who had been taught how to masturbate at the age of seven by an older servant girl. During this experience, she accidentally touched his erect penis with her shoe. An association was established between the female's shoe and sexual pleasure. From that time on, he masturbated while looking at women's shoes or while fantasizing about them. He became so obsessed that at school he repeatedly grasped his teachers' shoes. In spite of being punished, he found this extremely arousing. He eventually began ejaculating into women's shoes. Twice he had dissociative seizures (Chapter 11) while masturbating in this way. Nothing else sexually aroused him. He found the thought of coitus horrifying.

It was thought that marriage would cure him, and he was married to a pretty young woman. But because of his distaste for sexual intercourse, he was completely unable to become sexually aroused by his wife. Finally, he was advised to hang a woman's shoe over the head of his bed and stare at it during coitus with his wife, at the same time imagining that his wife was the shoe. The result was that he had no further seizures, and he was able to have sexual intercourse with his wife about once a week. Over time he also became less excited by women's shoes. This type of therapy is known as **orgasmic reconditioning** (Hyde, 1994). The individual is gradually reconditioned by having orgasm repeatedly associated with an appropriate sexual object, in this case, his wife.

Fetishes illustrate that humans can be classically conditioned to be sexually aroused by virtually anything. Moreover, the development of fetishes can occur in a more or less accidental fashion in societies where masturbation is the primary or sole sexual behavior allowed for adolescents.

Fetishes and cultural variations in sexual behavior also illustrate that humans are not necessarily heterosexual, homosexual, bisexual, pedophiliacs, exhibitionists, masochists, or sadists. All of these are potential behaviors in all humans that can be learned through classical sexual conditioning, especially at a young age.

Frotteurism

Frotteurism is characterized by rubbing against or touching a nonconsenting person in a sexual way. It usually occurs in crowded public spaces such as on buses or subway cars. Typically, a young man will spot an attractive woman about to enter a subway car during rush hour when the cars will be full and necessitate crowding. He will follow her onto the car, standing closely behind her. He will then rub his erect penis against her buttocks, imagining that he is in a loving, consensual sexual relationship with the woman. He may have an orgasm on the spot, or later masturbate to orgasm remembering his experience on the subway (Spitzer et al., 1994).

Frotteurism is obviously related to culture in that it occurs in large cities with crowded public transportation vehicles in societies that restrict the sexuality of young people. Frotteurism is more likely to occur in urban areas in societies with high levels of male dominance such as India or Japan.

Once young males learn to become orgasmic through masturbation, they look for ways to fulfill their sexual desires. If sexual fulfillment is not available with postpubescent females of similar age, or with older females, then other forms of sexual behavior will be learned as a substitute for copulation. As we have seen in the case of fetishisms, this can involve inanimate objects that substitute for a female. In the case of frotteurism, a female is the sexual object, but the male has learned a very crude, childish form of sexual expression and has become conditioned over time to be orgasmic in this socially limited fashion.

Pedophilia

Pedophilia is defined in DSM-IV as a person 16 years or older having sexual activity with a prepubescent child (legally this is generally 13 years or younger).

Most often, pedophiliacs are men (Finkelhor, 1984). Some pedophiliacs have a sexual preference for prepubescent females, some prefer males, and some either gender. Some are attracted only to prepubescent children, while others are sometimes attracted to postpubescent individuals.

The range of sexual activity with prepubescent children varies considerably. Some pedophiliacs only want to look at a naked child while they masturbate to orgasm. Others will fondle the genitals of the children, perform fellatio or cunnilingus on them, or insert their penis in the mouth, anus, or vagina of the child.

Pedophiliacs typically state and believe that the children derive sexual pleasure from the activities. They also claim that the children were sexually provocative, inviting sexual activity. Like most of the paraphilias, pedophilia has its origins in early adolescence.

Pedophilia is a complex topic from a cross-cultural perspective. The concept itself has meaning only in societies where all sexual contact with children is prohibited. Obviously, not all human societies practice this form of restriction on sexuality. In Mangaia, adults commonly fondled the genitals of children and performed fellatio and cunnilingus on the children as well. Likewise, in Sambian society postpubescent males had prepubescent boys perform fellatio on them as part of the boys' normal sexual and social development.

However, no society condones or regularly practices coitus with prepubescent children. Even in bonobo society, where individuals begin rubbing their genitals against those of others and performing oral sex around the age of one, coitus with prepubescent juveniles is not part of their regular sexual activities.

The concept of pedophilia is also related to cultural concepts of sexual development in children. Some people in North American society still believe that prepubescent children are not sexual and that sexuality suddenly emerges at the time of puberty. This is certainly not true. Humans are capable of sexual pleasure from the time of infancy. Human infants commonly fondle their own genitals, and in some nonwestern societies adults fondle the genitals of infants to keep them quiet, an effective pacifier (Hyde, 1994). Moreover, unless sexuality in children is actively suppressed by adults, humans will remain sexual throughout childhood.

Young children naturally experiment with immature forms of sexual play. In societies that mandate gender segregation among children, this play will usually be of a homosexual nature. In societies that allow mixing of the genders, the sexual play can be heterosexual or homosexual. Young boys remember these early sexual encounters, especially if they were enjoyable. Later, when the boy learns to be orgasmic, memories of earlier sexual encounters with young children may be sexually stimulating, prompting an initial experimental sexual contact with a young child (Barlow & Durand, 1995). This will usually emulate his own earlier sexual play as a young child. That means fondling the genitals or inserting fingers into the child's vagina or anus, or inserting his penis into the mouth, anus, or vagina of the child.

The young children who receive this sexual contact from an adolescent or adult learn about these forms of sexual activity. Those children will be much more likely to engage in sexual behavior with young children when they grow older because they have experienced being a sexual object for an older person. This may remain the preferred form of sexual expression if they have not subsequently learned how to have satisfying sex with persons of their own age.

As discussed above, because of the sociocultural restrictions placed on sexuality, adolescents are sometimes forced to express their sexuality surreptitiously with the sexual objects that are available to them. Just as an adolescent can develop a habit of sexual arousal and orgasm with an inanimate object (fetish), so too can he or she develop a habit of sexual arousal and orgasm with younger children if no more appropriate sexual object (another adolescent) is available.

Thus, having sex with young children is most likely a learned behavior, just as a sexual fetish is a learned behavior. It is probably acquired by repeated experience that classically conditions the person to experience sexual arousal and orgasm in that fashion. There is no evidence to indicate that pedophilia or sexual fetishes are caused by brain disease.

Pedophilia is most likely to be learned in early adolescence. If the person does not subsequently learn to have satisfying sexual relations with persons of his or her own age, then the pedophilia will likely be chronic, and the person will become an adult pedophiliac.

Because pedophilia is primarily a problem beginning in early adolescence, it is directly related to cooperative male dominance and the sociocultural restrictions placed on sexuality. For example, in societies like the Sambia, where restrictions on sexuality stemming from cooperative male dominance were so extreme that they resulted in complete gender segregation of children and adolescents for several years, virtually 100 percent of the adolescent males developed into pedophiliacs by western standards (Herdt, 1990).

Sexual Masochism

Sexual masochism is characterized by sexual arousal resulting from being humiliated, beaten, bound, or other forms of punishment. Typical acts of punishment sought by the sexual masochist are being tied up, paddled, spanked, whipped, being put on a leash and forced to bark like a dog, verbal punishment, being urinated or defecated on, and for men, being forced to dress like a woman while being physically and verbally abused (APA, 1994; Hyde, 1994). However, the punishment is arousing only when it is part of a scripted sexual fantasy (Gosselin & Wilson, 1980; Hyde, 1994).

Again, with sexual masochism we see a conditioned sexual behavior probably resulting from repeated personal experience. Sexual masochism is common in both males and females in western societies. It probably has its origins in prohibitions on childhood sexuality. As DSM-IV states, "Masochistic sexual fantasies are likely to have been present in childhood" (APA, 1994, p. 529).

When young children are caught in sex play in societies that prohibit this type of behavior, they are frequently punished. The punishment may be verbal or physical, or both. Children may be spanked, paddled, humiliated, whipped, or bound for their "bad" behavior. An association can thus be created between sexual arousal and corporal punishment. If this punishment happens repeatedly, a classically conditioned response may be created in which the punishment itself may evoke sexual arousal.

Masochism can probably also result from masturbatory conditioning if the child recalls the sexual activity and corporal punishment while masturbating. Moreover, if a child's sexual play involves a fetish, for example, women's underwear, an association between corporal punishment, women's underwear, and sexual activity and arousal may develop. These individuals may create sexual fantasies involving the fetish objects, corporal punishment, and sexual activity. These are the sexual fantasies that are acted out in sadomasochistic sexual encounters.

Because of the effects of conditioning, sexual masochism probably occurs only in societies where young children receive corporal punishment for sex play. Prepubescent children are not asexual. Young children are capable of sexual pleasure and will pursue that pleasure if given the opportunity. Corporal punishment is used by adults to suppress the sexual activities of children in some societies. However, the adults may unwittingly be creating conditioned responses in their children, linking the leather belts, verbal abuse, and so forth used in punishment with sexual activity and arousal. These same implements of punishment (leather belts and so forth) then become fetish objects in sexual masochism by early adulthood. Sexual masochism is probably a culture-bound syndrome in that it requires a set of cultural schemas that both prohibit childhood sexuality and suppress it with corporal punishment. Not all societies fit this cultural pattern.

Sexual Sadism

Sexual sadism is closely related to sexual masochism. It is characterized by sexual arousal resulting from inflicting physical or psychological punishment on someone else. The sadist is typically the partner of the sexual masochist, performing the spanking, paddling, whipping, and so on. In many cases, sadomasochists will be interested in playing both parts in a sadomasochistic fantasy, alternating between the "master" and "slave" roles (Moser & Levitt, 1987). The level of pain or physical harm is usually slight in these encounters, and it is more sexual play than anything else. Typically, the degree of pain inflicted will be under the control of the masochistic "slave" partner. Thus, the two are fulfilling fantasies of being "bad" and being punished for their misbehavior. In many cases, they could be building on childhood experiences that later developed into adult fantasies of sex play.

Occasionally, however, a person develops a taste for sexual arousal resulting from inflicting serious pain and injury on nonconsenting victims. This person may have a personal history similar to that of other sexual sadists but may have been more seriously punished in childhood to the point of physical and perhaps sexual abuse.

It is possible for this person to have fantasies of inflicting serious injury before actually engaging in sexual sadism. It is also possible for the person to develop fantasies of inflicting real pain and injury through repeated sexual encounters with masochists (Spitzer et al., 1994). In any case, the person derives sexual pleasure from inflicting serious pain and injury, and sometimes killing the victims.

If they kill their victims, the means of death may be especially brutal and violent, involving torture, dismemberment, disemboweling, decapitation, and sometimes cannibalism. Sexual fantasies carried out by the sadist may involve inserting his penis to orgasm in the dead body (necrophilia) or body parts. Serial murderers are frequently sexual sadists, and the murders involve fulfillment of their sexual fantasies (for example, Jeffrey Dahmer, Arthur Shawcross).

Sexual sadism is a culture-bound syndrome in that it likely occurs in societies that link sexual pleasure with punishment, pain, humiliation, and personal injury. Thus, it may be possible to view serious sexual sadism as resulting from a high degree of cooperative male dominance resulting in strict prohibitions on childhood and adolescent sexuality, enforced by severe physical punishment.

Transvestic Fetishism

Transvestic fetishism is characterized by males deriving sexual pleasure by intermittently wearing female clothing. While wearing the female clothing, the male masturbates to orgasm while imagining himself to be both the female sexual object and the male subject of the sexual encounter (APA, 1994). In a sense, he becomes his own sex partner in a heterosexual relationship.

This paraphilia occurs only in heterosexual males. It likely has its origins in childhood or early adolescence in a similar fashion to other fetishes. The only difference is that the male wears the article of female clothing rather than just holding it or smelling it. This enables the man to imagine being both the female and the male in the sexual encounter, while masturbating to orgasm.

Like the other fetishes discussed earlier, transvestic fetishism is most likely caused by adolescent males not having access to more appropriate sexual objects (adolescent females). They therefore rely on masturbation to fulfill their sexual desires, imagining themselves to be their own sexual partner with the aid of female clothing.

Voyeurism

Voyeurism is characterized by sexual arousal resulting from observing unsuspecting persons who are getting undressed, are naked, or are engaged in sexual activities (APA, 1994).

Voyeurism usually occurs in adolescent or young adult males who will masturbate to orgasm while watching the unsuspecting persons, or masturbate later imagining the memory of what they have witnessed. If the voyeurs do not learn to have satisfying sex with females, then voyeurism may be their primary form of sexual expression (Gebhard, Gagnon, Pomeroy, & Christenson, 1965).

Like fetishes, voyeurism is more likely to develop in societies that prohibit sexual access to adolescent females and suppress sexuality by requiring concealment of the human body with clothing and concealment of sexual acts in private places.

As mentioned earlier in the discussion of exhibitionism, observing genitals, especially genitals swollen in a state of sexual arousal, is sexually arousing in primates. Being sexually aroused by viewing naked persons or those engaged in sexual activities is considered a paraphilia only because it is occurring in a society that prohibits such viewing. Nudity and viewing sexual activities occur as a normal part of life in many tribal societies. These activities have probably occurred as a regular part of life for the majority of the cultural evolution of our species. However, because of extensive restrictions on sexuality in some societies, voyeurism can become the primary or only form of sexual expression for some males, and therefore a paraphilia.

Paraphilia Not Otherwise Specified

Under the category of **paraphilia not otherwise specified** are forms of sexual behavior closely related to the other paraphilias but with somewhat different sexual objects. These include but are not limited to *telephone scatologia* (obscene phone calls), *necrophilia (corpses)*, *partialism* (body parts), *zoophilia* (animals), *coprophilia* (feces), *klismaphilia* (enemas), and *urophilia* (urine).

In *telephone scatologia*, males make phone calls to females describing their sexual fantasies and masturbate to orgasm while on the phone or shortly thereafter. A profitable telephone service has developed in the United States in recent years, with women paid to receive the sexual phone calls and play along with the callers' sexual fantasies. In some cases, this may be the man's primary sexual activity.

Necrophilia is sexual arousal and orgasm by engaging in various sexual activities with a dead body. Necrophilia is closely related to sexual sadism and might be considered to be the most extreme form of sexual sadism. Like sexual sadism, necrophilia involves living out sexual fantasies of injury, pain, homicide, dismemberment, having sex with body parts, or eating parts of the body (vagina, anus, and so on) as part of the sexual fantasy (Spitzer et al., 1994). Necrophilia has the same origins as extreme forms of sexual sadism.

Partialism involves sexual arousal by contact with a specific body part, usually while masturbating to orgasm. Partialism is closely related to fetishism except that the sexual object is not an inanimate object but a particular part of a female body. A typical case is a young male who becomes highly aroused by women's toes. He will caress, kiss, and suck on the toes while masturbating to orgasm; or he may masturbate later while remembering the toes. Partialism probably has origins similar to those of fetishism. However, instead of an inanimate object related to females becoming the focus of sexual arousal, a part of the female body that is commonly available to an adolescent male becomes his source of arousal.

Zoophilia involves sexual activities with animals. This paraphilia is more prevalent in males but also occurs in females. Kinsey and colleagues (Kinsey, Pomeroy, & Martin, 1948; Kinsey, Pomeroy, Martin, & Gebhard, 1953) reported that 8 percent of the males and 3 to 4 percent of the females in their sample had sexual contact with animals. This disorder typically originates in early adolescence in males and somewhat later in females. It is especially prevalent in farming communities where adolescent males are prohibited from sexual access to adolescent females but do have access to female animals. Kinsey et al. (1948) found that 17 percent of boys raised on farms in the United States had sexual contact with farm animals resulting in orgasm. In urban communities, the animals that are most likely to be used as sexual objects are large dogs. Humans of both genders will masturbate dogs to orgasm, perform fellatio on the dogs, or in some cases even train their dogs to perform coitus on themselves (Spitzer et al., 1994). Alternatively, human males may perform coitus on female dogs. This is a culture-bound syndrome in that it typically occurs in societies that stringently limit access to human sexual partners, especially for adolescents, but allow them private relationships with animals.

Coprophilia and *urophilia* involve sexual arousal by feces and urine, respectively. Coprophilia and urophilia are in some cases etiologically related to sexual masochism and sexual sadism. Being urinated or defecated upon may form part of a sadomasochistic sexual fantasy. These are culture-bound syndromes in that they occur in societies that define sexuality as "dirty" or related to excretion.

Klismaphilia involves sexual arousal by enemas. Many people find penetration of the anus to be sexually stimulating. If a person receives repeated enemas and experiences sexual arousal as a result, he or she can become conditioned to experience and desire an enema as a preferred sexual activity. This is a culture-bound syndrome in that it occurs only in societies that use enemas and that also restrict other more appropriate forms of sexual behavior.

Gender Identity Disorder

Gender identity disorder (GID) is characterized by strong and persistent self-identification with the opposite gender. There is also a strong sense of the inappropriateness of one's assigned gender. The person may feel that he or she has been "trapped" in a body of the wrong gender and seek gender reassignment (transsexual) surgery (APA, 1994). The diagnosis in DSM-IV also requires significant distress or social or occupational impairment.

This disorder occurs in both males and females but is far more prevalent in males. It originates in early childhood with the child identifying with the opposite gender, wearing the clothing of the opposite gender, and taking on

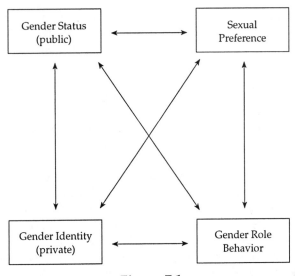

Figure 7.1
Factors Related to Gender Identity and Status

the opposite gender role behavior. If gender identification and role behavior consistent with physical gender is not acquired during adolescent development, this disorder will continue into adulthood.

Adults with gender identity disorder are preoccupied with wanting to live as a person of the opposite gender. In the typical case, a male will attempt to adopt the gender status of a female, perform female gender role behavior, have a sexual preference consistent with that of a female (that is, males), and have a gender identity of female.

Gender Identity and Status

To understand GID in its cultural context, it is first necessary to discuss factors related to gender identity and status. These factors and their interrelations are illustrated in Figure 7.1.

Gender status is the status that is publicly ascribed and recognized. Different societies have different means of ascribing gender status. Of course, having male or female genitals is the primary determinant, but many societies have further requirements for attaining a specific (particularly male) gender status.

These societies prescribe a particular pattern of gender role behavior and sexual preference for achieving male gender status. If a person with male genitals does not fit the male behavioral pattern, he is assigned to a third category in-between male and female for persons with male genitals who think, behave, and function in society as females (Callender & Kochems, 1993; Herdt, 1994; Levy, 1971; Nanda, 1993). Thus, although westerners tend to think of gender status as purely biological, it is, in fact, socially constructed.

In contrast to gender status, **gender identity** is the private subjective cognition of one's gender. In some cases, a person can be privately one gender but be publicly the opposite gender. For example, a person can be subjectively female but hold the public gender status of male. This can occur in the situation in which the person is physically male and performs male gender role behavior but has a female subjective self. Conversely, a person could be physically female, have a subjectively female self, but for economic or political reasons successfully impersonate a man with male gender role behavior and, therefore, possess a male gender status in public.

Gender role behavior refers to the gender-specific activities that are expected in any given society. This can include such things as wearing gender-specific clothing; having a gender-specific occupation; using gender-specific forms of speech, mannerisms, hairstyles, jewelry and accessories, cosmetics; performing gender-specific recreational activities, sexual behavior, household duties; and holding gender-specific social-political-religious offices. Societies all over the globe have varying degrees of gender division in all of these areas. Proper gender role behavior for any given society is learned during childhood.

Sexual preference refers to the gender the person finds sexually arousing. As discussed earlier, humans and other primates are not necessarily heterosexual. Although heterosexual activity is necessary for reproduction, most sexual activity in humans occurs for other purposes, including simply pleasure. Just as humans can be conditioned to be sexually aroused by inanimate objects, animals, body parts, and so on, they can also be conditioned to be sexually aroused by someone of the same gender. Thus, a person can be physically male, have a male gender status, a male gender identity, perform male gender role behavor, but have a sexual preference for men.

There are many complex interactions possible between these four factors. Each factor—gender status, gender identity, gender role behavior, and sexual preference—influences all the others to varying degrees.

In the typical case of gender identity disorder, a young male child is treated like a girl from infancy to puberty, usually by his mother. In one study of 17 male transsexuals, all had been treated as girls in childhood (Driscoll, 1971; see also Green, 1975). That is, the boy is dressed like a girl and raised either ambiguously or as a girl. In this case, the gender status is established as female even though the child is physically male. However, gender status influences all other factors. Because the child has the gender status of female, he is treated as a girl by society. The powerful forces of socialization shape the child such that female gender role behavior is learned and adopted as normal.

The adoption of female gender role behavior has a profound impact on gender identity. All of the messages that the child receives from society reinforce a female subjective identity. This includes messages about gender role behavior, appropriate sexual behavior, and sexual preference. These boys learn that the proper sexual partner for them is male. They are conditioned to be sexually attracted to males. As a result, the person thinks, acts, and functions as a female, except that he has the body of a male.

The Polynesian Mahu

In Polynesian societies, there is the tradition of the *mahu* (*mahu* in Hawaii and Tahiti, *fakaleiti* in Tonga, *faafafine* in Samoa). A *mahu* is a person born as a male but raised from infancy as a female (Besnier, 1994). This is a cultural practice in traditional Polynesian societies and does not carry the great stigma of transsexuality that occurs in western societies. In the traditional Hawaiian cultural context, an infant boy could be selected to be raised as a female simply because the family had too many boys and wanted a girl. Thus, *mahus* were very common in traditional Hawaiian society and are still sometimes seen today within the Native Hawaiian community. In contrast, in traditional Tahiti, it was customary to have one and only one *mahu* per village (Levy, 1971).

Mahus were valued as "substitute women" in traditional Polynesian society. There was no stigma of homosexuality attached to a man having sexual relations with a *mahu*. A man having sex with a *mahu* was not considered to be a homosexual, as this was seen as essentially the same as having sex with a woman. Levy (1971) indicates that sexual encounters in Tahiti traditionally consisted of the *mahu* performing fellatio on the man and that anal intercourse was not practiced. However, anal intercourse with *mahus* occurs in contemporary Polynesia (Besnier, 1994).

As there was little stigma attached with being a *mahu*, the type of emotional distress and social and occupational impairment found in persons with GID in western societies did not exist in traditional Polynesia. Thus, traditional *mahus* would not qualify for a diagnosis of gender identity disorder because they do not experience gender dysphoria. Because western values have now infiltrated Polynesian societies, especially in Hawaii, contemporary *mahus* in Hawaiian society do experience the gender dysphoria associated with GID, and some are now undergoing hormone treatments and gender reassignment surgery.

Relation to Transvestic Fetishism

Other factors besides being raised as a person of the opposite gender can be causes of GID. For example, some cases of GID may originate in transvestic fetishism. These are heterosexual males who fantasize about being their own female sexual object by cross-dressing in female clothing and masturbating to orgasm.

The fantasy of being female and being sexually aroused by that fantasy may lead to a persistent preoccupation with actually possessing a female body to be more fully sexually gratified by one's own masturbatory fantasies. These men are sexually attracted to females but want a female body to have a more realistic fantasy.

Relation to Homosexuality

In rarer cases, GID may originate in a man having a sexual preference for males. This is a homosexual male who feels such tremendous guilt and emotional distress about his homosexuality that he wishes to become female to be a "normal" heterosexual. In this case, the homosexuality probably originated in childhood sex play of a homosexual nature that was experienced as pleasurable. The boy probably continued with intermittent homosexual activity throughout childhood and adolescence, while at the same time being taught that homosexuality was sinful, wrong, disgusting, and so on. Simultaneously, he was being taught that the "natural" or "God-given" sexual partner for a man is a woman. Therefore, to have a man as a sexual partner and be a "good" person, it means that he must become a woman. It also means that because he is sexually attracted to males, "naturally" he must really be a female. Somehow, some "mistake" was made, and he was given the wrong body.

Gender identity disorder is a culture-bound syndrome, and the diagnosis requires emotional distress and social impairment. Traditional Polynesian *mahus* would not qualify for the diagnosis, but those influenced by western cultural values do qualify because of the stigma attached to homosexuality in western culture. For those developing GID as a result of transvestic fetishism, the same cultural factors promoting transvestic fetishism apply to GID as well. For those developing GID as a result of their homosexuality, the cultural factors operating are those defining homosexual activity as sinful, wrong, and so on.

The Sexual Dysfunctions

The sexual dysfunctions are characterized by disturbances in sexual arousal and orgasm, with accompanying emotional distress and interpersonal problems with sexual partners. Sexual dysfunctions can be caused by physical problems, or physical problems my contribute to a sexual dysfunction.

As seen with the paraphilias, the influence of cooperative male dominance and associated restrictions on sexuality can also result in sexual dysfunctions in both males and females. Comprehensive control of sexuality frequently results in an almost complete lack of sexual experience in young people. Also, the cultural schemas that construct such situations frequently define sexuality as sinful, dirty, unpleasant, to be avoided if possible, or practiced only for the sake of procreation. Sexual dysfunctions can be common in this type of cultural context.

Four primary factors involving cultural schemas about "proper" sexual activity can promote sexual dysfunctions: (1) proper sexual techniques; (2) proper morality; (3) proper ability to be orgasmic; and (4) proper amount of previous sexual experience.

Hypoactive Sexual Desire Disorder

Hypoactive sexual desire disorder is characterized by the absence of the desire for sexual activity. DSM-IV requires that emotional distress or interpersonal difficulty be present for the diagnosis to be made. Thus, someone who has no desire for sex and is not bothered by this, and has no interpersonal difficulty as a result, would not qualify for this diagnosis. Examples of this would be priests, monks, and nuns who have no desire for sex, or others who simply have no interest in sex and are not bothered by this. Having low sexual desire is not in itself pathological. However, married persons or those in sexual relationships who have no desire for sex will commonly have interpersonal problems because their partners want sex. This can cause emotional distress for both partners and cause problems for the relationship.

DSM-IV specifies four subtypes of this disorder: *lifelong, acquired, generalized,* and *situational.* Lifelong is diagnosed when the persons have never had a desire for sex as far as they can remember. Acquired is diagnosed when persons previously had a desire for sex but have now lost it. Generalized is diagnosed when persons have no desire for sex with anyone or anything, including masturbation. Situational is diagnosed when the lack of desire for sex is specific, that is, limited to a certain partner, sexual activity, or situation. Etiological factors specified as *due to psychological factors* and *due to combined factors* are also diagnosed when the disorder is exclusively psychological in origin or a combination of physical and psychological factors, respectively.

In societies such as Inis Beag, where the cultural schemas defined sexual activity as sinful and dirty, low sexual desire is likely to have been common, especially among the females. However, this lack of sexual desire would not cause emotional distress in the women because they did not expect to have sexual desires. In fact, having sexual desires might have caused them more emotional distress because they would have equated this with being crude, immoral, or sinful.

Moreover, the husbands, not expecting their wives to have sexual desires, would have made the minimum amount of sexual demands on them by ejaculating as quickly as possible so the wives need not endure the situation any longer than necessary. Thus, because low sexual desire in Inis Beag was normal and normative, hypoactive sexual desire disorder would not have been an appropriate diagnosis in this cultural context. It is not up to clinicians to pathologize a society's normal behavior.

However, if a married couple from Inis Beag were to immigrate to the United States where most people believe that females are supposed to desire sex and enjoy sexual activity, they would be exposed to different cultural schemas and might begin to question their own beliefs about proper sexuality, thus causing emotional distress.

Cross-cultural case study.   The *DSM-IV Casebook* includes a case titled "Mr. and Ms. B."* that is similar to this hypothetical example. This case involved a middle-aged couple from Scotland now living in the United States.

*Summarized with permission from the *Diagnostic and Statistical Manual of Mental Disorders Casebook,* Fourth Edition by R. L. Spitzer et al. (Eds.). Copyright © 1994 American Psychiatric Association, Washington, D.C.

Ms. B. reported that she had never enjoyed sex in her marriage, had never had an orgasm, and only passively engaged in sex "as a duty." She had never masturbated, was repulsed by the thought of any sexual variation such as oral sex, and was preoccupied by the thought of how disapproving her family would be if she engaged in such activity.

Ms. B. was positive that no respectable woman has ever enjoyed sex, and that only sleazy women act like "animals." She was horrified whenever she came close to being sexually aroused, thinking that she could not respect herself if she were to allow it, and thus became completely insensitive to sexual pleasure. Yet, in the United States she was exposed to modern feminist ideas about female sexuality and had come to wonder if there was something "wrong" with her.

This case illustrates very well the cultural factors that justify a diagnosis of hypoactive sexual desire disorder due to psychological factors, lifelong and generalized. She believed that no "respectable" woman desires or enjoys sex. Her lack of sexual desire clearly stemmed from her cultural upbringing in a highly male dominant society with tight controls on female sexuality. That this is a culture-bound disorder is evident from the fact that her lack of sexual desire became a problem causing emotional distress only after moving to the United States and being exposed to modern feminist ideas about female sexuality.

Sexual Aversion Disorder

Sexual aversion disorder is characterized by an aversion to and active avoidance of genital contact with a sexual partner. The typical case is a female who experiences anxiety, fear, or disgust from genital or other explicitly sexual contact. She may experience prominent anxiety symptoms such as feelings of terror, heart palpitations, dizziness, or hyperventilation (APA, 1994). In some cases, she may be able to have sex only by altering consciousness with psychoactive substances.

Persons with this disorder frequently have personal histories of sexual abuse, especially in childhood. The memories of the abuse may be dissociated from conscious memory. The *DSM-IV Casebook* includes a typical case titled "Music Lessons" (Spitzer et al., 1994, p. 213). This woman was sexually abused by her uncle from the ages of 9 to 12. However, the memories were dissociated and came back only many years later. The sexual encounters with her uncle consisted of her masturbating her uncle during music lessons with him. As a result, she developed an extreme aversion to male genitals in adulthood.

The cultural factors involved with this disorder are somewhat complex. The emotional trauma resulting from sexual abuse frequently results more from the *meaning* of what is happening than from the physical events themselves. In societies where sexuality in children is actively suppressed and punished by adults, an adult engaging in sexual activity with a child is by definition highly deviant and the sexual activity is prohibited, both for the child and the adult. In this situation, the child is placed in a kind of "double bind" because sexual activity by children is punished by adults, yet it is an adult who is the child's sexual partner, and children must obey adults. The sexual activity is prohibited, yet it is simultaneously required.

Children may not be able to cognitively accommodate this logical contradiction and may alter consciousness as a result, entering a spontaneous trance state. In "trance logic," mutually contradictory conditions may coexist simultaneously. The events occurring during this time may be dissociated from conscious memory yet manifest in consciousness later in life as symptoms of anxiety, mood, or sexual dysfunction syndromes such as sexual aversion disorder.

In this situation, it is the *meaning* of the events that is largely responsible for the manifestation of sexual dysfunction. In societies such as traditional Mangaia, where sexual behavior by children was not prohibited and sexual contact between children and adults did occur—but normally in a loving, non-traumatic fashion—there is no evidence that mental illness, especially sexual dysfunction, was caused by sexual contact between adults and children. Thus, the prevailing set of cultural schemas regarding proper sexuality can be largely responsible for the manifestation of emotional trauma associated with sexual aversion disorder.

Female Sexual Arousal Disorder

Female sexual arousal disorder is characterized by an inability of a woman to maintain sexual arousal during coitus. This typically results in pleasureless lovemaking, painful intercourse, avoidance of sexual activity, and marital or relationship problems (APA, 1994).

It is important to distinguish whether this disorder is situational or generalized, and lifelong or acquired. A generalized lifelong disorder is more serious and may be an indication of a problem related to sexual aversion disorder. A history of sexual trauma may be an etiological factor. A generalized lifelong disorder can also be related to hypoactive sexual desire disorder in females, indicating a possible relationship to the individual's cultural schemas about sexuality.

In contrast, a situational lifelong or acquired disorder may be related to the individual's spouse or usual sexual partner. In this case, the individual may have no trouble maintaining sexual arousal during masturbation, or with a different sexual partner. Thus, the problem may stem from the usual partner's inadequate sexual technique, lack of sexual attractiveness, or from general marital or relationship problems.

Obviously, female sexual arousal disorder will be an appropriate diagnosis only in those societies maintaining sufficient female sexual freedom to have a belief that females should be sexually aroused during coitus. In a society like Inis Beag, which placed little importance on female sexual arousal in their cutural schemas regarding proper sexuality, this diagnosis would be inappropriate.

Female Orgasmic Disorder

Female orgasmic disorder is characterized by a persistent absence of orgasm after normal sexual arousal that causes marked distress or interpersonal difficulty (APA, 1994). This disorder is highly sensitive to cultural factors because there are dramatic cultural differences in the ability of women to achieve orgasm and in their emotional response to being inorgasmic. For example, the typical woman in Inis Beag lived her entire life without ever having an orgasm or desiring to have one. In contrast, the typical woman in Mangaia experienced multiple orgasms with every sexual encounter. By far the most important factors in this discrepancy are the degree of male dominance in a society and the corresponding level of female sexual freedom. In some societies, females are not expected to have orgasms, and in some they are expected to be highly orgasmic.

For example, DSM-IV states that, "Because orgasmic capacity in females increases with age, Female Orgasmic Disorder may be more prevalent in younger women" (APA, 1994, p. 505). This statement is true in some societies, including the United States. Because young females in the United States have traditionally had their sexuality highly restricted, they usually achieve a high degree of sexual freedom only when they become middle-aged adults. Thus, the middle-aged period in a woman's life is typically when she achieves her peak of orgasmic ability. In contrast, females in Mangaia typically learned to have multiple orgasms shortly after puberty.

Once a female learns to be orgasmic, that ability is generally not lost. Thus, female orgasmic disorder is typically a lifelong disorder. Generally speaking, physically normal females are inorgasmic because they have not been allowed to learn the techniques of sexual stimulation and arousal that produce orgasm, either through masturbation or with a sexual partner. This ignorance results primarily from cooperative male dominance and associated social systems that restrict and control female sexuality.

Female orgasmic disorder is an excellent example of a culture-bound syndrome. It is not likely to occur in societies like Mangaia where females have a high degree of sexual freedom. And because virtually all females are inorgasmic in societies like Inis Beag, where female orgasm was deviant and undesired, female orgasmic disorder would not be an appropriate diagnosis in those societies.

The desire to be orgasmic is likely to be based on cultural norms and should not be considered an absolute requirement for mental health. If an individual woman does not desire to be orgasmic, then a lack of orgasm in itself should not be considered pathological. Female orgasmic disorder should be diagnosed only in cases in which a woman desires to be orgasmic and is experiencing significant distress because she is unable to achieve orgasm after a normal amount of sexual stimulation.

Female orgasmic disorder is common in particular societies such as the United States that allow a certain amount of sexual freedom in middle-aged females but restrict it in younger females. In these societies, most women desire to be orgasmic but have something of a struggle achieving the social and psychological freedom necessary to explore their full sexual capabilities.

Vaginismus and Dyspareunia

Vaginismus is characterized by recurrent involuntary contraction of the muscles surrounding the vagina whenever vaginal penetration is attempted. In some females, even the thought of vaginal penetration is enough to cause a muscle spasm in the vaginal area. This usually prevents coitus, and in some cases even the insertion of a tampon, speculum, or finger (APA, 1994).

Vaginismus is closely related to sexual aversion disorder, hypoactive sexual desire disorder, and dyspareunia. A typical case is a woman with a history of sexual trauma involving penetration of her vagina (APA, 1994). However, cultural beliefs about the dirtiness or sinfulness of sex can also be etiological in vaginismus (Spitzer et al., 1994). The cultural factors involved in sexual aversion disorder and hypoactive sexual desire disorder can thus also be operating in cases of vaginismus.

Dyspareunia is characterized by genital pain before, during, or after sexual intercourse (APA, 1994). It is closely related to sexual aversion disorder, hypoactive sexual desire disorder, and vaginismus. Individuals with dyspareunia may have had painful experiences of sexual intercourse during childhood. Also, cultural beliefs constructing sexual intercourse as sinful may cause it to be painful as well.

Male Erectile Disorder

Male erectile disorder is characterized by a persistent inability to attain or maintain an erection sufficient for the completion of coitus. Many physical problems can cause or contribute to the inability to attain or maintain an erection. However, the typical case involving psychological factors is characterized by fear and anxiety surrounding the man's sexual performance (APA, 1994).

A man may have difficulty attaining an erection because of some temporary physical cause such as alcohol intoxication. However, the embarrassment of not being able to achieve an erection with a willing sexual partner may sensitize the man to the possibility of further failure. At the next opportunity to engage in coitus, he might be so anxious about his ability to get an erection that he is no longer thinking about sex, only his possible failure to "perform," and the embarrassment that would cause him. Thus, performance anxiety can cause him to fail to attain or maintain an erection. If this occurs, the performance anxiety the next time he is in a similar situation is likely to be even greater, making the problem potentially chronic. This can lead to feelings of inadequacy, depression, and avoidance of sexual contact (Barlow, 1986; Kaplan, 1979).

The cultural factors in male erectile dysfunction are somewhat complex. This disorder is not likely to occur in a society like Inis Beag where there are no male "performance" expectations coming from females. Where females are reluctant to have sexual intercourse and chastity is viewed as virtuous, an erectile dysfunction might be viewed as a sign of spiritual merit.

Male erectile dysfunction is most likely to occur in societies such as the United States in which there are marginal controls on female sexuality. In these societies, females develop a demand for sexual performance from men, but because of social restrictions on sexuality, men are generally not well educated in sexual techniques, have relatively few opportunities to engage in sexual intercourse prior to marriage, and must sometimes "perform" in less than ideal conditions. The possibilities for erectile failure and consequent performance anxiety are greater in these societies.

Male Orgasmic Disorder

Male orgasmic disorder is characterized by a failure to achieve orgasm during coitus. However, in the typical generalized case, the man will be able to achieve orgasm by his partner's or self-masturbation or by fellatio. In some cases, a man may be able to achieve orgasm only by self-masturbation. If the case is situational, the man may simply be unaroused by his usual sexual partner and have no difficulty achieving orgasm with other sexual partners (APA, 1994).

In the case of generalized male orgasmic disorder, particulary if it is a life-long case, it is possible that some type of paraphiliac sexual practice, such as fetishism, may be occurring (APA, 1994). The man may be capable of having an orgasm only during fetishistic self-masturbation. In this case, coitus may not be sufficiently arousing to allow orgasm. This kind of situation is most likely to arise in societies that restrict female sexuality, especially in young females, thus requiring young males to find alternative sexual objects. The male then becomes conditioned to being orgasmic in some sexual activity other than coitus with a female. In some cases, he will then be unable to achieve coital orgasm with a female.

However, many medical conditions can cause or contribute to this disorder. Also, various types of drugs including alcohol, antihypertensives, antidepressants, and antipsychotics can cause an inability to achieve orgasm (APA, 1994). A person with symptoms of this disorder needs to be carefully assessed with regard to physiological and medical factors.

Premature Ejaculation

Premature ejaculation is characterized by persistent ejaculation after minimal sexual stimulation and before the person or the person's sexual partner wishes it. In the typical case, a young man will ejaculate immediately after initial penetration in coitus. This leaves his partner with insufficient sexual stimulation to achieve an orgasm, causing sexual frustration and difficulty for the relationship (APA, 1994).

This disorder is highly dependent on cultural factors. In a society like Inis Beag, the disorder of premature ejaculation would not occur because both the man and his wife want his ejaculation to occur as soon as possible—the quicker, the better. Because there is no emotional distress or interpersonal difficulty, this situation would not qualify for the diagnosis of premature ejaculation.

Likewise, premature ejaculation is also not likely to occur in societies with great sexual freedom such as Mangaia. In Mangaia, the young men received extensive training in how to give their sexual partners multiple orgasms before they have their own climax. This disorder is not likely to occur in Mangaia because the young men are so well trained.

Premature ejaculation is most likely to occur in societies such as the United States. In these societies, females expect to have coital orgasms, but because of social restrictions on sexuality, many young men are so inexperienced in lovemaking that they are unable to control their orgasm and ejaculate as soon as their penises touch their partners' vaginas. Moreover, these young men, and frequently their female partners, are so ignorant about sex that they do not realize that the young man can almost immediately get another erection and try again, and keep trying until he gets it right. Instead, they give up in frustration and humiliation.

It is clear that this and all of the other sexual disorders are highly sensitive to cultural factors. In many cases, the prevailing set of cultural schemas determines whether a certain sexual disorder will be present or not.

Overall, the cultural factors most important in determining the types and prevalence of sexual disorders in any given society are the level of male dominance and the corresponding level of social restrictions on female sexuality. In those societies with low levels of male dominance and few social restrictions on female sexuality, the prevalence of paraphilias and sexual dysfunctions in both males and females related to psychological factors is likely to be lower.

 Suggested Clinical Guidelines

1. Assess the Cultural Identity of the Individual

The diagnostic categories of the sexual disorders in DSM-IV should not be considered absolute natural entities. Sexuality is primarily cultural, not natural. Different cultures have differing patterns of sexual development as well as differing religious beliefs regarding proper sexual behavior. A foreign culture's normative sexual practices should not be judged pathological simply because they differ from the clinician's cultural norms. Assess the cultural identity of the individual before diagnosis.

2. Assess the Cultural Schemas Regarding Sexual Behavior

Sexual behaviors should be viewed as conditioned, learned expressions of sexual desire occurring within particular sociocultural contexts. Clinicians should explore with open ended questions the client's cultural schemas regarding sexuality to uncover why the client is motivated to behave in a particular fashion.

3. Assess Sexual Behavior within the Cultural and Psychosocial Environment

Clinicians need to see the client and his or her sexuality within the total sociocultural context. This should include assessment of culture-based sources of domination that could have an impact on sexual behavior and impairment. For example, the effects of male dominance on female clients could result in sexual dysfunctions such as female orgasmic disorder. Similarly, the effects of age restrictions on sexuality could have an impact on male adolescents resulting in the development of paraphilias such as fetishisms. Clinicians should not view sexual disorders as residing strictly within the client. Sexual disorders are maladaptations occurring within a particular sociocultural context.

4. Assess the Cultural Aspects of the Clinician-Client Relationship

Clinicians should critically assess their own concepts of normal sexual development and behavior and reflexively determine how these concepts may be projected onto the client. Clients with sexual disorders should not be viewed as "diseased." Human brain plasticity allows for a great variety of sexual behavior to be learned through repeated experience. A clinician should not diagnose a sexual disorder based strictly on a single notion of normal sexual development and behavior. Rather, clinicians should allow for cultural diversity in their concepts of normative sexuality, at the same time recognizing dysfunction and distress as pathology.

5. Negotiate Clinical Reality

Sexual disorders should not be viewed as disease categories that can be imposed on a client. However, certain forms of sexuality can be viewed as dysfunctional or illegal within particular sociocultural contexts, causing definite impairment and distress for the client. Problems may particularly arise in cases of immigrants moving between dramatically different cultures. Immigrants can be expected to obey the laws regarding sexuality of their adopted society. In these cases, the goal of clinical treatment should be to allow these individuals to conform their behavior to the dictates of the law.

However, clients should make a conscious choice to adapt to the sexual laws of the host society. Human brain plasticity allows for reconditioning of sexual behavior, especially in young people. This may require substantial resocialization, including changes in religion, ideas about proper gender roles, and sexual values. This should be done voluntarily. Therefore, a negotiation of clinical reality should be made between the clinician, the client, and ideally the client's family. A plan of treatment should be drawn up that is the result of a negotiated consensus of the problem and the appropriate treatment. This will provide the optimal environment for the formation of a therapeutic alliance and good treatment outcome.

Chapter Eight

Eating Disorders

Eating disorders are characterized by obsessive-compulsive or addictive type behavior involving food. In the eating disorders, the person is obsessed with ingesting or not ingesting food.

Mood alteration is also a factor in the eating disorders. Although mood alteration is obvious when taking mood altering drugs, many people overlook the fact that food, especially the high sugar and calorie content food that is typically ingested in the impulsive binge eating behavior of bulimics and some anorexics, is also mood altering. During the binge, mood is temporarily elevated from a low state, typically triggered by a stressful life event (Lingswiler, Crowther, & Stephens, 1989). Thus, the food is being used as a mood altering substance. Moreover, although the binge itself is pleasurable, it is followed by intense guilt and depression (Mizes & Arbitell, 1991). The mood of the person is thus moved radically up and down by the abuse of the food. In effect, this is substance abuse involving food.

Just as binge eating is mood altering, starving oneself and engaging in excessive exercise can also be mood altering. It has been found that many people with eating disorders have symptoms of dysthymia and major depression such as fatigue and low self-esteem (Beatty, Wonderlich, Staton, & Ternes, 1990; Ledoux, Choquet, & Manfredi, 1993). Semistarvation and great exercise can increase energy and can be subjectively viewed as an impressive achievement and a sign of great self-discipline, thus raising self-esteem (APA, 1994). But these activities can also be viewed as mood altering. It is the abuse of these mood altering methods that lead to the pathologies of the eating disorders.

Food is necessary for maintaining life, but it needs to be used in moderation. Too much food can be toxic, leading to obesity and various kinds of medical problems. Conversely, not enough food leads to the medical problems associated with anorexia nervosa. Bingeing-purging-starving behavior also leads to various medical problems associated with bulimia nervosa.

Anorexia Nervosa

The key features of **anorexia nervosa** are a refusal by the person to maintain a minimally normal body weight, an intense fear of being overweight, and a misperception of one's own body size or shape (APA, 1994). The usual case is an adolescent or young adult female who uses dieting, fasting, or exercise to lose an excessive amount of weight such that she is well below the normal for her age and height. This is called *restricting type* anorexia nervosa. Another type that is not as common is the *binge-eating/purging type* anorexia nervosa. These individuals (usually young females) also refuse to maintain a minimally normal body weight, but they occasionally engage in binge eating as well as purging and fasting. In some ways, this type of anorexia is like an alcoholic who is "on the wagon" but frequently "falls off" in compulsive binge drinking episodes triggered by times of stress.

Relation to Body Dysmorphic Disorder

Persons with *body dysmorphic disorder* (Chapter 11) may have experienced discrimination and humiliation concerning some aspect of their personal appearance, causing them significant emotional distress and preoccupation with appearance. Similarly, many anorexics have personal histories of being at least slightly overweight and being criticized or humiliated for this. As a result, they tend to have low self-esteem (Russell, 1981).

Also similar to persons with body dysmorphic disorder, persons with anorexia nervosa are obsessed with the perceived "defect" in their bodies, in this case "fat." Anorexics perceive themselves as being overweight, and therefore defective, unacceptable, unworthy, and so on. These are people who are experiencing significant emotional distress focusing on their perceived weight problem. They become obsessed with their weight and perform compulsive "checking" behavior, repeatedly examining themselves in a mirror looking for the offensive "fat." This obsession with their perceived inferiority may lead to self-imposed social isolation and other symptoms associated with *avoidant personality disorder* (Chapter 6).

Anorexia nervosa differs from body dysmorphic disorder in that anorexia is characterized by an obsessive concern about "fatness." Body dysmorphic disorder is used to define all other obsessive concerns about body shape and size. This difference might be seen as an arbitrary distinction. However, because anorexia deals with obsessive-compulsive behavior involving a substance (food) and sometimes has serious medical consequences (including death), this distinction is a valid one.

Anorexia nervosa can cause a range of serious medical problems associated with starvation. These can include amenorrhea in females, hypothermia, low blood pressure, low mineral levels, and electrolyte imbalances. Severe nutritional problems can cause death through circulatory system failure (Sharp & Freemen, 1993).

Bulimia Nervosa

The key features of **bulimia nervosa** are binge eating and inappropriate methods of preventing weight gain. Like anorexics, persons with bulimia also have an intense fear of being overweight. However, individuals with bulimia usually maintain their weight within the normal range, although some may be slightly over- or underweight (APA, 1994). Also like anorexics, bulimics may have a history of being overweight and receiving personal criticism because of their weight. Low self-esteem and the symptoms of dysthymia and major depression (Chapter 12) are common in bulimics. Sometimes the mood problems are present prior to the eating disorder, and sometimes they occur simultaneously or following the onset of the eating disorder. Abuse and dependence on stimulants initially used for controlling weight are also common in persons with bulimia (APA, 1994).

During a binge, persons with this disorder typically eat large amounts of sweet, high calorie foods in a single setting, and in secret. These binges are usually triggered by stressful life events. While the binge is occurring, the person usually feels out of control, sometimes even in a frenzied state (APA, 1994).

Binges are usually pleasurable, but after a binge, self-criticism, guilt, and a depressed mood set in. To compensate, in *purging type* bulimia the person engages in purging behavior. This can include vomiting, misuse of laxatives, diuretics, or enemas. The most common method is vomiting. There is also a *nonpurging type* of bulimia in which the person engages in fasting or excessive exercise to compensate for the binges.

The medical problems associated with bulimia nervosa can include fluid and electrolyte abnormalities, loss of stomach acid due to vomiting, and significant loss of dental enamel also due to vomiting (APA, 1994)

Culture and Eating Disorders

Both anorexia and bulimia occur far more commonly in modern, industrialized societies where there is an abundance of food and female beauty is associated with thinness. Females comprise 90 to 95 percent of the cases. These disorders are most common in the United States, Canada, Europe, Australia, Japan, New Zealand, and among the white population of South Africa (APA, 1994). However, a few cases have recently been identified in at least some nonindustrialized or premodern populations (Ritenbaugh, Shisslak, & Prince, 1992).

There has been an increase in the incidence of eating disorders in recent decades. This increase is very likely associated with changing cultural tastes regarding standards of female beauty in western society (Abramson & Valene, 1991; McGibbon, Handy, Ballard, & Silveira, 1991).

There have been notable changes over the past 100 years in standards of female beauty in western society. During the late 19th century, the ideal of female beauty consisted of a very "full figured" woman with large hips and breasts, far heavier than today's standards. Later, during the 1920s, the slim "flapper" style became the standard of female beauty in western societies. However, beginning in the mid-1930s during the Depression era when food was scarce for many people, a more rounded figure for women began to return as the ideal, possibly indicating that the person was well fed. This trend culminated in the 1950s, with the ideal of female beauty exemplified by "full-figured" actresses Marilyn Monroe and Jayne Mansfield.

However, since the 1960s, the ideal of female beauty in the United States and other western nations has become increasingly thin. This has been shown in studies of contestants in the Miss America Pageant and female models in both men's and women's magazines (Garner, Garfinkel, Schwartz, & Thompson, 1980; Wiseman, Gray, Mosimann, & Ahrens, 1992). This cultural trend toward thinness as the ideal of female beauty continues to the present day and indicates that women are under increasing pressure to lose weight to be considered physically attractive.

Not only is there an incentive to be thin coming from the desire to be attractive, but there is also great social pressure not to be considered obese. People who are considered obese run the risk of discrimination and humiliation by others. Research has indicated that prejudice against obese people in the United States is pervasive (Brownell & O'Neil, 1993). There are ample opportunities for people who consider themselves overweight to feel inferior, unacceptable, and so on, thus threatening self-esteem.

Nonwestern Anorexia Nervosa

Recent evidence indicates that a fear of fatness common to anorexics in western cultures may not be common in nonwestern forms of anorexia nervosa. Recent studies by Khandelwal, Sharan, and Saxena (1995), Lee, Ho, and Hsu (1993), Lee and Hsu (1995), and Toro, Salamero, and Martinez (1994) indicate that there can be variable reasons for persons to restrict food intake to the point of anorexic weight loss.

In a study of anorexic Chinese individuals in Hong Kong, Lee et al. (1993) found that fear of stomach bloating rather than fatness was a common motivating factor, a complaint that had more cultural significance in the Chinese context. Similarly, a study of anorexics in India by Khandelwal et al. (1995) did not find the excessive exercise or disturbances in body image typical of western anorexics. This Indian sample showed no desire to be thin, or fear of fatness. Rather, their restriction of food intake was related to fasting for religious purposes or eccentric nutritional ideas. Thus, it appears that a fear of fatness may be a common but nonessential feature of anorexia nervosa that is related to western cultural norms. Although DSM-IV requires a fear of fatness for making a diagnosis of anorexia nervosa, when assessing nonwestern cases, clinicians may want to make an exception (Weiss, 1995).

Gender Differences

It is highly significant that 90 to 95 percent of eating disorder cases are female. This is a clear effect of cultural influence. Traditionally in western society, there has been an emphasis on physical appearance as a measure of attractiveness for females. In contrast, male attractiveness has traditionally been measured more by wealth and social position. Thus, men have been under considerably less social pressure to conform to a standard of physical attractiveness. This is probably one factor that accounts for the great gender differential in the prevalence of eating disorders.

Another factor is the greater tolerance and cultural custom in western societies for males to use alcohol as a means of mood alteration. Males generally use alcohol to alter an anxious or depressed mood, whereas females may be using food more often for this purpose. Thus, eating disorders among males are less common, but alcohol abuse and dependence are more common.

However, there has also been an increase in the United States in the incidence of eating disorders among males in recent years (Seligmann, Rogers, & Annin, 1994). This increase in eating disorders among men is probably connected to two cultural factors. First, in recent years there has been a great increase in attention to diet and weight in connection to heart disease, hypertension, cancer, and other medical problems. Men who are overweight are now more likely to be seen as unhealthy by their society. Because of the great publicity in recent years surrounding weight and health, anyone who is significantly overweight is also likely to be perceived to be physically unfit and, perhaps, morally unfit. Thus, there is increasing pressure on men to be thin for health and social desirability reasons.

Second, with the progressive breakdown of the traditional gender dominance hierarchy in the United States, increasing numbers of females are becoming economically independent of men. Women who are economically independent can afford to be more selective in choosing a potential mate. Some women are now demanding attractive physical appearance in their romantic partners as well as the traditional financial assets. Therefore, a man's physical attractiveness can have greater importance in mate selection than in previous times. This puts more pressure on men to be thin. As these trends continue, it is likely that the number of eating disorders in men will increase.

Ethnic Differences

In a study of college students, Gray, Ford, and Kelly (1987) found that African American women were far less likely to indicate fear of being overweight than other women. In the past, eating disorders in the United States have been primarily found in white women of the upper socioeconomic classes. This is still generally the case, although the situation is changing as more ethnic minorities become assimilated into Anglo American culture (Abrams, Allen, & Gray, 1993). For example, some cases of eating disorders have been reported among

African American women and men (Anderson & Hay, 1985; Hsu, 1987; Silber, 1986).

Hispanic Americans also appear to have less risk for eating disorders. In a study of Hispanic American high school females in New Mexico, the risk for anorexia nervosa appeared to be low compared to Anglo American populations (Snow & Harris, 1989). However, some cases of eating disorders have been reported among Hispanics (Hiebert et al., 1988; Silber, 1986). In treatment outcome, no differences attributable to ethnic differences were reported (Hiebert et al., 1988).

Among Native American females, anorexia nervosa appears to be rare. However, the symptoms of bulimia nervosa are common (Rosen et al., 1988; Snow & Harris, 1989). Because the physical symptoms of bulimia are not as obvious as those of anorexia, clinicians should note this distinction.

Overall, the risk for eating disorders appears to rise with exposure to western culture (Ritenbaugh et al., 1992). Individuals from groups without a history of eating disorders, upon assimilating western values and patterns of thought, come to fear fatness in a fashion similar to that of westerners (Mumford, Whitehouse, & Choudry, 1992; Nasser, 1986). For example, in a study of female Egyptian university students in Cairo and London, the Cairo sample showed no evidence of eating disorders. However, the Egyptian students in London showed 12 percent positive for eating disorders (Nasser, 1986).

The prevalence of eating disorders seems to be directly related to the degree of western acculturation in any given population. As the influence of western culture continues to spread throughout the world, it is likely that eating disorders will become increasingly common in societies that assimilate western values and patterns of thinking.

 ## Suggested Clinical Guidelines

1. Assess the Cultural Identity of the Individual

Clinicians should be aware that although individuals from nonwestern cultural groups are at less risk for eating disorders than are westerners, the risk still exists. Especially in the case of bulimia nervosa, where the physical symptoms are more difficult to identify than in anorexia, clinicians should not assume that an individual from a nonwestern cultural group is not at risk. The level of risk for nonwesterners usually depends to some extent on the individual's degree of assimilation into western culture. Therefore, the cultural identity of every individual needs to be carefully assessed.

2. Assess the Cultural Schemas Regarding Eating Behavior

Fear of fatness common to anorexics in western cultures may not be common in some nonwestern forms of anorexia nervosa. There are a variety of reasons for persons to restrict food intake to the point of anorexic weight loss. Complaints based on nonwestern cultural schemas regarding food can have more cultural significance than fear of fatness in some societies. Thus, it appears that a fear of fatness may be a common but nonessential feature of anorexia nervosa that is related to western cultural norms.

3. Assess Eating Behavior with the Cultural and Psychosocial Environment

Clinicians need to see the client and her eating behavior within the total sociocultural context. It is highly significant that 90 to 95 percent of eating disorder cases involve a female. This is a clear effect of cultural influence. There has been an emphasis on thinness as a measure of attractiveness for females in western societies. Some females may have experienced discrimination and humiliation concerning their weight, causing them significant emotional distress and a preoccupation with thinness. Clinicians should therefore explore the client's cultural schemas regarding eating and appearance to uncover why the client is motivated to behave in a particular fashion.

4. Assess Cultural Aspects of the Clinician-Client Relationship

Clinicians should critically assess their own concepts of physical attractiveness and eating behavior and reflexively determine how these concepts may be projected onto the client. Clients with eating disorders should be viewed as being maladapted to a particular set of cultural schemas. Human brain plasticity allows for various values and eating behaviors to be learned through repeated exposure. It also allows for resocialization including alteration in values and behavior.

5. Negotiate Clinical Reality

Eating behavior causing impairment and emotional distress for the client or causing medical problems or even possible death should be viewed as pathological. Problems particularly arise in the internalization of western cultural values regarding thinness as a requirement for female beauty. Immigrants, especially young females, may adopt the values of western culture regarding female beauty and the need for extreme thinness. In these cases, the goal of clinical treatment should be to allow the clients to adapt to western culture in a way that is not dangerous to their health.

Eating disorders resulting from western acculturation are maladaptations. Maladaptation to western culture by young females may include changes in family relationships, ideas about proper gender roles, as well as ideas about female beauty. Therefore, negotiating clinical reality should consider the client's maladaptation to western cultural values and should involve the clinician, the client, and ideally the client's family. A plan of treatment should be drawn up that is the result of a negotiated consensus of the problem and the appropriate treatment. Creating a therapeutic alliance among the clinician, the client, and the client's family is especially important for a favorable treatment outcome for eating disorders.

Chapter Nine

Substance-Related Disorders

DSM-IV classifies **substance-related disorders** according to four major diagnostic groups: *substance intoxication, substance abuse, substance dependence,* and *substance withdrawal.* These four diagnostic groups are used with 11 classes of substances: (1) alcohol, (2) amphetamines, (3) caffeine, (4) cannabis, (5) cocaine, (6) hallucinogens, (7) inhalants, (8) nicotine, (9) opioids, (10) phencyclidine (PCP), and (11) sedatives, hypnotics, and anxiolytics. Not all classes include all four groups. For example, hallucinogens have no reported withdrawal syndrome. In addition, DSM-IV lists syndromes with the symptoms of other major mental disorders that are *induced* by substances, for example, substance-induced psychotic disorder. These substance-induced disorders are classified according to observed symptoms. Therefore, *substance-induced psychotic disorder* is included in the DSM-IV chapter on psychotic disorders.

Space does not permit a discussion of all four major groups in all 11 classes of substances. Therefore, the discussion here will focus on the four major diagnostic groups and a general discussion of culture and substance-related disorders.

Four Major Diagnostic Groups

The key features of **substance intoxication** are clinically significant maladaptive behavioral or psychological changes resulting from ingestion of a specific substance. These maladaptive changes can include social or occupational impairment, mood instability, cognitive impairment, or belligerence. Cognitive impairment can include changes in perception, wakefulness, attention, or judgment. These maladaptive changes must be present for a diagnosis to be made (APA, 1994).

The key features of **substance abuse** are repeated negative consequences resulting from a maladaptive pattern of substance use. The negative consequences can include multiple legal, social, and occupational problems. These problems must occur repeatedly during a 12-month period for the diagnosis to be made (APA, 1994).

The key features of **substance dependence** are multiple cognitive, behavioral, and physiological symptoms related to substance abuse, indicating that the person continues to abuse substances in spite of the negative consequences associated with that abuse. The symptoms can include physiological tolerance, which is the need for an increased amount of the substance to achieve the desired effect.

The symptoms of substance dependence can also include **substance withdrawal.** Substance withdrawal is classified in DSM-IV as both a symptom of substance dependence and as a disorder in its own right. The key features of substance withdrawal are cognitive, physiological, and behavioral changes that occur when bodily concentrations of a substance decline after cessation of prolonged use. The cognitive, physiological, and behavioral changes associated with substance withdrawal differ by substance.

When tolerance and withdrawal are present, it indicates that a person has become physiologically dependent on a substance. However, neither physiological tolerance nor withdrawal are required for a diagnosis of substance dependence (APA, 1994). There is a subtype of substance dependence classified as *without physiological dependence* that is used when physiological tolerance and withdrawal are not present but the person shows symptoms of *compulsive substance use.* Symptoms of compulsive substance use can include a desire but inability to quit or cut back on use; spending a great deal of time obtaining, using, or recovering from substances; or withdrawing from other important social or occupational activities to spend more time using substances (APA, 1994).

The American Disease Model

The classification of substance-related disorders in DSM-IV is based to a great extent on the model of alcoholism developed by E. M. Jellinek (1952, 1960). Consistent with the disease-centered paradigm of mental disorders adopted with DSM-III and continued in DSM-IV, the model developed by Jellinek has often been called the **American Disease Model** of alcoholism. As the name implies, alcoholism and other substance addictions are conceptualized as bodily diseases just as are cancer and heart disease. In contrast, prior to the 1950s, alcoholism was generally viewed as immoral behavior, not a disease (Doweiko, 1996).

Jellinek (1952) described the progression of alcoholism through four stages. The first stage was termed the *prealcoholic phase* and was characterized by the person using alcohol intoxication for relief of stress. The second stage was termed the *prodromal stage* and was characterized by repeated alcoholic blackouts, compulsive drinking, guilt over alcoholic behavior, and drinking in secret. The third stage was termed the *crucial phase* and was characterized by loss of control over drinking, loss of self-esteem, social withdrawal to allow more drinking, and neglect of proper nutrition. Also in this stage, the person may "go on the wagon" for short periods in an attempt to regain control and self-esteem but remains obsessed with thinking about alcohol and eventually returns to compulsive drinking. The fourth stage was termed the *chronic phase*. This stage was characterized by pronounced withdrawal symptoms such as motor tremors as well as downward social mobility, moral deterioration, and an obsession with drinking.

Jellinek's theory assumes that alcoholism is a progressive disorder. This idea has become gospel for many substance abuse counselors and clinicians and forms a major part of the disease model of alcoholism. However, the progression of alcohol-related symptoms is found in only a minority (25 to 30 percent) of cases (Toneatto, Sobell, Sobell, & Leo, 1991). Thus, the basis of the disease model of alcoholism is brought into question.

The four major diagnostic groups listed in DSM-IV regarding substance-related disorders—*substance intoxication, substance abuse, substance dependence,* and *substance withdrawal*—are clearly identifiable in Jellinek's disease model and correspond roughly to his four stages. Thus, it can be seen that the substance-related disorders in DSM-IV are based to a large extent on the American Disease Model of alcoholism. This disease model assumes that substance-related disorders have a biophysical etiology. Most research within the disease model of substance-related disorders has focused on genetic disease as the key factor in development of these disorders.

Genetic Studies

There have been numerous studies of the genetic factors involved in alcoholism. Some researchers have even claimed to discover an "alcoholism gene" (Blum et al., 1990; Noble et al., 1991). There has also been much media attention paid to the idea that alcoholism is a genetic disease, and the idea that alcoholism has a genetic basis has become widespread among the general public in the United States.

However, most genetic studies indicate that although there may be some genetic inheritance involved in the development of alcoholism, the majority of causative factors are environmental (Bolos et al., 1991; Cloninger, Gohman, & Sigvardsson, 1981; Murray, Clifford, & Gurling, 1983; Parsian & Cloninger, 1991; Pickens et al., 1991; Schuckit, 1987). For example, in an adoption study, Cloninger et al. (1981) found that if infants with high genetic risk for alcoholism were adopted by middle-class families, the number who actually became alcoholics in adulthood was no greater than chance. In contrast, they found that infants with high genetic risk for alcoholism adopted by poor families were more likely to become alcoholics in adulthood. This is strong evidence of the significance of environmental factors related to social class. Cloninger et al. labeled these alcoholics Type 1, which included both males and females.

However, there was another smaller subtype of alcoholics that Cloninger et al. (1981) labeled Type 2. These were exclusively male offspring of a "violent alcoholic" father, and they were found to have almost a 20 percent risk of becoming alcoholics regardless of the social class of their adoptive families. This is evidence of some genetic influence in the development of alcoholism. However, it should be noted that more than 80 percent of the males fathered by "violent alcoholics" in this study did not become alcoholics themselves. Although genetic risk for alcoholism can be a factor, it is neither necessary nor sufficient for the actual development of alcoholism.

Twin studies also show that there is some influence from genetic inheritance but that environmental factors must be playing an important role. For example, in a study of identical twins, Schuckit (1987) found a 58 percent concordance rate between identical twins when one was an alcoholic. However, if alcoholism was strictly a genetic disease, the concordance rate should be nearly 100 percent. Similarly, in another twin study, Pickens et al. (1991) concluded that "the influence of genetic factors appears to be somewhat weaker than the influence of shared environmental factors" (p. 25).

Recently, some researchers claimed to discover a specific gene responsible for alcoholism, which they referred to as the "dopamine D2 receptor gene" (Blum et al., 1990; Noble et al., 1991). However, in subsequent research these findings were not supported (Bolos et al., 1991; Parsian & Cloninger, 1991). Thus, this specific gene cannot be assumed to be the gene responsible for alcoholism.

The genetic basis of alcoholism is also not supported by cross-cultural epidemiological studies of alcoholism. Lifetime prevalence rates of alcoholism vary dramatically from one culture to another even when the same diagnostic criteria are used. For example, in a study of ten different regions of the world, the prevalence rates ranged from a high of 23 percent in a Native American population and 22 percent in Korea to a low of 3.5 percent in Taipei, Taiwan, and 0.45 percent in Shanghai, China (Helzer & Canino, 1992). Such great disparities between Chinese, Koreans, and Native Americans are not likely to be explained through genetic differences. Environmental factors, especially related to attitudes toward drinking, are more likely to be implicated in these findings. Low rates of alcoholism in China have been attributed to the importance of the Confucian moral ethic in Chinese culture (Westermeyer & Canino, 1992). In contrast, high rates of alcoholism among Native Americans have been attributed to high unemployment, racial prejudice, poverty, depression, and social alienation (Manson et al., 1992; O'Nell, 1993).

It should be noted that the American Disease Model of addiction is not widely accepted outside the United States; that is why it is commonly referred to as the *American* Disease Model (Miller & Hester, 1989). This peculiar way of thinking about addiction is most likely a product of Anglo American culture, including social and economic practices and institutions. Specifically, the treatment of addictive "diseases" has become a major industry in the United States that is dependent on the acceptance of the disease-centered paradigm for its profits. In the fee-for-service medical industry in the United States, there is profit to be made from insurance companies if addictions are classified as biological diseases. Thus, the American Disease Model of addictions is supported by the way health care is financed in the United States.

Classifying addictions as biological diseases also relieves the addicts, their families, and the society in general from searching for any environmental factors that might be responsible for addictions, or doing anything to change these factors. Treating addictions strictly as medical problems internal to the patient allows sources of significant environmental stress such as gender, race, and class dominance hierarchies to be ignored as causative factors and therefore maintained intact.

Culture and Substance-Related Disorders

A person's decision to use a mood altering substance is made within a socio-cultural context. Each society has its own values, beliefs, and customs regarding the use of mood altering substances, as well as differences in the availability of various substances (Westermeyer, 1995). For example, in many Islamic countries it is sinful, immoral and, in some cases, illegal to possess or drink alcohol. Yet in many of those same countries, smoking hashish is considered acceptable social behavior. Obviously, just the opposite is true in the United States.

The World Health Organization undertook a large-scale international study of how people from different cultures differentiate between normal and pathological drinking (Bennett, Janca, Grant, & Sartorius, 1993). This study was conducted in nine geographic settings selected for linguistic, religious, and geographic variation. Respondents in seven of the nine locations believed that normal drinking was possible in their culture. In particular, respondents in Athens, Greece, and Santander, Spain, reported that normal drinking was an essential part of social life. These respondents expected normal drinking to produce positive effects on physical and emotional well-being. In contrast, respondents in the Navajo Nation in Flagstaff, Arizona, and respondents in Bangalore, India, generally believed that normal drinking was not possible in their cultures. Both of these cultures have values defining abstinence from alcohol as good and ideal behavior. In the Navajo Nation it is illegal to sell, possess, or consume alcoholic beverages. The study found that terms such as *heavy drinking, alcohol abuse,* and *alcoholism* were used differently across cultures. Similar findings have been reported by other researchers (Babor, 1992; Heath, 1981, 1987; Murphy, 1992). When considering the topic of substance abuse, it is important to view any individual's substance taking behavior from within his or her own set of cultural schemas.

In DSM-IV, substance abuse is defined as repeated negative consequences resulting from a maladaptive pattern of substance use (APA, 1994, p. 182). The negative consequences can include legal, social, and occupational problems. However, negative consequences resulting from substance use can vary dramatically by sociocultural context. This is because laws regarding alcohol use, the social standards of drinking, and occupational standards differ in different societies. For instance, the United States and Saudi Arabia have radically different cultural standards for alcohol use and abuse. Drinking alcohol is normal and normative in the United States, yet immoral, illegal, and punishable in Saudi Arabia.

Also, even in societies where drinking alcohol is normative, there can be differences in attitudes toward alcohol use compared to norms in the United States. For example, in Puerto Rico, there is a large percentage of heavy drinking males who do not meet the DSM-IV criteria for alcohol abuse, mostly because they are not indigenously considered impaired in their social or occupational functioning. This is due to a great extent to the highly male dominant social structure that allows a permissive attitude toward heavy drinking in males (Canino, Burnam, & Caetano, 1992). These heavy drinking males do not face the kind of negative social and legal consequences that heavy drinkers in another society might encounter. A similar situation is also found in Ireland (Scheper-Hughes, 1979), Korea (Cho & Faulkner, 1993), and Japan (Hendry, 1994). In these societies, heavy alcohol use is expected and, to some extent, required by cultural custom for normal social interaction among males. Not engaging in heavy alcohol use would have negative social and occupational consequences for males in these societies. Therefore, using the DSM-IV definition of alcohol abuse, which is based on the presence of negative social consequences, means that the characteristics of alcohol abuse will vary by cultural context. This point needs to be appreciated by clinicians.

DSM-IV similarly defines substance intoxication in terms of significant maladaptive behavioral or psychological changes resulting from a specific substance. These maladaptive changes can include social or occupational impairment and cognitive impairment, including changes in perception, wakefulness, attention, or judgment (APA, 1994).

However, the behavioral response of any given individual to a specific drug is highly variable. The response of an individual to a given drug is dependent on three factors. First are the psychopharmacological effects of the drug. This is complicated by the type of substance used, the dose taken, the method of dosing, the duration of dosing, the individual's physiological tolerance for the drug, and time since the last dose. Second are the psychocultural characteristics of the individual. This refers to the person's cultural identity, personality traits, cultural beliefs about the behavioral effects of the drug, and the cultural meaning of taking the drug. Third is the sociocultural setting in which the drug is taken. This includes the people who are present, their beliefs, moods, and behaviors. All of these have an impact on the behavioral response of the individual to a drug.

For example, Mesoamerican Indians have for many centuries taken peyote as a sacrament in their tribal religions. Peyote is a hallucinogen that allows the Mesoamerican Indians to commune with their tribal gods. Similarly, we know from the sacred scripture of ancient India, the *Rig Veda*, that the Vedic priests took *soma*, a hallucinogenic drink derived from some still unknown plant, to commune with their tribal gods. In both cases, taking the drug is done in a ritual context. The type of drug, the amount taken, the method, and the duration are all controlled by the ritual. In both cases, the person's cultural identity specifies that the drug is being taken for sacred purposes, with the expectation of seeing and conversing with the tribal gods. Moreover, it is done collectively with others expecting the same things and who support use of the drugs.

Although the drug takers are hallucinating—therefore obviously intoxicated—with marked alterations in perception, attention, and cognition, they cannot be said to be engaging in maladaptive behavior. Because the intoxication in both cases is sacred behavior completely consistent with tribal beliefs and customs, these individuals should not be judged to be pathologically intoxicated by the standards of DSM-IV.

However, the same drug taken in the same amount could result in pathological intoxication if taken by a different individual in a different cultural context. For example, peyote has been used as a recreational hallucinogen by persons from Anglo American society since the 1960s. When peyote is used in this fashion, it is quite possible for persons to have "bad trips," characterized by clinically significant cognitive and social impairment. In this case, a diagnosis of substance intoxication is warranted by DSM-IV standards.

The intoxicating substance that is most traditional in western culture is alcohol. The intoxicating effects of alcohol are also quite variable, depending on the factors outlined above. For example, some individuals are capable of developing tremendous physical tolerance to alcohol. They are capable of drinking amounts of alcohol that would be toxic for other persons while still fulfilling all of their social and occupational obligations. Winston Churchill is said to have consumed a fifth of Scotch whiskey daily while fulfilling all of his duties as prime minister of Great Britain during World War II (Winick, 1986).

Also, patterns of drinking differ by culture. In France, alcohol consumption for an individual is typically spread out over the course of the day, and three to five glasses of wine might be consumed with meals on a daily basis. Thus, a considerable amount of alcohol is consumed during a one-week period, but the individual does not experience significant intoxication or impairment. In contrast, alcohol consumption in the United States is usually reserved for the end of the workday, weekends, or holidays. At these times, alcohol consumption can be heavy. This type of "partying" consumption can result in extreme intoxication because drinking is confined to a short period of time. The overall amount of alcohol consumed over a one-week period is usually less than in France, but it is more intoxicating because it is consumed all at once.

Similarly, the psychocultural effects of alcohol intoxication differ by culture. For example, there is a pervasive belief in the United States that alcohol intoxication instigates aggressive conduct or violence (Critchlow, 1986). And, in fact, alcohol has been implicated in violent crime in both offenders and victims in the United States (Bartol, 1995; Mayfield, 1976; Rada, 1975). However, the alcohol-violence connection appears to be strongest in the United States. In many countries, including France, Germany, Italy, Portugal, and Spain, more alcohol is consumed per capita than in the United States, but there is far less violence and crime. This is also probably related to the differences in the patterns of drinking behavior in which people in the United States experience more intoxication even though their overall consumption is less.

The psychological effects of alcohol intoxication can also vary by culture. For example, in Japan alcohol intoxication does not make people violent but rather brings out affectionate childishness (DeVos, 1984). The propensity toward violence during alcohol intoxication in the United States is probably related to the same factors that promote aggression and violence in overall personality development (Chapter 3). Thus, the negative behavioral effects of alcohol intoxication are influenced by the person's cultural identity, personality traits, cultural beliefs about the behavioral effects of alcohol, cultural patterns of drinking, and the sociocultural setting. Alcohol-related behavior becomes pathological by DSM-IV standards only with a proper combination of factors.

There has been a tendency in the United States to adhere strictly to the Alcoholics Anonymous (AA) definition of alcoholism. According to AA, alcoholism is a progressive physical disease for which there is no cure, and the only successful treatment strategy is complete abstinence. This AA definition of alcoholism is a cultural construction. Like other cultural constructions, it has the ability to affect subjective experience of illness, idioms of distress, culture-based diagnosis, culture-based treatment, and culture-based outcomes.

For example, if persons who abuse alcohol but are not physically dependent on alcohol enter an AA program, they are very likely to be classified as "alcoholics." If those persons accept this definition, their subjective experience of the problem will be affected. They are likely to view themselves as "diseased" and powerless over their condition. This can be detrimental to their confidence and self-esteem, promoting anxiety about drinking. They may become obsessed with either drinking too much or not at all.

Similarly, their idioms of distress, the way they express themselves and interact with others, will be affected. They may publicly present themselves as "recovering alcoholics" or "alcoholics" even though they have never been physically dependent on alcohol and may have been abstaining for months or even years.

The culture-based treatment in the AA model is "detoxification," consisting of inpatient stays of one month in a substance abuse treatment center. This is combined with indoctrination in the AA model in which individuals are repeatedly instructed to admit that they are powerless over their "disease" and that they should turn their will over to God or some higher power. The culture-based outcome of this treatment can result in abstinence from drinking. However, some people can become more convinced of their powerlessness and give in to their "disease," drinking even more and fulfilling the prophecy of a progressive course for their disorder. This progressive course can also be considered a culture-based outcome if their drinking habits were adversely affected by the AA treatment. More recently, new treatment programs emphasizing teaching alcohol abusers how to drink in moderation have been established and have shown some success (Kishline, 1996).

There are also cultural differences in substance dependence, primarily because DSM-IV defines substance dependence as continuing to abuse substances in spite of the negative consequences associated with that abuse (APA,

1994, p. 176). For example, in some societies, heavy drinking may be tolerated for males but significantly punished for females. Similarly, in some societies, upper-class persons may be given more leeway than lower-class persons, or vice versa. Therefore, the same cultural factors regarding the presence of negative consequences for substance abuse are also operating in cases of substance dependence. In some cultural contexts, there may be fewer negative social consequences.

Furthermore, a significant problem in definition of substance dependence arises when dealing with substances without noted physiological tolerance or withdrawal syndromes. For example, marijuana is known for having a more powerful effect on experienced users—just the opposite of physiological tolerance. This means that experienced users need to use less of the drug to achieve the desired result. Moreover, marijuana is not known for a pronounced withdrawal syndrome. Also, the negative social consequences that marijuana users encounter mostly arise from the fact that marijuana is illegal in some societies rather than from use of the drug itself. This implies that definitions relying on negative social consequences of substance abuse and substance dependence applied to marijuana are primarily dependent on local cultural values, customs, and legal statutes.

However, because the symptoms of substance dependence usually involve physiological changes such as substance tolerance and withdrawal that are relatively invariant regardless of cultural influences, the concept of substance dependence remains relatively constant across cultural boundaries for many substances. For example, the mean age of onset of alcoholism, the duration of the disorder, as well as patterns of comorbidity with other psychiatric disorders such as antisocial personality, depression, and anxiety are relatively invariant across cultures (Helzer & Canino, 1992; Westermeyer & Canino, 1992).

Personality and Substance-Related Disorders

Increasingly, theorists are viewing addictive behavior as a single concept encompassing all types of mood altering substances such as alcohol, drugs, food, and tobacco (Donovan, 1988; Doweiko, 1996; Franklin, 1987; Miller, 1980). Although theories about the etiology of addictions are still controversial, there has been a tendency in recent years to view persons with addictions as possessing an **addictive personality.** This means that persons are not necessarily addicted to any particular mood altering substance but generally feel the need to alter their moods with substances. Thus, they will have *substances of choice* based on substance effects, availability, and so on, but will use whatever mood altering substance is available if the substance of choice is not readily obtainable.

For example, Schmitz et al. (1991) found that 50 percent of persons seeking treatment for alcoholism were also regularly using other mood altering drugs. Doweiko (1996) has also noted that addiction to a single mood altering substance is becoming increasingly rare. If addicts can switch so easily between drugs, it implies that their problem is not addiction to a particular substance but an addictive personality.

Many theorists have also postulated a connection between substance-related disorders and personality development (Bradshaw, 1988; Coleman, 1988a, b; Horney, 1964; Kandel & Raveis, 1989; Kaufman, 1989; Khantzian, 1985, Shedler & Block, 1990; Ward, 1985). Generally speaking, these theorists believe that the problem of substance abuse can ultimately be traced back to early life experience, particularly parent-child relationships, and general personality development. This idea is supported by studies showing increased substance-related disorders in persons displaying symptoms of conduct disorder, antisocial personality disorder, and borderline personality disorder, as well as mood disorders and schizophrenia (APA, 1994).

Furthermore, it is increasingly being found that persons with other mental disorders are comorbid with substance-related disorders. Recent estimates of mentally ill persons comorbid for substance-related disorders range from 50 to 74 percent (Khalsa, Shaner, Anglin, & Wang, 1991; Leshner, 1991; Millman, 1991; Polcin, 1992; Robertson, 1992). Mentally ill persons who are also substance abusers tend to have low social functioning, low educational achievement, increased poverty and homelessness, increased medical problems, and increased arrests compared to mentally ill persons who are not substance abusers (Bartels et al., 1993; Kutcher et al., 1992; O'Hare, 1992). Whether these characteristics are a cause or an effect of substance abuse is unclear. They are probably both. However, it does seem clear that many of these people are trying to alter their moods with substances, in effect, attempting to self-medicate for their psychological problems.

It appears likely that environmental stress is an important factor in the etiology of substance-related disorders. Stress may be implicated in two ways. First, substance abuse may be a response to stress presently occurring in a person's life. An example of this would be using drugs to escape the emotional pain of some stressful life event such as the death of a loved one or an unexpected loss of employment. This can trigger a downward spiral in which substance abuse leads to further social or occupational impairment, which increases environmental stress, which leads to further substance abuse, and so on. Second, stress occurring earlier in a person's life during a critical period of personality development may cause that person to be more susceptible to subsequent stress. An example of this would be emotional trauma occurring early in life.

There is evidence that hypersensitivity to environmental stress can become structured into the neural networks of the brain as a result of emotional trauma early in life. For example, rhesus monkeys separated from their mothers for two six-day periods during infancy later as adults exhibited pathological behavior such as aggression, signs of depression, increased alcohol consumption when allowed to self-administer alcohol and, in females, neglect or abuse of offspring. In addition, these monkeys showed elevated levels of stress hormones (Suomi, 1991). Thus, the emotional trauma of early separation produced pathological changes in personality in the monkeys and hypersensitivity to further stress.

The effects of one environmental stressor that has been studied in humans is sexual abuse. In an NIMH study cited by Kramer (1993), 160 girls who had been subjected to legally documented sexual abuse by a family member had increased levels of stress hormones and exaggerated stress hormone responses to stimulation. These stress hormone abnormalities were correlated with high levels of depression in the girls, even years after the episodes of abuse.

Significantly, estimates of the number of female alcoholics who have been either neglected or sexually abused as children range from 40 to 75 percent (Coleman, 1988b; Fossum & Mason, 1986). Kaufman (1989) suggests that adults abused as children turn to mood altering substances to help them deal with the emotional pain of their abuse that is still remaining even after many years.

If persons traumatized as children are hypersensitive to environmental stress due to permanent changes in their stress hormone systems, then using mood altering substances may be their attempt to deal with a hypersensitive nervous system. This hypersensitive nervous system might be the biological basis of an addictive personality.

Genetic inheritance can also play a part in the development of an addictive personality. Suomi (1991) has shown that rhesus monkeys can be born hypersensitive to stress. These monkeys naturally displayed pathological behavior and elevated levels of stress hormones similar to monkeys that were traumatized in infancy. Like the traumatized monkeys, the monkeys born hypersensitive drank more under stress than the normal monkeys when allowed to self-administer alcohol.

These studies indicate that alcoholism as well as other addictive behaviors are related to hypersensitivity to stress, either acquired as a result of trauma or due to genetic inheritance. They also indicate that some types of pathological personality development as well as other forms of mental illness, such as depression, are related to hypersensitivity.

For example, if a person is born hypersensitive to stress or acquires hypersensitivity as a result of emotional trauma, that person will likely be at risk not only for substance-related disorders but also for other forms of mental disorder, particularly mood and anxiety disorders, as well as borderline personality disorder in females and antisocial personality disorder in males. This is illustrated by the frequent comorbidity of these disorders with substance-related disorders (APA, 1994).

Acquired hypersensitivity to stress is related to emotional trauma. This likely results from forms of social stress arising out of conflict associated with dominance hierarchies (Chapter 3). This hypersensitivity can affect behavior in a number of negative ways, only two of which are substance abuse and dependence. However, like the genetic risk for alcoholism, hypersensitivity to stress is neither necessary nor sufficient for the development of substance-related disorders.

Judging from a cross-cultural perspective, it is clear that there is no one reason people abuse or become addicted to mood altering substances. Substance abuse and dependence are most likely **final common pathways** of behavior (Carr & Vitaliano, 1985). This means that substance-related disorders might be caused by genetic risk, emotional trauma, personality development, personal misfortune, social conflict, cultural custom, or any combination of these factors. What these factors have in common is the final pathway—the addictive behavior. This implies that each person with a substance-related disorder should be carefully assessed in all of these areas of possible causation to tailor optimal treatment for that individual.

 # Suggested Clinical Guidelines

1. Assess the Cultural Identity of the Individual

Clinicians should be aware that individuals from differing cultural groups are at differential risk for substance-related disorders. This results from cultural customs regarding substance use. For example, in some cultures, such as France, alcohol consumption is higher per capita than it is in the United States, but negative effects of alcohol consumption are far less. In contrast, in Korea and Ireland it is normative for males to be very heavy drinkers, placing them at higher risk for physiological dependence on alcohol. However, because DSM-IV defines substance abuse and dependence in relation to negative social and occupational consequences that vary widely across cultures, there is no absolute standard of pathological substance use that is universally applicable. Therefore, the cultural identity of every individual needs to be carefully assessed.

2. Assess the Cultural Schemas Regarding Substance Use

There are a variety of reasons for persons to use mood altering substances. Some of these are religious, social, or economic reasons that are culturally supported for certain people within some societies. Thus, the *meaning* of taking mood altering substances varies dramatically by culture, from the American Disease Model to normative forms of substance use, intoxication, and dependence. Cultural schemas regarding alcohol consumption are a prime example. Therefore, the cultural schemas of each client regarding substance use need to be assessed.

3. Assess Substance Use within the Cultural and Psychosocial Environment

Clinicians need to see the client and his or her substance use within the total sociocultural context. Clinicians should particularly assess sources of social stress that might be motivating the use of mood altering substances for purposes of self-medication. Self-medication could be a response to stressful life events (for example, job loss) or a maladaptation to a stigmatized identity within race, class, or gender dominance hierarchies. Self-medication could also be a response to a hypersensitive nervous system resulting from emotional trauma that occurred early in life (for example, loss of a parent or sexual abuse).

Also, clinicians should keep in mind that a particular amount of substance use is not equivalent to a particular amount of social or occupational impairment. Substance use of varying amounts can cause social and occupational impairment in differing degrees in different societies. Some societies are very strict or tolerant for some substances but not others. These differences are based mostly on cultural schemas. For example, drinking alcohol or smoking marijuana is normative in some societies but prohibited and punished in others. These cultural differences will determine to some extent whether negative social or occupational consequences result from substance use.

Also, ideas about appropriate gender role behavior can determine the presence of negative social consequences to some extent. Females may sometimes experience social consequences for substance use whereas males do not. Clinicians should therefore explore the sociocultural context of the client to assess what behaviors are culturally supported or socially punished regarding substance use.

4. Assess the Cultural Aspects of the Clinician-Client Relationship

Clinicians should critically assess their own concepts of mood altering substance use and reflexively determine how these concepts may be projected onto the client. The American Disease Model of addictions should not be viewed as a universally applicable construct. Human brain plasticity allows for various patterns of mood altering substance use to be learned and unlearned through repeated experience. Treatment should take advantage of this behavioral plasticity.

5. Negotiate Clinical Reality

Mood altering substance use causing social or occupational impairment or emotional distress for the client, or causing medical problems and even possible death, should be viewed as pathological in all cases. However, these criteria will vary by substance and cultural context. Thus, a complex negotiation between the client and the clinician is necessary to arrive at a consensus of the problem and the appropriate treatment. This negotiation should take into account all of the above factors.

Those clients with comorbid diagnoses of other mental disorders should be assessed as to the relationship of the substance use disorder with the comorbid disorder. If substance use is determined to be an attempt at self-medication for the symptoms of the comorbid disorder (for example, heavy drinking in response to depression), then the comorbid disorder should be the primary focus of treatment. If the comorbid disorder appears to be a result of substance abuse (for example, depression resulting from life disruptions associated with alcohol dependence), then treatment of the substance disorder should take precedence. For a client in a downward spiral of substance dependence and emotional distress, both problems need to be treated, but the substance dependence problem should be addressed first.

Immigrants, racial and ethnic minorities, or others with differing cultural values or stigmatized social identity may especially experience difficulties adapting to the values of the dominant culture. These cultural differences can result in legal, social, and occupational consequences related to the use of mood altering substances. In these cases, the goal of clinical treatment should be to allow the clients to adapt to the dominant culture in a way that is not legally, socially, or occupationally impairing or dangerous to their health.

Chapter Ten

Anxiety Disorders

A great overlap of symptomatology exists between the general categories of anxiety, somatoform, and mood disorders. In actual cases, especially when viewed from a client-centered perspective, the rationale for dividing mental illnesses into these general diagnostic categories appears to be arbitrary and perhaps misleading. Cross-culturally, for many clients, their illnesses spread across the diagnostic categories of anxiety, somatoform, mood, and dissociative disorders rather indiscriminantly (Kirmayer, Young, & Hayton, 1995).

Moreover, the categories themselves are based on the disease-centered paradigm, which assumes that anxiety, somatoform, and mood disorders are based primarily in separate brain diseases. However, there is very little evidence to support this assumption. Throughout the three chapters in DSM-IV covering these disorders, one finds the statement: "No laboratory findings that are diagnostic of [these disorders] have been identified." Thus, the assumption that these disorders are caused by separate identifiable brain diseases is based more on ideology than on scientific evidence.

The DSM-IV classification system, based as it is on the disease-centered paradigm retained from DSM-III, structures the perceptions of clinicians by defining psychopathology in this fashion. The present system promotes the idea of **comorbidity** in complex cases. Comorbidity refers to the simultaneous existence of two or more disorders. In the same way that a person can simultaneously have heart disease and cancer, it is thought that a person can simultaneously have major depression and somatization disorder.

The disease-centered classification system promotes the view of mental disorders as separate diseases in a primarily biological matrix. Because of an assumed biological causation, until recently very little attention has been paid to how these disorders might be connected, either emotionally or culturally. Thus, the patient is sometimes abstracted from his or her social-cultural-emotional context and treated only as a biological organism with an imbalance in neurohormones.

However, these anxiety, somatoform, and mood disorders should be seen as connected because they are all related to disordered emotions. The anxiety and mood disorders are, of course, based on descriptions of emotions that are considered to be pathological. And the somatoform disorders are based on **somatization,** that is, an expression of emotional distress in somatic (bodily) symptoms.

In real-life clinical situations, it is extremely common to observe clients with anxiety, somatoform, and mood symptoms combined. Indeed, much of the space in the DSM-IV chapters on these disorders is devoted to a discussion of how to differentially diagnose individuals with symptoms crossing these boundaries. The very fine symptomatic distinctions made between these disorders was thought to be necessary for the research purposes of distinguishing the separate biochemical imbalances that were presumed to be the primary causes of the disorders. However, a simplistic one-to-one correspondence between a specific level of a neurotransmitter and a particular anxiety, somatoform, or mood disorder is no longer presumed to be true (Barlow & Durand, 1995).

Earlier theories targeted low levels of specific neurotransmitters such as norepinephrine (Schildkraut, 1965) or serotonin (Glassman & Platman, 1969) as the causes of depression. It is now known that these neurotransmitters interact in complex ways with other neurotransmitters and neurohormones, and no single neurotransmitter is responsible for depression in a simple relationship.

There is also now much evidence that anxiety, somatoform, and mood disorders are more alike than they are different. This is especially true of the relationship between anxiety and depression, and anxiety and somatization. It is now clear that almost everyone who is depressed is also anxious. However, not all anxious persons are depressed (Barlow, 1988; DiNardo & Barlow, 1990; Sanderson, DiNardo, Rapee, & Barlow, 1990).

The distinction and connection between anxiety and depression appear to be based in cognition. This is to be expected if anxiety and mood symptoms are conceptualized as manifestations of emotional distress. As was discussed in Chapter 4, emotion is not a purely biological process. Emotions are essentially cognitive in nature; therefore, they have meaning. The intentionality of persons bestows meaning on any experience in their lives. Those meanings are expressed in observable behavior and, therefore, in their symptoms of emotional distress.

In the discussion of emotion as a cognitive process (Chapter 4), it was seen that emotion manifests in a three-stage process: (1) initial appraisal, (2) emotional feeling, and (3) culture-based behavioral program. The key to this emotional process is Stage 1, the initial appraisal. This is where the meaning of a given event or situation is established for the individual. In research supporting the learned helplessness theory of depression (see Chapter 5), it was found that animals and people will first become anxious in a stressful situation but will subsequently become depressed if they cognitively construct the situation as one in which they have no control or are *helpless* (Abramson, Seligman, & Teasdale, 1978; Miller & Norman, 1979; Seligman, 1975). Thus, anxiety resulting from life stress can be followed by depression if the situation is cognized as *hopeless* (Barlow, 1988; Mineka & Kelly, 1989).

The key to the relationship between anxiety and depression appears to be cognition. If an individual cognitively constructs the cause of the stressful situation as something *internal* (that is, inside oneself) as well as *stable* (chronic) and *general* (affecting many areas of one's life), then that person is very likely to develop a sense of hopelessness and helplessness. This kind of cognitive style will add the emotional symptoms of depression onto those of anxiety.

According to the learned helplessness theory of depression, this kind of cognitive style can be learned. This directly connects depression with personality development and life experiences. As discussed in Chapter 3, stressful life events can have a negative impact on personality development and thus on cognitive style. This is especially true of persons with a stigmatized *moral career* or self-identity. A stigmatized person is more likely to view the cause of stressful events as internal, stable, and general. Thus, the stigmatized person is more likely to develop a sense of hopelessness and helplessness and, therefore exhibit symptoms of depression in addition to anxiety.

For example, in a recent five-year longitudinal study of children, Nolen-Hoeksema, Girgus, and Seligman (1992) found that stressful life events caused children to develop a negative cognitive style that was predictive of later depression when additional stressful events occurred. This is consistent with findings related to substance disorders (Chapter 9), wherein persons traumatized as children became hypersensitive to environmental stress due to permanent changes in their stress hormone systems. Thus, depression can probably also be related to an acquired hypersensitive nervous system. This hypersensitive nervous system would be theorized to be affecting both cognition and biochemistry simultaneously.

These same factors may also help explain gender differences in emotional distress. We have seen that the development of disordered emotions is closely related to the cognitive construction of situations as uncontrollable. In the United States, almost 70 percent of the persons with major depression and dysthymia are women (Nolen-Hoeksema, 1987; Weissman et al., 1991). Similar percentages are also found for most of the anxiety disorders (Barlow & Durand, 1995). These sex ratios are expectable in a male dominated society where females are socialized to be dependent, passive, and sensitive to the needs of others and males are raised to be independent, aggressive, and masterful. Moreover, members of dominated social groups such as women and racial and ethnic minorities are more likely to experience increased numbers of stressful events in the form of discrimination, poverty, humiliation, and harassment.

For example, a study by medical sociologist David Halpern (1993) found that being a member of a minority group increases an individual's risk for mental illness. The evidence reviewed suggests that it is the experience at the local level rather than the national level that is critical. That is, even if a person belongs to a racial or ethnic group that is the majority at the national level, if that group is a minority at the local level, then the personal experience of prejudice can increase perceived social stress and risk for mental illness. Conversely, a person who belongs to a racial or ethnic minority at the national level but lives in a local situation in which that group is the majority receives increased social support and is protected from prejudice and social stress. That person has less perceived social stress and less risk for mental illness. This points out the stressful effects of social dominance hierarchies on personality development, cognitive styles, and mental health.

Connections based on patterns of cognition between anxiety and depression can also be made between anxiety and symptoms of somatoform disorders (which are discussed in Chapter 11). In general, anxiety seems to be the common ground out of which most cases of mood and somatoform symptoms develop, and the connection between them is cognition. Cognition is highly influenced by cultural schemas. This could be the reason depressive symptoms seem to be more common in western societies, whereas somatoform symptoms appear to be more common in many nonwestern societies, and anxiety symptoms appear to be widespread in all parts of the world.

Anxiety

Anxiety disorders are the single most common psychiatric condition (Kirmayer, Young, & Hayton, 1995). **Anxiety** is essentially *future-oriented fear.* Barlow (1988) and Barlow, Brown, and Craske (1994) have analyzed the relationship between anxiety and fear. Their analyses conclude that anxiety is the emotion of fear linked to the anticipation of future danger or misfortune. In contrast, ordinary fear is linked to *present-oriented* danger or misfortune. Anxiety or future-oriented fear also seems to be connected to the cognition of uncontrollability (Barlow, 1988; Mineka, 1985a, b). Uncontrollability here means the cognition that an individual is not able to control upcoming stressful events. Anxiety is related to cognitive patterns constructing self-concept and ideas about personal competence, self-confidence, and the person's ability to deal effectively with events in his or her life. Therefore, anxiety is clearly connected to a specific cognitive process related to sociocultural factors influencing overall personality development (Chapter 3).

It appears that persons can possess a vulnerability to anxiety that can be either genetically inherited or acquired through traumatic experience. This vulnerability manifests simultaneously both biologically and psychologically in the form of a hypersensitive nervous system. Biologically, the person is hypersensitive to environmental stress due to abnormalities in his or her stress hormone system. Psychologically, hypersensitivity to environmental stress is structured into the neural networks of the brain as a result of emotional trauma. These neural networks structure cognitive schemas that promote anxiety-producing cognitions. These cognitions appear to produce the symptoms of anxiety disorders.

The basis for the *formation* of anxiety-producing cognitive schemas appears to be stressful life events. Similarly, the *triggers* for subsequent activation of anxiety schemas also appear to be stressful events. Most of these events are related to interpersonal relationships, for example, interactions with family, peers, superiors, and so on. Other types of stressful life events, such as illness or injury, financial problems, or the death of a loved one, can also be involved in producing or triggering anxiety schemas. Once these schemas are activated, they can produce negative misinterpretations in cognition, thus structuring a normal or less serious situation as something catastrophic, life threatening, or seriously embarrassing. This can result in a variety of symptoms conceptualized in DSM-IV within the general categories of anxiety, somatoform, and mood disorders. There is a tremendous overlap of symptomatology among these three general categories.

The overlap of anxiety, somatoform, mood, and, in some cases, dissociative symptoms is evident in the syndromes that DSM-IV designates as anxiety disorders. DSM-IV contains the following anxiety disorders: *panic disorder with and without agoraphobia, agoraphobia without history of panic disorder, specific phobia, social phobia, obsessive-compulsive disorder, posttraumatic stress disorder, acute stress disorder,* and *generalized anxiety disorder.*

Panic Attacks and Agoraphobia

Because panic attacks and agoraphobia occur in more than one disorder, there are separate diagnostic criteria in DSM-IV for these experiences.

Panic Attacks

Panic attacks are characterized by a discrete period of intense fear with at least four additional somatic or cognitive symptoms, including palpitations, sweating, trembling, shortness of breath, feelings of choking, chest pain, nausea or abdominal distress, dizziness, depersonalization, derealization, fear of going crazy, fear of dying, tactile sensations (paresthesias), and chills or hot flashes. It is clear from this list of symptoms that although the emotion of fear is central to a panic attack, the accompanying symptoms are primarily somatic and dissociative.

Once a person has developed anxiety related to panic attacks, various other symptoms and disorders can develop as a result of the way the situation is cognitively constructed. These include specific phobias, agoraphobia, obsessive-compulsive disorder, and major depressive episodes.

Agoraphobia

Agoraphobia is anxiety about being in places in which a panic attack or other anxiety reaction might occur, resulting in a pervasive avoidance of a variety of situations. This avoidance may cause social or occupational impairment. In clinical populations, more than 95 percent of patients with agoraphobia also have a current diagnosis or history of panic disorder. Thus, there is a definite cognitive connection between previous experience of panic and subsequent development of agoraphobia in most cases.

Panic Disorder

Panic disorder is characterized by recurrent and unexpected panic attacks. When a person has a panic attack, it is an extremely frightening experience. The person may feel that he or she is either going crazy or dying. The panic attack itself can be traumatic, and people can develop an intense fear of having another attack. This is future-oriented fear or anxiety. When persons develop anxiety over the possibility of having another panic attack, they form cognitive schemas about the attack. These schemas can connect the panic attack to various perceived triggers such as places, times, situations, or bodily sensations.

For example, if a panic attack occurred at a particular time or location (like flying in an airplane), the person may develop a phobia for air travel. Similarly, if the bodily sensations of palpitations, choking, chest pain, or depersonalization are most central to the person's panic attack schema, then the individual may minutely and continuously monitor bodily sensations and misinterpret normal events, such as a rapid heartbeat after exercising, as the onset of a panic attack (Clark, 1986, 1988). This cognitive misinterpretation structures normal events as catastrophic occurrences, sending the person into an anxiety state and possibly even triggering a full-blown panic attack. This is the creation of panic disorder. The person will now be continuously anxious, always fearing the onset of a new panic attack. Persons with panic disorder frequently develop situationally predisposed panic attacks by having a panic attack in a particular situation and then experiencing a similar situation as an emotional trigger.

The cognitive factors related to culture in both the triggering and treatment of panic attacks are illustrated in a case reported by Galanti (1991). In this case, a 22-year-old Mexican American inmate of a county jail was admitted for emergency services with the symptoms of a heart attack. He was examined, but no cardiac abnormalities were found. He was sent to the psychiatric unit in a state of acute panic, clutching his left side and speaking in incoherent Spanish. Later, he was lying on the floor, conscious, but shaking violently and in a state of terror. He claimed to be dying and begged the nurse to inform his mother. Instead, she asked the patient if he believed in God. Receiving an affirmative answer, she tore a picture of Jesus out of a Bible, showed it to the patient, and then held it on his heart. Slowly, the patient calmed down, and then surprised everyone by getting up and following the nurse into her office, still clutching the picture of Jesus to his chest. He later explained that he had been cursed by a *bruja* (witch) in Mexico. A former lover had paid the witch to place a curse on him to cause his death by heart attack. By morning the patient was fairly calm, convinced that his faith in God had saved him.

Understanding the patient's cultural identity and explanatory model was central to the treatment of this panic attack patient. Understanding and using the sources of illness and healing in the patient's cultural meaning system, the nurse was able to quickly alleviate the patient's symptoms through the use of symbolic healing (Chapter 5). The patient understood the clinical reality in his own terms and was now convinced that the danger had passed. Given the cognitive input necessary for the formation of panic disorder, it is highly unlikely that the panic attack in this particular patient would result in the onset of panic disorder. However, the attack would certainly convince the patient of the power of witchcraft. Because of his cultural identity and personal experience, this individual would be susceptible to further symptoms related to subsequent witchcraft activities. Treatment for any further difficulties should take this into account.

Demoralization leading to the symptoms of major depression is also a common consequence of panic disorder. This is especially true when individuals cognitively construct the problem as something *internal, stable,* and *general.* This can happen when individuals inaccurately construct the problem as an "incurable brain disease" (Chapter 5). Clients can become depressed as a result of generalizing their panic experiences to their entire lives. DSM-IV estimates that 50 to 65 percent of persons with panic disorder also have major depressive disorder, with two-thirds of these developing the depression coincident or following the onset of panic disorder. In this case, DSM-IV recommends that both disorders should be diagnosed. This comorbidity illustrates the close cognitive relationship between panic disorder and major depression in actual cases. This relationship should be assessed by the clinician and treated through cognitive-behavioral therapy.

Phobias

A **specific phobia** is characterized by a persistent fear of specific objects or situations, exposure to which almost invariably evokes an anxiety response. Adults with this disorder typically recognize that the fear is excessive or unreasonable but are unable to control their cognitive processes and, thus, are unable to control their emotions.

Specific phobias can be developed by experiencing panic in relation to a specific situation or object (for example, flying) or to a traumatic life event. Also, phobias can be developed by observing some extremely fearful event happening to someone else. In some cases, even hearing about some extreme danger can result in the formation of a phobia (Barlow & Durand, 1995). In all cases, it is the formation of a cognitive schema structuring the meaning of the object or situation as fearful that is operating in the thinking and emotions of the person.

Cultural factors that affect specific phobias are related to the meaning of objects and situations as defined by cultural schemas. Different sets of cultural schemas specify that certain objects or situations are fearful or dangerous, for example, witches, ghosts, and spirits in many premodern societies. Various specific cultural entities can cause what could be considered unreasonable fear by someone from a different culture.

Social phobia is characterized by a persistent fear of social situations in which extreme embarrassment may occur. Exposure to these situations provokes an anxiety response. There is frequently a circular pattern of conditioning in which fear of a social situation provokes an anxiety response in the person, which then results in embarrassment and further anxiety. This, in turn, results in more fear of similar situations, and so on.

Social phobia can be associated with panic disorder, obsessive-compulsive disorder, mood disorders, and somatization disorder, and usually precedes these disorders (APA, 1994). This illustrates the close cognitive connections among the anxiety disorders, mood disorders, and somatoform disorders in which one disorder may precede another and may be cognitively precipitating further symptoms.

Cultural factors influencing social phobia include systems of social and gender hierarchies, customs of social interaction, and consequences for improper social behavior. For example, in Japanese culture, because it is so important that individuals not be offensive to others in personal appearance or behavior, some people develop *taijin kyofusho,* a syndrome characterized by intense anxiety that one's appearance, body odor, or facial expressions will be found offensive. This phobia usually develops in a person in a subservient position in the Japanese social dominance hierarchy, illustrating the effects of social structure and cultural influences on cognition and emotions.

Social phobia is also very likely related to personality development and personality disorders, particularly avoidant personality disorder. As discussed in Chapter 6, persons with the symptoms of avoidant personality disorder are much more likely to develop in hierarchical societies. It is in this social context that persons are more likely to be labeled as inferior, inadequate, unacceptable, or some other form of stigmatization. In the United States, especially during the years of early adolescence, children may be taunted by their peers and be emotionally traumatized and humiliated. This can have a very detrimental effect on adult personality development. Persons who have internalized a stigmatized self-identity may experience extreme anxiety in social situations.

Generalized Anxiety Disorder

Generalized anxiety disorder (GAD) is characterized by excessive anxiety, restlessness, an inability to concentrate, and worry occurring more days than not for a period of at least six months. Worrying typically revolves around life activities such as work, finances, health, and family matters.

Unlike panic disorder, in which the somatic symptoms are generally confined to panic attacks, GAD is characterized by frequently recurring somatic symptoms including muscle aches and pains, feeling shaky, trembling, twitching, dry mouth, sweating, nausea, diarrhea, a lump in the throat, and frequent urination. Depressive mood symptoms are also quite common. Again, we see the great overlap of symptoms among anxiety, somatoform, and mood disorders in actual patients.

This disorder illustrates the direct connection between cognition and symptomatology. The typical cognitions of persons with GAD are centered around worrying about life events. The symptoms of difficulty concentrating and restlessness reflect the cognitive activity of anxiety. The common somatic symptoms are examples of the somatization of anxiety. As mentioned earlier, somatization is the expression of emotional distress in somatic symptoms. This illustrates the direct connection between anxiety and somatoform symptoms.

If the somatic symptoms of GAD are conceptualized within the three-stage cognitive model of emotion, they can be viewed as Stage 2, the *emotional feeling* stage. These are the bodily sensations associated with emotions. Also, any outward behavior initiated as a result of the emotion of anxiety would be considered to represent Stage 3, the culture-based behavioral program (see Chapter 4).

There are significant differences in the way generalized anxiety is experienced and expressed cross-culturally. The symptoms that are considered to be significant in western conceptions of anxiety may not be considered significant in other cultures, which may have their own symptoms not found in the West.

For example, a core symptom of generalized anxiety in Nigeria is the sensation of an insect crawling through the head and other parts of the body (Awaritefe, 1988; Ebigbo, 1986; Makanjuola, 1987). This is a somatic symptom that is not found in western societies. The typical western clinician looking for anxiety symptoms in a Nigerian is unlikely to ask about this particular symptom, but it may be central to the lived experience of the patient. In China and Malaysia, some persons experience the culture-bound syndrome *koro*, in which they have the sensation of their penises or breasts retracting into their bodies. They believe that if this retraction is allowed to proceed they will die (Leng, 1985). Again, we see how symptoms and disorders must be understood in relation to the person's cultural identity. Furthermore, this highlights the need to include indigenous symptom concepts in diagnostic interviews.

Obsessive-Compulsive Disorder

Obsessive-compulsive disorder (OCD) is characterized by persistent thoughts or impulses that are experienced as intrusive and inappropriate (obsessions), and repetitive behaviors (compulsions) that are performed to reduce the distress associated with obsessions.

Obsessive-compulsive disorder is obviously related to patterns of cognition. In fact, obsessions, the key symptom of OCD, are patterns of cognition. In this case, they are patterns of cognition that give rise to severe generalized anxiety, panic attacks, severe phobias, and various somatic symptoms. If we view OCD within the three-stage cognitive model of emotion, the obsessions constitute Stage 1, the *initial appraisal*. This is the cognitive construction of a given situation. The various somatic symptoms of generalized anxiety and panic attacks associated with OCD constitute Stage 2, the *emotional feeling*. And the compulsions associated with OCD constitute Stage 3, the *culture-based behavioral program*. Compulsions are the behaviors performed to reduce or control the fear and distress associated with obsessions. In OCD, anxiety has become such a crippling factor in the life of the individual that he or she is essentially resorting to magical or ritualistic behavior in an attempt to control events and thereby reduce anxiety.

The most common types of obsessions are thoughts of contamination, doubts about some behavior performed (for example, locking a door), need for orderliness, aggressive impulses, and sexual imagery. Some of these appear to be related to specific aspects of cultural schemas. For example, obsessions involving sexual content appear to be prevalent in persons involved with fundamentalist religions that severely restrict sexual behavior and prescribe serious punishment or even damnation for certain prohibited sexual behaviors. In these religions, just thinking about these sexual behaviors can be considered sinful and harmful. Thus, the thoughts themselves can be cognized as dangerous and needing suppression.

Believing that some behaviors and even some thoughts are dangerous motivates some people to engage in special ritual behavior to control them. This is illustrated in the case of Mr. Sinha, who had *dhat* syndrome (Chapter 2). He was made extremely anxious by recurrent sexual thoughts. The only way he could control these thoughts was to practice yoga meditation, which consisted of the ritual repetition of a mantra. As stated earlier, compulsions are repetitive behaviors that are performed to reduce the anxiety and distress associated with obsessions. Common compulsions are ritual washing, checking and ordering objects, praying, meditating, counting, and repeating words silently.

The above mentioned obsessions and compulsions have been found in such culturally diverse societies as Egypt, India, Israel, Taiwan, Puerto Rico, and England, which indicates that the clinical characteristics of OCD are similar across cultures (Okasha et al., 1994; Staley & Wand, 1995). However, in cultures that place a high value on ritual purity as part of their religious beliefs (for example, Egypt, India, Israel), thoughts of contamination and the resulting ritual washing may be deemed normal and normative in the cultural schemas, even though they would be considered excessive or unreasonable in the United States.

Egyptian Moslems are required to pray five times a day. Each time of prayer must be preceded by a ritual washing to purify the worshipper, making him or her fit to commune with the deity. The ritual purification is nullified by any bodily excretion and must be redone before prayer begins. Also, for strict Moslems, even casual contact with a person of the opposite gender is contaminating and requires purifications before prayer. In a non-Moslem setting, the prayers themselves might be viewed as compulsive rituals with obsessive rules about proper content and number of repetitions. But if many of these people did not perform their rituals, they would experience significant anxiety until they were able to perform the proper purifications and prayers.

If the average non-Moslem person in the United States were to behave in this fashion five times a day, the behavior would probably be considered obsessive-compulsive and socially impairing. However, many religious practices that some Americans perform consist of repetitive ritualistic behaviors, for example, praying on a rosary or chanting "Hail Marys" silently to oneself. These behaviors are also typically used to relieve the symptoms of anxiety arising from life events or the perceived commission of sin.

Thus, normative, repetitive, and ritualistic behaviors used for relieving or preventing anxiety are found in many different societies. Judging whether something is excessive or unreasonable depends on the prevailing set of cultural schemas. Clinicians need to keep this in mind when making assessments and diagnoses. Diagnostic decisions should be made based on a familiarity with the cultural schemas of the client and his or her cultural norms of behavior.

Posttraumatic Stress Disorder

Posttraumatic stress disorder (PTSD) is characterized by prominent anxiety and dissociative symptoms following exposure to an extreme traumatic stressor. The traumatic stressor typically involves direct personal experience of serious injury, life-threatening danger, witnessing death or injury of another person, or learning about death or serious harm to a family member or close associate. Examples are military combat, violent personal assault, being kidnapped or tortured, experiencing natural or manmade disasters, or severe car or airplane crashes. For young children, sexual abuse with or without threatened or actual violence or injury can also be traumatic.

Common symptoms of PTSD include the anxiety symptoms of insomnia, irritability, difficulty concentrating, hypervigilance, an increased startle response, and avoidance of stimuli associated with the traumatic events. Dissociative symptoms common in cases of PTSD include flashbacks in which the person relives the experience (including in dreams), physical and emotional numbing, detachment, reduction in awareness of surroundings, depersonalization, derealization, and dissociative amnesia (APA, 1994).

Individuals with PTSD also commonly experience numerous somatic symptoms as well as the symptoms of major depression. There also may be impaired relationships, loss of previously held beliefs, social withdrawal, and a possible change in personality characteristics.

The symptomatology of PSTD illustrates a major overlap between anxiety, somatoform, mood, and dissociative symptoms. Persons with PTSD have all four types of symptoms, with the dissociative symptoms being especially prominent. In fact, it probably makes just as much sense to classify PTSD as a dissociative disorder as it does an anxiety disorder. Of course, the dissociation is occurring as an adaptive response to the anxiety associated with traumatic stress (see Chapter 13).

Posttraumatic stress disorder clearly illustrates the pathological effects of traumatic events. Of course, vulnerability to the effects of traumatic events is variable. Because persons can apparently be born with hypersensitive nervous systems (Chapter 9), those persons will be genetically more vulnerable to the effects of all types of stressful events. Also, hypersensitivity can be acquired, especially through the experience of trauma early in life. Persons with traumatic early life histories will also be more vulnerable to stressful events later in life.

The symptoms of PTSD have been found to be very common in refugee populations (Boehnlein & Kinzie, 1995). These are usually people who experienced high levels of traumatic stress due to war-related events, either as soldiers or as civilians. The traumatic events experienced by these people can include bombing of one's village or home, witnessing deaths of family members, recovering bodies of dead family members, beatings, starvation, forced labor, rapes, combat, and so on.

Because of cultural schemas regarding shame and a fatalistic view of life, many Southeast Asian refugees may be uncomfortable volunteering information about these traumatic life events unless specifically asked. Also, because of cultural schemas regarding the shamefulness of emotional illness that is common to many Asians, these individuals are more likely to report somatic rather than emotional symptoms (Kinzie et al., 1990). Clinicians should specifically inquire about personal trauma when assessing refugees. Additionally, clinicians should be aware that some clients may be amnesic for specific traumas (Boehnlein & Kinzie, 1995).

Posttraumatic stress syndromes are very common in many nonwestern societies. This is especially true in extremely hierarchical societies where dominant groups maintain their status through coercion and violence. For example, severe wife abuse in highly patriarchal societies can result in a high prevalence of PTSD in women (Kinzie et al., 1990). However, because of differing cultural schemas, the subjective experience, idioms of distress, indigenous diagnoses, treatments, and clinical outcomes of posttraumatic stress syndromes may vary considerably. In many premodern societies, PTSD is most likely to manifest as variations of *dissociative trance disorder* (Chapter 13).

Acute Stress Disorder

Closely related to PTSD is **acute stress disorder (ASD).** The symptoms of acute stress disorder and PTSD are almost identical, the only major distinctions are in duration and point of onset. By definition, ASD has an onset within one month after the traumatic event and does not persist beyond four weeks after the event. In contrast, the symptoms of PTSD must persist for at least one month and may have a delayed onset. Clients with symptoms of ASD that persist for more than one month will have their diagnoses changed to PTSD.

If hallucinations or delusions occur in cases of ASD, DSM-IV recommends the diagnosis of *brief psychotic disorder* (Chapter 14) instead of ASD. However, diagnosing patients with brief psychotic disorder instead of ASD may result in treatment for psychosis instead of treatment for the effects of emotional trauma. This may lead to inappropriate treatment and a poor outcome.

Like PTSD syndromes, in premodern societies brief mental illnesses with hallucinations and delusions resulting from traumatic stress are most likely to be structured according to the cognitive schemas of the indigenous culture.

These are usually manifested in brief dissociative type culture-bound syndromes. These are most appropriately diagnosed as forms of *dissociative trance disorder* (Chapter 13) and should be treated as cases of dissociation, not psychosis. For example, some cases of the Latin American syndrome *ataques de nervios* might appear to fit the diagnostic criteria for ASD, panic disorder, brief psychotic disorder, or dissociative trance disorder. Clinicians should anticipate that syndromes from nonwestern societies will not exactly fit the diagnostic criteria of DSM-IV disorders and may include symptoms that cross different categories.

Nonwestern Syndromes

The boundaries between the anxiety, somatoform, and mood disorders are very porous. This is demonstrated by the fact that clients very frequently have symptoms running across these three general categories. In nonwestern societies, there is no inclination to construct illness categories within these DSM-IV boundaries, and single folk categories of illness frequently include anxiety, somatic, and depressive symptoms in a unified syndrome.

For example, *dhat* syndrome in India (see Chapter 2) is characterized by fatigue, physical weakness, insomnia, head and body aches, the various symptoms of generalized anxiety, as well as dysthymia, and it is thought to be caused by excessive loss of semen. Is this an anxiety disorder, a somatoform disorder, or a mood disorder? *Dhat* syndrome is probably best classified as an anxiety disorder because the essential problem is anxiety about the consequences of "losing too much semen." However, it has elements of all three general categories and demonstrates that the symptoms manifesting from emotional distress can be experienced in virtually any combination and are not required to follow the diagnostic boundaries of DSM-IV. This illustrates the limitations of the disease-centered paradigm applied cross-culturally.

Nervios

Other nonwestern syndromes also demonstrate the ethnocentricity of DSM-IV diagnostic boundaries and the tremendous overlap of anxiety, somatoform, and depressive symptoms. For example, *nervios* ("nerves") is a Latin American syndrome characterized by a chronic and generalized sense of emotional distress with a range of symptoms, including headaches, body aches, heart palpitations, heat in the chest, irritability, gastrointestinal disturbances, insomnia, nervousness, inability to concentrate, persistent worrying, trembling, and dizziness. *Nervios* is indigenously attributed to a loss of key personal relationships (Dresp, 1985; Guarnaccia & Farias, 1988; Lock, 1989; Low, 1989).

According to DSM-IV, various presentations of *nervios* can resemble adjustment, anxiety, depressive, dissociative, somatoform, and psychotic disorders (APA, 1994, p. 847). However, giving a patient with *nervios* multiple diagnoses, following the DSM-IV notion of comorbidity, would ignore the cultural identity of the client, the client's explanatory model, and would probably be of little clinical value to the client. It makes little sense to split up symptoms into separate unfamiliar diagnoses when a unified diagnosis already exists within the client's indigenous set of cultural schemas.

Susto

Susto is another Latin American syndrome. It is characterized by loss of appetite and weight, physical weakness, restlessness in sleep, depression, introversion, and apathy. It is indigenously attributed to *soul loss* resulting from frightful or traumatic experiences (Bolton, 1981; Clark, 1959; Rubel, O'Nell, & Collado, 1985; Uzzell, 1974).

Among Native Indian populations of Latin America, *susto* may be conceptualized as a case of *spirit attack*. Among non-Indian cultural groups, *susto* is perceived to be a result of a person's soul becoming separated from his or her body because the individual has been seriously frightened. Recovery from *susto* is thought to be dependent on returning the person's soul to the body. If allowed to persist untreated, it is believed that *susto* will result in the victim's death.

Susto manifests as a result of being frightened, an etiology related to anxiety disorders such as PTSD and acute stress disorder, but the symptoms are primarily related to major depression. This again illustrates the connection between anxiety and mood disorders. Should *susto* be classified as an anxiety disorder or a mood disorder? It is tempting to view *susto* as a cultural variant of PTSD or acute stress disorder. However, these diagnoses would not take into account the client's cultural schemas. Furthermore, how should it be treated? In the folk treatment of *susto*, it is believed that only native folk healers can retrieve lost souls. Therefore, to treat *susto* as one would PTSD, acute stress disorder, or major depression may not be appropriate. Because of the client's set of cultural schemas, cooperation of folk healers in treatment of *susto* may be required for the best clinical outcome.

Koro

Koro is a Malay and southern Chinese syndrome (although similar cases have been reported elsewhere). It is characterized by the patient's fear that the penis or breasts are shrinking and will disappear into the body, causing death. The usual symptoms are intense anxiety, palpitations, sweating, numbness in limbs, faintness, stiffening of the body, and sometimes loss of consciousness. To prevent their penises from retracting into their bodies, some men will manually hold onto the penis or tie it onto some object with a piece of string or tie weights onto the penis. Sometimes severe trauma of the penis results. *Koro* is indigenously attributed to excessive or inappropriate sexual intercourse or sudden exposure of the penis to cold air or water, and at times it occurs in localized epidemic form (Edwards, 1985; Gang-Ming, Guo-Qian, Li-Xum, & Tseng, 1995; Rin, 1965; Yap, 1965).

The symptoms of *koro* are primarily anxiety symptoms. One possibility is to view *koro* as a cultural variant of panic disorder. However, *koro* is directly related to ideas about a part of the body (penis or breasts) retracting into the body and disappearing. This makes sense only within the cultural schemas of the client. To diagnose a client suffering from *koro* with panic disorder would ignore the cultural identity and explanatory model of the client.

Tseng et al. (1992) conducted psychometric testing on a group of victims of Chinese *koro* epidemics, a group of psychiatric patients with anxiety disorders, and a control group. They found that the *koro* group had significantly elevated anxiety and phobic subscale scores compared to the control group. However, the psychiatric group was significantly elevated on almost all of the somatic, anxiety, depression, anger/hostility, interpersonal sensitivity, obsessive-compulsive, neurasthenia, and hypochondriasis subscales. These findings indicated that the *koro* group was not similar to the psychiatric group. Thus, the proper diagnosis for a client with *koro*, from a client-centered perspective, should probably be *koro*. Also, culturally appropriate treatment for *koro* should address the explanatory model of the client.

Taijin Kyofusho

Taijin kyofusho is a Japanese syndrome characterized by intense fear that one's appearance, body odor, facial expressions, or bodily movements may be offensive to someone. This leads to social withdrawal and avoidance. Japanese psychiatrists generally take the view that *taijin kyofusho* is a special kind of social phobia with a unique set of symptoms such as eye contact phobia or body smell phobia. Because of Japanese cultural traits such as fear of offending others, denial of the self, and the importance of harmonious social interactions, *taijin kyofusho* should be viewed as a pathological amplification of cultural concerns about the self in social interaction (Kirmayer, 1991; Russell, 1989; Tseng, Mo, et al., 1992). Therefore, treatment should address the cultural schemas of the client, with appropriate symbolic healing.

Hwa-Byung

Hwa-byung is a Korean syndrome characterized by prominent anxiety, somatoform, and mood symptoms such as insomnia, fatigue, panic, fear of impending death, indigestion, palpitations, "heat sensation," flushing, "pushing-up" sensations in the chest, irritability, epigastric mass, difficulty in concentration, dysphoria, and generalized aches and pains. This is a very common condition, especially among less educated, middle-aged Korean women who are trapped in marriages to unfaithful, domineering, violent, alcoholic husbands, or with abusive mothers-in-law. These family conditions are frequently found in both

Korean and Korean American families that are extremely patriarchal (Kendall, 1987; Lin et al., 1992).

Hwa-byung can be literally translated as "anger syndrome," and it is indigenously attributed to the suppression of anger. A married Korean woman is expected to fulfill her roles as hardworking wife and daughter-in-law in a patrilocal marriage in an obedient fashion. Anger is not an emotion that she is allowed to directly express toward her husband or her in-laws. As a result, she develops *hwa-byung,* a syndrome that cuts across the boundaries of DSM-IV anxiety, somatoform, and mood disorders. Assessment and treatment of *hwa-byung* needs to take into account the gender and family dominance hierarchies present in Korean society. Symbolic healing altering family dynamics may be necessary in treatment.

 # Suggested Clinical Guidelines

1. Assess the Cultural Identity of the Individual

Clinicians should be aware that anxiety disorders may manifest differently across cultures. Behaviors that appear to be obsessive-compulsive may be deemed normal and normative in the cultural schemas of some societies but would be considered excessive or unreasonable in the United States. For instance, if the average non-Moslem person in the United States were to ritually bathe and pray five times a day, the behavior would probably be considered obsessive-compulsive. Therefore, the cultural identity of every individual needs to be carefully assessed.

2. Assess the Cognitive Schemas Regarding Anxiety

Anxiety is the emotion of fear linked to the anticipation of future danger or misfortune. In contrast, ordinary fear is linked to present-oriented danger or misfortune. Anxiety or future-oriented fear also seems to be connected to the cognition of uncontrollability. Anxiety is thus related to cognitive patterns constructing self-concept and ideas about personal competence, self-confidence, and an individual's ability to deal effectively with events in his or her life.

These meanings surrounding the self can be structured in unique cultural schemas. Many culture-bound syndromes in nonwestern societies have prominent anxiety symptoms combined with somatoform and mood symptoms in unified folk diagnostic categories. Examples include *hwa-byung* in Korea and *taijin kyofusho* in Japan. These are meaningful categories of illness for persons from these cultures. Because disordered emotions are so closely bound up with cultural schemas, recognizing these culture-bound syndromes and their indigenous meanings may be important in treatment. Therefore, the cognitive schemas of each client regarding anxiety need to be assessed.

3. *Assess Anxiety within the Cultural and Psychosocial Environment*

Clinicians need to see the client and his or her anxiety within the total socio-cultural context. The basis for the formation of anxiety-producing cognitive schemas appears to be stressful life events. Similarly, the triggers for subsequent activation of anxiety schemas also appears to be stressful events. Most of these events are related to interpersonal relationships, for example, interactions with family, peers, superiors, and so on. Other types of stressful life events, such as illness or injury, financial problems, or death of a loved one, can also be involved in producing or triggering anxiety schemas. Once these schemas are activated, they can produce negative misinterpretations in cognition, thus structuring a normal or less serious situation as something catastrophic, life threatening, or seriously embarrassing.

Clinicians should particularly assess sources of social stress that might be promoting anxiety. For example, anxiety could be a response to stressful life events or a maladaptation to a stigmatized identity within race, class, family, or gender dominance hierarchies. Clinicians should assess verifiable instances of abuse, assault, or intimidation. If those are continuing, successful treatment may require some form of culturally appropriate family therapy or other social intervention. Anxiety could also be a response to a hypersensitive nervous system resulting from emotional trauma that occurred earlier in life, for example, loss of a parent, sexual abuse, and war trauma in veterans and refugees.

4. *Assess the Cultural Aspects of the Clinician-Client Relationship*

Clinicians should critically assess their own concepts of anxiety disorders and reflexively determine how these concepts may be projected onto the client. The standard DSM-IV disorders should not be viewed as the only acceptable diagnoses for a client from a nonwestern cultural background. Human brain plasticity allows for various patterns of symptomatology with culturally specific combinations of anxiety, somatoform, and mood symptoms. Therefore, clinicians should consider diagnostic categories from the client's indigenous culture when making diagnoses. These may be conceptualized within the category of anxiety disorder not otherwise specified, if necessary.

Clinicians should also be aware that something in their appearance may be anxiety provoking for clients. For example, a Vietnam veteran with PTSD may react with anxiety when interviewed by an Asian American clinician.

5. *Negotiate Clinical Reality*

Clients with anxiety symptoms may not find western categories of illness to be meaningful. For example, diagnosing and treating a South Asian client who presents with *dhat* syndrome with one of the standard DSM-IV disorders may result in noncompliance by the client. Thus, a negotiation between the client and the clinician is necessary to arrive at a consensus of the problem and the appropriate treatment. This negotiation should take into account all of the above factors.

Also, clients with comorbid symptoms of somatoform and mood disorders should be assessed as to the cognitive relationship of the anxiety disorder with the comorbid symptoms. For example, the key to the relationship between anxiety and depression appears to be cognition. If an individual cognitively constructs the cause of the anxiety as something *internal* (that is, inside oneself), as well as *stable* (chronic), and *general* (affecting many areas of one's life), then that person is very likely to develop a sense of hopelessness and helplessness. This pattern of cognition will add the emotional symptoms of depression to those of anxiety. A negotiation of clinical reality that avoids this pattern of cognition is recommended.

Chapter Eleven

Somatoform Disorders

DSM-IV includes the following **somatoform disorders:** *somatization disorder, undifferentiated somatoform disorder, conversion disorder, pain disorder, hypochondriasis,* and *body dysmorphic disorder.* All of these disorders are characterized by prominent somatic (bodily) symptoms as their central problem. However, as discussed in Chapter 10, somatoform symptoms appear to be directly related to anxiety. As we know from the discussion of anxiety as emotion, anxiety is based in a cognitive process. Recurrent or generalized anxiety is based in deep-seated anxiety-producing cognitive schemas.

We also know that the basis for the formation of anxiety-producing cognitive schemas appears to be stressful or traumatic life events. Similarly, the triggers for the subsequent activation of anxiety schemas also appears to be stressful events. Most stressful events are related to interpersonal relationships, work problems, illness or injury, financial problems, or death of a loved one. Once these schemas are activated, they can produce negative misinterpretations in cognition, thus structuring the symptoms of anxiety disorders as well as somatoform disorders.

Cross-cultural studies indicate that somatic symptoms are the most common clinical manifestation of anxiety disorders worldwide (Kirmayer, 1984; Kirmayer & Weiss, 1994). The somatization of anxiety is also very common among North American and British patients in primary care settings (Goldberg & Bridges, 1988; Kirmayer & Robins, 1991). This widespread expression of anxiety in the form of somatic symptoms challenges the classification system in DSM-IV that places syndromes with prominent somatic symptoms in a separate category distinct from the anxiety disorders. There is no etiological basis for this distinction, nor does there seem to be much clinical utility in this grouping. Looking at mental illnesses from a client-centered perspective, separating mental disorders expressing emotional distress into distinct anxiety, somatoform, and mood groupings is questionable.

Somatization Disorder

In earlier conceptualizations of mental illness, **somatization disorder** was referred to as **hysteria** and **Briquet's syndrome**. In the latter half of the 19th century in Europe, hysteria was a commonly diagnosed mental disorder characterized by extreme anxiety and chronic and recurrent somatic symptoms such as paralyses, anesthesias, blindness, seizures, and head and body aches, with no medical explanation. Hallucinations and multiple personalities were also commonly observed in persons diagnosed with hysteria (North et al., 1993).

Paul Briquet (1859) provided the first systematic description of hysteria and recommended that the term *hysteria* be abandoned because of the pejorative connotations associated with it. This recommendation was not to be followed until Guze (1970) proposed that hysteria be labeled *Briquet's syndrome* in recognition of Briquet's contribution. This suggestion has met with only partial acceptance.

Perley and Guze (1962) systematized the diagnostic criteria for Briquet's syndrome (hysteria). According to their criteria, 25 symptoms without medical explanation distributed across 9 of 10 categories were necessary for a diagnosis. Their symptom list included anxiety, somatic, depressive, and dissociative type symptoms.

In DSM-IV, Briquet's syndrome is called *somatization disorder*. However, the diagnostic criteria for somatization disorder are significantly restricted compared to Perley and Guze's (1962) criteria. In DSM-IV, somatization disorder requires pain symptoms in four areas of the body, two gastrointestinal disturbances other than pain, one sexual symptom other than pain (for example, sexual indifference), and one pseudoneurological (dissociative) symptom (for example, paralysis or seizures). Noticeably absent from the DSM-IV criteria for somatization disorder are anxiety and depressive symptoms, that is, the emotional or *psychoform* (as opposed to *somatoform*) symptoms that are prominent in Briquet's syndrome.

The absence of emotional symptoms in the diagnostic criteria is not because persons with somatization disorder do not have symptoms of emotional distress. It is just that those symptoms have been categorized as separate disorders in DSM-IV. Therefore, instead of having a single diagnosis of Briquet's syndrome, individuals are frequently given a diagnosis of somatization disorder with comorbid diagnoses of panic disorder, generalized anxiety disorder, or major depressive disorder. Thus, the illness is divided up into several distinct disorders.

This diagnostic practice appears to be based on the disease-centered paradigm, which assumes that each symptom cluster has a separate biological cause that can best be treated with a separate medication. This leads to the administration of several medications designed to alleviate specific symptoms. As a result, it is not uncommon for individuals to receive separate medications for pain, anxiety, depression, and insomnia all at the same time.

Thus, it appears that hysteria or Briquet's syndrome has been divided into separate disorders in DSM-IV. The somatic symptoms have been classified as somatization disorder, whereas the emotional symptoms have been classified primarily as panic disorder, generalized anxiety disorder, or major depressive disorder. Thus, the client receives multiple comorbid diagnoses instead of a unified illness description. This diagnostic practice is based on the disease-centered paradigm, and its clinical utility is doubtful.

In premodern societies, because of differing cultural schemas, hysteria-like syndromes are most likely to manifest in trance or spirit possession syndromes that include a cluster of anxiety, somatic, dissociative, and possibly depressive symptoms, with the dissociative symptoms frequently being most prominent (for example, *ataques de nervios*). Somatization disorder is an inadequate diagnosis for these premodern hysteria-type syndromes. A better diagnosis for these syndromes would probably be *dissociative trance disorder* (Chapter 13).

Undifferentiated Somatoform Disorder

Undifferentiated somatoform disorder is a residual category for persistent somatoform type illnesses that do not meet the full criteria for somatization disorder. This is an important category for cross-cultural assessment because patients may present with only those symptoms that are associated with a culture-bound syndrome and ignore other symptoms that are not part of the traditional syndrome (Janca, Isaac, Bennett, & Tacchini, 1995). Most frequently, this disorder is characterized by chronic fatigue, loss of appetite, bodily pains, and gastrointestinal symptoms without medical explanation. The example given both in DSM-IV and the *DSM-IV Casebook* (Spitzer et al., 1994) is **neurasthenia** in China.

Neurasthenia in China

The example in the *DSM-IV Casebook* titled "Tired Technician"* is a 36-year-old technician with insomnia, weakness, headaches, difficulty concentrating, poor memory, irritability, and nervousness. He sometimes feels depressed and is unable to enjoy anything. When he feels depressed, he experiences guilt, slowed thinking, appetite disturbance, and psychomotor retardation. His periods of depression never last more than two weeks and occur about five or six times a year.

In their discussion of this case, the *DSM-IV Casebook* editors comment that neurasthenia is one of the most commonly diagnosed disorders in China and that this individual's symptoms represent a typical case. They observe that his symptoms suggest a depressive syndrome and that a western-trained clinician

---

*Summarized with permission from the *Diagnostic and Statistical Manual of Mental Disorders Casebook*, Fourth Edition by R. L. Spitzer et al. (Eds.). Copyright © 1994 American Psychiatric Association, Washington D.C.

might well have diagnosed the patient with *depressive disorder NOS*. However, because mood disorders are relatively rare in China, and due to the Chinese use of physical symptoms as cultural idioms expressing emotional distress, the editors conclude that this individual should be diagnosed with *undifferentiated somatoform disorder*.

This case illustrates the effects of culture on subjective experience, idioms of distress, and professional diagnosis. Because depressive symptoms are not important in Chinese cultural schemas, little attention is paid to them, either in subjective experience or in interpersonal expressions of distress. Somatic symptoms have far more importance in the Chinese schemas. Therefore, the patient primarily notices and reports somatic symptoms. Likewise, clinicians trained in their own set of professional schemas will pay attention to the symptoms they are trained to consider significant. The editors mention that a western-trained clinician would likely diagnose a mood disorder. However, a Chinese-trained clinician would have no trouble diagnosing *neurasthenia*, a diagnosis that does not exist in western medicine. This illustrates the effects of culture on both subjective experience of illness and professional diagnosis. The obvious factor is patterns of cognition.

Cultural schemas construct emotional distress as depressive symptoms in western patients and clinicians, and as neurasthenia in Chinese patients and clinicians. This case illustrates the close relationship of mood, anxiety, and somatic symptoms and the effects of culture on the construction of a mental disorder. By having a subjective experience of illness validated by a professional diagnosis, the disorder *neurasthenia* becomes reified in the Chinese cultural context. It is a disorder that is both subjectively experienced and medically validated. This is not to say that neurasthenia is a fictitious disorder. Neurasthenia in China is certainly real, and people definitely suffer from it. However, the constellation of subjective experience and professional diagnosis is a cultural entity, a reification.

In all likelihood, most of the diagnostic categories in DSM-IV have a similar level of validity as neurasthenia in China. The cultural schemas in western culture have identified certain symptoms as signifying a particular disorder, which in turn are subjectively attended to because of their cultural significance. These symptoms are then reported to a clinician who validates a particular disorder from the professional schemas with his or her diagnosis. This reifies the cultural entity and creates a recognized category of mental disorder. Because cultural schemas differ, varying disorders in separate cultures can be constructed and reified from mostly the same basic symptoms of human suffering and emotional distress.

Conversion Disorder

Conversion disorder is characterized by pseudoneurological (dissociative) symptoms such as amnesia, paralysis, impaired coordination or balance, localized anesthesia, blindness, deafness, double vision, hallucinations, tremors, or seizures without medical explanation.

The pseudoneurological symptoms of conversion disorder are dissociative somatic symptoms. In fact, the *International Classification of Diseases* (ICD-10) lists conversion disorder symptoms as dissociative disorders such as dissociative motor disorders, dissociative convulsions, and dissociative anesthesia and sensory loss (WHO, 1989). Thus, conversion disorder is actually a manifestation of dissociation in somatic symptoms (Escobar, 1995). Dissociation is a splitting of consciousness based on trance (Chapter 13). Trance is a narrow focusing of attention. In the case of conversion symptoms, the sensory information (sight, hearing, touch, pain, and so forth), or motor ability in the case of paralysis, is placed outside of a narrow focus of attention and therefore outside of conscious awareness.

The contents of consciousness are determined by attention (see Chapter 13). Thus, sensory or motor modalities can be temporarily "forgotten" or "lost" to conscious awareness. Likewise, dissociative hallucinations are the product of attention narrowly placed on memory or imagination, shutting out external reality. Similarly, dissociative amnesia is attention focused away from memory or some aspect of memory. And dissociative seizures are actually pseudoseizures that are not related to brain pathology. Dissociative seizures result from narrowly focusing attention away from the bodily functions that normally maintain balance, muscle tone, posture, and overall body movement.

Conversion symptoms are the product of spontaneous trances resulting from emotional stress or trauma. Because of their emotional distress, some people enter a spontaneous trance and temporarily "lose" a sensory or motor modality or experience dissociative hallucinations or seizures to avoid or escape some extremely stressful or traumatic situation.

In premodern societies, these symptoms are typically structured in culture-based trance and possession trance syndromes and are probably most appropriately diagnosed as *dissociative trance disorder* (Chapter 13).

Hysteria in India

The case titled "Fits" in the *DSM-IV Casebook** illustrates the effects of culture in conversion disorder. The patient is a 26-year-old married woman from a middle-class urban family in New Delhi, India, who has experienced "fits" for the last four years. Her fits have a sudden onset, last 30 to 60 minutes, and are characterized by her becoming unresponsive and rigid throughout her body, with convulsions, frothing at the mouth, crying, shouts of abuse, and amnesia for the episodes. The fits recur once or twice a month. She and her family believe she is suffering from a physical illness. However, they recognize that the fits often occur after some social stressor such as family arguments. An EEG shows no seizure activity. The Indian psychiatrist who submitted the case diagnosed *hysteria* and noted that similar syndromes are very common in South

---

*Summarized with permission from the *Diagnostic and Statistical Manual of Mental Disorders Casebook*, Fourth Edition by R. L. Spitzer et al. (Eds.). Copyright © 1994 American Psychiatric Association, Washington D.C.

Asia, with 5 to 8 percent of all patients seen in the psychiatric unit of his general hospital receiving a diagnosis of hysteria.

In their comments on this case, the *DSM-IV Casebook* editors note that the seizures are not occurring in association with any culturally sanctioned behaviors and recur in response to stressful situations, with a normal EEG. Therefore, they diagnose *conversion disorder with seizures or convulsions*. However, they state that they "would not quarrel with a clinician who diagnosed a Dissociative Disorder Not Otherwise Specified" (Spitzer et al., 1994, p. 470).

Because the patient in this case was a middle-class urban woman in India, she did not experience her fits the same way as would a woman in rural India. Middle-class urban Indians are educated and modern. Therefore, their mental illnesses will differ from the mostly uneducated, premodern Indians in rural villages.

A dissociative response to emotional distress is extremely common in South Asia, as the Indian psychiatrist rightly points out. The woman in this case has this in common with her rural counterparts. The differences are in the subjective experience, explanatory models, indigenous diagnoses, and indigenous treatments. In the present case, the woman experienced her illness as a physical problem, which is the explanatory model of her family. This is consistent with their middle-class, modern cultural identity. The indigenous diagnosis in this case is *hysteria*, a diagnosis given to 5 to 8 percent of the patients in the psychiatric unit of this general hospital. Again, this is consistent with the cultural context. Dissociative symptoms are extremely common in this clinical setting, but they are understood within the concept of hysteria, a diagnostic category taken from late 19th and early 20th century western psychiatry.

These urban Indian patients have hysteria in a similar fashion to how patients in China have neurasthenia. Both of these diagnostic categories originated in 19th century western psychiatry but are no longer recognized mental disorders in their culture of origin. Yet neurasthenia still exists in China, and hysteria still exists in India. This is probably due to the colonial history of China and India. The indigenous elites adopted illness concepts from the colonizing culture that, after time and decolonization, became part of the indigenous culture. In the meantime, western psychiatry has evolved, abandoning the concepts of neurasthenia and hysteria. Nevertheless, these illnesses continue to be prominent in Chinese and Indian psychiatry, respectively, because they are meaningful concepts in those cultural contexts.

A woman in the villages of rural India with similar dissociative symptoms would almost invariably experience the problem as spirit possession. This would also be the explanatory model of her family. A local folk healer would undoubtedly diagnose spirit possession and identify the spirits responsible. Appropriate exorcism rituals would be performed, probably highlighting the need for the family members to treat the patient with greater respect or risk further supernatural attacks. Most likely, the outcome of such treatment would be good, with no further symptoms.

In the case from the *DSM-IV Casebook*, the woman was treated with family therapy in which her husband was instructed to protect his wife from her in-laws and to pay more attention to her in general. The patient had a remission of symptoms. In both this case and the hypothetical rural case, the individual's status in the family is altered, relieving her from significant further stress, resulting in remission of symptoms. However, although the results of the two treatments are similar, they are not interchangeable. Treating the modern, middle-class patient with exorcism, or treating the premodern, village woman with family therapy would not be consistent with the families' explanatory models or with the cultural schemas of the patients. Therefore, outcome is likely to be poor. Because the individuals have different cultural identities and explanatory models, they require different forms of culture-based symbolic healing. These differences highlight the need for treatment to be client-centered and culturally appropriate.

This case illustrates the dissociative nature of conversion disorder. Nevertheless, DSM-IV categorizes conversion disorder as a somatoform disorder. There appears to be very little scientific justification for this classification.

Pain Disorder

Pain disorder is characterized by the subjective experience of pain that does not have sufficient medical justification. DSM-IV specifies two subtypes. The first subtype is *pain disorder with psychological factors*. This subtype is characterized by pain that has little or no medical justification. The second subtype is *pain disorder with both psychological factors and a general medical condition*. This subtype is characterized by the confirmed presence of a medical condition causing pain, but with psychological factors playing a role in the onset, severity, exacerbation, or maintenance of the pain.

This disorder is another demonstration of the power of cognition to create subjective suffering. The example given in the *DSM-IV Casebook* (Spitzer et al., 1994, p. 300) is of a woman who experiences pain after discovering her husband's marital infidelity. She was also in a minor car accident, but all medical tests were negative.

In pain disorder, the experience of pain becomes the center of a person's cognitive processes. The experience of pain thereby becomes amplified. By focusing attention on pain or any other physical sensation, that sensation can be heightened, altered, or maintained in consciousness.

Persons with this disorder are also in danger of entering a downward spiral in which their pain leads to inactivity, which causes further pain, as well as social isolation, which leads to further psychological problems and social stress, which both lead to disability, loss of employment, and stress in family relations. However, this downward spiral does not necessarily start with pain. It can start with anxiety, leading to depressive symptoms, that can lead to inactivity, that can lead to pain, and so on. Because of this downward spiral process, persons with chronic pain disorder frequently have anxiety and mood disorders that precede, co-occur, or result from the pain disorder. Again, we see the close cognitive relationships between anxiety, somatoform, and mood disorders.

Although it is almost impossible to judge the severity of pain objectively, it is known that the expression of pain varies cross-culturally. For example, East Asians in general are taught self-restraint and may be reluctant to express pain. In contrast, Jewish patients in American hospitals are known for openly expressing pain (Galanti, 1991).

Also, the meaning of pain to an individual can vary dramatically. For example, a professional musician may view the pain of arthritis in her hands with great dread and emotional distress, thus heightening the experience of pain. This could be quite different from the experience of arthritis for someone who is not dependent on manual dexterity for his or her livelihood.

The clinical expression of pain is not dependent on any absolute scale of severity of pain but on the subjective experience of individuals and their culture-based idioms of distress. Therefore, clinicians should keep in mind cultural patterns in the expression of pain as well as the individual's personal meanings associated with pain when evaluating anyone for pain disorder.

Hypochondriasis

Hypochondriasis is characterized by persistent and unfounded fears of having a serious disease based on a misinterpretation of normal bodily functions or minor symptoms. Repeated negative medical examinations, laboratory tests, and reassurances from physicians do not alleviate the individual's fears. Patients will typically see many clinicians in an attempt to find the "right one" who can properly diagnose and treat their imagined serious diseases. As DSM-IV states, "Individuals with Hypochondriasis often have other mental disorders (particularly Anxiety and Depressive Disorders)" (APA, 1994, p. 464).

Hypochondriasis again illustrates the close relationship between anxiety and somatoform disorders. In the case of hypochondriasis, persons develop severe anxiety symptoms resulting from the false cognition that they have a serious medical condition. Thus, the central problem in hypochondriasis is actually anxiety.

Should hypochondriasis be classified as an anxiety or somatoform disorder? DSM-IV classifies it as a somatoform disorder, but it is obviously based in cognitive processes leading to anxiety reactions. This illustrates the rather arbitrary distinctions between these general diagnostic categories and the broad overlap of symptomatology among them.

In cross-cultural situations, particularly where the clinician has a different cultural background from the client, it is important to recognize and treat the client's construction of the illness experience. In all illness, but especially in mental illness, the disorder may be a symbolic construction of the individual consistent with the prevailing cultural schemas. If this illness is not treated through a process of symbolic healing, the client will not be satisfied, will not have his or her suffering relieved, and will continue to look for the "right" clinician—someone who can successfully treat the illness.

For example, attempting to treat a South Asian man with *dhat* syndrome by telling him it is something he has imagined, diagnosing major depression, and prescribing antidepressant medications is not likely to satisfy him. This treatment strategy completely ignores the client's cultural schemas and explanatory model and will result in the individual going to a different doctor to receive the treatment he wants (Singh, 1985).

Clinicians should explore the client's cognitive construction of the suffering, and ideally, the source of the distress should be treated through a process of symbolic healing in addition to any medications that might be appropriate. For individuals with premodern cultural schemas, this can be facilitated by the use of folk healers in collaboration with modern clinicians. For individuals with modern scientific explanatory models, treatment should proceed through the use of appropriate cognitive-behavioral psychotherapy in conjunction with appropriate biomedical treatment.

Body Dysmorphic Disorder

Body dysmorphic disorder is characterized by a persistent belief that the person's appearance is somehow seriously defective. Complaints commonly involve perceived defects in the face or head but can involve any body part. Persons with this disorder typically describe their emotional experience as " 'intensely painful,' 'tormenting,' or 'devastating' " (APA, 1994, p. 466).

These people are experiencing significant anxiety symptoms resulting from a cognitive process focusing on some aspect of their appearance. They become obsessed with their perceived physical defects and may perform compulsive "checking" behavior, repeatedly examining themselves in a mirror. This obsession may lead to self-imposed social isolation, loss of marital-romantic and employment opportunities, and depression.

The use of clothing, cosmetics, and, in industrialized societies, cosmetic surgery to hide or eliminate the perceived defect is common. In the United States, where cosmetic surgery is increasingly commonplace, some persons with this disorder may end up with numerous surgically altered body parts. In some cases, the cosmetic surgery may improve the person's body image. In other cases, the person may remain dissatisfied and emotionally distressed. Body dysmorphic disorder is frequently associated with major depressive disorder, delusional disorder, social phobia, and obsessive-compulsive disorder (APA, 1994).

According to DSM-IV, body dysmorphic disorder differs from normal concerns about appearance in that the preoccupation with appearance is associated with significant emotional distress and social or occupational impairment. Clinicians should realize, however, that persons who experience emotional distress regarding their appearance may have concerns based in real experiences of racial or ethnic discrimination and humiliation. These experiences can cause significant anxiety, depression, and preoccupation with appearance.

For example, in a racially and ethnically diverse society like the United States, persons from racial and ethnic minorities may experience very real instances of verbal or behavioral discrimination or harassment based on their appearance. If this occurs repeatedly, it is not irrational to have a preoccupation with one's appearance and, particularly, the "defects" as defined not by the person but by the dominant ethnic or racial group.

Consider how many Jewish American women born with a "Jewish nose" have had cosmetic surgery to fix their "defect." The notion of the defect in their appearance has been imposed upon them by the larger society. In cases such as this, the "defect" is not imagined but is a *cultural entity* constructed by the prevailing cultural schemas.

Obviously, standards of "normal" appearance and beauty differ by culture. In a multicultural society such as the United States, having an appearance consistent with the dominant ethnic standards of beauty may bring tangible rewards in the form of potential marital-romantic partners and employment opportunities. Therefore, persons who differ from this standard should not be considered pathological for wanting to alter their appearance. However, multiple major surgeries undertaken to alter racial or ethnic appearance in a type of "Michael Jackson syndrome" should probably be considered as an example of body dysmorphic disorder.

Body dysmorphic disorder again illustrates the arbitrariness of the distinctions between anxiety, somatoform, and mood disorders. Body dysmorphic disorder is characterized by prominent anxiety symptoms, is frequently associated with depressive symptoms, yet is classified as a somatoform disorder. The boundaries between these three general categories appear to be nothing more than cultural constructions.

 ## Suggested Clinical Guidelines

1. Assess the Cultural Identity of the Individual

Clinicians should be aware that somatoform disorders may manifest differently across cultures. For example, neurasthenia in China, hysteria in India, and body dysmorphic disorder in the United States are all disorders with symptomatology shaped by cultural schemas. Therefore, the cultural identity of every individual needs to be carefully assessed.

2. Assess the Cognitive Schemas Constructing Anxiety Regarding Bodily Concerns

Anxiety is closely linked to somatoform symptoms. For example, in body dysmorphic disorder, anxiety is experienced in relation to concerns about

personal appearance. In hypochondriasis, anxiety is experienced in relation to concerns about imagined diseases. The experience of anxiety is
related to cognitive patterns constructing ideas about personal competence, self-confidence, and an individual's ability to deal effectively with
events in his or her life. Therefore, the cognitive schemas of each person
regarding anxiety need to be assessed.

Also, these cognitive schemas can construct culture-bound syndromes.
Examples of culture-bound somatoform syndromes include neurasthenia
in China and hysteria in India. These are meaningful categories of illness for persons from these cultures. Because disordered emotions are
so closely bound up with cultural schemas, recognizing these culture-
bound syndromes and their indigenous meanings may be important in
treatment.

3. Assess the Anxiety Connected with Bodily Concerns within the Cultural and Psychosocial Environment

Clinicians need to see the client and his or her anxiety within the total
sociocultural context. The basis for the formation of anxiety-producing
cognitive schemas appears to be stressful life events. Similarly, the triggers
for subsequent activation of anxiety schemas also appear to be stressful
events. Most of these events are related to interpersonal relationships or
other types of stressful life events such as illness. Once these schemas are
activated, they can produce negative misinterpretations in cognition, thus
structuring a normal or less serious situation as something catastrophic,
life threatening, or seriously embarrassing. This appears to be the cognitive process occurring in many somatoform illnesses including body dysmorphic disorder and hypochondriasis.

Clinicians should also assess sources of social stress that might be promoting anxiety and dissociative somatic symptoms. For example, anxiety
could be prompting a dissociative response to stressful life events such as
family conflict. Somatic symptoms could also result from emotional or
physical trauma that occurred earlier in life (for example, loss of a parent,
sexual abuse, or war trauma in veterans and refugees).

4. Assess the Cultural Aspects of the Clinician-Client Relationship

Clinicians should critically assess their own concepts of somatoform disorders and reflexively determine how these concepts may be projected
onto the client. Human brain plasticity allows for various patterns of
symptomatology with culturally specific combinations of anxiety, somatoform, and mood symptoms. Therefore, clinicians should consider other
diagnostic categories such as PTSD, dissociative trance disorder, or syndromes from the individual's indigenous culture when making diagnoses
for individuals with prominent somatic symptoms.

5. *Negotiate Clinical Reality*

Persons with somatoform symptoms may not find western categories of illness to be meaningful. For example, diagnosing and treating a South Asian person who presents with a spirit possession illness with conversion disorder may result in a poor outcome. A negotiation between the individual and the clinician is necessary to arrive at a consensus of the problem and the appropriate treatment. This negotiation should take into account all of the above factors.

Chapter Twelve

Mood Disorders

The chapter on **mood disorders** in DSM-IV includes disorders that have depressive or manic symptoms as their primary feature. However, as discussed in Chapters 10 and 11, in real life clinical situations, it is extremely common to observe persons with anxiety, somatoform, and mood symptoms combined. There appear to be cognitive connections among all three types of symptoms, which would be expected if these symptoms are conceptualized as disorders of emotion rather than diseases. Emotions are essentially cognitive and are associated with meanings. The differential meanings of situations and events are expressed in differing symptoms of emotional distress.

The cognitive relationship between anxiety and depression appears to be especially strong. As was mentioned earlier, it is now clear that almost everyone who is depressed is also anxious. However, not everyone who is anxious is depressed (Barlow, 1988; DiNardo & Barlow, 1990; Sanderson et al., 1990). The key to the relationship between anxiety and depression as a chronic problem appears to be cognition. This kind of cognitive relationship will add the emotional symptoms of major depression onto those of anxiety.

This is especially likely in persons with a stigmatized *moral career* or self-identity (Chapter 3). A stigmatized person is more likely to view the cause of stressful events as internal, stable, and general. For example, in a hierarchical society, a person with a stigmatized moral career could have very low self-esteem and a hypersensitive nervous system resulting from emotionally traumatic experiences of discrimination, humiliation, exploitation, or rejection. In hierarchical societies, there can be very real conditions of economic exploitation, degradation, extreme poverty, illness, and political domination associated with the symptoms of anxiety, somatoform, and mood disorders (Kleinman, 1986; Kleinman & Kleinman, 1995).

Stigmatized persons in hierarchical societies can be of the "wrong" race, gender, religion, ethnic group, social class, sexual orientation, and so on. These *social* causes of emotional distress can be internalized in the form of cultural schemas. Cultural schemas can construct an experience of social distress as having an *internal* cause. For example, cultural schemas stigmatizing certain groups can be internalized to the point where individuals subjectively experience that they *really are* the "wrong" race, gender, religion, and so on. They experience the problem as being internal to themselves rather than as a sociocultural construction.

Moreover, because the problem may be something that is not easily changed, such as race, gender, religion, or social class, these persons view the problem as stable. On top of this, because their stigmatized status affects many areas of social interaction, they view their situation as being a general problem affecting most aspects of their lives. Stigmatized persons are more likely to develop a sense of hopelessness and helplessness and, therefore, depression in addition to anxiety.

In the United States, almost 70 percent of the persons with major depression and dysthymia are women (Nolen-Hoeksema, 1987; Weissman et al., 1991). These sex ratios are probably at least partially related to a social organization with male dominance wherein females are raised to be dependent and passive and males are raised to be independent and aggressive. Women in the United States are more likely to experience increased stress in the form of discrimination, poverty, and harassment. Similar kinds of situations are found in all hierarchical societies, however, the cognitive construction of the situation and the meanings and emotions associated with that construction will vary.

Mood Episodes

The diagnostic criteria for mood disorders in DSM-IV are based on the presence or absence of one or more of the following **mood episodes**: *major depressive episode, manic episode, mixed episode,* or *hypomanic episode.* Therefore, the mood disorders refer to emotional illness and distress characterized by depression, mania, or hypomania, or some combination of these.

Major depressive disorder is characterized by one or more major depressive episodes. *Dysthymic disorder* is characterized by at least two years of depressed mood without a major depressive episode. *Bipolar I disorder* is characterized by one or more manic or mixed episodes, which may be accompanied by major depressive episodes. *Bipolar II disorder* is characterized by one or more major depressive episodes accompanied by at least one hypomanic episode.

Major Depressive Episode

A **major depressive episode** is required for the diagnosis of *major depressive disorder* and *bipolar II disorder,* and may be present in *bipolar I disorder.* A major depressive episode is characterized by at least two weeks of depressed mood with at least four additional symptoms of depression. These additional symptoms can include changes in appetite, weight, sleep, or psychomotor activity as well as fatigue, feelings of worthlessness or guilt, difficulty thinking, and recurrent thoughts of suicide or suicide attempts. Some individuals may emphasize somatic complaints such as bodily aches and pains. There is almost always a loss of interest in pleasure. Some persons may also experience a loss of interest in sexual activity (APA, 1994).

As discussed earlier, there is a great overlap of symptoms among anxiety, somatoform, and mood disorders. According to DSM-IV:

> Individuals with a Major Depressive Episode frequently present with tearfulness, irritability, brooding, obsessive rumination, anxiety, phobias, excessive worry over physical health, and complaints of pain (e.g., headaches, or joint, abdominal, or other pains). During a Major Depressive Episode, some individuals have Panic Attacks that occur in a pattern that meets criteria for Panic Disorder. (APA, 1994, p. 323)

As can be seen from this list of symptoms associated with a major depressive episode, individuals frequently present with significant anxiety and somatoform symptoms combined with depressive symptoms. The notion that these constitute separate disorders comes from the disease-centered paradigm retained from DSM-III, which assumes that there are separate biological causes for depressive, anxiety, and somatoform symptoms, which therefore must be treated as separate disorders.

This is the notion of comorbidity. The client experiences a singular illness experience, but the clinician dissects that experience into separate disorders, providing treatment for each disorder. This leads to treatment using multiple medications, each designed to control a different type of symptom.

However, the same medications have also been found to be effective in treating supposedly different disorders. For example, monoamine oxidase inhibitors as well as serotonin reuptake inhibitors have been shown to be effective in the treatment of panic disorder, agoraphobia, bulimia, obsessive-compulsive disorder, premenstrual syndrome, substance abuse, attention-deficit disorder, and major depressive disorder. This argues against the notion that all these disorders are based in differing biological diseases. If the same medications are effective in treating so many supposedly separate diseases ranging across the boundaries of mood, anxiety, and somatoform disorders, then we have to wonder how, in fact, the drugs are working and what is being treated. Moreover, this brings into question the clinical utility of diagnosing these illnesses as separate disorders.

Cultural Differences

Sadness and other depressed emotions can have different meanings and can be based in different sociocultural contexts. In some societies, a depressive syndrome is not recognized as an illness at all, and the people have no concept for it in their set of cultural schemas (Furnham & Malik, 1994; Leighton et al., 1963; Marsella, 1979; Marsella et al., 1985; Resner & Hartog, 1970; Schieffelin, 1985; Tanaka-Matsumi & Marsella, 1976; Terminsen & Ryan, 1970; Tseng & Hsu, 1969). In these and other societies, somatic symptoms may be more meaningful and therefore primarily experienced by individuals and diagnosed by local clinicians (Crittenden et al., 1992; Ebert & Martus, 1994; Ulusahin, Basoglu, & Paykel, 1994). This does not mean that a western-trained clinician could not find dysphoric symptoms that would be labeled depression in the West. However, these depressive symptoms would be structured by nonwestern cultural schemas, and the subjective experience would be different from the concept of depressive disorder developed in the West (Bebbington, 1993; Schieffelin, 1985).

The question is how to conceptualize depression from a cross-cultural perspective. Is it one disorder with different cultural shapings? Or is it several different disorders categorized by a single name? Or is it possibly a culture-bound syndrome related to western culture? Most researchers have taken the disease-centered position that it is a single brain disease with cultural shapings.

However, as discussed earlier, anxiety seems to be the common ground out of which most cases of mood and somatoform symptoms develop. The connection between them appears to be cognition, and cognition is highly influenced by cultural schemas. Many studies have found a reduced frequency or absence of the typical western psychological components of depression in nonwestern societies. This is especially true for the emotions of guilt, existential despair, self-denigration, and suicidal ideation (Ebigbo, 1982; Kleinman, 1982; Ohara, 1973; Pfeiffer, 1968; Rao, 1973; Sethi & Gupta, 1970; Shinfuku et al., 1973; Teja & Narang, 1970). In these nonwestern societies, somatic symptoms, appear to be dominant.

Guilt, one emotion associated with major depression in western countries, is less likely to be found in nonwestern societies. For example, the World Health Organization Collaborative Study on Depression represents one of the most extensive cross-cultural comparisons of depressive symtomatology (Jablensky et al., 1981; Sartorius et al., 1980; Thornicroft & Sartorius, 1993; WHO, 1983). Depressed patients from five countries (Canada, India, Iran, Japan, and Switzerland) were interviewed concerning their subjective experience of depression. Guilt feelings were found in 68 percent of the Swiss sample, but only in 32 percent of the Iranian sample. Thus, highly significant cultural differences were found even though all the individuals from the various countries were highly educated and westernized. It may be that guilt is a more culturally salient concept in western societies. In contrast, somatization was present in 57 percent of the Iranian sample but in only 27 percent of the Canadian sample.

From a cross-cultural perspective, it appears that differing sets of cultural schemas are shaping cognition and the experience of anxiety or emotional distress. This is probably the reason depressive symptoms such as guilt seem to be more common in western societies and somatic symptoms appear to be more common in many nonwestern societies, whereas anxiety symptoms appear to be widespread in all parts of the world. It appears that anxiety can be either *somaticized* or *psychologized*. That is, anxiety resulting from stressful life events can further manifest in the form of somatic symptoms or depressive symptoms, or both. The differences will depend on the cultural schemas of the persons involved. Westerners tend to psychologize, whereas many nonwesterners tend to somaticize their anxiety and emotional distress.

As discussed in the case of neurasthenia in China (Chapter 11), mood disorders are relatively rare in China due to the use of physical symptoms as cultural idioms expressing emotional distress. Somatic symptoms have far more importance in the Chinese meaning system. Therefore, the individual primarily notices and reports somatic symptoms. The obvious factor is patterns of cognition. Cultural schemas can construct emotional distress as major depression in western patients and clinicians and as neurasthenia in Chinese patients and clinicians.

Even when a depressed mood is experienced, the depression itself may not have the same meaning in a nonwestern society. For example, generalized hopelessness and what westerners would call major depression can have a completely different meaning in South Asian Hindu and Buddhist cultural schemas. In this cultural context, depression is not an illness but an accomplishment, a spiritual insight about the true nature of the world (Castillo, 1991b; Obeyesekere, 1985).

Hindus and Buddhists believe that the point at which an individual realizes the utter hopelessness of life in the world is a sacred moment. It is at this point that the person is ready to renounce worldly life and take up the path of asceticism and meditation. Traditional forms of meditation even use thoughts of corpses or actual corpses as the focus of meditation to instill in the person the idea of the hopelessness of life in the world and to promote emotional detachment from all persons and physical objects, including one's own body. For these people, profound depression is a good thing, a profound insight into ultimate reality. In fact, Hindu yogis believe that anyone who is not depressed about life in the world is merely self-deluded (Castillo, 1991a).

Cross-cultural studies indicate that depression can have a different subjective experience, idioms of distress, culture-based diagnosis, treatment, and outcome. For example, Catherine Lutz (1985), in her study of Micronesians, found that their subjective experience of depression is somewhat different from that of westerners.

The Micronesians are highly sociocentric, and their depressive emotions are focused around loss of important personal relationships. For example, the Micronesian emotion *fago* is feeling sorrow and compassion for others' loss of loved ones. The emotion *lalomweiu* appears to be the closest thing to the western idea of major depression and is conceptualized as loneliness or sadness caused by a loss of a loved one. It is characterized by excessive thinking about the missed person, loss of appetite, loss of interest in pleasurable activities, and fatigue. Also, the emotion *liyemam* is conceptualized as longing for a missing loved one, but it also includes the nostalgia evoked by places, persons, and objects that are associated with the missing person. Similarly, the emotion *pak* is conceptualized as the homesickness experienced by travelers who are missing their loved ones back home. And finally, the Micronesians also have an emotion called *tang lanal* that is conceptualized as frustration, grief, and self-pity. *Tang lanal* is associated with being treated unfairly, being abused, or being excluded by the social group. In this highly sociocentric society, depressive emotions are all centered around the quality or loss of close personal relationships.

However, none of these emotions are conceptualized by the Micronesians as an illness. All of these emotions are considered to be normal states. If an individual has a longer than usual period of depressed mood following the loss of a personal relationship, the problem is defined by the Micronesians as that of an inadequate replacement of the lost relationship with another. Thus, the indigenous diagnosis of the problem is quite different from the western disease-centered paradigm. The treatment also differs from disease-centered psychiatry. In the United States, we would recommend psychotherapy and antidepressant medications. This is appropriate in our highly egocentric society where the illness is viewed as being internal to the individual and where individuals are responsible for their own well-being. However, in the sociocentric society of Micronesia, the appropriate treatment is to get the person focused on his or her remaining personal relationships or to replace the lost personal relationship with a new one. This reintegrates the sociocentric individual into the social life of the community and relieves the depressed mood.

However, the Micronesians have been undergoing dramatic social and cultural change in recent decades. This has resulted from cultural contact with the West and has been correlated with an explosion in the annual suicide rate. In the years between 1960 and 1980, there was an eightfold increase in suicide rates for 15- to 24-year-old males on the island of Truk. This rate soared to 200 per 100,000 between 1974 and 1983, compared to a rate of 13.3 per 100,000 for all 15- to 24-year-olds in the United States in 1989 (Desjarlais et al., 1995).

The disease-centered paradigm would tend to view the Truk suicides in terms of individual biological pathology. However, the client-centered approach would view each case within the sociocultural context. Micronesia has become increasingly westernized with the introduction of a wage labor system. Traditional religious and social organizations have disappeared, leaving individuals with fewer traditional means of dealing with depressed emotions. This breakdown of traditional sociocultural structures has resulted in alienation in the younger generation in a society that is highly sociocentric. In the local explanatory model, a completed suicide by a Micronesian teenager is viewed as an act expressing anger but also soliciting support, reconciliation, and nurturance (Desjarlais et al., 1995).

Although completed suicides are strongly correlated with psychopathology in western societies (usually substance abuse, depression, or psychosis), in nonwestern societies, completed suicides are less likely to be associated with a psychiatric problem. For example, official statistics for suicide in India highlight social stressors. The top known causes of suicide in India for 1990 were; "Dreadful disease" (leprosy and so forth), "Quarrel with in-laws," "Quarrel with spouse," "Love affairs," "Insanity," "Poverty," and "Dowry dispute." Only 3 percent of suicides were attributed to "insanity," the only category of mental disorder on the list (Desjarlais et al., 1995).

Several other studies indicate that disruptions in social relationships are a strong predictor for suicide attempts (Grossi & Violato, 1992; Hart & Williams, 1987; Hawton, 1986; Magne-lgvar, Ojehagen, & Traskman-Bendz, 1992; Shaffer et al., 1988). Social factors can play a very important role in suicidal acts in nonwestern societies. In many of these cultures, sadness arising from social stress is not seen as a psychiatric problem. For a clinician to view a suicide attempt strictly as the consequence of a psychiatric disorder may aggravate the situation. Psychiatric explanations are stigmatizing and may promote feelings of alienation, devaluation, and powerlessness (Kirmayer, 1994). Suicidal acts relate to a range of social, political, and psychological factors and should not automatically be viewed as a symptom of major depression.

Diagnosing a major depressive episode outside of western culture can be problematic. The belief that depression is a psychiatric disorder appears to be a western cultural construction (Lutz, 1985; Obeyesekere, 1985). This may be tied to the peculiarly western notions of Cartesian dualism and the modern individual's right to the "pursuit of happiness." First, the Cartesian mind-body split that permeates throughout western thought appears to make westerners very mind- and mood-oriented as opposed to body- or group-oriented (Manson, 1995). This probably goes back to the traditional importance Christians placed on the "condition of the soul" and the idea that sin exists in the mind or soul of the individual. This Christian emphasis probably also influenced the idea of Descartes' *cogito* "I think, therefore, I am" and resulted in a mind- and mood-centered emphasis in western culture. During the 18th century Enlightenment, this preoccupation with mind and mood became codified in the inalienable right to the individual's "pursuit of happiness." The pursuit of happiness has become the primary goal of western culture. "Are you happy?" is a question that people in the United States are constantly asking each other. In western culture, if persons are not happy, or at least pursuing happiness with some degree of initiative, it is presumed that something is wrong with them.

Moreover, the pursuit of happiness that is virtually required of all people in Anglo American culture for them to be considered normal is viewed as an *individual* right and responsibility. This is a product of Anglo American egocentrism (see Chapter 3). This egocentrism also structures the meaning of depression. As we know, not all cultures are egocentric. Most nonwestern cultures are sociocentric. This means that an individual's personal identity is centered in the social group rather than in the self. In sociocentric societies, individual wants and desires are subjugated to the benefit of the group. Individual *rights* have very little meaning in this cultural context; rather, individuals focus on personal *obligations* to the group. Self-sacrifice for the good of the group is usually seen as the greatest virtue and responsibility—not the pursuit of personal happiness. Thus, in a sociocentric context, sadness is not usually seen as a psychiatric disorder but as a disruption in social relations. Furthermore, sadness in this context need not be a personal event but could be a group experience. Persons might not say, "I feel depressed," but they may say, "Our life has lost meaning" (Manson & Good, 1992).

An example of this sociocentric experience is Theresa O'Nell's (1993) study of depression among Native Americans on the Flathead Reservation. For the tribe as a whole, their life has lost its traditional meaning. She found that depression could have positive connotations among Native Americans on the reservation because it signified maturity and recognition of the tremendous loss they experienced through domination by Anglo American society.

Depression is not necessarily an illness. The idea of depression as illness is probably related to the modern western idea that individuals should rightly pursue and achieve their own personal happiness. For example, in a study of depression in Britain, middle-aged immigrants from South Asia differed from middle-aged British and young South Asian immigrants in their beliefs about depression. The middle-aged immigrants scored significantly higher than did the middle-aged British or young immigrants on a measure of depression but did not consider themselves or others to be suffering from an illness. In contrast, the young South Asian immigrants appeared to have adopted a western definition of depression similar to that of the British (Furnham & Malik, 1994). The recognition of symptoms of depression as an illness appears to be mediated by cultural schemas that are internalized during an individual's formative years.

In contrast to the modern West, in premodern or sociocentric cultural contexts, the pursuit of personal happiness may be considered deviant or sinful. For example, in premodern Christianity, intense emotional suffering was considered beneficial for the soul, and the pursuit of personal pleasure was considered sinful. The symptoms of major depressive episodes need to be assessed within their sociocultural contexts.

Manic Episode

A **manic episode** is required for a diagnosis of *bipolar I disorder*. Manic episodes are characterized by an abnormally elevated, euphoric, or irritable mood lasting at least one week, or less if hospitalization is required. There must also be at least three additional manic symptoms to make the diagnosis according to DSM-IV. The manic symptoms include grandiosity, decreased need for sleep, pressure of speech, flight of ideas, distractibility, increased goal-directed activity, and excessive involvement in pleasurable activity with a high potential for painful consequences. The disturbance must cause social or occupational impairment and may involve hallucinations and grandiose delusions (APA, 1994). However, because cultural ideas determine what kind of behavior is considered inappropriately grandiose or excessively pleasure-seeking, it is very important that persons be judged by the norms of behavior in their own culture.

During a manic episode, persons may feel they have a special message from God (grandiose delusions) or may hear the voice of God (hallucinations). Typically, the persons do not believe there is anything wrong with them, nor do they believe they require any medical attention. If others try to control them, they may become irritable and angry. An example of a manic episode in the *DSM-IV Casebook* is the case titled "I Am Vishnu" (Spitzer et al., 1994, p. 137). This man was euphoric, had tremendous energy, and rapid speech. He had a religious message from the Hindu god Vishnu that he preached to everyone around him. If anyone tried to control him, he became loud and angry. During some of the manic episodes, he believed he was the god Vishnu.

There has been very little research on mania in premodern societies. This is probably because mania in premodern societies is understood and structured in culture-bound idioms of distress, in many cases as spirit possession syndromes. In these cases, a person in a state of mania, having lost his or her normal personality, would be considered possessed by a demon, a ghost, or another supernatural entity. A person who would be considered manic in the United States might not be considered ill at all but rather as being in a state of religious ecstasy. Hearing the voices of gods or other spiritual beings or having a special message or religious insight might be seen as normal in these premodern societies. The person could be revered as an inspired prophet or religious seer. This is especially true in societies undergoing serious social upheavals such as war, military occupation, famine, drought, epidemic disease, or rapid social change. People under these kinds of stressful conditions often need to attach some kind of religious meaning to their suffering, thus making them more accepting of a "prophet" or "seer."

Viewing manic episodes from this cross-cultural perspective, it appears that manic episodes could be temporary ecstatic trance states (Chapter 13). Some pathological trance states are characterized by persons turning from external reality and focusing their attention on something internal that allows relief or salvation from whatever is causing them suffering. This usually involves a transformation of their personal status from a typically painful social existence to an elevated, grandiose, happy, and powerful condition. This is accomplished by focusing attention away from their painful reality and toward a euphoric, pain-free, grandiose internal fantasy created in a temporary trance state.

This internal fantasy is usually so different from their external reality that it can be sustained only briefly (a few hours to a few days). The external reality intrudes on their fantasy, and they are brought back with a crash. Because their euphoria is gone, which is invariably interpreted in their own cultural idiom (for example, the gods have abandoned me), they become emotionally desolate, sinking to an extreme low (for example, Christian mysticism's "dark night of the soul").

The paradigm of disease-centered psychiatry interprets manic episodes as a neurochemical imbalance in the brain. However, as DSM-IV states, "No laboratory findings that are diagnostic of a Manic Episode have been identified" (APA, 1994, p. 330). I believe it makes more sense to look for the explanation of manic experiences in psychobiological rather than in purely biochemical terms.

Mixed Episode

A **mixed episode** is defined by DSM-IV as a period of at least one week in which diagnostic criteria are met for both a manic episode and a major depressive episode. In a mixed episode, the individual experiences rapidly alternating depressed, euphoric, and irritable moods. There is also typically agitation, insomnia, appetite disturbance, hallucinations and delusions, and suicidal thinking (APA, 1994).

Hypomanic Episode

DSM-IV defines a **hypomanic episode** as a period of at least four days in which the person experiences an abnormal and persistently elevated, expansive, or irritable mood. There must also be at least three additional symptoms, such as nondelusional grandiosity, decreased need for sleep, pressure of speech, flight of ideas, distractibility, increased involvement in goal-directed activities, and excessive involvement in pleasurable activities that have high potential for painful consequences. It must also be clear that the state is a distinct change from the person's usual personality (APA, 1994).

In contrast to a manic episode, a hypomanic episode does not cause social or occupational impairment, and there are no hallucinations or delusions. In fact, there may even be a marked increase in efficiency, accomplishments, or creativity (APA, 1994). A hypomanic state is characterized by euphoria without the functional impairment of a manic episode.

One or more hypomanic episodes are required for a diagnosis of *bipolar II disorder*, which is characterized by recurrent major depressive episodes with accompanying hypomanic episodes. Hypomanic episodes are also required for a diagnosis of *cyclothymic disorder*, which is characterized by numerous hypomanic periods interspersed with periods of depressive symptoms that are not severe enough to meet the criteria for a major depressive episode.

In both bipolar II disorder and cyclothymic disorder, hypomania is associated with depression. Hypomania not associated with depression should not be considered a symptom of mental illness (APA, 1994). In some cultural contexts, permanent hypomania can be a highly valued emotional state, for example, in Hindu yogis.

Depression and Hypomania in Hindu Yogis

Hindu yogis use their meditative trances to achieve a permanent hypomanic state. In the Hindu cultural context, this is experienced as "spiritual bliss" and can be generally described as a euphoric state sought after and actively cultivated by the yogis as part of their religious discipline.

The yogi's hypomania is usually associated with an earlier experience of major depression that is eliminated by the deliberately induced hypomania. If the yogi is successful in his meditation practice, the depression does not return and is permanently replaced by a hypomanic, euphoric state. Thus, yogic practice can be seen as a type of religious healing, and it provides some insight into the experiences of hypomania in mood disorder patients.

Yogis use meditative trance and the resulting hypomanic state to escape problems in life as well as the symptoms of depression and anxiety. They create a hypomanic state through the use of trance to escape from emotional suffering, thus enabling the individual yogi to achieve a higher level of happiness, self-esteem, and social and occupational functioning. The success of the meditative trance in overcoming generalized anxiety and depression by inducing a long-term hypomanic state suggests that this type of emotional experience should not be considered psychopathology. Hypomania should not be considered abnormal in itself, and it might even be viewed as a highly desirable state (Castillo, 1991b).

Depressive Disorders

The depressive disorders consist of *major depressive disorder* and *dysthymic disorder*. These disorders are characterized primarily by sadness or low mood without the presence of mania or hypomania. Sometimes clients are diagnosed with both major depressive disorder and dysthymic disorder. These persons are said to have *double depression*. This is usually associated with more severe pschopathology, longer course, and more frequent relapse (Barlow & Durand, 1995).

Major Depressive Disorder

Major depressive disorder is characterized by one or more major depressive episodes without a history of manic, mixed, or hypomanic episodes. If a major depressive episode is accompanied by a manic, mixed, or hypomanic episode, the appropriate diagnosis would be *bipolar I* or *bipolar II* disorder. In addition, the major depressive episodes must not be better accounted for by a psychotic disorder (APA, 1994).

Four of the more significant findings in the cross-cultural study of major depressive disorder are that the incidence of major depression increases with age, the total prevalence varies by culture and is increasing over time, and the age for people developing major depression is becoming increasingly younger across cultures (Cross-National Collaborative Group, 1992). Some of these data from the United States, Puerto Rico, Taiwan, and Lebanon are depicted in Figure 12.1.

The data in Figure 12.1 indicate that only 1 percent of Americans born before 1905 developed major depression by age 75. In contrast, 6 percent of those born after 1955 had developed major depression by age 24, with even higher rates expected as these people grow older. Similar trends are found cross-culturally. These data from various societies are strong evidence for sociocultural factors in the etiology of major depression. If this illness was based exclusively in a genetically inherited brain disease, the great increases in prevalence and the rapidly decreasing age of onset observed in societies around the world during the 20th century would not be found.

These data indicate that rapid changes in the sociocultural environment are detrimentally affecting the mental health of persons in many societies. Modernization brings with it increasing individualism, the breakdown of traditional social support systems such as family and religious structures, and injects the influence of market-driven values into all aspects of life (see Chapter 3). It is most likely that these macro-level factors in the sociocultural environment are largely responsible for the significant changes in age of onset and prevalence of major depression over the last several decades.

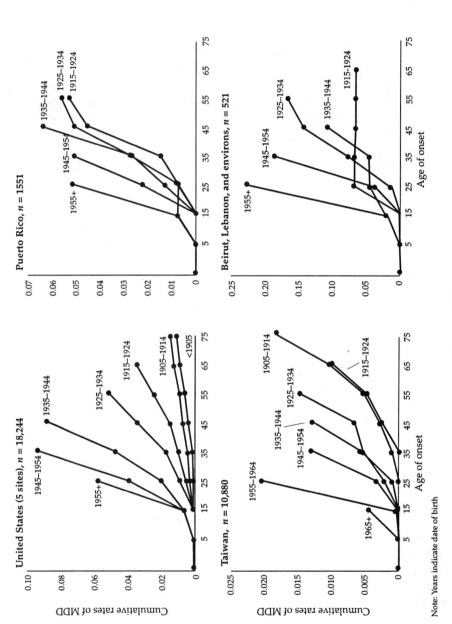

Figure 12.1

Cross-Cultural Data on the Age of Onset and Cumulative Rates of Major Depressive Disorder

Note: Years indicate date of birth

SOURCE: Adapted from "The Changing Rate of Major Depression: Cross-National Comparisons," by the Cross-National Collaborative Group, 1992, *Journal of the American Medical Association,* 268, 3098–3105. Copyright © 1992 by the American Medical Association. Used by permission. Adaptation appears in *Abnormal Psychology,* by D. H. Barlow and V. Mark Durand, p. 247, Brooks/Cole Publishing, 1995.

Suicide is common in persons with major depressive disorder and is also increasing across cultures (Cross-National Collaborative Group, 1992). As many as 15 percent of persons in western societies with this disorder kill themselves. This high rate of mortality is probably due to the cognitive processes of the individuals wherein they structure their situations as hopeless and themselves as helpless. These people may cognize that they have nothing to live for and that their lives have become meaningless. This is especially true for persons over the age of 55, who may feel that their lives are no longer worth living. This suicide differential in older people can be related to chronic or serious physical health problems in many cases. However, the cultural construction of the meaning of old age is probably also a factor. Some societies treat the elderly with great respect and reverence. Other societies view old age as a time of infirmity, incompetence, and impotence and treat older people with little respect. This sociocultural construction of old age can have a profound effect on a person's self-esteem and chances for suicide.

Stress and the nervous system. Episodes of major depressive disorder often follow stressful life events such as death of a loved one or some other loss of an important personal relationship. A precipitating stressful event appears to be an important factor in the first or second depressive episode of this disorder but plays less of a role in triggering later depressive episodes. DSM-IV estimates that 50 to 60 percent of individuals experiencing a single major depressive episode will experience a second episode. Also, individuals who have had two episodes have a 70 percent chance of having a third, and those experiencing three have a 90 percent chance of a fourth. This is suggestive of an acquired hypersensitive nervous system. That is, emotional trauma alters the nervous system, making it more sensitive to subsequent stress. The resulting experiences of anxiety and depression alter neural networks, making the person more likely to experience further anxiety and depression. It is possible that recurring depressive episodes are structured in what Lex (1979, following Gellhorn, 1969) calls alternative *tunings* of the central nervous system.

Tuning refers to a long-term change in the central nervous system resulting from repeated experience of a particular condition of the nervous system that makes the individual more susceptible to reestablishment of that same condition (Gellhorn, 1969; Lex, 1979; Winkelman, 1986). This is analogous to the concept of *kindling*. Robert Post (1990) has theorized that recurrent mood disorders may result from a *kindling effect* in the brain related to traumatic stress. In this theory, an original traumatic life event, such as an important loss or personal assault, could have a long-term effect on neural pathways in the brain, making the individual more sensitive to further stressful events. The person then has a lower response threshold for stress. As a result, less stressful events are capable of triggering a stress response, and more events are experienced as stressful. The result is a heightened sensitivity to stress and its effects on the brain. As the brain experiences more stress, there will be a continuously diminishing threshold for stimuli to trigger a stress response. Eventually, the stress response may not require any stimulus at all and simply take an independent course as the underlying neural structures become stronger with repeated experience. This could explain why a person who has had more depressive episodes is more likely to have another one, and why that subsequent episode may be linked to only minor or nonexistent stressful events.

This acquired hypersensitivity is referred to as a kindling effect because of its similarity to experiments done on the brains of animals in which electricity was applied to the brains, causing seizures. With repeated application of electricity and consequent uncontrolled neuronal firing, less electricity was required to cause a seizure. After enough periodic application of electricity the animals began to have spontaneous seizures without application of electricity. Also, seizures occurred with increasing rapidity and with greater parts of the brain being affected. The initial applications of electricity are the "kindling," which gets the seizure process going. Kindling affects neural pathways by strengthening the connections between neurons, making the neurons more likely to fire an action potential (send a bioelectrical message to neighboring neurons). Thus, in reaction to stress, the brain can become changed anatomically on the micro-level, particularly in dendritic branching and in the strength of neurotransmitter properties and stress hormone systems.

As mentioned in Chapter 9, girls who had been subjected to legally documented sexual abuse by a family member had increased levels of stress hormones and exaggerated stress hormone responses to stimulation. These stress hormone abnormalities were correlated with high levels of depression in the girls, even years after the episodes of abuse. Thus, a personal history of traumatic or stressful experiences affecting the microbiology of the brain should be considered as possible etiological elements in the development of mood disorders.

Differential diagnosis. Major depressive disorder can also occur with accompanying psychotic symptoms. In this case, the symptoms need to be distinguished from those of *schizoaffective disorder* (Chapter 14) and *bipolar I disorder.* In **major depresssive disorder with psychotic features,** hallucinations and delusions only occur within the context of major depressive episodes. In contrast, in schizoaffective disorder, psychotic symptoms occur outside of depressive episodes. However, hallucinations and delusions can also occur during manic episodes. If these psychotic type symptoms occur only within the context of manic episodes, then bipolar I disorder is the appropriate diagnosis. Also, if the psychotic symptoms occur outside of manic or depressive episodes but are accompanied by prominent mood symptoms, then schizoaffective disorder is the appropriate diagnosis (APA, 1994). However, the fact that mood and psychotic symptoms can overlap to such an extent suggests the appropriateness of viewing symptoms as occurring along a spectrum of mental illnesses.

Dysthymic Disorder

The essential feature of **dysthymic disorder** is a chronically depressed mood lasting for at least two years. Dysthymic disorder differs from major depressive disorder in that a depressed mood must be present most of the time, nearly every day for two weeks, for a diagnosis of major depressive disorder. In contrast, dysthymic disorder is characterized by a depressed mood more days than not, over at least two years. Thus, dysthymic disorder is a chronic illness with generally less severe depressive symptoms. If symptoms are severe enough for diagnosis of a major depressive episode, then the appropriate diagnosis is major depressive disorder, chronic (APA, 1994).

However, as discussed earlier, a depressed mood can mean different things in different cultural contexts. Moreover, in many situations, very real conditions of political domination, economic exploitation, discrimination, extreme poverty, and emotional trauma can rightly justify a chronically depressed mood. To view these people as suffering from a brain disease may be medicalizing and internalizing what are actually social problems and, in effect, blaming the victims.

Bipolar Disorders

The bipolar disorders include *bipolar I disorder, bipolar II disorder,* and *cyclothymic disorder.* All of these disorders are associated with elevated or irritable mood. Persons with these disorders can go from the heights of euphoria to the profound depths of despair.

Bipolar I Disorder

The essential feature of **bipolar I disorder** is the presence of one or more manic or mixed episodes. Frequently, individuals will also have had one or more major depressive episodes. If bipolar I disorder is not accompanied by major depressive symptoms, it may be difficult to distinguish the symptoms of bipolar I disorder from those of schizophrenia (Chapter 14). Grandiose and persecutory delusions, irritability, agitation, and hallucinations are common in both disorders. And there is some evidence that clinicians in the United States misdiagnose bipolar I disorder as schizophrenia when treating African Americans and younger individuals (APA, 1994). However, psychotic-type symptoms in bipolar I disorder occur only during manic episodes. If psychotic symptoms are occurring outside of mood episodes, then a diagnosis of a psychotic disorder (for example, schizophreniform disorder, schizophrenia, schizoaffective disorder) is probably justified.

However, because cultural schemas determine what kind of behavior is considered inappropriately grandiose, or excessively pleasure-seeking, it is very important that persons be judged by the norms of behavior in their own culture. What is judged to be mania in a western culture may be culturally appropriate religious ecstasy in another society. It is important not to pathologize cultural differences. Because there has been very little research on mania in premodern societies, it is best to consult with persons knowledgeable about a premodern individual's indigenous behavioral norms before making this diagnosis. Many societies have culturally normal practices of possession by ancestral spirits during times of illness, healing ceremonies, or rituals of divination. Agitation, grandiosity, hallucinations, and other manifestations that might be considered symptoms of mania can occur during these times. These should not be confused with the symptoms of pathological manic episodes.

Bipolar II Disorder

The key features of **bipolar II disorder** are the presence of at least one major depressive episode accompanied by at least one hypomanic episode. The symptoms must cause significant distress or impairment in social or occupational functioning (APA, 1994).

Hypomania in itself need not cause social or occupational impairment. Indeed, there may even be an increase in efficiency, accomplishments, or creativity. Hypomania is considered pathological only when it is associated with major depression and causes significant distress or dysfunction. In some cultural contexts, hypomania is a highly valued emotional state associated with religious experience, aesthetic pleasure, artistic expression, creativity, or peak experiences during athletic endeavors.

Mihaly Csikszentmihalyi (1988) has coined the term *flow experience* for episodes that appear to be very similar to episodes of nonpathological hypomania. It is notable that these flow experiences occur during periods of highly focused attention. This is consistent with the hypomania observed in Hindu yogis resulting from meditative trance, which is based on highly focused attention.

Cyclothymic Disorder

The key features of **cyclothymic disorder** are numerous hypomanic symptoms alternating with numerous depressive symptoms occurring over a two-year period. In addition, the depressive symptoms must not be severe enough to warrant a diagnosis of a major depressive episode. If a major depressive episode is present, then the appropriate diagnosis would be bipolar II disorder.

The same cautions concerning dysthymic disorder and bipolar II disorder apply to cyclothymic disorder when diagnosing someone from a nonwestern culture. Emotional states considered normal and justifiable differ by sociocultural context. It is important to assess an individual's cultural identity and social context and to understand the cultural norms of behavior and emotion appropriate for that person. Only then can a judgment be made that observed emotions are abnormal or dysfunctional. The person's emotions need to be placed within cultural schemas to be fully understood. This is true for all of the mood disorders.

Suggested Clinical Guidelines

1. Assess the Cultural Identity of the Individual

Clinicians should be aware that mood symptoms may manifest differently and have different meanings across cultures. For example, Hindu yogis use their meditative trances to achieve a permanent hypomanic state. In the Hindu cultural context, this is experienced as "spiritual bliss" and can be described generally as a euphoric state sought after and actively cultivated by the yogis as part of their religious discipline. Therefore, the cultural identity of every individual needs to be carefully assessed.

2. Assess the Cognitive Schemas Constructing Mood Symptoms

Anxiety is closely linked to depressive symptoms. The experience of anxiety is related to cognitive patterns constructing ideas about personal competence, self-confidence, and an individual's ability to deal effectively with events in his or her life. If the problem is viewed as internal, stable, and general, depressive symptoms may be added onto anxiety. Therefore, the cognitive schemas of each client regarding connections between anxiety and depression need to be assessed.

Also, cultural schemas can construct culture-bound manifestations of depression. For example, depressive emotions are not conceptualized by Micronesians as an illness. If an individual has a longer than usual period of depressed mood following the loss of a personal relationship, the problem is defined by the Micronesians as that of an inadequate replacement of the lost relationship with another. Therefore, cultural schemas regarding mood symptoms need to be assessed.

3. Assess the Mood Symptoms within the Cultural and Psychosocial Environment

Clinicians need to see the client and his or her anxiety within the total sociocultural context. The basis for the formation of anxiety-producing cognitive schemas appears to be stressful life events. Similarly, the triggers for the subsequent activation of anxiety schemas also appear to be stressful events. Most of these events are related to interpersonal relationships or other types of stressful life events such as physical illness. Clinicians should assess sources of social stress that might be promoting anxiety and mood symptoms. For example, mood symptoms could be resulting from current stressful situations related to dominance hierarchies or emotional or physical trauma that occurred earlier in life (loss of a parent, sexual abuse, or war trauma in veterans and refugees).

4. *Assess the Cultural Aspects of the Clinician-Client Relationship*

Clinicians should critically assess their own concepts of mood disorders and reflexively determine how these concepts may be projected onto the client. Clinicians should avoid the western tendency to psychologize human suffering and view syndromes with mixed mood, anxiety, and somatoform symptoms as major depressive disorder. Human brain plasticity allows for various patterns of symptomatology with culturally specific combinations of mood, anxiety, and somatoform symptoms. Therefore, clinicians should consider other diagnostic categories from the individual's indigenous culture when making diagnoses with prominent mood, anxiety, and somatoform symptoms.

5. *Negotiate Clinical Reality*

Clients with mood symptoms may not find western categories of illness to be meaningful. For example, diagnosing and treating a South Asian client with major depression who presents with *dhat* syndrome may result in a poor outcome. A negotiation between the client and the clinician is necessary to arrive at a consensus of the problem and the appropriate treatment. This negotiation should take into account all of the above factors.

Chapter Thirteen

Dissociative Disorders

Dissociation

Dissociation is characterized by a loss of the integration of faculties or functions that are normally integrated in consciousness. This lack of integration or division in consciousness can affect memory, sensory modalities, motor functions, cognitive functions, and personal identity or sense of self. Cultural schemas affect the subjective experience and expression of dissociation. There are particular differences between modern and premodern societies.

Dissociation is based in trance behavior, either spontaneous or voluntary. Trance and dissociation in themselves are not pathological. Institutionalized forms of trance have been identified in 437 societies, 89 percent of the societies for which adequate ethnographic data are available (Bourguignon, 1972). These forms of trance are voluntarily practiced within the context of cultural institutions such as religious and healing rituals. These are nonpathological forms of trance and dissociation that allow people in these societies to access the spiritual forces existing in their culture. They serve many valuable functions in maintaining social structures, actualizing religious systems, providing healing and comfort to the sick and grieving, and in providing meaning in life (Castillo, 1990, 1991a, b, 1995; Ludwig, 1983).

As with most behavior, practice improves performance, and many people in premodern cultures become highly skilled at dissociative experience. These are the shamans, mystics, and religious leaders found in premodern societies all over the world. Generally speaking, these people are not mentally ill, even though they may be permanently dissociated, hear voices of spirits, and believe they have supernatural powers. These can be normal experiences within their cultural contexts (Bourguignon, 1994; Price-Williams & Hughes, 1994).

Trance as Adaptation

Trance is essentially a narrowed focus of attention such that what is outside of attention is lost to consciousness (Beere, 1995; Bliss, 1986; Castillo, 1985,

---

Box 13.1

Major Functions of Trance

1. Automatization of certain behaviors
2. Efficiency and economy of effort
3. Resolution of irreconcilable conflicts
4. Escape from the constraints of reality
5. Isolation of catastrophic experiences
6. Cathartic discharge of certain feelings
7. Submersion of ego into group identity

SOURCE: Based on Ludwig, 1983.

1991a, b, 1995). Ludwig (1983) argued that trance is essentially an adaptation with great individual and species survival value. He identified seven major functions that trance serves to facilitate. These are summarized in Box 13.1. According to Ludwig:

> While there is reason to suspect that the classical dissociative states may reflect a unitary, underlying process, the wide variety of manifestations appears due to the molding influence of individual psychological needs and conflicts, social forces and cultural factors. Given an individual's capacity for dissociation, these molding influences will determine whether the outward manifestations will be that of hypnosis, mediumistic trance, arctic hysteria, fugue or multiple personality. (1983, p. 95)

Trance allows for persons to escape from the constraints of reality. It is well known that hypnotized subjects can experience both positive and negative hallucinations. Positive hallucinations are the experience of something that is not there, for example, seeing someone sitting in a chair when the chair is actually empty. Negative hallucinations are not experiencing something that is there, for example, not seeing someone sitting in a chair who is in plain view (see Sparks, 1962). Ludwig (1983) particularly noted the use of trance in ritual and religion as successful adaptations and as escapes from reality. For example, trance allows persons to transcend the subjective limitations of time and space and permits direct personal experience with supernatural beings. This can be highly adaptive in times of personal or social stress, providing opportunities for healing, maintaining group cohesion, and so on.

However, when considering trance as an escape from the constraints of reality, the question of mental illness also arises. Raymond Prince (1979–80) argues that psychoses are more or less unsuccessful attempts at adaptation. He states:

> Looked at in this way, we can see that the psychoses presenting themselves at the psychiatrist's office are merely the tip of the iceberg as it were, they are only a small proportion of the most unsuccessful endogenous attempts at resolving life problems. . . . Occasionally the psychosis may result in a rebirth into a socially acceptable belief system so that the individual is able to take up

his life within the mainstream of the community at a level even superior to his earlier adjustment. With this last type, the psychosis is already merging with the more widely distributed forms of religious experience. (pp. 179–180)

Prince's point, that if the psychotic's psychological rebirth is into a socially acceptable religious system he will not be considered mentally ill, has also been made by Obeyesekere (1981). Thus, some psychotic experiences may be unsuccessful attempts at adaptation to life problems through the behavior of profound trance.

Trance as Focused Attention

In normal consciousness, attention can be placed on four major areas of experience: the external environment, the body, memory, and imagination. In normal consciousness, attention is placed in a combination of all four of these areas. However, by learning how to precisely direct and focus attention, the contents of consciousness can be controlled, creating opportunities for unusual subjective experiences. This is the essential mechanism of trance and related phenomena (Castillo, 1985, 1991a, b, 1994a, b, 1995).

Classic Yoga Meditation

Yoga meditation is an ancient religious practice from India that is based on narrowly focused attention. Although yoga meditation is a culture-specific religious practice, an analysis of the psychological techniques of yoga meditation provides insight into the mental processes associated with directing and focusing attention and how those mental processes construct the elements of consciousness and, thus, subjective reality.

The essential point in the practice of classical yoga meditation is that attention determines the contents of consciousness. By controlling attention, the contents of consciousness can be controlled. Yoga meditation is simply the practice of intense focusing of attention (Castillo, 1985, 1991b). This is especially relevant in consideration of trance and possession syndromes; it is possible to subjectively become a god, a demon, or another supernatural entity through intensive focusing of attention on that mental object. A similar process probably takes place spontaneously in the formation of possession trance syndromes throughout the world.

The goal of yoga meditation is primarily the loss of self in subjective awareness, that is, the loss of the body, senses, memory, and all else that goes to make up the normal experience of the self. It is this loss of self that yogis interpret as loss of the personal self and the liberation of the spiritual self (*atman*), which the primary yogic text, the *Yoga-Sutra* (YS:2:20), describes as "pure perception" or "pure attention" (*drishi-matra*). In this state, the yogi loses awareness of the external environment, his or her physical body, and his or her "personal" consciousness. In effect, the yogi is in a dissociative catatonic state.

The yogi is still awake but has no awareness of anything other than his or her own pure consciousness (Castillo, 1985).

Meditative Dissociation

The *Yoga-Sutra* describes a fundamental duality in consciousness, the personal self (*jiva*) and the spiritual self (*atman*). According to the yogic cultural schemas, these two parts of consciousness are two separate entities that exist simultaneously but are normally fused in everyday awareness such that they are subjectively experienced as a single self. The goal of yoga meditation is to separate these two selves in the subjective awareness of the individual. By accomplishing this, the yogi becomes a dual personality or a person with divided consciousness (Castillo, 1991b).

According to the yogic cultural schemas, all persons do in fact have this dual nature, but most are simply not aware of it. It is necessary to separate out the spiritual self from its assimilation by the personal self for the individual to realize this dual nature in subjective experience. This separation is described as "liberation" (*moksha*), that is, liberation from the boundaries, limitations, pains, and suffering of the personal self.

It is experienced as liberation from suffering because the spiritual self, the newly isolated consciousness, is as if one step removed from the everyday events of life. The events of the world are subjectively experienced as occurring to and around the personal self. In contrast, the spiritual self only *witnesses* the events that happen to the personal self but does not participate in them. By identifying the "true self" as the witnessing consciousness, the yogi experiences the events of the world as if they were happening to someone else—"like a movie." The yogi is in effect "liberated" from the personal self and from ordinary life in the world.

This experience of dissociation (divided consciousness) has occurred because the yogi has learned how to control and divide attention. He or she has learned how to continuously focus attention on an object of choice, regardless of what else is happening in the environment. Thus, the yogi is able to continuously keep enough attention inwardly on the spiritual self to isolate this "witness" from the personal self, while simultaneously giving enough attention to the personal self to be engaged in everyday activities. The yogi has mastered the ability to divide attention and thereby divide consciousness. The yogi has deliberately divided his or her consciousness, and if the yogi is successful, this dissociation will be permanent (Castillo, 1991b).

Altering Subjective Reality

Divided consciousness is not the only cognitive alteration that occurs through precisely controlling attention. Through this process, the yogi also acquires the ability to significantly alter subjective reality. This is because attention can be focused on anything, including imagination and memory. For the accomplished yogi, anything that can be remembered can be reexperienced with lifelike realism through the ability to precisely control the focus of attention. Likewise, anything that can be imagined can be experienced with lifelike realism through this same mechanism of focusing out external reality and concentrating attention only on the contents of imagination or fantasy.

Thus, subjective reality can be altered, and the yogi can live in a deliberately created religious fantasy. The religious visions and other meaningful events of the yogi's spiritual life are essentially of this nature. These are religious hallucinations structured according to cultural schemas that in a psychiatric context might be mistaken for psychotic hallucinations and delusions. Indeed, most psychiatric symptoms—from mood symptoms such as depression and mania to anxiety symptoms such as obsessions and panic attacks to the psychotic symptoms of autistic withdrawal, hallucinations, and delusions—can be produced from intensely focusing attention, usually on some internal content of consciousness.

Hypnosis

Those familiar with the techniques of **hypnosis** will immediately recognize the similarities between yogic meditative techniques and those of hypnosis. Research on hypnotic trance also leads to the conclusion that hypnosis is based on the process of focusing attention. There have been many experimental studies of hypnosis, as well as summaries and reviews (for example, Bliss, 1986; Burrows & Dennerstein, 1980; Frankel & Zamansky, 1978; Fromm & Shor, 1979; Hilgard, 1971, 1977; Kihlstrom, 1979). Spiegel and Spiegel (1980) reviewed information about trance induction techniques. They concluded that hypnotic trance is not so much induced as it is evoked in subjects who already have the ability to enter a trance. Likewise, working with hypnotized psychiatric patients, Bliss (1986) concluded that well-known hypnotic phenomena such as hypersuggestibility, vivid images, realistic memories, realistic fantasies or hallucinations, and reduction in reality testing (trance logic) result from an intensification of inward attention—what he calls a "virtually unwavering concentration of attention" that "creates a realistic illusion or delusion" (p. 107).

Induction techniques among hypnotists have varied, but the most common have been such things as having subjects focus attention on sleep or relaxation or focus on a sense of lightness or heaviness, having subjects listen to repetitive or monotonous speech, and having subjects fix their vision on a particular object (Spiegel & Spiegel 1980). Other behaviors to induce trance observed by anthropologists in the field include auditory driving, fasting, social isolation, sensory deprivation, meditation, and extensive motor behavior (Winkelman, 1986). It has been suggested that all the above-mentioned methods of trance induction have a common element of focused attention (Castillo, 1995).

The Dissociative Disorders

The **dissociative disorders** in DSM-IV are: *dissociative amnesia, dissociative fugue, dissociative identity disorder* (formerly multiple personality disorder), *depersonalization disorder*, and *dissociative disorder not otherwise specified* with a subtype most relevant to premodern societies of *dissociative trance disorder.*

Dissociative Amnesia

Dissociative amnesia is characterized by an inability to recall important information that is too extensive to be explained by ordinary forgetfulness. This information is usually of a traumatic or stressful nature. Dissociative amnesia is typically a spontaneous trance response to some sort of emotional trauma or extreme stress (APA, 1994).

Cross-culturally, dissociative amnesia is quite common. However, it is usually indigenously seen as a symptom of some larger culture-bound syndrome, such as *amok* in Malaysia or spirit possession in South Asia. It is not usually perceived as a separate disorder in itself, as it is in DSM-IV. This is probably because the symptom of amnesia will always be seen in the context of a local explanatory model such as sorcery or attack by spirits. Although the symptom of dissociative amnesia is very common cross-culturally, dissociative amnesia as a separate disorder is found mostly in modern societies.

Dissociative Fugue

Dissociative fugue is characterized by sudden, unexpected travel away from home or one's customary place of work. It is accompanied by an inability to recall one's past and confusion about personal identity. In some cases, a person moves away from home and assumes a new identity with no memory of his or her former self. Fugues can last from a few hours to several months. Once the individual returns to the prefugue state, it is typical that he or she has no memory for the events that occurred during the fugue. During the fugue, a separate stream of consciousness takes over control of the body and personal identity. Individuals act as if they are a different person or are unsure of their identity. In the typical case seen in modern societies, a person in a fugue condition does not act in an overtly unusual fashion indicating psychopathology. Thus, they do not attract attention and appear to be normal unless questioned carefully about their personal identity or personal history (APA, 1994).

Cross-culturally, taking on a new identity for brief periods of time and leaving one's home is a common type of dissociative behavior. However, in many premodern societies, this type of behavior can be structured in a culture-bound trance syndrome that differs from the usual modern case.

For example, *pibloktoq* among the native Arctic peoples, or *grisi siknis* among the Miskito Indians of Central America are characterized by trance, amnesia, and leaving home. However, in these syndromes the individuals act wildly, running aimlessly and sometimes assaulting others or harming themselves (Dennis, 1985; Gussow, 1985). Moreover, these syndromes are indigenously seen as spirit attack (*grisi siknis*), or no illness at all (*pibloktoq*). They have their own typical subjective experience, idioms of distress, indigenous diagnosis, treatments, and outcomes. Thus, it is probably inappropriate to classify these "running" syndromes as dissociative fugue. In general, dissociative-type syndromes resembling dissociative fugue are common in many cultures, but they may have their own culture-bound presentations. *Dissociative trance disorder* should be considered as an alternative diagnosis for premodern syndromes.

Dissociative Identity Disorder

Dissociative identity disorder (DID) is characterized by the presence of two or more distinct identities or personality states that recurrently take control of the individual's behavior. This is accompanied by dissociative amnesia (APA, 1994). Dissociative identity disorder is an illness caused by spontaneous trance reactions to traumatic stress, usually occurring in childhood.

Dissociative identity disorder has shown a particularly strong overlap of symptoms with schizophrenia (Fink & Golinkoff, 1990; Kluft, 1987; Ross & Anderson, 1988; Ross & Gahan, 1988; Ross, Heber, Norton, & Anderson, 1989; Steinberg et al., 1994). In one study that the authors describe as "potentially paradigm-threatening," DID patients were found to have more of Kurt Schneider's *first-rank* symptoms of schizophrenia than schizophrenics have (Ross & Heber et al., 1989). In another study, DID patients did not differ statistically in the number of first-rank symptoms from patients diagnosed with schizophrenia (Fink & Golinkoff, 1990). Schneider's first-rank symptoms form a major portion of the diagnostic criteria for schizophrenia in DSM-IV (see Chapter 14).

Mental patients with dissociative pathology have frequently been misdiagnosed with schizophrenia. This is hardly surprising as they report such a high number of first-rank symptoms. This misdiagnosis usually occurs on the basis of *auditory hallucinations* (primarily voices), *made feelings* (feelings that appear to have been imposed by some external entity), *made impulses* (impulses to carry out an action imposed by an outside entity), and *made volitional acts* (acts experienced as being under the control of an external agency). In the DID patient, these are the voices and influences of the alternate personalities, usually arguing or commenting on the patient's activities or interfering with the actions and emotions of the patient's primary personality.

The studies of first-rank symptoms in dissociative patients have yet to make a significant impact on official psychiatric nosology. DSM-IV still largely ignores the presence of first-rank symptoms in DID. This is because schizophrenia is considered to be a psychotic disorder, and DID is classified as a dissociative disorder. Psychosis and dissociation are presumed to be two separate processes in the disease-centered paradigm, one biological and the other psychological, and any similarities in symptomatology have been largely ignored.

However, the current expansion of the disease-centered paradigm to include social and cultural factors is also likely to reincorporate psychological factors such as dissociative processes as the basis for many psychotic symptoms.

In general, dissociative identity disorder appears to be primarily a modern syndrome. In premodern societies, individuals tend to dissociate into gods, ghosts, demons, and other supernatural entities. This is in contrast to the mostly human personalities of dissociative identity disorder observed in modern societies. This makes for important differences in subjective experience, idioms of distress, indigenous diagnoses, treatments, and outcomes.

Depersonalization Disorder

Depersonalization disorder is characterized by a persistent or recurrent feeling of being detached from one's mental processes or body accompanied by clinically significant emotional distress or impairment. Typically, individuals feel as if they are separate from their bodies, thinking processes, or emotions. Individuals may feel a lack of control of their actions, speech, or thoughts, as if someone or something else was in control. Individuals usually experience a feeling of passively observing their actions or thoughts, as if someone else was performing them (much like the Hindu yogis divided consciousness described previously). Reality testing remains intact (APA, 1994).

Depersonalization is a very common experience all over the world, both in psychiatric and normal populations. Depersonalization in itself is not an indication of psychopathology. However, depersonalization is a symptom common to many types of mental disorders, including all of the dissociative disorders, schizophrenia and other psychotic disorders, posttraumatic stress disorder, panic disorder, and various phobias. Depersonalization is probably a spontaneous trance response to extreme stress or anxiety.

Cross-culturally, depersonalization is a very common experience. However, depersonalization disorder is found primarily in modern societies. In premodern societies, depersonalization is typically experienced and diagnosed in various culture-bound syndromes related to spirit attack or spirit possession. Alternatively, depersonalization forms the basis of many religious experiences deliberately induced through trance practices, for example, yogic meditation. These voluntary forms of depersonalization should not be confused with depersonalization disorder.

Cross-Cultural Differences

Like mental illnesses in Bali (Suryani & Jensen, 1993; Thong, 1993; see Chapter 4), mental illnesses in many premodern cultures are predominantly of a dissociative type (Levine & Gaw, 1995). Dissociative disorders are generally based in spontaneous trance reactions to repeated or extreme stress in the environment. This etiology appears to be a universal psychological process with much cultural variation. Dissociation can be viewed as an adaptation and survival behavior that can operate in situations of life-threatening danger or other instances of extreme or repeated stressful situations in the environment. Examples of this are victims of accidents, soldiers in intense combat situations, victims of physical or sexual abuse, severe emotional abuse, or cases of sudden loss of a parent or sibling. These trances, if prolonged or repeated, can result in the creation of separate streams of consciousness, which in turn can develop into separate conscious entities with their own sense of identity, behavior, memories, and desires. These dissociative experiences are likely to be structured in culture-bound syndromes.

Saxena and Prasad (1989) reviewed the cases of 62 psychiatric outpatients in India whose symptoms fit the diagnostic criteria for dissociative disorders in DSM-III (APA, 1980), which are essentially the same in DSM-IV. Based on these criteria, 56 cases (90.3 percent) fell into the *atypical dissociative disorder* category. The psychocultural differences between Anglo America and India are illustrated by the fact that only 10 percent of the Indian cases fit the DSM diagnostic criteria for dissociative disorders. This is probably because of the difference in cultural schemas. Because India has an extensive cultural repertoire of supernatural beings (gods, ghosts, demons, and so forth) that are accepted as real entities by the vast majority of the population, the experiences of dissociation in India typically center around spirit possession. This is very different from the modern cultural schemas and results in differences in subjective experience, idioms of distress, indigenous diagnoses, treatments, and outcomes (see Chapter 11).

Teja, Khanna, and Subrahmanyam (1970) summarized the typical case of pathological spirit possession seen by Indian psychiatrists:

> The usual clinical picture of our cases of spirit possession is as follows. A young female, usually in the third decade of her life, presents with features of unusual behaviour. Suddenly she has started having periods of altered consciousness when she behaves as if she is a different person possessed by the spirit of a dead relative or a neighbour or a god. (p. 73)

Cases of spirit possession in South Asia following this general pattern with associated symptoms of seizure-type episodes and auditory and visual hallucinations similar to those observed in Anglo American DID patients have been widely reported by anthropologists and psychiatrists (for example, Berreman, 1963; Claus, 1979, 1983; Freed & Freed, 1964, 1990; Harper, 1963; McDaniel, 1989; Obeyesekere, 1970, 1977, 1981; Teja, Khanna, & Subrahmanyam, 1970; Varma, Srivastava, & Sahay, 1970).

Judging from the available ethnographic and psychiatric literature on spirit possession in South Asia, two factors determine how a particular episode of possession will be perceived in the South Asian cultural context. First, is the possessing entity a supernatural being (for example, ghost, demon, or god)? If the possessing entity is *not* a supernatural being but rather a *human* personality, the episode will be perceived as mental illness, and psychiatric treatment will be sought. In the case of possession by human personalities, the patient will in all likelihood be diagnosed with dissociative identity disorder (DID). However, this is an exceedingly rare occurrence in India (Adityanjee, Raju, & Khandelwal, 1989). It is far more likely that in cases of possession the secondary consciousness will manifest as a supernatural being structured by the South Asian cultural schemas (that is, a ghost, demon, or god). This phenomenon is viewed in the general population as a case of supernatural intervention, not mental illness.

Furthermore, supernatural intervention can be viewed either as a spiritual illness, in the case of an evil spirit taking possession of the person, or as a spiritual gift, in the case of possession by a god or goddess. In the case of benevolent possession by a god or goddess, treatment is usually not sought as this is not seen as a problem. And in the case of a malevolent possession by a demon or other evil spirit, treatment is sought, usually from a traditional folk healer, sometimes from a psychiatrist, or both (Amarasingham, 1980; Babb, 1975; Berreman, 1963; Carstairs & Kapur, 1976; Claus, 1979; Freed & Freed, 1964; Harper, 1963; Kakar, 1982; McDaniel, 1989; Obeyesekere, 1970, 1977, 1981; Varma et al., 1970; Wadley, 1976).

Because the possibility of ghosts and demons possessing a person is part of the cultural schemas of South Asia, this illness is immediately recognized in that cultural context as spirit possession. Both the subjective experience and the outward behavior of dissociation are constructed in the forms of the ghosts of a known dead person and demons. Likewise, shamans called in to treat pathological spirit possession validate this diagnosis.

Dissociative Trance Disorder

As a result of observed cross-cultural differences in dissociative disorders, a new diagnostic category called **dissociative trance disorder (DTD)** was proposed for DSM-IV to accommodate premodern dissociative syndromes. The diagnostic criteria for dissociative trance disorder are presented in Box 13.2.

The diagnostic criteria for dissociative trance disorder highlight the distinction between *trance* and *possession trance* made by Bourguignon (1973). This new diagnostic category has a dual structure, subsuming pathological dissociation of two overall types—trance syndromes and possession trance syndromes.

Trance, defined in DSM-IV as a temporary marked alteration of consciousness based on a narrowing of awareness, can manifest in a wide variety of symptoms and syndromes across cultures. Many of these culture-bound syndromes would qualify for a diagnosis of dissociative trance disorder (DTD).

For example, *ataques de nervios,* a Latin American trance syndrome, is characterized by trembling, heart palpitations, heat in the chest rising to the head, faintness and seizure-like episodes, and sometimes hallucinations. It is indigenously attributed to acute anxiety-provoking experiences, particularly related to family conflict, fear, and grief (Garrison, 1977; Guarnaccia, De La

---

Box 13.2

Diagnostic Criteria for Dissociative Trance Disorder

A. Either (1) or (2)
  (1) trance, i.e., temporary marked alteration in the state of consciousness or loss of customary sense of personal identity without replacement by an alternate identity, associated with at least one of the following:
    (a) narrowing of awareness of immediate surroundings, or unusually narrow and selective focusing on environmental stimuli;
    (b) stereotyped behaviors or movements that are experienced as being beyond one's control.
  (2) possession trance, a single or episodic alteration in the state of consciousness characterized by the replacement of customary personal identity by a new identity. This is attributed to the influence of a spirit, power, deity, or other person, as evidenced by one (or more) of the following:
    (a) stereotyped and culturally determined behaviors that are experienced as being controlled by the possessing agent;
    (b) full or partial amnesia for the event.
B. The trance or possession trance state is not accepted as a normal part of a collective cultural ritual or religious practice.
C. The trance or possession state causes clinically significant distress or impairment in social, occupational, or other important areas of functioning.
D. The trance or possession trance state does not occur exclusively during the course of a Psychotic Disorder (including Mood Disorder With Psychotic Features and Brief Psychotic Disorder) or Dissociative Identity Disorder and is not due to the direct physiological effects of a substance or a general medical condition.

SOURCE: Reprinted with permission from the *Diagnostic and Statistical Manual of Mental Disorders*, Fourth Edition, pp. 728–729. Copyright © 1994 American Psychiatric Association, Washington D.C.

Cancela, & Carrillo, 1989; Harwood, 1987; Lewis-Fernández, 1992, 1994; Spitzer et al., 1994).

Latah (which is usually thought of as a Malay-Indonesian syndrome, although similar syndromes are found elsewhere) is a trance syndrome characterized by an extreme response to startling stimuli. Attention becomes highly focused, and the person exhibits anxiety and trance-related behavior such as violent body movements, assumption of defensive postures, striking out, throwing or dropping held objects, mimicking observed movements, and sometimes extreme suggestibility or obedience (Geertz, 1968; Kenny, 1978; Simons, 1985).

Pibloktoq, also sometimes called *arctic hysteria*, is a Polar Eskimo trance syndrome. It is characterized by short-lived episodes (5 minutes to 1 hour) of extreme anxiety responses in which the person will tear off his or her clothes and go running into the snow or across the ice, screaming incoherently. There is amnesia for the episodes. It is indigenously attributed to sudden fright, intense fear, and imagined or actual personal abuse (Foulks, 1985; Gussow, 1985; Parker, 1962).

Amok (see Chapter 4), a Southeast Asian trance syndrome, is characterized by a short-lived (a few minutes to several hours) sudden outburst of unrestrained violence, usually of a homicidal nature, preceded by a period of anxious brooding and ending with exhaustion. There is amnesia for the episodes. It is indigenously attributed to interpersonal conflict, intolerably embarrassing or shameful situations, loss of honor, and personal abuse (Burton-Bradley, 1968; Carr, 1985; Carr & Tan, 1976).

Trance syndromes can be distinguished from **possession trance** syndromes, which are characterized by replacement of the primary personality by a new identity, usually a ghost, demon, or deity. The behavior of persons with possession trance syndrome is usually more complex, with a more complete alternate personality whose behavior follows preestablished cultural patterns. Thus, persons will behave as a particular spirit or demon from the indigenous cultural repertoire, in most cases speaking and performing actions as the spirit or demon, sometimes over lengthy periods of time.

However, there is no clear boundary between these two variations, and some syndromes fall in between. For example, spirit possession among female factory workers in Malaysia is characterized by extreme anxiety episodes in which the victims are screaming, crying, and flailing about uncontrollably, with apparently great strength. This is attributed to spirit possession, but the behavior exhibited is relatively simple compared to the elaborated behavioral characteristics of spirits that possess persons in India (Castillo, 1994b; Lewis-Fernández, 1994).

The same thing can be said of *amok*. Amok is also attributed to spirit possession, but the behavior displayed is relatively simple in contrast to the fully developed supernatural personalities that carry on long negotiations with the families and healers of possessed persons in India, and who may remain in the victim for years (Lewis-Fernández, 1992).

Given the wide variety of possible symptoms, diagnosticians should not consider DTD to be a single disorder but a variety of disorders based on a common dissociative process with various types of cultural structuring. The symptoms of trance and possession trance syndromes that would be appropriately diagnosed as DTD can vary widely in different cultures. For example, North American Charismatic Christians can be possessed by satanic demons, while Taiwanese are possessed by local gods and ghosts. In the multi-ethnic population of India, symptoms vary by religion, region, and caste.

What is clear is that populations form cultural repertoires of dissociative experience. A cultural repertoire of possessing agents may include stable characteristics of gender, personality, behavior, and social (supernatural or natural) status. Therefore, the cultural complexity of pathological trance syndromes should be noted in diagnosis and treatment of premodern forms of dissociative disorders.

Cross-Cultural Case Studies

The *DSM-IV Casebook** (Spitzer et al., 1994) includes typical cases of dissociative trance disorder. The case titled "Cultural Healing" (p. 471) is a relatively simple case of DTD. In this New Zealand case, a 26-year-old female Polynesian bus driver was hospitalized in a trance state when she became highly anxious after a traffic accident in which she hit, but did not injure, a pedestrian while driving her bus. Her family decided to take her to a Polynesian folk healer who diagnosed possession by the ghost of her ex-father-in-law who was mad at her for deserting his son. The folk healer gave her a traditional healing massage as treatment, and within a few hours her symptoms disappeared.

A more serious and complex case is the one titled "Evil Spirits and Funeral Cars" (Spitzer et al., 1994, p. 440). In this case, a 28-year-old woman, an immigrant from Surinam, South America, now living in the Netherlands, was referred to a psychiatrist because she was hallucinating, seeing funeral cars everywhere, and was suicidal. She also experienced brief (5 minute) trance states during which her eyes rolled back in her head, she no longer understood Dutch, and for which she had amnesia.

She was highly agitated because she believed she was being attacked by evil spirits. One of the evil spirits wanted to rape her. When she went to sleep, the spirit would lie on top of her and try to have sex with her. He pressed on her and sucked her nipples. She went to two Surinamese folk healers living in Amsterdam who performed an appropriate symbolic healing ritual, and her symptoms disappeared.

However, three months after the birth of an unexpected baby, she had pains over her body and was too fatigued to have sex with her husband. She also began to hallucinate the voices of spirits threatening her and her children, and she began to see funeral cars following her and was contemplating suicide. Her brother took her to another folk healer who diagnosed neglect of ancestral spirits. The healing ritual consisted of an herb bath, tearing a white sheet in two over her body, smashing an egg on her head, and removing the mucus from her mouth. The symbolic healing improved her condition, but she still heard the voices of the evil spirits as well as the voices of her dead ancestors who were trying to help her.

This case is similar to other cases of young women in premodern societies in many parts of the world. These women do not have memories of childhood sexual abuse. Neither has any therapist or healer suggested childhood abuse, nor is child abuse a salient concept in these cultures. However, the sexual nature of the hallucinations makes it possible that these women are reexperiencing dissociated memories of childhood sexual abuse, but they are structuring

---

*Case studies cited on pp. 232–233 are summarized with permission from the *Diagnostic and Statistical Manual of Mental Disorders Casebook*, Fourth Edition by R. L. Spitzer et al. (Eds.). Copyright © 1994 American Psychiatric Association, Washington, D.C.

the memories in the form of spirit attack or possession, which is consistent with their cultural schemas. The spirit possession could also be an idiom of distress related to fear of further pregnancies and the desire to avoid sex.

In their comments on this case, the *DSM-IV Casebook* editors state that the patient has "bizarre psychotic symptoms," yet they conclude their discussion with a diagnosis of *dissociative trance disorder*. This illustrates the possible confusion between dissociative and psychotic symptoms.

It is important to note that the psychiatrist who treated the patient in this case treated her with culturally appropriate psychotherapy, and after one month she was much improved. She then went back to Surinam and was treated by a folk healer and was completely cured. This illustrates the effectiveness of culturally appropriate symbolic healing in the treatment of dissociative disorders.

Another case in the *DSM-IV Casebook* is relevant to this discussion. That is the case titled "Leader of the Movement" (Spitzer et al., 1994, p. 419). This case involves a 35-year-old woman, the leader of a large religious movement in West Africa that is based on spirit possession. Significantly, the woman in this case is not a patient. She has no illness as defined by herself or by her culture. She is not engaged in any help-seeking behavior, but is herself a healer. She is interviewed by a psychiatrist who is interested in the movement.

Years earlier, one month after the death of her only child, she had an extreme dissociative reaction in which she suddenly began running aimlessly and shaking wildly. She stated that at this time "God opened her mouth" and made her announce that He was calling her. She currently hears the voice of God, the voices of dead ancestors, and sees visions "like a cinema." God speaks through her and gives religious instructions through her to her numerous followers. God also gave her the power to heal and showed her where to find healing roots. If she resists the religious visions, she feels very ill. If she accepts them, she feels fine.

In their comments on this case, the *DSM-IV Casebook* editors conclude that because she has auditory, visual, tactile, and olfactory hallucinations, she has "symptoms that would be considered psychotic if they were experienced by someone from a society that did not share the beliefs of her culture" (Spitzer et al., 1994, p. 421). Indeed, what would have happened to this woman if she had been hallucinating as an immigrant in the United States?

In the modern cultural context, she probably would have been diagnosed with a psychotic disorder, most likely schizophrenia, due to the long-term presence of her hallucinations. However, because this case occurred in West Africa, in a society that accepts this woman's hallucinations as spiritual gifts, Spitzer et al. (1994) are reluctant to diagnose her with a psychotic disorder. Therefore, their conclusion is to view her hallucinations as trance states and to give her a diagnosis of *dissociative disorder not otherwise specified*.

This diagnosis illustrates the possible confusion between dissociative and psychotic hallucinations, but it also highlights the ethnocentric biases of those making the diagnosis. Although the editors are trying to be culturally sensitive in not giving this woman a diagnosis of a psychotic disorder, they simply cannot accept the idea that this woman is hearing voices as well as having other types of hallucinations without suffering from a psychotic or dissociative disorder.

However, her dissociative experiences are accepted as a normal part of a collective religious practice, and they do not cause any distress or impairment in social or occupational functioning. In fact, the hallucinations form the very basis of her social and occupational functioning. This woman is typical of shamans and many traditional folk healers in premodern societies. These healers have had what we would call mental disorders, but they have managed to become healed by gaining some control over their hallucinations and using them for a culturally acceptable purpose. These people serve an important function in their communities by contacting the gods and other spiritual forces that are meaningful to the lives of the people. Shamans and spiritual leaders should not be considered mentally ill because of their ability to act as mediums for spirits. Dissociation without distress or impairment should not be considered psychopathology. Therefore, the correct diagnosis in this case should be *no mental disorder.*

Dissociative Disorder Not Otherwise Specified

Dissociative disorder not otherwise specified is a residual category for syndromes that do not meet the full diagnostic criteria of the other dissociative disorders. The above cross-cultural cases illustrate the importance of dissociative trance disorder as an alternative diagnostic category appropriate to premodern societies. Unfortunately, DTD was not included as an independent diagnostic category in DSM-IV but was included as a variation of dissociative disorder not otherwise specified (DDNOS).

However, the placement of DTD within the category of DDNOS is probably inappropriate. Because a large portion of the world's population live in premodern societies that generally do not experience dissociation in the same way as modern psychiatric patients do, DTD should have been an independent diagnostic category. Placing DTD within the category of DDNOS implies that the modern patterns of dissociation are the normative ones and the premodern syndromes are somehow "atypical." This is ethnocentric because the major DSM-IV dissociative disorders are generally limited to modern cultures and the modernized segments of premodern societies. This represents only part of the world's population. Syndromes appropriate for a diagnosis of DTD are found in both premodern societies and those segments of modern societies holding a premodern worldview.

Satanic Ritual Abuse and False Memory Syndrome

One syndrome in the United States that is probably appropriate for a diagnosis of dissociative trance disorder is **satanic ritual abuse syndrome.** Beginning in the mid-1980s, literally hundreds of people in North America began to report dissociated memories of childhood abuse during satanic rituals that occurred years earlier (Greaves, 1992). Some clinicians practicing in the area of dissociative disorders accepted these accounts of satanic abuse at face value, validating their clients' abuse experiences. This validation of experiences led to accusations by clients of satanic and sexual abuse directed at family members in many cases. This prompted creation of the False Memory Syndrome Foundation, an organization of persons and families accused of child abuse, usually by their adult children. Their position is that incompetent clinicians have suggested or inappropriately validated claims of child abuse in therapy sessions, thus causing harm to the parents and the families of clients.

Judging from the evidence, it is likely that some clinicians have inappropriately suggested child abuse, or perhaps even satanic abuse, to individuals as possible etiological factors in their illnesses. It also is possible that persons experiencing dissociative or other types of psychiatric symptoms may be influenced by numerous accounts in the media of childhood abuse causing adult mental illness. For example, an emotionally distressed person influenced by the cultural schemas of the "wounded inner child" or "satanic cults" may focus attention on ideas of childhood abuse in imagination and subjectively experience those events as actually having happened. The ability to focus attention on imagination can create lifelike realism in subjective experience, creating "memories" of abuse.

From a cross-cultural perspective, memories of satanic ritual abuse either occurring spontaneously or uncovered in therapy appear to be the North American version of dissociative disorders structured within the symbols of premodern cultural schemas. Belief in Satan and satanism are part of the American Charismatic Christian subculture and provide meaningful symbolic structures for the expression of emotional distress. Thus, dissociated memories of satanic ritual abuse or attack by satanic demons should probably be seen as idioms of distress relevant to a particular set of cultural schemas in American society and diagnosed as dissociative trance disorder or dissociative disorder not otherwise specified.

The power of cultural schemas to create subjective reality needs to be recognized in the creation of illness experience and in explanatory models for illness. The current epidemic of psychiatric patients who have experienced childhood sexual and satanic abuse in the United States may be a manifestation of an American culture-bound syndrome related to the extensive publicity regarding child abuse in recent years.

However, the etiological connection between dissociation and child abuse cannot be dismissed. A direct connection between documented child abuse and dissociative identity disorder has been observed in abused children (Coons, 1994; Hornstein, 1993; Hornstein & Tyson, 1991; Peterson, 1991; Putnam, 1991). Also, there is considerable evidence that DID observed in adults had its initial onset in childhood, long before the individuals were ever exposed to hypnotherapy or psychological concepts regarding child abuse and mental illness (Bliss, 1988; Coons, Bowman, & Milstein, 1988). Thus, there is a documentable connection between childhood abuse and dissociative disorders.

Not all dissociative symptoms are attributable to child abuse, however. Dissociation in psychiatric patients is used as a spontaneous coping or adaptive mechanism to escape anxiety and other associated emotional distress. The sources of stress and trauma associated with dissociative disorders are numerous. Child abuse is only one source of traumatic stress that may have a detrimental effect on mental health. At no time should clinicians ever suggest to an individual that he or she was abused as a child unless this can be independently documented by medical or court records or eyewitness testimony. Nor should dissociated memories of childhood abuse uncovered in therapy be accepted at face value unless they can be reliably corroborated.

Dissociative Hallucinations and Delusions

Dissociative hallucinations and delusions are psychotic-type symptoms based on the mental processes of trance. Dissociative trance disorder has been included as a disorder requiring further study in the appendix of DSM-IV (APA, 1994, p. 727). Criteria for the disorder are provided for further research. Most appropriately, in the section on differential diagnosis, DSM-IV states that the symptoms of DTD can be confused with the hallucinations and delusions of schizophrenia and other psychotic disorders. This point is very important because the hallucinations of trance and possession syndromes can easily be interpreted by clinicians as psychotic symptoms, as is seen in the *DSM-IV Casebook.*

Because there is as yet no definitive understanding of the etiology of schizophrenia, combined with the poor prognosis for clients who receive this diagnosis, it is probably in the best interest of clients who show symptoms of trance or possession trance to avoid the diagnosis of schizophrenia or the other psychotic disorders. In these individuals, DTD (or another culturally consistent dissociative disorder) should be the preferred diagnosis, and treatment appropriate to this diagnosis should be attempted before making a diagnosis of a psychotic disorder. Trance and possession syndromes generally have a better prognosis than do psychotic disorders, especially when treated with culturally appropriate psychotherapy or symbolic healing.

DSM-IV also makes the statement that the hallucinations and delusions of DTD can be distinguished from the hallucinations and delusions of schizophrenia by the **cultural congruency** of the trance, its briefer duration, and the absence of the characteristic symptoms of the psychotic disorders (APA, 1994, p. 728). However, as is seen in the *DSM-IV Casebook* (Spitzer et al., 1994), distinguishing **dissociative hallucinations and delusions** from psychotic hallucinations and delusions is easier said than done. Even the most experienced diagnosticians (like the *DSM-IV Casebook* editors) can have difficulty. This is because the content of hallucinations will always be based on a person's cultural schemas, whatever those are.

Cultural congruency is a problematic concept when talking about hallucinations and delusions. Culturally congruent hallucinations can mean two things: First, that the hallucinations are *typical* of the culture, indicating limited cultural congruency; second, that the hallucinations are considered to be *true and real* in that cultural context, indicating high cultural congruency. This is problematic because hallucinations and delusions are by definition *false perceptions* and *untrue beliefs*. If a hallucination is highly congruent with the culture, it may be accepted as being real or true. Thus, persons can hear voices and yet have their voices accepted as "the gospel" if the hallucinated voices say the right things.

However, if the hallucinated voices are slightly off, not as congruent with the culture, they are not likely to be accepted. The person may then be seen as mentally ill or demonically possessed, depending on the cultural context. In the case of demonic possession, the voices are *typical* of the culture but not as culturally congruent as the voices of a *saint* or *prophet*, whose voices are accepted as the word of God.

Probably the best way to understand the notion of cultural congruency in hallucinations and delusions is to examine how well they fit the cultural norms of beliefs and behavior. For example, the "Leader of the Movement" heard voices but was not considered mentally ill. Her voices were highly congruent with the culture and not considered to be hallucinations by her followers but the actual voice of God.

If mental pathology is determined by what is culturally incongruent, this presents a problem with immigrants, minority subcultures, religious heretics, and political dissidents. The prevailing culture, simply by use of its political power, can define certain experiences or beliefs as mental pathology. For example, in the "Crimes Against the State" case in the *DSM-IV Casebook* (Spitzer et al., 1994, p. 449), a political dissident in the former USSR was diagnosed with schizophrenia.

It is possible that with the new diagnostic criteria for dissociative trance disorder in DSM-IV, persons with culturally typical spirit possession who previously would have been diagnosed and treated for schizophrenia will now be diagnosed with DTD and treated with culturally appropriate psychotherapy or symbolic healing. This would certainly be an improvement in clinical practice.

However, the question still remains about those persons who hallucinate in a typically modern fashion. After all, the content of hallucinations and delusions is determined by cultural schemas. DSM-IV is willing to grant the idea that premodern individuals, hallucinating in a way that is typical of their culture (for example, possessed by demons and ghosts), may be experiencing dissociative trance disorder and not schizophrenia. However, those persons who hallucinate in typically modern ways (for example, hearing the voices of space aliens) are likely to be diagnosed with schizophrenia. This situation is probably based on a modern cultural construction of clinical reality. It may be that *schizophrenia* is the name given for the culturally typical way of hallucinating for people from modern societies and modernized segments of premodern societies.

Dissociative Trance Disorder versus Dissociative Identity Disorder

DSM-IV also distinguishes dissociative trance disorder (DTD) from dissociative identity disorder (DID), noting that there are culture-based differences in the type of alternates in DTD and DID. Dissociative identity disorder patients typically have living human personalities as opposed to the ghosts, demons, and deities of DTD patients. However, it should also be noted that DID patients typically have numerous alternates, whereas DTD patients usually have only two or three. Also, it should be noted that DID typically has a chronic course with gradual response to treatment, whereas DTD can be of brief duration and highly responsive to culturally appropriate folk treatment (for example, exorcism or other symbolic healing).

DSM-IV also notes that the prevalence of DTD decreases in modern societies. The prevalence is also likely to be higher in premodern societies and in some ethnic minorities in modern societies (for example, Puerto Ricans in the United States and Charismatic Christians). This is consistent with the symptomatic differences between DID and DTD. Persons with cultural schemas based on a modern meaning system will not get possessed by ghosts, demons, or deities. However, they may dissociate into separate human personalities. Just the opposite is true in premodern societies.

This highlights the problem of precedence of diagnosis, which exists in the diagnostic criteria for DTD in DSM-IV. In criterion "D" for DTD, DSM-IV states that "The trance or possession trance state does not occur exclusively during the course of a Psychotic Disorder (including Mood Disorder With Psychotic Features and Brief Psychotic Disorder) or Dissociative Identity Disorder" (APA, 1994, p. 729). Thus, the criteria for DTD indicate that if an individual's symptoms fit the diagnostic criteria for schizophrenia or DID, then schizophrenia or DID should be the preferred diagnosis, even if the symptoms also fit the criteria for DTD. This is an inappropriate and ethnocentric perspective, taking the modern forms as the normative patterns of illness and as the suggested diagnoses. This could result in misdiagnosis, inappropriate treatment, and poor outcome (Castillo, 1992; Lewis-Fernández, 1992).

Other Nonwestern Syndromes

Some other examples of syndromes appropriate for a diagnosis of DTD beside the ones already mentioned include **falling out,** a trance syndrome among Southern blacks in the United States and the Bahamas, characterized by falling down in a trance, not being able to move, yet being able to hear and understand surrounding events (Weidman, 1979).

A similar syndrome known as **indisposition** occurs in Haitians in which the person falls to the ground in a trance but is not able to understand anything said or heard (Philippe & Romain, 1979).

There is also *grisi siknis* (mentioned earlier), a trance syndrome of the Miskito Indian culture of Nicaragua. This is found almost exclusively in teenage girls and young women and is characterized by running wildly with a machete or other sharp instrument with some assaultive behavior, self-mutilation, and amnesia; it is attributed to spirit possession (Dennis, 1985).

And, of course, there are a number of possession trance syndromes globally characterized by the replacement of the person's usual personality by a spirit, deity, or demon from the cultural repertoire, in which the person behaves in a complex fashion as the spirit or demon (Akhtar, 1988; Bourguignon, 1976; Chandrashekar, 1989; Crapanzano & Garrison, 1977; Gussler, 1973; Kleinman, 1980; Lewis, 1989; McDaniel, 1989; Obeyesekere, 1977; Salisbury, 1968; Stoller, 1989; Suryani, 1984; Suryani & Jensen, 1993; Suwanlert, 1976; Walker, 1972; Yap, 1960).

It is clear from looking at dissociation cross-culturally that dissociative disorders are bound up with cultural schemas and may include culturally formed patterns of illness experience, unique culturally meaningful illness categories, and culturally specific idioms of distress. They may respond to indigenous treatments and may be expressed in many forms of nonpathological hallucinations and culturally "bizarre" belief systems.

 # Suggested Clinical Guidelines

1. Determine the Cultural Identity of the Individual

Dissociative disorders vary by culture, and normative forms of dissociation will be found in each culture. What is normative in one culture may be exotic in another. For example, the behavior of a South Asian woman who is possessed by the ghost of her dead grandmother makes sense only with reference to her cultural identity.

Furthermore, subcultural groups will have differing forms of mental illness. Charismatic Christians may have the potential to be possessed by satanic demons. Malay immigrants to the United States may or may not have the potential to run *amok*. Immigrants in North America may have varying degrees of involvement with the culture of their country of origin and Anglo American culture in the United States. Therefore, they will behave with varying degrees of consistency to cultural norms of mental illness. The same can also be said for ethnic minorities.

Premodern societies may contain modernized minority segments. These individuals possess a more modern cultural identity, and they may present with modern forms of dissociation, such as DID. Therefore, it is vital that the cultural identity of each client be assessed individually.

2. Assess the Cultural Schemas Structuring Dissociative Symptoms

The prevalence of dissociative trance disorder decreases in modern societies, but dissociative trance disorder is often encountered in premodern societies and in some ethnic minorities in modern societies (for example, Puerto Ricans in the United States and Charismatic Christians). This is consistent with the symptomatic differences between dissociative trance disorder and dissociative identity disorder. Persons with cultural schemas based on a modern meaning system will not usually be possessed by ghosts, demons, or deities. However, they may dissociate into separate human personalities. Just the opposite is true in premodern societies, as cultural schemas structure dissociative symptoms. This has important implications for treatment and outcome. Therefore, cultural schemas structuring dissociative experience need to be assessed.

3. Assess the Cultural and Psychosocial Environment

Dissociative symptoms are usually spontaneous adaptations to environmental stress or trauma. Clinicians should assess culture-based sources of social and environmental stress as well as social supports that may have an impact on functioning, impairment, recovery, and relapse. Clinicians need to see the client and his or her dissociative symptoms within the total sociocultural context. This includes looking for unusual or severe stressors in the social environment that may be affecting the client.

4. Do Not Accept Dissociative Experience at Face Value

Cultural schemas contain symbolic structures that shape cognition and memory. These culture-bound symbolic structures will shape subjective experience of illness and idioms of distress. That is why dissociation can manifest in consciousness as benevolent gods, satanic demons, ghosts, spirit attack, soul loss, alternate human personalities, memories of child abuse, and so on. Dissociated memories should be assumed to be filtered through cultural schemas. Therefore, memories of child abuse need to be corroborated before being accepted. Clinicians should explore the symbolic structure of the client's cultural schemas to assess the meaning of the dissociative experience.

5. Assess the Cultural Aspects of the Clinician-Client Relationship

Clinicians should critically assess their own concepts of dissociation and dissociative disorders and reflexively determine how these concepts may be projected onto the client. Clinicians should avoid the modern tendency to pathologize divided consciousness and to view all dissociative experience as pathological. Most dissociation in premodern societies is based in normative religious and healing traditions. Thus, most dissociative experience in premodern individuals is nonpathological. No dissociative experience considered normal in the person's indigenous culture should be considered to be a mental disorder.

Also, clinicians should not ignore premodern concepts of pathological dissociative experience. For example, a clinician trained in modern psychiatry might diagnose a dissociative illness based strictly on modern concepts. However, the client will be better served if the clinician allows for the influence of premodern concepts such as spirit possession.

6. *Do Not Assume Psychosis*

Clinicians should not automatically assume the presence of a psychotic disorder because the client presents with first-rank symptoms of schizophrenia. First-rank symptoms are common in some forms of dissociative trance disorder and dissociative identity disorder. A presumption of psychosis can contribute to a misdiagnosis and less than optimal treatment and outcome.

7. *Negotiate Clinical Reality*

Individuals with dissociative symptoms may not find modern categories of illness to be meaningful. For example, diagnosing and treating a South Asian person for dissociative identity disorder when he or she presents with the symptoms of spirit possession may result in inappropriate treatment and poor outcome. For successful symbolic healing to occur, a consensus of the problem needs to be established. A negotiation between the client and the clinician is necessary to agree on the problem and the appropriate treatment. This negotiation should take into account all of the above factors.

Chapter Fourteen

Psychotic Disorders

In DSM-IV, the term **psychotic** refers to the presence of delusions, prominent hallucinations, disorganized speech, and disorganized or catatonic behavior. As discussed in Chapter 6, psychotic behavior is usually characterized by a loss of reality testing. With a loss of reality testing, the person has a disturbance in the experience of self and his or her relationship with the external physical and social environments. The presence of hallucinations or delusions is usually viewed as a loss of reality testing. The **psychotic disorders** listed in DSM-IV are: *schizophrenia, schizophreniform disorder, schizoaffective disorder, delusional disorder, brief psychotic disorder,* and *shared psychotic disorder.*

Cultural meaning systems shape the experience of self through the construction of cultural schemas, and they structure the physical and social environments as well. The fundamental consequence of recognizing this cultural influence is realizing that symptomatic manifestations may be interpreted differently by individuals, healers, and societies (Fabrega, 1989b). This is especially true when dealing with psychotic symptoms such as hallucinations and delusions. These symptoms do not stand alone as universally pathological phenomena. These symptoms occur within a sociocultural context and have important implications for adaptive functioning, subjective experience, idioms of distress, culture-based diagnoses, treatments, and outcomes. The clinical reality of any mental illness experience is a constructed entity that is dependent on the prevailing cultural schemas and power relationships of the persons involved (Fabrega, 1992, 1993a, b). The cultural interpretation of hallucinations and delusions in premodern societies can draw on local traditions of mysticism, sorcery, witchcraft, spirit attack, or spirit possession (see Chapter 13). These cultural realities shape the subjective experience and social reaction to hallucinations and delusions.

Schizophrenia

Schizophrenia is characterized by the presence of psychotic symptoms for a significant portion of time during a one-month period and some signs of the disorder for at least a six-month period. Subtypes include paranoid, disorganized, catatonic, and undifferentiated schizophrenia. *Paranoid schizophrenia* is characterized by hallucinations and delusions of persecution by others. *Disorganized schizophrenia* is characterized by extreme disruption in cognitive associations such that the person displays disorganized speech and behavior. *Catatonic schizophrenia* is characterized by fixed postural position or physical rigidity without awareness of surroundings, or by excessively excited activity. *Undifferentiated schizophrenia* is an alternative category for persons who display atypical patterns of schizophrenic symptoms. The diagnosis of schizophrenia also requires occupational or social dysfunction (APA, 1994).

In addition to the psychotic symptoms listed here, broadly categorized as *positive symptoms*, there is also a group of symptoms categorized as *negative symptoms* of schizophrenia. The negative symptoms include: flattening of emotions (*affective flattening*), reduction in the amount of thought and speech (*alogia*), and reduction in goal directed activity (*avolition*).

In the diagnosis of schizophrenia in DSM-IV, no one particular positive or negative symptom is considered to be necessary for the diagnosis. The diagnostic criteria specify that two or more symptoms must be present for the diagnosis to be made. However, only a single symptom is necessary to satisfy the psychotic criterion for diagnosis under certain circumstances. These single symptoms include cases in which delusions are considered to be *bizarre*. Bizarre delusions are defined as those that are "clearly implausible and not understandable and do not derive from ordinary life experiences" (APA, 1994, p. 275). If the individual's hallucinations consist of a voice separate from his or her own thoughts that provides a running commentary on the individual's behavior or thoughts or consists of two or more voices conversing with each other, then this single symptom is sufficient to satisfy the psychotic criterion for diagnosis (APA, 1994).

Culture and Psychosis

The World Health Organization has conducted two major international comparisons of persons with psychoses. These are the International Pilot Study of Schizophrenia (WHO, 1973) and Schizophrenia: An International Follow-Up Study (WHO, 1979). These two studies were carried out in nine and ten countries, respectively, and represented both economically developed and less developed societies. These studies found important cross-cultural differences in symptomatology. Overall, paranoid schizophrenia was the most commonly diagnosed subtype, followed by undifferentiated and acute schizophrenia. However, in the less developed societies, acute schizophrenia was found almost twice as often (40 percent) as paranoid schizophrenia (23 percent). Also, catatonic schizophrenia was found in 10 percent of the cases in the less developed societies but in only a handful of cases in the developed societies. In contrast, undifferentiated schizophrenia was found in 13 percent of the cases from developed societies and in only 4 percent of the cases from less developed societies. Thus, the WHO researchers have found significant differences in symptomatology across cultures. These differences are most likely attributable to the cognitive structuring of cultural schemas, which produce different cultural experiences of the self, illness, and the environment.

Unfortunately, the DSM-IV diagnostic criteria assume a modern universalistic perspective on psychotic symptoms. As discussed in Chapter 4, the meaning of hearing voices is not the same across all cultures. In some cultures, persons hear voices as part of their normal psychological experience. These voices can be the voices of ancestors who help family members in their daily lives, or the voices can be associated with deities, in which case, the person is not considered to be mentally ill but a spirit medium possessed by a god. In some cultural contexts, these persons may even be considered *to be a god*. For example, in India persons known as *avatars* are spirit mediums who permanently take on the role of a particular god from the Hindu pantheon. That is, in the Indian sociocultural context, they are considered to be a human incarnation of a god or a deity-saint.

In June McDaniel's (1989) analysis of the biographies of Indian deity-saints, she demonstrates that many of them were profoundly affected by their possession experiences and in a modern psychiatric context would have been considered psychotic. However, in India they were worshiped as gods in human form. Krishna Chaitanya (b. 1486), revered in India as an incarnation of the Hindu god Vishnu, is an excellent example of the deity-saint who would today be seen as suffering from catatonic symptoms according to the diagnostic criteria in DSM-IV. Quoting McDaniel (1989)*:

> He had strange physical symptoms of his intense love—his body would become distorted, stretched and compressed, sweat and blood oozing from his pores and saliva foaming at the mouth. Sometimes he was totally lost in ecstatic trance, sometimes he was half conscious, and sometimes he was in a normal state. . . . His love [of God] was not a peaceful state, but a continuous fluctuation between divine and human personalities, between love and loneliness. . . . He would mistake his environment for Vrindavana [Vishnu's home], sing and dance, and then faint. He would later return to normal consciousness and ask, "Am I conscious? . . . What have I seen in this near-dream state? What sort of madness have I spoken?"

McDaniel (1989) also included this description from an Indian biography:

> "Caitanya's body was paralyzed, trembled, perspired, paled, wept and choked. He was thrilled. He would laugh, cry, dance and sing, running here and there, and sometimes he would fall unconscious on the ground. . . . When

---

*From *The Madness of the Saints: Ecstatic Religion in Bengal*, by J. McDaniel, pp. 35–37. Copyright © 1989 The University of Chicago Press. Reprinted with permission.

Prabhu [Krishna Chaitanya] cries, he cries for hours. He rolls on the ground, his hair completely dishevelled. . . . When Prabhu laughs, he does so loudly, enjoying the bliss for hours. . . . On other occasions he emits haunting, deep sighs, sending everyone away to remain alone. . . . From time to time his entire body would become rigid so that he could not even bend over."

In her study of the lives of some of India's most famous deity-saints, such as Ramakrishna Paramahansa, Ananda Mayi Ma, Krishna Chaitanya, and others, McDaniel (1989, p. 4) finds that virtually all were at first thought to be possessed by malevolent spirits or were thought to be insane. It was only later, after extensive ritual healing, that the individuals were accepted as *avatars*.

According to McDaniel, the individual's acceptance as a deity-saint may occur because the subjective experience and behavior of the possessed person is shaped by healing rituals to conform with culturally orthodox theology and patterns of religious behavior. That is, the healing process of a possessed person may involve altering the subjective experience of that individual to conform with established cultural categories defining appropriate subjective experience and outward behavior. Thus, the possessed person is taught how to be possessed by a socially acceptable "god" rather than by an evil "demon." Through this type of training, the person can learn to control his or her possession experiences and become a religious practitioner (shaman, oracle, or *avatar*). The training transforms the person's subjective experience of possession to a form that is highly congruent with the culture, thus *healing* the psychotic person.

According to McDaniel, it is the training the individual receives during healing rituals that shapes his or her internal schemas in a way that is highly congruent with the accepted cultural reality and allows the person's reintegration into the larger society. Thus, she says, "experience may come to imitate ritual" (1989, p. 5). Other similar examples are found in *Medusa's Hair* (Obeyesekere, 1981), in which the author describes the transformation of possessed patients into priestesses (see also Claus, 1979, 1983).

The symptoms of hallucinations and catatonic behavior, such as those experienced by Krishna Chaitanya, are certainly identifiable across cultures, but the meaning of these symptoms is determined by cultural schemas. Moreover, it is clear that individuals can learn through training to control these symptoms in ways that allow them to be socially acceptable and functional in some cultures.

Culture and Delusions

Another single symptom that will satisfy the diagnostic criteria for schizophrenia is *bizarre delusions*. Delusions are by definition erroneous beliefs. Bizarre delusions are defined in DSM-IV as those that are "clearly implausible and not understandable and do not derive from ordinary life experiences" (APA, 1994, p. 275). Studies have shown that the content of schizophrenic delusions varies significantly by cultural context (Kim et al., 1993; Tateyama et al., 1993). The example contained in DSM-IV for a bizarre delusion is a person believing that a stranger has removed his or her internal organs without leaving any wounds or scars. This example clearly demonstrates that the definition of *bizarreness* is a cultural construction.

The belief that an individual can remove objects and illnesses from inside the body without leaving scars or wounds may seem to be a bizarre belief to many in modern cultures, but it is one of the most common shamanic practices throughout the premodern world. Thus, the bizarre in one culture can be the accepted truth in another. This healing technique and many other types of supernatural powers are believed to be real and normal in many societies.

For example, all of the Hindu yogis that I interviewed during fieldwork in India, and virtually all the Indian people who are religiously devout, believe that persons can have supernatural powers. These powers can be bestowed by a god or be developed through yogic practice. Some yogis in India believe that they have supernatural powers. To them, and to most people in Indian culture, this is not a *bizarre* belief at all but quite natural. Believing in supernatural powers may seem bizarre to someone with a modern set of cultural schemas, but it does not seem so to most people in premodern societies.

Other behaviors that can appear to be bizarre are also common among Hindu ascetics. For example, McDaniel (1989) describes Hindu ascetics who eat human feces merely to demonstrate that their state of consciousness is beyond any conception of good or bad, pure or impure. Likewise, it is traditional for some Hindu ascetics to smear their bodies with the ashes of cremated corpses to signify that they themselves have burned up their personal selves (*jiva*) and are now the spiritual self (*atman*). Similarly, other ascetics stand for years without ever sitting or lying down. Others keep one arm raised above the head for years; eventually the arm withers and becomes completely useless. Others tie weights or place metal rings around their penises to transcend their human sexuality. Still others emulate their chosen deity, dressing like the god or goddess and taking on as much as possible the personality of the deity (Hartsuiker, 1993). All of these behaviors would be considered bizarre in a modern western culture. In India they are seen as extreme but nevertheless respected and in no way pathological. Clinicians should be aware that certain behaviors or beliefs that seem bizarre by modern standards may be respected parts of premodern cultural meaning systems.

Culture and Negative Symptoms

The negative symptoms of schizophrenia include flattening of emotions (*affective flattening*), reduction in the amount of thought and speech (*alogia*), and reduction in goal directed activity (*avolition*). However, all of these negative symptoms of schizophrenia are also found in normal forms of religious asceticism. Indeed, religious asceticism in various premodern cultures and subcultures involves withdrawal of attention from the environment and society so that the person appears to have little emotional response, little thought or speech, and little desire to perform purposeful actions.

Hindu asceticism and meditation are designed to produce just this state of mind in the ascetic on a permanent basis. Asceticism is by definition a withdrawal from worldly activities and social contacts. To be unemotional and completely detached from events, either good or bad, is one of the primary goals of religious asceticism. Likewise, having a mind that does not move is the explicit goal of meditation. Some ascetics practice mutism (nonspeaking) for many years as part of their religious endeavors. The overall goal of this practice is to have no desires and, therefore, no need to perform action. Ascetics from various religions believe this will result in spiritual enlightenment or salvation.

In the Hindu ascetics, these beliefs and practices are based on their cultural schemas; they are not psychosis. Yet yogis do these things to escape suffering in life. The motivation and the general psychological process may not be so different from modern psychiatric patients if psychosis is viewed as a withdrawal from reality. Religious monasticism is outwardly very similar to the type of autistic withdrawal seen in schizophrenia. However, the ascetics have a highly structured, institutionalized, and socially respected form of withdrawal from the world.

People diagnosed as psychotics may be autistically withdrawing from the world in their own idiosyncratic fashion without the guidance, structure, or social acceptance accorded religious ascetics (McDaniel, 1989). It may be that the psychotics develop mental illness because of this lack of guidance, structure, and social acceptance. And, of course, in modern societies persons can be defined as ill because these societies generally do not value or easily tolerate withdrawal from productive economic activity. To be able to support oneself is part of the definition of a healthy person in modern capitalist societies.

Schizophrenia and Dissociation

The disease term *schizophrenia* was coined by Swiss psychiatrist Eugen Bleuler (1908) and is a combination of the Greek words *skhizein* (split) and *phren* (mind). It literally means "split mind." This term is appropriate given Bleuler's understanding of the underlying psychological basis of schizophrenia. Bleuler believed that the symptoms of schizophrenia involved the *associative splitting* of the basic functions of personality. However, the concept of *dissociation* is also defined as the splitting of the associative functions of personality (see Chapter 13). The two concepts are virtually identical, and there is evidence that Bleuler himself saw little, if any, difference between them. For example, Bleuler wrote that "it is not alone in hysteria that one finds an arrangement of different personalities one *succeeding* the other: through similar mechanisms schizophrenia produces different personalities existing *side by side*" (1924, p. 138). Thus, we see that Bleuler himself tended to merge the concepts of dissociation and schizophrenia, which are today considered to be two separate illness categories.

In the disease-centered paradigm, schizophrenia was assumed to have a primarily biological basis. In contrast, dissociation is viewed as being primarily a psychological process. In the past few decades, research on schizophrenia has focused almost exclusively on biological factors, and no assumption was made about a relationship to dissociation. However, the current expansion of the disease-centered paradigm is now more inclusive of psychological factors in the definition of mental disorders. Thus, the relationship between dissociation and schizophrenia is now being actively studied.

There is increasing evidence that schizophrenia and dissociation should be considered as related concepts. For example, German psychiatrist Kurt Schneider (1959) proposed that particular forms of hallucinations and delusions should be considered central to the definition of schizophrenia. He called these symptoms the **first-rank symptoms** of schizophrenia. Today, Schneider's first-rank symptoms form a major portion of the diagnostic criteria for schizophrenia in DSM-IV (APA, 1994). The first-rank symptoms are:

1. *Audible thoughts:* the experience of auditory hallucinations in which voices external to the individual's own thoughts speak his or her thoughts aloud.
2. *Voices arguing:* two or more hallucinated voices external to the individual's own thoughts in argument or discussion. The subject of the discussion is usually the patient.
3. *Voices commenting on the individual's action:* the content of the hallucinated discussion is a description of the patient's activities as they occur.
4. *Influences playing on the body:* the patient is a reluctant recipient of bodily sensations imposed by some external agency.
5. *Thought withdrawal:* the patient experiences thoughts being taken from his or her mind, as if withdrawn by some external agency.
6. *Thoughts ascribed to others* (also called *thought insertion*): the patient experiences thoughts in the mind that appear to have been imposed by some external agency.
7. *Thought broadcasting:* the patient has the experience that his or her thoughts can be heard by others.
8. *Made feelings:* the patient experiences feelings that appear to have been imposed by some external agency.
9. *Made impulses:* the imposition by an external agency of an impulse to carry out an action.
10. *Made volitional acts:* the patient experiences his or her actions as being under the control of an external agency. The movements are initiated and directed throughout by the controlling influence, and the patient experiences him or herself as an automaton or the passive observer of his or her own actions.
11. *Delusional perception:* the production of an elaborate, but false, meaning system based on experienced perceptions.

Persons with dissociative identity disorder have been found to display just as many or more first-rank symptoms as do patients diagnosed with schizophrenia (see Chapter 13). In related research, DID patients were found to have significantly more positive symptoms of schizophrenia than schizophrenics had, whereas the schizophrenics had more negative symptoms than the DID patients had (Ellason & Ross, 1995). This great overlap in symptomatology indicates that there may be a common psychological process underlying both schizophrenia and dissociative identity disorder. Moreover, numerous types of dissociative disorders in nonwestern societies that are now being diagnosed as dissociative trance disorder in DSM-IV can be very similar in their symptomatology to psychotic disorders, including schizophrenia. These similarities indicate that the concept of schizophrenia needs to be expanded beyond its disease-centered formulations to include Bleuler's original view that focused on splitting the associative functions of consciousness.

In Scandinavia, for example, the concept of "reactive" or "psychogenic" psychoses is still widely used in clinical practice. The types of syndromes commonly considered to be psychogenic psychoses in Scandinavia are spread over the general diagnostic categories in the DSM-IV classification system. These include schizophreniform disorder, brief psychotic disorder, schizoaffective disorder, delusional disorder, major depression with psychotic features, PTSD, dissociative identity disorder, and dissociative trance disorder (Stromgren, 1994). It is possible for all of these disorders to be considered psychogenic psychoses. It is also possible that they have dissociative processes in common.

Culture, Course, and Outcome

The need for a reconceptualization of schizophrenia is also indicated by cross-cultural course and outcome studies of schizophrenia. Schizophrenia is found throughout the world, but it may be more prevalent in industrialized societies—where it also typically has a longer course and worse outcome.

Full recoveries from schizophrenia are not unknown in economically developed societies (Angst, 1988; Harding et al., 1987; McGlashan, 1988), but they are more common in less developed societies. Two major, multinational, longitudinal studies of schizophrenia have been sponsored by the World Health Organization (1973, 1979). In these studies, a core schizophrenic syndrome, as defined by the presence of one or more of Schneider's first-rank symptoms, was identifiable in all societies. The most important finding of these studies was that the clinical course and social impairment of schizophrenia are more benign in premodern societies, regardless of the nature of onset or the presenting symptoms. This finding was especially true in the least economically developed nations in the study (Nigeria and India).

The patients in the less developed countries had a better course and outcome than did patients in the most economically developed countries (Great Britain, United States, and Denmark). This finding was confirmed during both two-year and five-year follow-up studies (Sartorius et al., 1986; WHO, 1979). In the economically developed countries, only 25 percent of the patients were classified in the best two outcome categories, and 65 percent were classified in the worst two outcome categories. In contrast, in economically less developed countries, 39 percent were classified in the best two categories, and only 38 per-

Table 14.1
Outcome for Schizophrenia

	Best outcome	Worst outcome
Developed Countries	25%	65%
Less Developed Countries	39%	38%

SOURCE: Based on Sartorius et al., 1986.

Table 14.2
Social Impairment from Schizophrenia

	Least impaired	Most impaired
Developed Countries	43%	56%
Less Developed Countries	65%	33%

SOURCE: Based on Sartorius et al., 1986.

cent were in the worst two categories (Sartorius et al., 1986). This is summarized in Table 14.1.

In the area of social impairment, 43 percent displayed no or mild impairment and 56 percent displayed moderate or severe impairment in the developed countries. In contrast, in the less developed countries, 65 percent displayed no or mild impairment and only 33 percent displayed moderate or severe impairment (Sartorius et al., 1986). This is summarized in Table 14.2.

A similar benign course and outcome for schizophrenia was also found in previous studies in the developing nations of Mauritius (Murphy & Raman, 1971) and Sri Lanka (Mendis, 1986). In subsequent analyses of the WHO data, Susser and Wanderling (1994) found that the incidence of nonaffective psychoses with acute onset and full recovery was about twice as high in women across the various research centers, and about *ten times* higher in the less developed societies versus the developed societies.

There is a strong preponderance of evidence to indicate that psychoses including schizophrenia have a more benign course and better outcome in less economically developed nations. Moreover, prevalence rates for schizophrenia appear to be higher in economically developed societies than they are in premodern agrarian or hunter-gatherer societies. In fact, schizophrenia seems to be relatively uncommon in any society without a system of wage labor (Warner, 1985). Also one study's findings indicate that the chances of developing schizophrenia are higher for persons raised in cities compared to those raised in rural areas (Lewis, David, Andreasson, & Allsbeck, 1992).

The reasons for the differences in prevalence, course, and outcome of schizophrenia across cultures remain unclear. However, the differences appear to be related to the distinctions between *sociocentric* and *egocentric* societies, and *premodern* versus *modern* cultural meaning systems (Chapter 3).

Sociocentrism versus egocentrism is especially important when considering the effects that families may have on the course and outcome of schizophrenic illness. The concept of **expressed emotion (EE)** has been developed to describe the influence of family life on the individual with schizophrenia (Brown et al., 1962). Expressed emotion refers to criticism, hostility, and emotional over-involvement directed at the individual by his or her family. Numerous studies have shown that schizophrenic persons who live in homes with high levels of EE are significantly more likely to suffer relapses of psychotic symptoms (Jenkins, 1991, 1992; Karno et al., 1987; Leff, 1989; Leff & Vaughn, 1985; Martins, de Lemos, & Bebbington, 1992; Vaughn & Leff, 1976; Vaughn & Doyle et al., 1992; Vaughn & Snyder et al., 1984; Wig et al., 1987a, b).

Levels of EE in families with a schizophrenic member appear to vary by culture. In cultural groups studied thus far, families in India have shown the lowest rates of high EE (23 percent), followed by Mexican Americans (41 percent), British (48 percent), and Anglo Americans (67 percent) (Karno et al., 1987; Vaughn & Leff, 1976; Wig et al., 1987a, b). The highly significant difference between Indians, Mexican Americans, and Anglo Americans on levels of EE appears to provide support for the hypothesis that behavioral factors within the family are affecting the course and outcome of schizophrenia across cultures (Karno et al., 1987).

Low levels of EE could be one of the reasons schizophrenia has a relatively benign course and outcome in economically less developed countries. In most less developed countries, the societies are premodern and sociocentric, with the sense of self, personal identity, and sense of well-being all centered in the extended family. This also means that the ill person will have a larger and more effective social support network than do persons living in modern egocentric societies. In a premodern sociocentric context, a schizophrenic person will receive more personal attention and caring because there are typically much larger families with more individuals available to care for the sick person. Thus, the person is less likely to be perceived as an undue burden, as he or she might be in the small nuclear family typical of modern egocentric societies. Therefore, there is likely to be less hostility and criticism of the individual in a premodern sociocentric family, and more hostility and criticism in a modern egocentric family (Karno & Jenkins, 1993).

Also, the autistic withdrawal characteristic of schizophrenia is less acceptable and more noticeable in a sociocentric family, and therefore more quickly identified and treated. In an egocentric family, individuals are more isolated and have more personal latitude to withdraw into themselves as long as they do not become occupationally impaired. Thus, autistic withdrawal may proceed further, with more deterioration in the person's condition, in egocentric societies before it is perceived to merit treatment (El Islam, 1979).

The presence of modern versus premodern meaning systems may also be related to levels of EE. In a family with a premodern meaning system, psychotic symptoms are likely to be conceptualized within their own indigenous illness categories, such as witchcraft, sorcery, or demonic possession. In such cases, the cause of the illnesses is always *external* to the individual. This means that the illness is not the person's fault. It is assumed that the individual has been attacked by some external force and is not responsible for his or her behavior or for being sick in the first place. Also, because the cause of the illness is cognized as external, the cure is seen as relatively simple, and the illness is expected to be not chronic, but *short-lived* (Waxler, 1974, 1979). Thus, hostility and criticism are less likely to be directed at the individual than in a family with a modern meaning system.

In the modern egocentric families of Anglo American society, schizophrenia is typically cognized as *internal* to the individual and almost always *incurable*. This is consistent with disease-centered explanations of schizophrenia. Moreover, because a high degree of independence and self-sufficiency is expected of all individuals in egocentric Anglo American society, these individuals are viewed as personally inadequate and therefore stigmatized. Thus, family hostility and criticism directed at the patient is more likely in this type of sociocultural context. The very high levels of EE reported in Anglo American families with a schizophrenic member is perhaps a manifestation of these cultural factors. The high level of hostility and criticism indicative of social stress in the environment is correlated with a more serious course and poor outcome for schizophrenia in modern societies such as the United States.

Similarly, in a WHO-sponsored cross-cultural study of life events and schizophrenia, it was found that social stress in the environment may precipitate psychotic episodes in schizophrenic patients. It was found that stressful events tend to cluster in a two- to three-week period immediately preceding onset of a psychotic episode (Day et al., 1987).

Schizoaffective Disorder

Schizoaffective disorder is characterized by a combination of psychotic and mood symptoms. The diagnosis in DSM-IV requires the presence of psychotic symptoms occurring in conjunction with either a manic or depressive episode, followed by at least two weeks of psychotic symptoms *without* prominent mood symptoms. If the psychotic symptoms occur only during major depressive episodes, the proper diagnosis would be *major depressive disorder with psychotic features*. If the psychotic symptoms occur only during manic or mixed episodes, or during major depressive *and* manic or mixed episodes, the proper diagnosis would be *bipolar I disorder* (APA, 1994).

Cross-Cultural Case Study

Schizoaffective disorder is best illustrated by a case study. The case titled "I Am Vishnu" in the *DSM-IV Casebook** (Spitzer et al., 1994, p. 137) illustrates the

---

*Case studies on pp. 251–256 are summarized with permission from the *Diagnostic and Statistical Manual of Mental Disorders Casebook*, Fourth Edition by R. L. Spitzer et al. (Eds.). Copyright © 1994 American Psychiatric Association, Washington D.C.

combination of psychotic and mood symptoms as well as the cultural factors involved in this disorder.

The patient is a 32-year-old male, an unemployed immigrant from India now living in Atlanta, Georgia. He is unemployed because he has been hearing voices almost continuously for five years. Recently, the voices have been telling him that he is the Hindu god Vishnu and that he should begin a new religious epoch in human history. He also has brief euphoric episodes in which he becomes possessed by Vishnu and emphatically preaches his religious insights to his family and neighbors. At these times, he can become loud and angry if others attempt to control his behavior. Outside of these episodes, he is well behaved and well liked in the neighborhood. When the psychiatrist saw him, he kept repeating, "I am Vishnu."

The *DSM-IV Casebook* editors note that the individual is unable to work, therefore he is occupationally dysfunctional. They diagnose his euphoric experiences as manic episodes. Because he has experienced voices for five years, accompanied by manic episodes, they diagnose *schizoaffective disorder, bipolar type*, and note the need to rule out schizophrenia.

The prevailing cultural context is of key importance in this case. Because this person is living in the United States, a modern capitalist society where all people are expected to be productive unless they are disabled, he is by definition dysfunctional because he is not able to work. However, if he was still living in his native India, he would have other options. He could become one of the thousands of religious ascetics there, who do not work. Indian society is structured so that the ascetics are provided for. They receive money, food, and other gifts from people who give because they believe it is good karma to give to a religious ascetic. Thus, his inability to hold a regular job would not be seen as occupational dysfunction in the Indian cultural context. In fact, he would be considered holy because he has renounced worldly life. Likewise, his ability to hear the voice of the god Vishnu could become an asset, and he might become a respected and high functioning spiritual leader with many followers.

Even if this individual chose not to become a religious ascetic, the voices he hears would not necessarily be seen as mental illness in India. It would depend on his sociocultural context. If he was in a middle-class, modern segment of the Indian population, he probably would be seen as mentally ill and taken for psychiatric treatment. In this case, he would probably be described as psychotic and given the diagnosis of schizoaffective disorder.

However, if he was in a premodern Indian cultural context (75 percent of the population), he would probably be described as demonically possessed (with the demon impersonating the god Vishnu). In this case, culturally appropriate healing rituals would be attempted. These rituals are frequently effective, either getting rid of the demons or allowing the individual to control his hallucinations in a culturally congruent way. In that case, he probably would become some type of religious specialist (oracle, exorcist, healer, or so forth). Thus, the cultural context can have an important impact on the subjective structure of the symptoms of schizoaffective disorder as well as on how the illness is indigenously diagnosed and treated. These cultural factors also have the potential to affect the level of impairment and outcome.

Brief Psychotic
and Schizophreniform Disorders

Brief psychotic disorder is a psychotic disturbance that lasts more than one day but less than one month. **Schizophreniform disorder** is a psychotic disturbance that lasts at least one month but less than six months. The symptoms for these disorders are essentially the same as for schizophrenia; the only significant difference in diagnostic criteria is the *duration* of symptoms.

Cross-Cultural Case Studies

Cases from the *DSM-IV Casebook* can be analyzed to illustrate cultural factors in brief psychotic and schizophreniform disorders. In the case titled "Ataques de Nervios" (Spitzer et al., 1994, p. 74), the patient is a woman from the Dominican Republic who is treated in a hospital in the United States. She is alternately screaming, mute, and mumbling unintelligibly in Spanish and English. On the ward, she attempts to grab another patient's purse and the gold chains around another patient's neck. She appears to be terrified and has auditory hallucinations of her daughter's voice telling her to kill herself. She receives antipsychotic medications, but these are only mildly effective. A few days earlier, she had learned that her former husband had remarried. She was afraid he would no longer provide child support for her daughter, but the next day she learned that her ex-husband still intended to provide her with child support payments. Immediately upon learning that her financial support would still be forthcoming, her symptoms remitted and she was discharged after one week of hospitalization.

The *DSM-IV Casebook* editors state that they are aware that *ataques de nervios* is a Latin American culture-bound syndrome listed in the Glossary of Culture-Bound Syndromes in DSM-IV (APA, 1994, p. 845). They also recognize that the symptoms in this case are dissociative in nature, prompted by socioenvironmental stress, and that administration of antipsychotic medication for this patient was inappropriate. They must also be aware that the DSM-IV Glossary does not mention psychotic disorders at all as a possible diagnosis for cases of *ataques de nervios*. Nonetheless, their suggested diagnosis for this case is *brief psychotic disorder, with marked stressor*. I suggest that this is an inappropriate diagnosis. *Ataques de nervios* is one of the prototype syndromes for *dissociative trance disorder* (Chapter 13) in DSM-IV (Lewis-Fernández, 1992, 1994). This case is an obvious example of DTD, trance type. However, diagnosing this woman as psychotic is an example of how dissociative reactions can be misinterpreted as psychotic episodes.

The case titled "International Spirit" in the *DSM-IV Casebook* (Spitzer et al., 1994, p. 422) is also relevant to this discussion. This case is related to the "Leader of the Movement" case discussed earlier (Chapter 13). In this case, a 20-year-old man who lives in the region of Africa where the "movement" is active felt ill. He swam across a turbulent bay to go to a folk healer he knew but was unable to find the healer. He walked naked into the city to find a doctor he was familiar with. A policeman tried to stop him, but he bit the policeman's hand. It took seven strong men to subdue him and carry him to the hospital. His family wanted to take him to the leader of the movement for healing, but the police refused. He told the doctor that hundreds of people were going to die and that he could kill people by pointing at them with his finger.

The patient's problems began two days earlier, after a slight but rare earthquake. He says he saw a spirit that looked like a white woman with long hair. He told a fellow patient that they were both "international spirits." He was given antipsychotic medication and released after one week's hospitalization, with his symptoms in remission. On his way home he participated in a religious ritual with the "leader of the movement," who concluded that his illness was a sign from God that he should become a healer in the movement, which he agreed to do. He stopped taking his medication after two weeks. Three months after this, his symptoms returned. But three months after that, he was back to normal and is soon to be initiated as a healer in the movement.

In their discussion of this case, the *DSM-IV Casebook* editors conclude that his behavior (nudism, indiscriminate aggression) is deviant and bizarre—even for those involved in the movement. Therefore, they are inclined to diagnose a psychotic disorder. Because his initial episode lasts only about ten days, they conclude that *brief psychotic disorder* is the appropriate initial diagnosis. However, because his symptoms return and last more than one month but less than six months, they conclude that the diagnosis should be changed to *schizophreniform disorder.*

However, I would suggest a different diagnosis. When individuals are possessed by "evil spirits," it is quite usual for them to tear off their clothes, assault people, throw things, behave incoherently, and believe that they can harm or kill people with their supernatural powers. This is the typical behavior of an "evil spirit" and may not be perceived as bizarre but as demonic possession by people in a premodern society. Furthermore, this type of behavior is seen all over the world wherever the cultural schemas support the behavior of possession trance. For example, this person's behavior did not seem bizarre to the leader of the movement, who completely accepted him and decided that he should become a healer in the movement. The leader obviously recognized his ability to contact "spirits," and she will train him in the appropriate rituals so that he can use his abilities in the service of the movement.

Again, we have an illustration of how easy it is to diagnose psychotic disorders in cases in which the patients display trance and possession symptoms. Because of his spirit possession symptoms, I suggest an alternative diagnosis for this patient of *dissociative trance disorder, possession type.*

Another spirit possession case in the *DSM-IV Casebook* also illustrates an important point. This is the case titled "El Duende" (Spitzer et al., 1994, p. 435). The patient in this case is a 14-year-old girl living with her aunt and uncle in Cali, Colombia. She is possessed by a "ghost" (*el duende*). The ghost assaults her continuously. She feels the hands of the ghost on her body, squeezing her breasts and pinching and scratching her arms and legs. Every night, he comes to her bed and rapes her savagely, despite her struggling. She experiences violent seizures that her family interprets as levitation. She is constantly tormented by the ghost's threats and blasphemous language that only she can hear.

The symptoms go on for one month. Her family thinks she is demonically possessed, but the local priest orders the relatives to take her to the mental hospital. She is treated there with antipsychotic medications, and an EEG shows episodic discharges in the frontal-temporal area of the right hemisphere. She is diagnosed with temporal lobe epilepsy. Her symptoms improve, and she is released after 20 days of hospitalization.

However, she never returns for a follow-up appointment. Instead, she is taken by her family to a brotherhood of spiritualists. The spiritualists are impressed with her ability to contact "spirits" and teach her to develop this ability and control it. With this religious training and symbolic healing, she later becomes a gifted spirit medium and the leader of a spiritualist cult. As more time passes, she reduces her trance behavior, gets married, has a child, and lives a normal life free from further symptoms.

In their discussion of this case, the *DSM-IV Casebook* editors state that because of the psychotic symptoms a strict application of DSM-IV criteria would result in a diagnosis of *schizophreniform disorder*. However, because of the cultural context of this case, in which it is common to believe in possession by ghosts, they reject this option and instead suggest a diagnosis of *psychotic disorder not otherwise specified*, and on Axis III add, *complex partial seizures* (temporal lobe epilepsy) (provisional diagnosis).

In their assessment and diagnosis of this case, the *DSM-IV Casebook* editors ignore the obvious sexual content of the patient's hallucinations. She is violently raped every night by the ghost. There is no discussion of this by the editors. In cases such as this, a possible history of sexual abuse should be investigated. If this can be corroborated, it should be considered in diagnosis. The patient could be experiencing flashbacks of traumatic sexual abuse occurring earlier in her childhood, which she structures in a cultural idiom of distress, that is, demonic possession and attack.

Similar syndromes of prominently sexual demonic possession and attack afflicting adolescent females and young women are common in many parts of the world. These syndromes should be recognized as possibly dissociative in nature and not psychotic. Merely diagnosing this girl with a psychotic disorder and prescribing antipsychotic medications does not address the possibility of psychological trauma and the need for emotional healing.

In this case, the symbolic healing the patient received from the spiritualists allowed her to control and eventually end her trance behavior, allowing her to live a normal life with no further symptoms. This is another illustration of the effectiveness of symbolic healing of mental illness.

However, if this young woman had been treated in the United States, she could have been misdiagnosed with a psychotic disorder, probably schizophreniform disorder and possibly schizophrenia. The result of this type of misdiagnosis is likely to be a poor outcome with chronic illness and possible complications resulting from long-term use of neuroleptic medications. Again, we see how easy it is to confuse psychotic and dissociative disorders in individuals with premodern cultural schemas. I suggest that a possible diagnosis for this case is *dissociative trance disorder, possession type.*

Delusional Disorder

Delusional disorder is characterized by at least one month of nonbizarre delusions, without other psychotic symptoms. Social or occupational impairment is not required for a diagnosis of delusional disorder. In fact, DSM-IV states that "a common characteristic of individuals with Delusional Disorder is the apparent normality of their behavior and appearance when their delusional ideas are not being discussed or acted on" (APA, 1994, p. 297).

Because the delusions are nonbizarre in cases of delusional disorder, knowledge of the cultural identity of the individual is required along with some familiarity with the prevailing cultural meaning system. By definition, delusions are false beliefs, but what is considered false and true varies by culture.

Cross-Cultural Case Study

The case titled "Pseudocyesis" in the *DSM-IV Casebook* (Spitzer et al., 1994, p. 431) is an excellent illustration of this disorder. The patient is a 24-year-old single, Xhosa man from a rural village in South Africa who has been referred for psychiatric evaluation after murdering a male witch doctor.

He had initially seen the witch doctor to be treated for a cough. However, the witch doctor performed anal intercourse with the man over three successive days, and the man came to believe that he was pregnant with the witch doctor's baby. A few weeks later, he went back to the witch doctor to get him to abort the pregnancy, but the witch doctor refused. The man became angry and fatally stabbed the witch doctor. This was the man's only homosexual experience, and he felt guilty about it. When he saw the psychiatrist, he was convinced that he was still pregnant. The man had no other functional impairment.

In their discussion of this case, the *DSM-IV Casebook* editors conclude that a delusion such as this would be bizarre in most other cultures. This would indicate a diagnosis of *schizophrenia* or *schizophreniform disorder.* However, because witch doctors are commonly believed to have supernatural powers in this man's culture, they conclude that his delusion is nonbizarre. Therefore, based on the man's cultural identity, they appropriately conclude with a diagnosis of *delusional disorder, somatic type.*

Shared Psychotic Disorder

Shared psychotic disorder is characterized by a delusional belief in an individual who is influenced by someone else who has an established delusion. The essential feature of shared psychotic disorder is a delusion that develops in a person as a result of a close relationship with another person (called the "primary case") who already has a psychotic disorder characterized by promi-nent delusions. The primary case is usually dominant in the relationship and imposes the delusional belief system on the second person. There is typically a close relationship between the two, sometimes characterized by social isola-tion. The delusions can be bizarre or nonbizarre (APA, 1994).

This disorder generally involves only two people, but it can involve larger numbers of people. The number of people involved is an important factor. For example, how many people does it take for a shared delusion to no longer be considered pathological? Cases of shared psychotic disorder are highly depen-dent on cultural schemas. It is clear from the diagnostic methodology in DSM-IV that if a belief considered bizarre in western culture is held by a sufficiently large enough group of people, it is no longer a delusion but counts as a set of cultural schemas. Therefore, it is no longer a sign of mental pathology.

This disorder illustrates the ability of humans to collectively believe virtu-ally anything, create cultural entities, and experience those entities as real, "natural" objects separate from their own intentionality. The process usually starts with a single person. If that person can convince enough other people to believe in his or her "insight" about the nature of the world, a cult can be started that over time can turn into a whole new culture.

For example, take the belief that a man can be executed, rise from the dead after three days, and remove the sins of all those who believe in his resurrec-tion. When this belief first began, it was perhaps a "shared delusion," yet over time it spread to millions of people and is not now seen as a sign of mental pathology.

The same thing can be said about the "movement" in the West African *DSM-IV Casebook* examples. Their cognitive schemas are not considered delu-sional because so many people share this set of schemas. Yet the "movement" began only recently, with the "Leader" who introduced ideas not wholly con-sistent with tribal culture. For example, she believes that her people should abandon their traditional ancestor spirits. If this belief was held only by the leader and one or two followers, it could have been considered a shared delu-sion. However, now that the belief system has spread to many people, what started as a few people with a shared delusion is now an identifiable cultural group.

This illustrates the ethnocentric effects of our own intentionality in looking at the cognitive schemas of other cultural groups. What we consider to be delu-sional, bizarre, or reasonable is dependent on our own collectively created cul-tural definitions of reality.

   ## Suggested Clinical Guidelines

1. Determine the Cultural Identity of the Individual

Psychotic symptoms such as hallucinations and delusions can be inter-preted very differently across cultures. There may be nonpathological forms of hallucination in some cultures. Also, what is a "bizarre" belief in one culture may be normative in another. For example, believing that one can remove objects and illnesses from inside the body without leaving scars or wounds is one of the most common shamanic practices throughout the premodern world. Therefore, it is vital that the cultural identity of each individual be carefully assessed.

2. Assess the Cultural Schemas Structuring Psychotic Symptoms

The meaning of hearing voices is not the same across all cultures. In some cultures, persons hear voices as part of their normal psychological experience. These voices can be the voices of ancestors who help family members in their daily lives or voices associated with deities, in which case, the person is not considered to be mentally ill but a spirit medium possessed by a god. In some cultural contexts, these persons may even be considered *to be a god.* Thus, hallucinations and delusions need to be placed within the context of indigenous cultural schemas to judge if they are pathological. Hallucinations and delusions should not in themselves be judged to be pathological without regard to cultural context.

3. Assess the Cultural and Psychosocial Environment

Psychotic symptoms may be adaptations to environmental stress or trauma. Therefore, clinicians should assess culture-based sources of social and environmental stress as well as social supports that may have an impact on functioning, impairment, recovery, and relapse. Clinicians need to see the individual and his or her psychotic symptoms within the total sociocultural context. This includes looking for unusual or severe stressors or high levels of "expressed emotion" in the social environment affecting the individual.

4. Assess the Cultural Aspects of the Clinician-Client Relationship

Clinicians should critically assess their own concepts of psychosis and psychotic disorders and reflexively determine how these concepts may be projected onto the client. Clinicians should avoid the modern tendency to view schizophrenia as an incurable brain disease. In less developed countries, schizophrenia generally has a more benign course and better outcome than it does in the most economically developed countries. This should cause clinicians to rethink their conceptions regarding the curability of schizophrenia. It is inadvisable to project the notion of incurability onto a patient.

5. *Consider the Possibility of Dissociation*

Clinicians should not automatically assume the presence of a psychotic disorder because the person presents with first-rank symptoms of schizophrenia. First-rank symptoms are common in some forms of dissociative trance disorder and dissociative identity disorder. A presumption of psychosis can contribute to misdiagnosis and less than optimal treatment and outcome.

6. *Negotiate Clinical Reality*

Persons with psychotic symptoms may not find modern categories of illness to be meaningful. For example, diagnosing and treating a West African for schizophrenia when that individual presents with the symptoms of spirit possession may result in inappropriate treatment and poor outcome. For successful symbolic healing to occur, a consensus of the problem needs to be established. Thus, a negotiation between the client and the clinician is necessary to agree on the problem and the appropriate treatment. This negotiation should take into account all of the above factors.

Chapter Fifteen

Toward a Client-Centered Paradigm: A Holistic Synthesis

Disease-centered psychiatry conceptualized mental disorders as being caused by brain diseases, primarily "chemical imbalances" in neurotransmitters. It has been found, however, that attributing mental disorders primarily to chemical imbalances in the brain is too simplistic an explanation to accommodate recent research findings or to serve as a basis for consistently successful treatment. It is now known that psychiatric medications treat *symptoms* and not *diseases* (Guttmacher, 1994). Also, it has been found that psychotherapy can alter the brain (Schwartz et al., 1996).

Clinical reality is created by the clinician and the client within a clinical context employing their learned cultural schemas. Treatment of mental disorders with medications—on the assumption that this reversed the effects of a genetically based chemical imbalance—was based on the disease-centered paradigm and led to conclusions in assessment and diagnosis that are unwarranted. For example, this disease-centered view of mental illness promoted the conclusion that complete recovery from schizophrenia was unlikely if not impossible. We now know that this is not necessarily true. Complete recoveries from schizophrenia are uncommon in economically developed countries but significantly more common in less developed societies (Chapter 14). This indicates that complete recovery from schizophrenia is possible; therefore, schizophrenia needs to be conceptualized in a more complex, holistic fashion.

The realization has slowly dawned that the etiology, structure, course, and outcome of mental disorders are far more complexly integrated than was previously imagined. It is now becoming clear that mental disorders need to be defined in a holistic manner that includes the interactions of the individual's sociocultural environment and the effects of diagnosis and treatment on the individual's brain. All of these factors combine and interact to produce an actual illness experience in a given individual. The traditional disease-centered paradigm in psychiatry is now being expanded to include the neurobiology of adaptation and learning. This theoretical expansion includes the effects of neuronal changes in the brain resulting from psychotropic medications and psychotherapy as well as the neurobiological effects of individual and cultural learning.

In this book, I have taken an essentially anthropological viewpoint of mental illness, utilizing anthropology's deliberately holistic perspective and methodology, combining neurobiological, psychological, social, and cultural theories and data. I have specifically attempted to embrace a holistic, client-centered approach to assessment and diagnosis. In client-centered psychiatry, rather than diagnosis and treatment being concerned with a *disease*, diagnosis and treatment are concerned with an individual who has thoughts, emotions, a social context, and a set of cultural schemas. In this final chapter, I will define a client-centered model for psychopathology with an emphasis on the relationship between culture, brain plasticity, and mental illness.

The cultural information in DSM-IV (APA, 1994) demonstrates official recognition of the important role sociocultural forces play in the etiology, structure, and treatment of mental illness. It also indicates an expansion beyond the disease-centered paradigm of psychopathology. As was pointed out in Chapter 1, a paradigm is never superseded until an adequate replacement has been formulated. Therefore, new client-centered models of mental illness need to be constructed that integrate and synthesize known biological, psychological, social, and cultural factors. The following is one possible client-centered model synthesizing the key points of this text. In this chapter, I have combined information on brain plasticity with elements from various parts of this book into a single statement about the nature of mental illness.

Based on recent studies, I suggest that a client-centered model of mental illness should be used as a basis for assessment and diagnosis and that it should integrate the eight factors, presented in Box 15.1. Each of these factors will be discussed in detail in the sections that follow.

Culture-Based Stress and Emotional Trauma

Culture is not just a set of beliefs but a meaning system that structures thought, experience of the world, and social organizations (Clifford & Marcus, 1986; D'Andrade, 1984; Shweder, 1990). As a result, everyday patterns of life, norms of behavior, and things that are taken for granted are all different in different cultures. Likewise, the types of socioenvironmental stress that have an impact on individuals can vary dramatically.

For example, in economically developed societies, the need to make a living within the context of a wage labor system creates different types of social and economic stressors than those experienced by individuals in agrarian or hunter-gatherer societies. In a WHO-sponsored cross-cultural study of life events and schizophrenia, it was found that social stress in the environment may precipitate psychotic episodes in schizophrenic patients. It was found that stressful events tend to cluster in a two- to three-week period immediately pre-

---

Box 15.1

A Holistic Paradigm for
Mental Illness and Treatment

1. Culture-based socioenvironmental stress and emotional trauma affecting groups, and differential individual experience of stress and emotional trauma affecting the microstructures of neural networks in the brain.
2. Individual genetic sensitivity to socioenvironmental stress and emotional trauma.
3. Individual culture-based thinking-feeling responses to the environment structured in and altering neural networks in the brain.
4. Fluid boundary between mental health and mental illness.
5. Factors affecting the duration of illness: that is, self-limiting, adaptive, maladaptive, and progressive influences (biological and sociocultural).
6. Culture-based clinical realities: that is, culture-bound syndromes, idioms of distress, professional diagnoses, and forms of deviant behavior structured in neural networks.
7. Culture-based treatments affecting the psychology and neurology of the client.
8. Culture-based psychological and neurological outcomes.

SOURCE: Adapted from Castillo, 1994c.

---

ceding onset of a psychotic episode (Day et al., 1987). Significantly, prevalence rates for schizophrenia are much higher in industrialized societies than they are in some premodern societies. In fact, schizophrenia seems to be relatively uncommon in any society without a system of wage labor (Warner, 1985). Further, one recent study indicates that the chances of developing schizophrenia are higher for persons raised in cities than for those raised in rural areas (Lewis et al.,1992). Moreover, as discussed in Chapter 14, schizophrenia appears to have a more benign course and outcome in less economically developed countries that have sociocentric societies and premodern meaning systems. Also, as discussed in Chapter 3, the types of social stressors differ across cultures and are likely to be greater in societies that are hierarchical rather than egalitarian.

Social Stress for Females

One example of culture-based social stress created by social dominance hierarchies is that experienced by females in various societies that are characterized by high levels of male dominance. The culture-based structure of dominance hierarchies has a differential impact on various groups within the hierarchy.

In India's hierarchical society, the social structure places women and low caste persons in typically difficult situations with highly restricted avenues of social and psychological adaptation. The only means of escape for a newlywed Indian woman living in the context of an abusive affinal family may be a culture-bound dissociative disorder such as spirit possession or, in some extreme cases, suicide (Harper, 1963). Hindu family structure places younger females at the bottom of the family hierarchy. Quite simply, younger females are the most vulnerable members of any family group in India, possessing the lowest status in the family hierarchy and the least power. As such, they are unprotected from serious abuse and neglect within families.

In India all females in a subordinate position are expected to be obedient, submissive, hardworking, and noncomplaining. Ordinarily, if a female is able to maintain this type of behavior outwardly, the amount of physical and verbal abuse directed against her by her family will be tolerable. However, in cases where she is unable to maintain her constant attitude of submissiveness, or when the amount or severity of abuse is simply intolerable, the female typically has two options—suicide or dissociation in the form of spirit possession (Harper, 1963). The customary method of suicide is to jump into the family well (Freed & Freed 1964; Harper, 1963), although hanging is also used in urban areas (Gandhy, 1988).

Ceaseless demands for dowry ensure a lucrative source of income for a woman's affinal family. If the natal family refuses to pay continuing demands for more money, a "cooking accident" with the kerosene stove will occur in which the young woman is deliberately burned to death, leaving the husband free to marry again and start the whole process anew. Dowry deaths in India have increased 170 percent since 1984. During 1994, 6,200 dowry deaths were recorded—an average of 17 young married women killed each day by their affinal families (Moore, 1995). The sheer number of excess deaths or aborted births of females in India is illustrated by the male-female ratio in a population of 900 million. In nearly all other countries of the world, there are more females than males. In contrast, in India the male-female ratio is 1000:935. Millions of females are missing from the population (Ghandy, 1988; see also Pachauri, 1988, concerning female infanticide, and Menon, 1989, concerning child prostitution). This extreme male dominance in South Asian social organization may help to explain the high incidence of dissociative disorders in females observed on the subcontinent (Akhtar, 1988; Carstairs & Kapur, 1976; Khanna, Wig, & Varma, 1974; Varma, Bouri, & Wig, 1981).

It is clear that some types of culture-based socioenvironmental stressors affect particular groups differentially within dominance hierarchies. This point needs to be recognized and included in any client-centered assessment of psychopathology.

Psychological Trauma

A person's own individual life history also needs to be examined when determining the etiology of mental illness. Numerous recent studies have shown a direct connection between psychological trauma, especially early in life, and various symptoms of psychopathology (Kleinman & Kleinman, 1995; Nolen-Hoeksema, Girgus, & Seligman, 1992; North et al., 1993; Post, 1992; Post et al., 1989).

For example, the presence of extreme or repeated psychological trauma in the personal histories of many psychiatric patients with various diagnoses indicates the possibility that *highly focused attention* may be the common psychological mechanism at the basis of numerous symptoms. Several researchers have come to the conclusion that spontaneous trance (highly focused attention) occurring during times of extreme stress or life-threatening danger can be related to many subsequent psychiatric symptoms (Bliss, 1986; Kleinman & Kleinman, 1995; Price, 1987; Putnam, 1989, 1993; Ross, 1989; Spiegel, 1991; van der Kolk & van der Hart 1989).

Because of a common background of physical and emotional trauma and a great overlap in symptoms, van der Kolk and van der Hart (1989) have suggested the existence of a continuum of *trauma spectrum disorders* with:

> multiple personality disorder [dissociative identity disorder in DSM-IV] at one end of the spectrum, representing an extreme adaptation to very severe chronic childhood abuse, borderline personality disorder as an intermediate adaptation, and some forms of somatoform, conversion, panic, and anxiety disorders representing dissociated somatic reexperiencing of more circumscribed traumatic events. (p. 1537)

This position was also taken by Price (1987) and by Ross (1989).

Thus, many different symptoms may have a common element of highly focused attention. For example, a list of symptoms common in dissociative identity disorder (a syndrome linked directly to traumatic stress) includes symptoms from many different DSM-IV disorders, namely: voices arguing, voices commenting on one's actions, influences playing on one's body, thought withdrawal, thoughts ascribed to others, made feelings, made impulses, made volitional acts, delusions, visual hallucinations, amnesia, fugues, depersonalization, derealization, depression, mania, anxiety, panic, suicide attempts, intractable headaches, dissociative seizures, dissociative sensory loss, dissociative paralysis, sexual dysfunction, sexual promiscuity, recurrent nightmares, self-mutilation, antisocial behavior, and substance abuse (Bliss, 1986; Coons, 1988; Coons et al., 1988; Escobar, 1995; Kluft, 1985, 1987; Lowenstein & Putnam, 1990; North et al., 1993; Putnam 1989, 1993; Ross & Anderson, 1988; Ross & Heber et al., 1989; Ross, Norton, & Wozney, 1989).

The great overlap of symptoms between dissociative identity disorder and schizophrenia suggests that highly focused attention directed inwardly may be implicated in the symptoms of schizophrenia. For example, it is known that people with schizophrenia perform poorly on tests of outwardly focused attention such as being able to track objects across the visual field (Clementz & Sweeney, 1990; Holzman & Levy, 1977; Iacono, 1988). It is possible that this well-studied deficit in attention tasks may be related to these individuals having highly focused inward attention.

Considerable evidence also exists that environmental stress and emotional trauma alter the microstructure and biochemistry of the brain, including anatomical changes in neuronal microstructures such as dendritic branching and neurotransmitter receptor systems and changes in brain hormone levels. Extreme or long-term stress may also result in alterations in brain memory systems making persons more sensitive to further stress. Table 15.1 summarizes

Table 15.1

Changes in Brain Neurotransmitter and Neurohormonal Systems with Stress

Neurotransmitter	Acute stress	Chronic stress	Brain regions involved	PTSD symptoms
Norepinephrine	Increased turnover	Increased responsive-ness of LC neurons	Hipp, Hypo, LC, Cor, Amyg	Anxiety, fear, hypervigilance, hyperarousal, irritability, encoding of traumatic memories
CRF-HPA axis Brain CRF	Increase	Increase/ decrease	Hipp, Hypo, Cor, LC	Anxiety and fear, memory
Peripheral ACTH	Increase	Increase/ decrease	Amyg	alterations, hyper-arousal
Peripheral cortisol	Increase	Increase/ decrease		
Dopamine	Increased release	Increase	PFC, NA	Hypervigilance, paranoia, altera-tions in memory
Benzodiazepines	Increased release	Decrease[a]	Hipp, Hypo, Cor, Stria, MB	Anxiety
Endogenous opiates	Increased release	Decrease[a]	MB, Hipp	Analgesia, emotional blunt-ing, encoding of traumatic memories

NOTE: LC = loeus coeruleus, Hipp = hippocampus. Hypo = hypothalamus. Cor = cerebral cortex. Amyg = amygdala. CRF = corticotropin-releasing factor. HPA = hypothalamic-pituitary-adrenal axis. ACTH = adrenocorticotropic hormone. PFC = prefrontal cortex. NA = nucleus accumbens. Stria = striatum. MB = midbrain.
[a]Decrease in receptor binding measured by B_{max}.
SOURCE: From "Neurobiology of Posttraumatic Stress Disorder," by Bremner et al. In J. M. Oldham et al., *Review of Psychiatry, 12.* Copyright © 1993 American Psychiatric Association. Reprinted with permission.

the changes in brain neurotransmitter and neurohormonal systems resulting from stress that have been discovered thus far.

The studies summarized in Table 15.1 by Bremner et al. (1994) show that multiple brain neurotransmitter and neurohormonal systems develop long-term changes as a result of stress. These changes are sure to be related to anatomical changes in neurotransmitter and neurohormonal receptor systems.

In related research, Robert Post (1990) has theorized that recurrent mood disorders may result from a kindling effect in the brain related to traumatic emotional stress. In this theory, an original traumatic life event, such as an important loss or a personal assault, could have a long-term effect on neural pathways in the brain, making the individual hypersensitive to subsequent stressful events. Thus, the person has a lower response threshold for stress. As a result, less stressful events are capable of triggering a stress response, and more events are experienced as stressful.

As the brain experiences more stress, there will be a continuously diminishing threshold for stimuli to trigger a stress response. Eventually, the stress response may not require any stimulus at all and simply take an independent course as the underlying neural structures become stronger with repeated experience. This is referred to as a "kindling" effect because of its similarity to experiments done on the brains of animals in which electricity was applied to the brains, causing seizures. With repeated application of electricity and consequent uncontrolled neuronal firing, less electricity was required to cause a seizure. After enough periodic applications of electricity, the animals began to have spontaneous seizures without electricity. These seizures occurred with increasing rapidity and affected greater parts of the brain. The initial applications of electricity are the "kindling," which gets the seizure process going. Post theorizes that this is analogous to what is happening in the brains of rapid-cycling bipolar disorder patients. Kindling affects neural pathways by strengthening the connections between neurons, making the neurons more likely to fire an action potential. Thus, the brain becomes changed anatomically on the microlevel, particularly in dendritic branching and in the efficacy of neurotransmitter receptor systems.

Because of these factors, a personal history of traumatic or stressful experiences affecting the microstructures of dendritic branching and neurotransmitter systems in the brain should be considered as possible etiological elements in any client-centered model of mental illness.

Individual Sensitivity to Stress and Emotional Trauma

Studies in monkeys and rats have shown evidence for genetically determined individual variations in sensitivity to environmental stress and emotional trauma (Robertson, Martin & Candy, 1978; Suomi, 1991). Likewise, numerous studies have shown a higher concordance rate of psychopathology between identical twins over fraternal twins or other siblings. Although various methodological objections have been raised concerning the twin studies, it is generally accepted that genetic inheritance makes certain individuals more susceptible to mental illness.

However, the twin studies have also made it abundantly clear that mental illness is not purely genetic in origin. It is now known that genetic factors contribute less than half of the explanation for mental disorders. For example, the percentage of identical twins who both have schizophrenia is less than 50 percent (Gottesman, 1991). Similar or lower rates also exist for other mental disorders. Therefore, the full explanation for the origin of mental pathology needs to focus on the interaction between genetic sensitivity and environmental factors. Based on results from animal studies, it is likely that some individuals are neurologically more sensitive to environmental stress and emotional trauma as a result of genetic variation, or as a result of personal history. Those with greater genetic vulnerability would presumably require less stress to develop a mental disorder.

Brain Plasticity and Individual Experience

In the last few decades, the relationship between mind and body has become increasingly observable. Some neuroscientists now use the term **mind-brain** to convey a monistic vision of the relationship between the mind and the brain (Hobson, 1988). In this new monistic perspective, the associations of memory can be seen as organizations of ideas structured simultaneously in both the mind and the neural networks of the brain (Thompson, 1987). This monistic conception of mind-brain has obvious implications for a client-centered model of mental illness because the mind-brain can be seen to be the repository of culture and personal experience.

Culture and the Mind-Brain

As a result of enculturation, every individual learns a language, a religion or other meaning system specifying the forces of nature operating in the world, norms of behavior, and patterns of experiencing the environment. All of this knowledge is structured in neural networks in the mind-brain.

Connections between individual neurons and the strength of synaptic connections are determined by use patterns (Thompson, Donegan, & Lavond, 1986). By the habitual act of thinking in a particular language or believing in the forms of a particular religion, those forms of thought become a physical reality in the brain in the organization of neural networks. In a very real sense, the sociocultural environment becomes physically structured in the brains of individuals.

This process has frequently been referred to as **downward causation** (for example, Sperry, 1987). That is, thinking, as an activity pattern, is causal in that it alters the brain at the level of dendritic branching and strengthens the neurotransmitter systems in individual synapses. Thus, people walk around with their culture and their personal history literally inside their heads. Therefore, it can be said that the individual mind-brain becomes "cultured" through experience of the world. This means that the organization of culture has its psychobiological correlates in the organization of the mind-brain. Culture-specific organizations will exist, not in gross anatomy but in the microanatomy of individual dendritic branching, synaptic receptor systems, and in the organizational formation of neural networks.

To speak Chinese, you must have the neural networks for speaking Chinese structured in the brain—no Chinese neural networks, no speaking Chinese. The presence of Chinese neural networks results, of course, from enculturation. Someone who is genetically Chinese but born and raised in the United States and fully assimilated into American culture will have American neural networks—an American mind-brain. It is these culture-specific systems of neural structure that influence most aspects of cognitive processing by individuals in the form of cultural schemas. These cultural schemas structure experience of the world, including the experience of mental illness.

Neural Network Plasticity

The study of plasticity in the neural networks of individual animals resulting from life experience is now possible (Aoki & Siekevitz, 1988; Cotman & Lynch, 1989; Kandel, 1989; Leon, 1992; Thompson, Donegan, & Lavond, 1986; Usherwood, 1993; Woodruff-Pak, Logan, & Thompson, 1990). The plasticity of the brain occurs primarily in the structure of dendritic branching between the neurons and in the structure and functional efficacy of synaptic neurotransmitter release and receptor systems.

It is a widely held working hypothesis that modifications at synapses are, to a large extent, responsible for the overall plasticity of nervous system circuitry and, therefore, behavioral plasticity (Nieto-Sampedro & Cotman, 1987). Synaptic modifications occur in a number of ways and can be linked directly to types of behavior and experience. Types of synaptic modifications include *synapse turnover*, changes in *synaptic transmission*, and *long-term potentiation*.

Synapse turnover includes both synapse replacement and overall changes in synapse number. The process of turnover includes:

1. synapse disconnection and degeneration,
2. new axonal growth and differentiation of new presynaptic endings,
3. establishment of new synaptic structures, and
4. maturation of the new synapses.

Synapse turnover is an ongoing process in the normal adult nervous system. It may be evoked by stimuli such as life experiences (that is, learning, memory, psychological trauma), environmental changes, normal physiological activity of the organism, or disease and injury (Nieto-Sampedro & Cotman, 1987).

Synaptic transmission refers to the "message" (neurotransmitter substance) transmitted between the presynaptic and postsynaptic membranes. Synaptic transmission is plastic in normal usage in that it strengthens or weakens as a function of the amount of previous activity of the synapse. Such changes are referred to as *use-dependent* or historical effects because the previous history or use of the synapse determines its current strength. Generally, repetitive use of a synapse results in an increase of its functional strength characterized by an increase in efficacy of neurotransmitter release and receptor systems.

The most important form of synaptic plasticity with regard to the formation of neural networks in the human nervous system is **long-term potentiation (LTP)**. LTP refers to an enduring increase in functional synaptic strength. It is now generally accepted that LTP plays an important role in memory formation (Swanson, Teyler, & Thompson, 1982). LTP requires the repetitive, nearly synchronous coactivation of adjacent nerve fibers on the postsynaptic membrane. The result is typically a doubling in functional strength of the post-synaptic response. It is likely that the coactivation of adjacent nerve fibers on the postsynaptic membrane structures neural networks at that location for incoming messages from two or more sources in the brain. LTP appears to be the underlying biophysical mechanism for the formation of neural networks responsible for learning and memory (that is, associations). Research in the neurobiology of LTP suggests that it is accompanied by an increase in presy-naptic neurotransmitter release, an increase in postsynaptic neurotransmitter receptors, and growth in postsynaptic dendrites associated with increases in dendritic cytoskeletal proteins (Aoki & Siekevitz, 1988; Teyler, 1987).

Adult patterns of cognition, thought, and emotion are not inborn but develop over the course of time through the experience of the environment. This means that experience itself places its own imprint on the microstructures of the brain, particularly in dendritic branching and in the strength of neuro-transmitter systems. Even though the basic organization of the brain is deter-mined by genetics, details of its microstructure and function remain plastic and modifiable throughout the lifetime of the individual. Personal experience based in a cultural context reinforces specific neural pathways while others fall into disuse.

Tuning the Central Nervous System

In addition to the differences in mind-brain that are expected to exist in persons from different cultures, the use-dependent plasticity of neural net-works also plays a pivotal role in creation of individual differences in mind-brain in persons belonging to the same culture. These differences of mind-brain will be based on differences in individual behavior and personal experience. This is important in understanding the neurobiology of mental ill-ness because of the possibility that recurring states of consciousness are struc-tured in what Lex (1979, following Gellhorn, 1969) calls alternative *tunings* of the mind-brain.

Tuning refers to a long-term change in the central nervous system (CNS) that results from repeated experience of a particular condition of the nervous system, which makes the individual more susceptible to reestablishment of that same condition (see Gellhorn, 1969; Lex, 1979; Winkelman, 1986). This is analogous to the concept of kindling. It has been suggested that an alternative tuning of the CNS can operate in substitution of the tuning and organizational processes (or behaviors of mind-brain) that sustain the usual, familiar experi-ence of body, self, and environment (Castillo, 1995). This hypothesis is based on the well-supported assumption that the "mind" is in fact a particular orga-nizational process based on the central nervous system. It is the organizational process that is key, not the neurons themselves. According to the *Encyclopedia of Neuroscience:*

The key word linking brain and mind is organization (or in a loose sense, information) and the key level of analysis is that of the interaction of the network of individual neurons. In other words, mind, despite its apparently molar and continuous nature, is a process that is embodied within the interaction of the extremely complex, yet fundamentally discrete neuronal network. It is the ebb and flow of signals among the vast number of neurons in the brain that is most likely to emerge as the actual psychoneural equivalent of mind. (Uttal, 1988, p. 57)

If the mind and, by extension, normal consciousness are organizational processes—that is, the "ebb and flow of signals" in plastic neural networks—and if these neural networks are established and stabilized by repeated use, then the connection between habitual use and tuning is established. Thus, relatively stable tunings of the mind-brain are created through repeated experience or behavior.

Mental Illness as Tuning of the Mind-Brain

The property of use-dependent plasticity in neural networks suggests the possibility of the establishment of alternative tunings of the individual mind-brain based on the process of habitual patterns of thinking, behavior, or experience. Thus, new abnormal tunings of the mind-brain can be structured in neural networks through the repetition of thought, behavior, or experience that is abnormal.

From this perspective of a dynamic mind-brain, a major depressive episode could be seen as being identical with a particular pattern of thought or organization of signals in the neural networks of the mind-brain. Therefore, pathological states of consciousness such as a major depressive episode could be seen as patterns of *pathological thought* in the dynamic mind-brain. In other words, the organizational processes of the mind-brain that are commonly referred to as brain disease could be viewed as the thought patterns or *thinking behaviors* of a dynamic mind-brain.

Thus, it is suggested that mental illness results from a pattern of thinking, behavior, or experience in a dynamic mind-brain, which will, with sufficient repetition, result in its own unique tuning of the central nervous system. This abnormal tuning will have its own related psychophysiological characteristics contrasting to those that sustain normal consciousness. This could explain why the neurobiological correlates of major depressive episodes are *state dependent* (APA, 1994).

For example, habitual thinking about distressing things, such as traumatic memories, can be an activity pattern in the brain that can cause alterations in neurotransmitter release and receptor properties and microanatomical structures in neural networks, which strengthen the biological substrates of that particular pattern of thought. In this way, a depressing pattern of thinking can become "tuned" into the mind-brain and become more powerful in relation to other nondepressing patterns of thinking, eventually coming to dominate the subjective experience of consciousness.

Tuning of Dissociation

Parallel to the example of major depression, it has been suggested that highly focused attention is a behavior of the mind-brain, manifesting in various types of trance, that with habitual repetition will result in altered tunings of the CNS. It has been further suggested that this process can be intentional and is based on behavioral norms such as religious practices (Castillo, 1995).

The phenomena commonly recognized as examples of dissociation (see Box 15.2) are primarily specific behaviors associated with trance (highly focused attention). Most of these items are recognizable as culture-based behaviors (for example, shamanism, asceticism, crystal gazing, hypnosis). The most problematic items on this list are the medical trances—amnesia, fugues, dissociative identity, hallucinations, delusions, and depersonalization. These are usually thought of as symptoms of mental illness and not as behaviors. However, it may be possible to view these medical trances as habitual patterns of thinking, a habitual focusing of attention to the point of entering trance and altering consciousness. This type of thought behavior can be hypothesized to be an activity pattern in the brain that can cause alterations in neurotransmitter release and receptor properties and microanatomical structures in neural neworks, which strengthens the biological substrates of that particular pattern of thought. In this way, dissociative patterns of thinking can become "tuned" into the mind-brain and become more powerful in relation to more integrated patterns of thinking, coming to dominate the subjective experience of consciousness.

Cultural and personal patterns of abnormal thinking and their downward causation effects on the biochemistry and microanatomy of the brain should have a central place in a client-centered model of mental illness. These abnormal patterns of thought can include habitually focusing attention inward on distressing topics, causing anxiety and depression, or trance-related behavior resulting in dissociative symptoms.

Boundary Between
Mental Health and Mental Illness

The client-centered model suggested here accepts the psychodynamic principle that mentally healthy people can become ill if they are exposed to severe enough emotional trauma. Combined with this psychodynamic principle is the assumption that mental illnesses exist on a continuum or spectrum from normality, to mild mental illness, to severe mental illness. Specific syndromes can be identified on this spectrum, but individuals may move over time on the spectrum from one syndrome or disorder to another. This is significantly different from the disease-centered paradigm, which assumes separate brain diseases as the causes for discrete mental disorders.

The client-centered model also assumes that personality development and mental functioning have their psychobiological correlates based in the plastic

---

Box 15.2

The Phenomena of Trance

A. Varieties of Religious Trance
   1. Shamanism
   2. Asceticism and meditation (for example, yoga)
   3. Spirit possession
   4. Revivalism and conversion
   5. Glossolalia or speaking in tongues
   6. Spiritualistic medium (for example, channeling)
   7. Near death experiences
   8. Crystal gazing
   9. Religious visions and hallucinations
   10. Religious ecstasy
B. Secular and Medical Trances
   1. Spontaneous trances (ecstasy, catalepsy, and somnambulism)
   2. Induced trances (hypnosis)
   3. Dissociative amnesia
   4. Dissociative fugue
   5. Dissociative identity (multiple personality)
   6. Dissociative hallucinations and delusions
   7. Depersonalization and derealization
C. Trances of Everyday Life
   1. Dreams and other sleep association phenomena
   2. Reverie (daydreaming)
   3. Absentmindedness and inattention
   4. Habitual actions
   5. Automatisms, the planchette, and the ouija board

SOURCE: Based on Carlson, 1986, p. 9.

---

microanatomy of the neural networks of the brain. Abnormalities in personality and mental functioning will always have some psychobiological basis, but this can be viewed as a modifiable condition resulting from patterns of thinking, behavior, or experience, and not necessarily brain disease.

Factors That Affect Duration of Illness

Some mental illnesses are self-limiting, occurring in response to a particular environmental stressor. When the stressor is removed, the pathologic condition is alleviated. Similarly, some mental illnesses may simply run their course, with natural healing processes and the passage of time the only treatment.

In other cases, a mental illness may prove to be adaptive for an individual. For example, in some spirit possession cases in India, a woman's position in the family or village may be permanently altered and enhanced by her mental illness. This is an adaptive change usually validated and solidified in healing rituals that can sometimes allow the individual to function from then on without a recurrence of psychopathology (Castillo, 1994b). For example, Lewis

(1989) has analyzed the relationship between spirit possession and social structure, cross-culturally and observes that women appear to be possessed more often than men:

> It will now be clear, I think, that we are dealing with a widespread spiritual interpretation of female problems common to many cultures, whose diagnosis and treatment gives women the opportunity to gain ends (material and non-material) which they cannot readily secure more directly. Women are, in effect, making a special virtue of adversity and affliction, and, often quite literally, capitalizing on their distress. (p. 77)

Although the capitalistic emphasis of Lewis's interpretation is probably somewhat overstated, the idea that women in positions of subservience are using the behavior of trance and possession as mechanisms of adaptation and survival is probably correct. As Harper (1963) points out, the possessing spirit frequently demands expensive gifts and ceremonies from family members as an inducement to depart, and may threaten the family with supernatural harm if they do not comply. In any case, the abused female is invariably treated less harshly by her family as a result of the spirit possession, mostly in an attempt to avert the need for more costly rituals. This can be seen as a mental illness that is adaptive for the sick individual. It results in a permanent improvement of her status in the family and in her living conditions. In this case, the illness is no longer required, and it disappears.

However, for most patients, mental illness is maladaptive. Disturbances in consciousness and behavior can impair social and occupational functioning with the result that socioenvironmental stress is increased, sometimes dramatically. This increase in environmental stress can greatly exacerbate symptoms, which in turn can further increase sources of environmental stress. A snowball effect is created in which the illness condition becomes chronic, with frequent relapses. This appears to be the situation in cases of schizophrenia within families exhibiting high levels of *expressed emotion* (Chapter 14). This circular process needs to be recognized and assessed in its sociocultural context.

Mental illness can also be maladaptive in situations in which individuals become dependent on the symptomatology of illness for their livelihood. Some individuals learn to "make it" in the world by "being crazy," thereby qualifying for permanent public financial assistance. This is maladaptive in that their financial situation can require them to remain seriously ill. Thus, they may take on the "career" of a chronic mental patient (Estroff, 1981).

Influences that promote a progressive course in mental illness also need to be recognized. Included here would be any identifiable brain disease that is determining a progressive course of illness. However, although much progress has been made in recent decades concerning the physiology of the brain, discovery of an independent brain disease as the cause of any of the major psychiatric syndromes has yet to be confirmed.

Even though many people (including some scientists) believe that schizophrenia is based on an incurable brain disease, no such disease has ever been determined. As DSM-IV states, "No laboratory findings have been identified that are diagnostic of Schizophrenia" (APA, 1994, p. 280). Moreover, there is considerable cross-cultural evidence against such a conclusion. If an incurable brain disease is not at the basis of schizophrenia, the factors that are progressive in influence need to be identified.

The presence of a modern versus premodern meaning system may also be related to high levels of expressed emotion. As discussed in Chapter 14, in the modern egocentric families of Anglo American society, schizophrenia is frequently cognized as *internal* to the individual and almost always as *incurable*. This is consistent with modern disease-centered explanations of schizophrenia. Moreover, because a high degree of independence and self-sufficiency is expected of all individuals in Anglo American society, these individuals are viewed as personally inadequate and therefore stigmatized. Thus, high levels of family hostility and criticism directed at the ill person are more likely in this context. The high levels of hostility and criticism are probably instrumental in determining a progressive course for schizophrenia in modern egocentric societies such as the United States.

Culture-Based Clinical Realities

As I have shown in this book, patterns of mental illness vary across cultures. During enculturation, patterns of thinking, experiencing the world, and norms of behavior become structured in the neural networks of the brain. This is true not only for normal patterns of functioning but also for abnormal functioning. Thus, there are culturally specific ways of being abnormal. These cultural forms of mental illness are learned through the process of enculturation and are structured in cognitive schemas in neural networks. They are based on differing sets of cultural schemas. For example, spirit possession is commonplace in India but dissociative identity disorder is rare. In contrast, spirit possession is rare and exotic in the United States but dissociative identity disorder is increasingly common.

Culture-Bound Dissociative Syndromes

Dissociative identity disorder (DID) appears to occur primarily in persons holding a modern set of cultural schemas. These modern individuals typically dissociate into separate human personalities. In contrast, dissociation in premodern societies and in those individuals in western society holding premodern, supernatural worldviews is typically manifest as demons, ghosts, deities, or other supernatural entities. These differences in mental illness are based on differing sets of cultural schemas.

Although what would be considered DID according to DSM-IV criteria has been reported in India, it is a rare illness. There appear to be two reasons for the rarity of DID in India. First, cases of dissociation are almost always subjectively experienced as spirit possession in India (Varma et al., 1981). Varma et al. conclude that this is related to the Hindu cultural schemas in which poly-theism, reincarnation, and possession by spirits are generally accepted. Second, the idea that spirits can come in and out of a person is quite consistent with the Hindu concept of human nature, which is viewed as porous, transac-tional, and fluid (Daniel, 1984; Marriott, 1976; Zimmerman, 1980). In subjective experience of the world, the Hindu person is susceptible to all sorts of pene-trations by outside influences in a process of continuous exchange with the environment and other beings.

Varma et al. (1981) contrast this with the North American subjective expe-rience of dissociation as taking on a new human role or "personality." They attribute this to the American penchant for "role-playing," that is, experiment-ing and assuming different personal identities and roles in a society that allows relatively great flexibility in the formation of the individual identity (see Goffman, 1959). This is structured by a modern set of cultural schemas in which the person is a solid physical entity separate from the environment with a relative lack of belief of spirits, ghosts, or demons interfering in the affairs or bodies of living persons. Thus, dissociation is manifest as alternate *personal-ities*—that is, common alternative human identities.

This pattern is contrasted with Indian cultural schemas in which many alternative supernatural identities are available in the cultural repertoire—gods, demons, ghosts, and so on—but there is a relative lack of human alter-natives. For the average individual in the rigid hierarchical social structure of India, "There is but one role, namely, to simply live and act like a good human being, and not a variety of roles that a person should adopt" (Varma et al., 1981, p. 118).

It is clear that these two illnesses, South Asian spirit possession and North American DID, although closely related dissociative disorders, are psychocul-turally distinct, with different subjective experiences, idioms of distress, and indigenous diagnoses and forms of treatment.

Effects of Culture-Based Clinical Realities

Cultural schemas structure mental illnesses along cultural lines. This point is especially relevant to the diagnosis of personality disorders. Standards of nor-mative personality development can vary widely by cultural context. For example, diagnosis of antisocial personality disorder is dependent on a partic-ular pattern of behavior that is considered deviant in most cultures. However, this same pattern of behavior can be considered normal and normative in a particular cultural context. As discussed in Chapter 3, the Swat Pukthun of northern Pakistan teach all their children to lie, cheat, steal, and fight. Individuals feel no guilt in any of these activities, and the only shame is in being caught (Lindholm, 1997).

Similarly, diagnostic categories such as avoidant personality disorder or dependent personality disorder are based on the western cultural ideal of an extroverted and independent personality. Not all cultures value this type of personality development. Each culture socializes its individuals to conform to its own cultural ideal.

Idioms of distress also vary by culture. In American society, dysphoria or sadness is an extremely common symptom in psychiatric populations reacting to socioenvironmental stress. However, in many nonwestern societies, somatic symptoms are more common in persons reacting to environmental stress (Kirmayer, 1984; Kleinman, 1988a). There are also cultural differences in types of somatic symptoms experienced and reported (Janca et al., 1995). These differences in symptomatology should be seen as idioms of distress related to culture-based patterns of thinking, experience, and behavior. Deviant behavior should always be judged in relation to the cultural identity of the client.

Conceptions of mental illness are based in culturally divergent meaning systems, and modern psychiatry is no exception. Modern psychiatry is a product of western cultural conceptions of human nature and pathology. You need only look at the history of western psychiatry to realize that as western cultural schemas changed, notions about the nature of mental illness changed. Former etiological factors in psychiatry, such as imbalances in black and yellow bile, wandering uteruses, and oedipus complexes, have given way to modern notions of imbalances in neurotransmitters.

These cultural conceptions can affect the individual after the onset of illness and become part of the phenomenology of the illness. An individual diagnosed with schizophrenia might be told that this is an incurable brain disease that can be only partially controlled by medications. This professional conception of the illness could have a self-fulfilling influence on the individual. If the client comes to view him- or herself as an incurably diseased person, projecting that diseased identity into the future, the client's family and society might also accept this view, treating the individual with increased amounts of expressed emotion. Society might view this individual as frightening or undesirable, based on existing cultural biases. In contrast, in many premodern societies, mental illness is generally thought to have a brief duration, and individuals are treated in a more accepting fashion by their families and society (Waxler, 1974, 1979).

The conception of a mental illness in the mind of the clinician, given in the form of a diagnosis, can influence the subjective experience of the client (Kleinman 1988a, b). Thus, the diagnosis and the illness itself come to be intertwined. Culture-based clinical realities, including professional diagnoses, cultural biases, culture-bound syndromes, idioms of distress, and forms of deviance should be recognized as preexisting, culture-specific patterns of abnormality and included in any client-centered model of mental illness.

Culture-Based Treatments

Because conceptions of mental illness are culture-based, so are treatments. A folk healer treating a case of spirit possession by means of exorcism is practicing a culture-based treatment, just as is a psychiatrist treating schizophrenia exclusively with neuroleptic medications. Both of these are based on cultural constructions of illness. In both cases, the effects of treatment can alter the mind-brain of the individual and become part of the subjective experience of illness.

Exorcism as Culture-Based Treatment

In the case of treatment by exorcism, the individual is submerged in a culture-based world of deities, ghosts, and demons, which serves to structure the subjective experience of the illness (Castillo, 1994b; McDaniel, 1989).

In her study of the lives of some of India's most famous deity-saints such as Ramakrishna Paramahansa, Ananda Mayi Ma, Krishna Chaitanya, and others, McDaniel (1989) found that virtually all were at first thought to be possessed by malevolent spirits, or were thought to be insane. It was only later, after extensive treatment and the failure of healing rituals to banish the possessing spirit, that the individuals were accepted as deity-saints.

In the hierarchy of spiritual entities in India, a "spirit" of a higher status controlled by the exorcist may cast out the lower "spirit" possessing a person. If the "spirit" possessing the person claims to be of a high status in the hierarchy (that is, a god or goddess), then the "spirit" controlled by the exorcist will have to be of a still higher status in the cultural hierarchy of spirits for the ritual to be successful. This is because the exorcism ritual is essentially *a clash of symbols* in the minds of the individual and the exorcist (see the analysis of healing rituals in Chapter 5).

If the "spirit" possessing an individual claims the highest status (for example, Shiva or Kali), then only an exorcist who also claims to be possessed by these highest divinities will be able to exorcise the individual's "spirit." If the exorcist fails, it is often concluded that the possessing "spirit" *really is* Shiva or Kali and not a "demon" lying about its identity, otherwise the "spirit" would have been successfully banished.

By having the divine presence confirmed in this manner, an individual may come to be accepted as a god in human form and thus be healed—that is, the possessing "spirit" is now recognized in the society as a deity instead of a demon. Even though trance and possession behavior continue, the individual is no longer a patient but a spiritual adept or even an *avatar* (incarnation of a god). The cognitive construction of the possession both in the individual and for the society is transformed from a spiritual attack to a spiritual gift (McDaniel, 1989). The patient is healed, but dissociative experiences continue.

According to McDaniel (1989), acceptance as a deity-saint also may occur because the subjective experience and behavior of the possessed individual is shaped by the healing rituals to conform with culturally orthodox theology and dogma. Thus, the possessed person is taught how to be possessed by a benevolent "god" rather than a malevolent "demon," channeling the individual's ability and tendency to dissociate in a culturally appropriate and socially acceptable direction. Through this type of training, an individual can learn to control his or her trance ability and become a religious practitioner (exorcist,

oracle, *avatar*, and so forth). In this case, the patient is also healed, but dissociative experiences continue.

Neuroleptics as Culture-Based Treatment

In disease-centered psychiatry, even decades-long use of neuroleptics for the
treatment of schizophrenia was normative. Schizophrenia is an illness with a
typically progressive course in economically developed societies, but this may
not be the result of a natural disease process. However, with the assumption
that schizophrenia is caused by an incurable brain disease, the long-term use
of neuroleptics was justified. Neuroleptic medications have well-known side
effects of slowed thinking, slowed speech, akathisia, and other types of dystonias
frequently seen both by the patient and by untrained observers as symptoms
of the illness (APA, 1994, p. 742). These side effects of treatment can become part
of the subjective experience of the illness. Therefore, any client-centered model
of mental illness should take into account the psychological and neurological
side effects of culture-based treatments because these can become part of the
overall illness experience.

For example, it is now understood that neuroleptic medications can affect
neuronal structures. Neuroleptic medications administered over a long term
cause the brain to adapt to the neuroleptics by upregulating the dopamine
receptor system. This means the brain increases the number of dopamine
receptors as well as increasing the avidity with which receptors seek the
dopamine (Guttmacher, 1994). Although blocking dopamine receptors with
neuroleptics does reduce psychotic symptoms in a majority of patients, leading to short-term improvement, over the long term an upregulated dopamine
receptor system has the potential of escalating and prolonging the illness.

Birley and Brown (1970) found that schizophrenic patients who reduced or
discontinued the use of neuroleptics were more likely to relapse without the
involvement of stressful life events than were patients who had taken no neuroleptics for at least 12 months. Similar findings have been reported by
Chouinard and Jones (1980) and also by Chouinard, Annable, and Ross-
Chouinard (1986). Moreover, upregulated dopamine receptors in the motor
cortex caused by prolonged neuroleptic dopamine blockage cause various
kinds of movement disorders such as tardive dyskinesia, characterized by
abnormal, involuntary movements. In recent years, a growing awareness of the
serious side effects of neuroleptics has allowed most clinicians to realize that
neuroleptics may be overprescribed and should be used judiciously
(Guttmacher, 1994).

Significantly, this change in view has resulted in the inclusion of listings
for medication-induced movement disorders in the appendix of DSM-IV (APA,
1994, pp. 735–751). The disorders listed are: neuroleptic-induced parkinsonism, neuroleptic malignant syndrome, neuroleptic-induced acute dystonia,
neuroleptic-induced acute akathisia, neuroleptic-induced tardive dyskinesia,
and medication-induced postural tremor. This is the first time that a discussion

of the impairments caused by psychiatric medications has been included in the official manual. This is an indication of movement beyond the boundaries of the disease-centered biomedical paradigm.

Culture-Based Outcomes

Outcomes can be a defining factor in some mental disorders. For example, the distinction between schizophrenia and schizophreniform disorder in DSM-IV is strictly one of outcome. The symptoms of schizophreniform disorder are identical to those of schizophrenia; the difference is in the duration of the illness. Schizophreniform disorder requires at least one month of illness, but less than six months. If the illness goes on for six months or more, the diagnosis changes to schizophrenia. If the psychotic symptoms last less than one month, the diagnosis is brief psychotic disorder. Thus, it is hypothetically possible for an individual with unchanging psychotic symptoms to go from a diagnosis of brief psychotic disorder to schizophreniform disorder to schizophrenia simply by the passage of time. This is hardly an intellectually satisfying method of classification but, nevertheless, true.

Similarly, an individual might be provisionally diagnosed with schizophrenia, but if the individual recovers before six months, the diagnosis will be changed to schizophreniform disorder. This is equivalent to the clinician telling the patient, "Oh, you've recovered. I guess you didn't have schizophrenia after all." In this case, a poor outcome means the patient has schizophrenia, but a recovery within six months means the patient did not have schizophrenia.

This time-based distinction is an arbitrary method of classification. There is nothing special about one-month or six-month durations in psychotic symptomatology. These arbitrary categories are cultural entities, objects that exist because of a cultural agreement that something counts as that entity. Also, when we see that the outcome for schizophrenia varies by culture, we can surmise that sociocultural factors are affecting outcome. Thus, there are culture-based outcomes for mental illness.

Summary

A general trend toward client-centered practice in American medicine is now also being expressed in psychiatry. The explicit recognition in DSM-IV that cultural factors structure subjective experience, symptom patterns, types of dysfunctions, social correlates, course, and outcome of mental illness ushers in a new era of research. A narrow brain disease model for mental illness is no longer considered to be adequate by most researchers. New holistic models of mental illness and treatment are needed to guide research. Mental illness should be seen as a complex interaction between all eight of the factors discussed here, with a particular emphasis on the effects that habitual patterns of thinking and experience have on the biochemistry and microanatomy of the brain. The neural networks of the brain, particularly dendritic branching and neurotransmitter release and receptor systems, are continuously being altered because of influences from all of these factors. Therefore, each client's illness should be considered as a unique and changing experience occurring within specific social, cultural, and medical contexts.

The disease-centered diagnostic categories that separate psychopathology into mood disorders, psychotic disorders, dissociative disorders, somatoform disorders, anxiety disorders, and so on may be too inflexible to accommodate a client-centered conception of mental illness. The disease-centered classification system may also be based on a false biological determinism. As psychiatry moves into a new era of holistic research, the data that will inform future editions of the DSM may require a different, more client-centered system of classification.

acute stress disorder (ASD)   Syndrome closely related to *posttraumatic stress disorder* characterized by *anxiety* and *dissociative* symptoms after exposure to extreme stress. The only major distinctions are in duration and point of onset. By definition, ASD has an onset within one month after the traumatic event and does not persist beyond four weeks after the event.

addictive personality   Personality development in which an individual generally feels the need to alter his or her moods with substances but is not necessarily addicted to any particular mood altering substance and thus will use whatever substance is available.

adolescence   The period between the onset of puberty and the attainment of adulthood. Determined by cultural factors that define behavior expected of the adolescent and the length of time spent in this period.

agoraphobia   Syndrome characterized by *anxiety* about being in places in which a *panic attack* or other anxiety reaction might occur resulting in a pervasive avoidance of a variety of situations.

American Disease Model   Theoretical model in which alcoholism and other substance addictions are conceptualized as bodily diseases like cancer or heart disease.

amok   A Southeast Asian *trance* syndrome, usually characterized by a short-lived (a few minutes to several hours), sudden outburst of unrestrained violence, usually of a homicidal nature, preceded by a period of brooding, and ending with exhaustion. There is typically *dissociative amnesia*.

anomaly   A deviation from the usual or normal in scientific research. Something that cannot be explained according to the existing *theory*, *model*, or *paradigm*.

anorexia nervosa   Syndrome characterized by a refusal of the person to maintain a minimally normal body weight, an intense fear of being overweight, and a misperception of the individual's own body size or shape.

antisocial personality disorder   Personality characterized by a persistent pattern of victimizing others through theft or destruction of property, physical assault (including spouse or child abuse), or deceit to gain personal profit or pleasure.

anxiety   The emotion of fear linked to the anticipation of future danger or misfortune.

ataques de nervios   Latin American *trance* syndrome that is characterized by trembling, heart palpitations, heat in the chest rising to the head, faintness and seizure-like episodes, and sometimes hallucinations.

avoidant personality disorder Personality characterized by extreme social *anxiety,* low self-esteem, and hypersensitivity to criticism to the point that the individual purposely avoids interpersonal contact.

biopsychosocial paradigm The view that mental disorders are reactions of the personality to a combination of biological, psychological, and social factors.

bipolar I disorder Syndrome characterized by the presence of one or more *manic* or *mixed episodes.*

bipolar II disorder Syndrome characterized by the presence of at least one *major depressive episode* accompanied by at least one *hypomanic episode.*

body dysmorphic disorder Syndrome characterized by a persistent belief that the person's appearance is somehow seriously defective. Complaints commonly involve perceived defects in the face or head but can involve any body part.

borderline personality disorder Personality characterized by a persistent instability in social relationships, self-image, and emotions. Central to this instability is fear of abandonment and rejection.

brief clinical ethnography A narrative summary of a client's illness from the client's point of view, including the individual's cultural background, cultural explanations of illness, cultural factors related to psychosocial environment and levels of functioning, clinician-client relationship, and treatment options.

brief psychotic disorder Syndrome characterized by a *psychotic* disturbance that lasts more than one day but less than one month.

Briquet's syndrome Alternate name for *hysteria,* an obsolete diagnostic category characterized by *anxiety, somatoform, depressive,* and *dissociative* symptoms.

bulimia nervosa Syndrome characterized by binge eating and inappropriate methods of preventing weight gain including vomiting, misuse of laxatives, diuretics, or enemas.

category fallacy The *reification* of one culture's diagnostic categories and their projection onto individuals in another culture, where those categories lack coherence and their *validity* has not been established.

client-centered psychiatry The clinical perspective that diagnosis and treatment should be concerned with an individual's thoughts, emotions, social context, and cultural identity rather than diagnosis and treatment of only a brain *disease.*

clinical reality The cognitive construction of reality in the clinical setting. Clinical reality is created by the clinician and the client within a clinical context employing their learned *cultural schemas.*

cognitive schemas Learned structures of cognition used by an individual to make sense of and construct to some extent his or her subjective experience of the world.

coherence (in healing) Psychotherapeutic technique of convincing an individual that his or her internal and external environments are predictable and reasonably under control. By gaining coherence, the ill person gains hope and thereby avoids hopelessness. There are three components to the concept of coherence: *comprehensibility, manageability,* and *meaningfulness.*

comorbidity The simultaneous existence of two or more disorders in the same individual.

competitive male dominance A social organization characterized by males competing with each other through combat or other means for the exclusive sexual rights to a group of females. Thus, there is one dominant male controlling a harem of females.

comprehensibility (in healing) A sense of order. It means that the ill person can understand the source of the illness, the mechanism of illness, and its effects on the body and on his or her life. Thus, the illness is known and understood.

constructive function (of cultural meaning systems) The ability of cultural groups to make up explanations of the world and thereby create the subjective and intersubjective world they inhabit. This function constructs things that would not exist without a particular *cultural meaning system* (for example, tribal gods).

conversion disorder Syndrome characterized by pseudoneurological (*somatoform* and *dissociative*) symptoms such as amnesia, paralysis, impaired coordination or balance, localized anesthesia, blindness, deafness, double vision, hallucinations, tremors, or seizures without medical explanation.

cooperative egalitarianism Social organization in which the two genders are roughly equal and there is no gender dominance hierarchy. As a result, female sexuality is not controlled by male dominance or by a female *dominance hierarchy.*

cooperative female dominance Social organization in which females cooperate to control the lives of males. These societies are formed around large female family groups.

cooperative male dominance Social organization characterized by high levels of cooperation among males to dominate females and control female sexuality. Competition between males is controlled through typically elaborate systems of rules and rituals; sharing the sexuality of females is generally compulsory.

cultural congruency (of symptoms) Degree to which symptoms of mental disorders are consistent with the norms of the prevailing *cultural meaning system.*

cultural constructionist Philosophical view that adult human experiences depend on *cultural schemas* that mediate between sensory stimuli and experience. Thus, the meaning of events and norms of behavioral responses for adult humans are not uniform across cultures.

cultural entities Objects created by the social agreement that something counts as that entity.

cultural learning Learning that occurs as a result of primary socialization such as native language, religion, norms of behavior, and so on within specific cultural contexts. Cultural learning is presumed to have an effect on the brain in the formation of culture-specific neural networks.

cultural meaning systems The organization of cultural knowledge in a semantic system. Analogous to scientific *paradigms*, but much larger. A cultural meaning system generally structures cognitive reality for an entire society.

cultural schemas A set of culture-specific *cognitive schemas* formed within the *mind-brains* of individuals in cultural groups. These cultural schemas can result in cognitive differences across cultures. These differences in cognitive construction result from *cultural learning* and are stored in plastic neuronal structures.

cultural significance (of mental illness) The meanings projected onto the mental patient by the surrounding society, which then structure the experience of suffering by the patient. These meanings include what the society thinks about the ill person, about his or her particular mental disorder, and about mental illness in general.

culture The sum total of knowledge passed on from generation to generation within any given society. This body of knowledge includes language, forms of art and expression, religion, social and political structures, economic systems, legal systems, norms of behavior, ideas about illness and healing, and so on.

culture-based diagnosis A diagnosis of a mental disorder based on a particular *cultural meaning system.*

culture-based idioms of distress   The ways *culture* structures an individual's expressions of illness. This can include culture-based physical actions, including unusual behavior, seeking out clinical care, mannerisms, figures of speech, and cognitive emphasis on certain symptoms while ignoring others.

culture-based outcome   The outcome that occurs because an illness has been cognitively constructed and treated in a particular cultural fashion.

culture-based subjective experience   The tendency of *cultural schemas* to structure an individual's experience of illness.

culture-based treatment   The appropriate treatment for an illness as defined by a particular *cultural meaning system*.

culture-bound syndromes   Mental illnesses structured by indigenous sets of *cultural schemas*. Some of the mental illnesses are in fact *cultural entities*. They exist primarily in particular cultural contexts or are responses to certain precipitants in the indigenous meaning systems.

curing   Treating only the *disease* as defined by the clinician.

cyclothymic disorder   Syndrome characterized by numerous *hypomanic* symptoms alternating with numerous *depressive* symptoms not severe enough to warrant a diagnosis of a *major depressive episode* occurring over a two-year period.

delusional disorder   Syndrome characterized by at least one month of nonbizarre delusions without other *psychotic* symptoms.

dependent personality disorder   Personality characterized by an excessive need to be taken care of, associated with submissive, clinging behavior, and fear of independence.

depersonalization   Mental condition based in divided consciousness characterized by an individual's persistent or recurrent feeling of being detached from his or her mental processes or body.

depersonalization disorder   Syndrome characterized by *depersonalization* accompanied by clinically significant emotional distress or impairment.

dhat **syndrome**   A *culture-bound* semen-loss syndrome in South Asia. It is indigenously thought that a loss of semen leads to physical and mental weakness and susceptibility to illness. Excessive masturbation or sexual intercourse is thought to produce mental and physical illness. The most common symptoms are fatigue, weakness, body aches, severe headaches, depression, anxiety, loss of appetite, insomnia, heart palpitations, and suicidal feelings.

diagnostic ethnocentrism   Clinical diagnosis of a client's problem according to professional training without regard to the individual's cultural identity or cultural differences in subjective experience of illness.

directive function (of cultural meaning systems)   The ability of culture-based semantic systems to have an impact on people's motivations and to direct their behavior.

disease   In medical anthropology this refers to the diagnosis of the doctor or folk healer. It is the clinician's definition of the client's problem, always taken from the *paradigm* of disease in which the clinician was trained.

disease-centered psychiatry   A biomedical *paradigm* in psychiatry in which mental disorders are conceptualized as brain diseases and treatment is aimed primarily at treating the *disease* instead of the patient.

dissociation   Mental condition characterized by a loss of the integration of faculties or functions that are normally integrated in consciousness. Can affect memory, sensory modalities, motor functions, cognitive functions, and personal identity or sense of self.

dissociative amnesia   Syndrome characterized by divided consciousness in which there is an inability to recall important information that is held in a separate part of consciousness.

dissociative disorders   Syndromes characterized by divided consciousness including *dissociative amnesia, dissociative fugue, dissociative identity disorder* (formerly multiple personality disorder), *depersonalization disorder, dissociative trance disorder,* and *dissociative disorder not otherwise specified.*

dissociative fugue   Syndrome based in divided consciousness characterized by sudden, unexpected travel away from home or one's customary place of work, accompanied by an inability to recall one's past and also a confusion about personal identity.

dissociative hallucinations and delusions   *Psychotic*-type symptoms based on the mental processes of *trance.*

dissociative identity disorder (DID)   Syndrome characterized by the presence of two or more distinct identities or personality states in consciousness that recurrently take control of the individual's behavior, accompanied by *dissociative amnesia.*

dissociative trance disorder (DTD)   New diagnostic category included in the appendix of DSM-IV to accommodate premodern dissociative syndromes, characterized by *trance* or *possession trance* symptoms.

dominance hierarchies   Systems of social stratification and social control based on physical or economic power or political or religious legitimacy. In large-scale societies, there can be gender, class, age, race, and ethnic dominance hierarchies.

downward causation   The effects that thinking as an activity pattern has on the structure of the brain in altering dendritic branching and the strengths of neurotransmitter systems in individual synapses.

dyspareunia   Syndrome characterized by genital pain before, during, or after sexual intercourse. Closely related to *sexual aversion disorder, hypoactive sexual desire disorder,* and *vaginismus.*

dysthymic disorder   Syndrome characterized by a chronically depressed mood lasting for at least two years. Differs from *major depressive disorder* in that dysthymic disorder is a chronic illness with generally less severe depressive symptoms.

eating disorders   Syndromes characterized by obsessive-compulsive or addictive type behavior involving food. Persons are obsessed with ingesting or not ingesting food.

egocentric (personality or society)   Refers to personal identity centered in the self. Persons perceive themselves as autonomous individuals with personal choices, desires, and rights and see dependence as undesirable. In an egocentric society, the "self" becomes the primary object of interest, and personal freedom and power become the supreme values.

emic   Indigenous or native categories and interpretations of life experience.

etic   Nonindigenous or foreign categories and interpretations of life experience.

evocative function (of cultural meaning systems)   The ability of culture-based semantic systems to define life situations and evoke certain emotions.

exhibitionism   Syndrome characterized by a compulsion to expose one's genitals to a stranger. The typical case is a young man exposing his erect penis to unsuspecting females.

explanatory model (of mental illness)   The ways a set of *cultural schemas* explain the cause of mental illness, why the onset occurred when it did, the effects of the illness, what course the illness will take, and what treatments are appropriate. These meanings dramatically affect the lived experiences of mental patients, in many ways structuring their subjective experiences.

expressed emotion (EE) Criticism, hostility, and emotional over-involvement directed at a mental patient by his or her family members.

extraordinary science The period when formerly standard scientific methods and expectations are called into question, and researchers begin looking outside the established *paradigm* for answers to unresolved problems.

falling out A *culture-bound syndrome* among Southern blacks in the United States and the Bahamas, characterized by falling down in a *trance*, not being able to move, yet being able to hear and understand surrounding events.

female dominance A social condition in which the lives of males are by and large controlled by females.

female orgasmic disorder Syndrome characterized by a persistent absence of orgasm after normal sexual arousal that causes marked distress or interpersonal difficulty.

female sexual arousal disorder Syndrome characterized by an inability of a woman to maintain sexual arousal during coitus. This typically results in pleasureless lovemaking, painful intercourse, avoidance of sexual activity, and marital or relationship problems.

fetishism Syndrome involving the use of inanimate objects (the fetish) for sexual arousal. This is typically a male disorder. Commonly used fetishes are objects associated with females, for example, women's undergarments, stockings, shoes, or other articles of clothing.

final common pathways (of behavior) The theoretical idea that pathological behavior can be caused by genetic risk, emotional trauma, personality development, personal misfortune, social conflict, cultural custom, or any possible combination of these factors. What these factors have in common is the final pathway—the pathological behavior.

first-rank symptoms (of schizophrenia) Particular forms of hallucinations and delusions considered by German psychiatrist Kurt Schneider to be central to the definition of *schizophrenia.*

frotteurism Syndrome characterized by a compulsion to rub against or touch a nonconsenting person in a sexual way. It usually occurs in crowded public spaces such as buses or subway cars.

gender identity The private subjective cognition of one's gender.

gender identity disorder Syndrome characterized by an intense and persistent sense of identity as someone of the opposite gender, causing significant emotional distress and social or occupational impairment.

gender role behavior The gender-specific activities that are expected in any given society. This can include such things as wearing gender-specific clothing, having a gender-specific occupation, using gender-specific forms of speech, mannerisms, hairstyles, jewelry and accessories, cosmetics, performing gender-specific recreational activities, sexual behavior, household duties, and holding gender-specific sociopolitical-religious offices.

gender status The gender that is publicly ascribed and recognized for an individual.

generalized anxiety disorder (GAD) Syndrome characterized by excessive *anxiety*, restlessness, inability to concentrate, and worry occurring more days than not for a period of at least six months.

grisi siknis *Culture-bound syndrome* of the Miskito Indian culture of Nicaragua found almost exclusively in teenage girls and young women. Characterized by *trance*, running wildly with a machete or other sharp instrument, with some assaultive behavior, self-mutilation, and *dissociative amnesia.*

healing In medical anthropology, the treatment of *illness,* that is, the patient's subjective experience of being sick.

histrionic personality disorder Personality characterized by excessive emotionality and attention-seeking behavior.

hwa-byung A Korean *culture-bound syndrome* characterized by prominent *anxiety, somatoform,* and *mood* symptoms such as insomnia, fatigue, panic, fear of impending death, indigestion, palpitations, "heat sensation," flushing, "pushing-up" sensations in the chest, irritability, epigastric mass, difficulty in concentration, dysphoria, and generalized aches and pains.

hypnosis A modern form of *trance.*

hypoactive sexual desire disorder Syndrome characterized by the absence of the desire for sexual activity resulting in emotional distress or interpersonal difficulty.

hypochondriasis Syndrome characterized by persistent and unfounded fears of having a serious disease based on a misinterpretation of normal bodily functions or minor symptoms.

hypomanic episode A period of at least four days in which the person experiences an abnormal and persistently elevated, expansive, or irritable mood, with at least three additional symptoms such as: nondelusional grandiosity, decreased need for sleep, pressure of speech, flight of ideas, distractibility, or increased involvement in goal directed activities. Differs from a *manic episode* in that a hypomanic episode does not cause social or occupational impairment, and there are no hallucinations or delusions.

hypotheses The lowest level, most specific, testable explanations for unanswered scientific problems.

hysteria Obsolete diagnostic category used commonly in the latter half of the 19th century, characterized by extreme *anxiety, somatoform, depressive,* and *dissociative* symptoms such as paralyses, anesthesias, blindness, seizures, and head and body aches, with no medical explanation, as well as dysphoria, hallucinations, and multiple personalities.

icon A sign that actually looks like the thing it represents. An example would be a photograph, a drawing, or a statue of a person.

illness In medical anthropology, this refers to the subjective experience of being sick, including the experience of symptoms, suffering, help seeking, side effects of treatment, social stigma, explanations of causes, diagnosis, prognosis, as well as personal consequences in family life and occupation.

index A sign that does not look like the thing it represents but has a direct connection to it. In many cases, an index may be something that was physically connected to the represented object at some time.

indisposition Haitian *culture-bound syndrome* in which the person falls to the ground in a *trance* and is not able to understand anything said or heard.

intentionality The processing that goes on in the brain between the intake of raw sensory data and the end product of cognition of an object. Intentionality is the primary object of study in *phenomenology.*

koro Chinese and Malaysian *culture-bound syndrome* (although similar syndromes are found elsewhere) in which persons have the sensation of their penises or breasts retracting into their bodies. They believe that if this retraction is allowed to proceed they will die.

latah Malay-Indonesian *trance* syndrome (although similar syndromes are found else-where) characterized by an extreme response to startling stimuli such as violent body movements, assumption of defensive postures, striking out, throwing or dropping held objects, mimicking observed movements, and sometimes extreme suggestibility or obedience.

liminality A difficult period "betwixt and between" two social categories and states of being. An example is an adolescent who has reached sexual maturity but is not yet an adult until socially recognized as an adult.

long-term potentiation An enduring increase in functional synaptic strength gener-ally accepted to play an important role in memory formation based on the repeti-tive, nearly synchronous coactivation of adjacent nerve fibers onto the postsynaptic membrane.

mahu In Polynesian societies, a person born as a male but raised from infancy as a female (*mahu* in Hawaii and Tahiti, *fakaleiti* in Tonga, *faafafine* in Samoa).

major depressive disorder Syndrome characterized by one or more *major depressive episodes* without a history of *manic, mixed,* or *hypomanic episodes.*

major depressive disorder with psychotic features Syndrome in which hallucina-tions and delusions occur only within the context of *major depressive episodes.*

major depressive episode At least two weeks of depressed mood with at least four additional symptoms of depression, which can include changes in appetite, weight, sleep, or psychomotor activity, fatigue, feelings of worthlessness or guilt, difficulty thinking, and recurrent thoughts of suicide or suicide attempts.

male dominance A social condition in which the lives of females are by and large con-trolled by males.

male erectile disorder Syndrome characterized by a persistent inability to attain or maintain an erection sufficient for the completion of coitus.

male orgasmic disorder Syndrome characterized by a failure to achieve orgasm dur-ing coitus.

manageability (in healing) Refers to a psychotherapeutic technique of providing a sense of control or competence to meet the demands of the illness.

manic episode Episode characterized by an abnormally elevated, euphoric, or irri-table mood lasting at least one week, or less if hospitalization is required, with at least three additional manic symptoms, which can include grandiosity, decreased need for sleep, pressure of speech, flight of ideas, distractibility, increased goal directed activity, and excessive involvement in pleasurable activity with a high potential for painful consequences. There may be grandiose delusions and halluci-nations.

masturbatory conditioning Process in which the person becomes classically condi-tioned to experience sexual pleasure through repeated occurrences of masturbation associated with some object or situation.

meaningfulness (in healing) A psychotherapeutic technique of providing a sense of purpose to the *illness* experience. Found in various forms of religious healing of mental illness.

mind-brain Monistic theoretical view in which the mind and brain are not separate.

mixed episode Episode characterized by a period of at least one week in which diag-nostic criteria are met for both a *manic episode* and a *major depressive episode.*

models General theories that explain a large part of the field of inquiry within a sci-entific discipline.

modernism A philosophical school that views modernization (essentially westerniza-tion) as a type of universal social solvent that will transform all societies it contacts into something resembling a modern western society. It is based on the assumption that western forms of thinking, social organization, and personality development are inherently superior.

modern personality Personality development dependent on at least a minimum level of education in modern standards of literacy, science, technology, history, politics, and a general acceptance of the scientific view of the world. A sense of personal efficacy in controlling and being responsible for one's own life, independence from traditional (particularly religious or parental) sources of authority, and cognitive flexibility to accommodate new experiences and change are also necessary attributes.

modern society A society with a relatively high level of technology, great specialization in social and economic organization, large-scale interdependency in the flow of goods and services, a permanent bureaucracy controlling many aspects of social life, a dependence on rationality and scientific reasoning for solving problems, and an attitude of expecting material progress and change.

mood disorders Syndromes that have depressive or manic symptoms as their primary feature.

mood episodes Episodes of emotional illness and distress characterized by depression, mania, or hypomania, or some combination of these, including *major depressive episode, manic episode, mixed episode,* or *hypomanic episode.*

moral career Refers simultaneously to the moral status as well as to the morale of an individual. The moral status of an individual is an indication of that person's perceived value in society judged by the cultural definitions of morality within the context of a social *dominance hierarchy*. Someone in a stigmatized social group can be a "bad" person by definition of the *cultural meaning system*. By having one's moral status compromised in this fashion, the individual's morale or self-esteem can be negatively affected.

narcissistic personality disorder Personality characterized by an obsession with grandiosity, an intense need for admiration, and a lack of empathy for others.

natural attitude A society's own unique cultural way of experiencing the world. Refers to the way someone "naturally" experiences the world. "Naturally" is put in quotes because the way the person is experiencing the world is not actually natural at all, but cultural.

nervios ("nerves") A Latin American *culture-bound syndrome* characterized by a chronic and generalized sense of emotional distress with a range of symptoms including headaches, body aches, heart palpitations, heat in the chest, irritability, gastrointestinal disturbances, insomnia, nervousness, inability to concentrate, persistent worrying, trembling, and dizziness.

neurasthenia A disorder referring to "tired nerves" and including symptoms of fatigue, *anxiety*, and various somatic complaints. This disorder originated in the United States but is no longer a part of the DSM classification system. However, it remains a very common diagnosis in China.

neuroses Mental disorders presumed to have psychodynamic origins existing toward the mild to moderate end of a spectrum of mental illnesses in the *biopsychosocial paradigm.*

noetic pole A metaphorical conceptualization of a conscious experience as a physical pole with two ends—the *noesis* (cognizer) and the *noema* (cognized). Husserl used the Greek terms *noesis* and *noema* deliberately to avoid using the terms *subject* and *object*, which would imply two separate entities. The noetic pole is a single thing, an experience with two ends.

normal science Scientific research within an accepted *paradigm.* All researchers assume that the paradigm is an accurate description of the field of study and do not question its basic premises. They seek only to refine problems and answer unanswered questions.

object-in-itself   An object free of all human *intentionality* or cognitive processing.

obsessive-compulsive disorder (OCD)   Syndrome characterized by persistent thoughts or impulses that are experienced as intrusive and inappropriate (obsessions) and by repetitive behaviors (compulsions) that are performed to reduce the emotional distress associated with obsessions.

obsessive-compulsive personality disorder   Personality characterized by a persistent preoccupation with order, perfection, attention to detail, rules, and control.

orgasmic reconditioning   Therapy technique for *paraphilias* in which the patient is gradually reconditioned by having orgasm repeatedly associated with an appropriate sexual object.

Outline for Cultural Formulation   Contained in the Appendix of DSM-IV, this section outlines factors to consider for cultural assessment of mental disorders.

pain disorder   Syndrome characterized by the subjective experience of pain that does not have sufficient medical justification.

panic attacks   Experiences characterized by a discrete period of intense fear with at least four additional somatic or cognitive symptoms including palpitations, sweating, trembling, shortness of breath, feelings of choking, chest pain, nausea or abdominal distress, dizziness, *depersonalization*, derealization, fear of going crazy, fear of dying, tactile sensations (paresthesias), and chills or hot flashes.

panic disorder   Syndrome characterized by recurrent and unexpected *panic attacks.*

paradigm   The highest, most general level in a hierarchy of scientific intellectual structures. A paradigm is a generally accepted view of the nature of a scientific discipline.

paradigm crisis   The period when *anomalies* last a long time and penetrate deeply into a *paradigm*, in effect demanding the large-scale alteration of the paradigm and major shifts in the problems and methods of *normal science.*

paradigm shift   At least a partial reconstruction of a scientific discipline that can include alterations in basic theoretical generalizations and methods of research.

paranoid personality disorder   Personality characterized by a pervasive distrust of other people such that others are virtually always perceived as being threatening or hostile.

paraphilia not otherwise specified   Syndromes closely related to the other *paraphilias* but with somewhat different sexual objects. These include but are not limited to telephone scatologia (obscene phone calls), necrophilia (corpses), partialism (body parts), zoophilia (animals), coprophilia (feces), klismaphilia (enemas), and urophilia (urine).

paraphilias   Syndromes characterized by recurrent sexual fantasies and behaviors involving objects, persons, or situations that are considered deviant in the prevailing *cultural meaning system*, causing significant emotional distress or social impairment.

pedophilia   Syndrome characterized by a person 16 years or older having recurrent sexual activity with a prepubescent child (legally this is generally 13 years or younger).

personal and social meanings (of mental illness)   The interpersonal relations and social life of the mentally ill person. Interpersonal relationships, particularly family relations, possess meanings that can add to or shape the suffering associated with mental illness.

personality disorders Enduring patterns of pathological subjective experience and behavior based in personality development rather than in some specific disease entity.

phenomenology The study of phenomena; that is, the mental construction of cognition out of raw sensory data. A phenomenon is an experience of an object by a subject. In phenomenology, it is the experience of the object that is the focus of study, not the object itself.

pibloktoq (arctic hysteria) Polar Eskimo *trance* syndrome characterized by short-lived episodes (five minutes to one hour) of extreme agitation in which the person will tear off his or her clothes and go running into the snow or across the ice screaming incoherently. This is accompanied by *dissociative amnesia*.

possession trance Mental condition characterized by replacement of the primary personality by a new identity, usually a ghost, demon, or deity.

postmodernism A philosophical school that views *modernism* as being ethnocentric and tied to western intellectual and economic colonialism. The view that wholesale adoption of modern western cultural values, economic practices, social organizations, ways of thinking, and personality development are not necessary or even desirable for all peoples.

posttraumatic stress disorder (PTSD) Syndrome characterized by prominent *anxiety* and *dissociative* symptoms following exposure to an extreme traumatic stressor.

premature ejaculation Syndrome characterized by persistent ejaculation after minimal sexual stimulation and before the person or the person's sexual partner wishes it.

premodern personality Individuals in a *premodern society* who lack a sense of personal efficacy to change conditions, who accept traditional (religious and familial) sources of authority, and who rely on divine intervention for any change in their lives. Causes of illness and healing are generally accepted as coming from supernatural sources.

premodern society A society in which the level of technology is relatively low, there is little specialization in social or economic organization, and a subsistence economy exists with the flow of goods and services occurring on a relatively small scale. Social organization is based primarily on kinship systems, there is a great reliance on traditional religious-familial authorities, and supernatural causation is used to explain life events consistent with the local religious tradition.

primary role identification A particular status and correlated behavior assigned to an individual by a society structured in a *dominance hierarchy*. It structures elements of individual personality development in relation to positions in the social structure.

psychic unity of humankind The assumption that all people have the same basic brain structure and, therefore, universally have the same basic mental processes and ways of experiencing the world.

psychoses Severe forms of the mental illness characterized by a loss of *reality testing*, such as hallucinations and delusions.

psychotic The presence of delusions, prominent hallucinations, disorganized speech, and disorganized or catatonic behavior.

psychotic disorders Syndromes characterized by a loss of *reality testing* including *schizophrenia, schizophreniform disorder, schizoaffective disorder, delusional disorder, brief psychotic disorder*, and *shared psychotic disorder*.

reality testing (loss of) A disturbance in the experience of self and the individual's relationship with the external physical and social environments. The presence of hallucinations or delusions is usually viewed as a loss of reality testing.

reification   The collective projection onto an object of a level of reality it does not actually possess, yet the people themselves are not aware that it is their own collective cognitive process accomplishing this. The object invariably appears in cognition as a completely separate entity with its own qualities independent of the cognizers, even though the cognizers have been active participants in construction of the experience, shaping the form, content, and meaning of the object.

reliability   The ability of separate clinicians or researchers to consistently diagnose the same disorder after observing the same pattern of symptoms in patients.

representational function (of cultural meaning systems)   The ability of individuals within a cultural group to represent the world symbolically to themselves and to others.

satanic ritual abuse syndrome   North American *culture-bound syndrome* in which individuals report traumatic memories of satanic ritual abuse that may have been hidden for many years by *dissociative amnesia.*

schizoaffective disorder   Syndrome characterized by a combination of *psychotic* and *mood* symptoms in which psychotic symptoms occur in conjunction with either a *manic* or *major depressive episode*, followed by at least two weeks of psychotic symptoms without prominent mood symptoms.

schizoid personality disorder   Personality characterized by a pervasive detachment from social relationships and a restricted range of emotions.

schizophrenia   Syndrome characterized by the presence of *psychotic* symptoms for a significant portion of the time during a one-month period and some signs of the disorder for at least a six-month period.

schizophreniform disorder   Syndrome characterized by a *psychotic* disturbance that lasts at least one month but less than six months.

schizotypal personality disorder   Personality characterized by *anxiety* in social relationships accompanied by eccentricities of behavior such as superstitiousness, preoccupation with paranormal phenomena, magical thinking, or use of rituals in everyday situations.

semicooperative male dominance   A social organization characterized by competition, aggression, and violence among males and toward females but with somewhat more cooperation between males, larger social groups, and more sharing of sexual partners than in *competitive male dominant* societies.

semiotics   The study of signs. Signs are objects that represent something else. In semiotics, there are three kinds of signs: *icons*, *indexes*, and *symbols.*

sexual aversion disorder   Syndrome characterized by an aversion to and active avoidance of genital contact with a sexual partner. The typical case is a female who experiences *anxiety*, fear, or disgust from genital or other explicitly sexual contact.

sexual dysfunctions   Syndromes characterized by psychophysiological problems that have an impact on an individual's ability to have satisfying sexual relations, causing marked emotional distress and interpersonal difficulties.

sexual masochism   Syndrome characterized by sexual arousal resulting from being humiliated, beaten, bound, or subjected to other forms of corporal punishment.

sexual preference   The gender an individual finds sexually arousing.

sexual sadism   Syndrome characterized by sexual arousal resulting from inflicting physical or psychological punishment on another person.

shared psychotic disorder   Syndrome characterized by a delusional belief in an individual who is influenced by someone else who has an established delusion.

social phobia Syndrome characterized by a persistent fear of social situations in which extreme embarrassment may occur. Exposure to these situations provokes an *anxiety* response.

sociobiology Philosophical school that presumes that all individuals want to maximize their chances of passing on their genetic material, which, in turn, unconsciously controls their behavior.

sociocentric (personality or society) A personality with an identity centered in the group or society. This individual derives his or her primary identity from membership in a social group, usually the extended family. In a sociocentric society, there are strict rules of interdependence. Social obligations are of paramount importance, and proper behavior is determined by an individual's position in the social structure.

somatization The expression of emotional distress in somatic (bodily) symptoms.

somatization disorder Syndrome characterized by chronic and recurrent *somatoform* symptoms such as paralyses, anesthesias, blindness, seizures, and head and body aches, with no medical explanation.

somatoform disorders Syndromes characterized by prominent somatic (bodily) symptoms as their central problem.

specific phobia Syndrome characterized by a persistent fear of specific objects or situations, exposure to which almost invariably evokes an *anxiety* response.

state dependent The observation that the presence or absence of alterations in brain biochemistry or behavior associated with a particular mental state such as depression are dependent on the presence or absence of that mental state.

structured diagnostic interview schedules Diagnostic questionnaires with standardized lists of questions inquiring about the presence of specific symptoms.

substance abuse Syndrome associated with repeated negative consequences resulting from a maladaptive pattern of substance use, such as multiple legal, social, and occupational problems.

substance dependence Multiple cognitive, behavioral, and physiological symptoms that indicate that an individual continues to abuse substances despite the negative consequences associated with that abuse.

substance intoxication Condition characterized by clinically significant maladaptive behavioral or psychological changes resulting from ingestion of a specific substance, such as social or occupational impairment, mood instability, cognitive impairment, or belligerence.

substance-related disorders Syndromes associated with *substance intoxication, substance abuse, substance dependence,* or *substance withdrawal.*

substance withdrawal Condition characterized by negative cognitive, physiological, and behavioral changes that occur when bodily concentrations of a substance decline after cessation of prolonged use.

susto A Latin American *culture-bound syndrome* characterized by loss of appetite and weight, physical weakness, restlessness in sleep, depression, introversion, and apathy. It is indigenously attributed to "soul loss" resulting from frightful or traumatic experiences.

symbol A sign that has no logical connection to the thing it represents, an arbitrary sign. It is used simply out of convention, and its use results primarily out of historical accident.

symbolic healing The use of transformational *symbols* used in *healing* rituals for purposes of therapeutically altering the meaning of life events, emotional experience, and mental disorders.

symptom as a symptom The fact that a particular experience, for example, a sensation, thought, emotion, or behavior, becomes a symptom (an indication of illness) only when it is cognized as such. Cognizing something as a symptom is an interpretation. This interpretation occurs within a *cultural meaning system.*

taijin kyofusho Japanese *culture-bound syndrome* characterized by intense *anxiety* that a person's appearance, body odor, or facial expressions will be found offensive.

theories Specific explanations for large unanswered scientific problems.

therapeutic use of hope Psychotherapeutic technique of providing hope to patients, thereby creating a therapeutic effect on the patients' emotions and, therefore, on their mental disorders.

trance Mental condition based on a narrowed focus of attention such that what is outside of attention is lost to consciousness.

transvestic fetishism Syndrome characterized by males deriving sexual pleasure by intermittently wearing female clothing.

tuning A long-term change in the central nervous system resulting from repeated experience of a particular condition of the nervous system that makes the individual more susceptible to reestablishment of that same condition.

undifferentiated somatoform disorder A residual category for persistent *somatoform*-type illnesses that do not meet the full criteria for *somatization disorder.*

upregulation (of neurotransmitter systems) An increase in the number of neurotransmitter receptors as well as an increase in the avidity with which receptors seek the neurotransmitter. This can result from use of psychiatric medications such as neuroleptics.

vaginismus Syndrome characterized by recurrent involuntary contraction of the muscles surrounding the vagina whenever vaginal penetration is attempted.

validity The reality of diagnostic categories. A diagnostic category (for example, schizophrenia) is valid when it refers to a real clinical entity independent of diagnosis and is an appropriate means of naming that entity.

voyeurism Syndrome characterized by a compulsion to achieve sexual arousal by observing unsuspecting persons who are getting undressed or are naked or are engaged in sexual activities.

yoga meditation An ancient religious practice from India based on *trance.*

References

ABRAMS, K. K., ALLEN, L. A., & GRAY, J. J. (1993). Disordered eating attitudes and behaviors, psychological adjustment, and ethnic identity: A comparison of black and white female college students. *International Journal of Eating Disorders, 14,* 49–57.

ABRAMSON, E. E., & VALENE, P. (1991). Media use, dietary restraint, bulimia and attitudes towards obesity: A preliminary study. *British Review of Bulimia and Anorexia Nervosa, 5,* 73–76.

ABRAMSON, L. Y., SELIGMAN, M. E. P., & TEASDALE, J. D. (1978). Learned helplessness in humans: Critique and reformulation. *Journal of Abnormal Psychology, 87,* 49–74.

ADITYANJEE, RAJU, G. S. P., & KHANDELWAL, S. K. (1989). Current status of multiple personality disorder in India. *American Journal of Psychiatry, 146,* 1607–1610.

AKHTAR, S. (1988). Four culture-bound psychiatric syndromes in India. *International Journal of Social Psychiatry, 34,* 70–74.

AMARASINGHAM, L. R. (1980). Movement among healers in Sri Lanka: A case study of a Sinhalese patient. *Culture, Medicine and Psychiatry, 4,* 71–92.

AMERICAN PSYCHIATRIC ASSOCIATION. (1952). *Diagnostic and statistical manual of mental disorders.* Washington, DC: American Psychiatric Association.

AMERICAN PSYCHIATRIC ASSOCIATION. (1968). *Diagnostic and statistical manual of mental disorders* (2nd ed.). Washington, DC: American Psychiatric Association.

AMERICAN PSYCHIATRIC ASSOCIATION. (1980). *Diagnostic and statistical manual of mental disorders* (3rd ed.). Washington, DC: American Psychiatric Association.

AMERICAN PSYCHIATRIC ASSOCIATION. (1987). *Diagnostic and statistical manual of mental disorders* (3rd ed., revised). Washington, DC: American Psychiatric Association.

AMERICAN PSYCHIATRIC ASSOCIATION. (1994). *Diagnostic and statistical manual of mental disorders* (4th ed.). Washington, DC: American Psychiatric Association.

ANDERSON, A. E., & HAY, A. (1985). Racial and socioeconomic influences in anorexia nervosa and bulimia. *International Journal of Eating Disorders, 4* (4), 479–487.

ANDREASEN, N. C. (1984). *The broken brain: The biological revolution in psychiatry.* New York: Harper & Row.

ANGST, J. (1988). European long-term follow-up studies of schizophrenia. *Schizophrenia Bulletin, 14,* 501–513.

ANTONOVSKY, A. (1979). *Health, stress, and coping.* San Francisco: Jossey-Bass.

AOKI, C., & SIEKEVITZ, P. (1988, December). Plasticity in brain development. *Scientific American*, pp. 56–64.

ASUNI, T. (1979). Modern medicine and traditional medicine. In Z. A. Ademuwagun (Ed.), *African therapeutic systems* (pp. 176–181). Waltham, MA: Brandeis University Crossroads Press.

AWANBOR, D. (1982). The healing process in African psychotherapy. *American Journal of Psychotherapy, 36*, 206–213.

AWARITEFE, A. (1988). Clinical anxiety in Nigeria. *Acta Psychiatrica Scandinavica, 77*, 729–735.

BABB, L. A. (1975). *The divine hierarchy: Popular Hinduism in central India*. New York: Columbia University Press.

BABOR, T. F. (1992). Cross-cultural research on alcohol: A quoi bon? In J. F. Helzer & G. J. Canino (Eds.), *Alcoholism in North America, Europe, and Asia* (pp. 33–52). New York: Oxford University Press.

BADDELEY, J. (1985). Traditional healing practices of Rarotonga, Cook Islands. In C. Parsons (Ed.), *Healing practices in the South Pacific* (pp. 129–143). Honolulu: University of Hawaii Press.

BANCROFT, J. (1974). *Deviant sexual behavior: Modification and assessment*. New York: Oxford University Press.

BARLOW, D. H. (1986). Causes of sexual dysfunction: The role of anxiety and cognitive interference. *Journal of Consulting and Clinical Psychology, 54*, 140–148.

BARLOW, D. H. (1988). *Anxiety and its disorders: The nature and treatment of anxiety and panic*. New York: Guilford Press.

BARLOW, D. H., BROWN, T. A., & CRASKE, M. G. (1994). Definitions of panic attacks and panic disorder in DSM-IV: Implications for research. *Journal of Abnormal Psychology, 103*, 553–554.

BARLOW, D. H., & DURAND, V. M. (1995). *Abnormal psychology: An integrative approach*. Pacific Grove, CA: Brooks/Cole.

BARTELS, S., TEAGUE, G., DRAKE, R., CLARK, R., BUSH, P., & NOORDSY, D. (1993). Substance abuse in schizophrenia: Service utilization and costs. *Journal of Nervous and Mental Disease, 181*, 227–232.

BARTOL, C. R. (1995). *Criminal behavior: A psychosocial approach* (4th ed.). Englewood Cliffs, NJ: Prentice Hall.

BAYES, M. (1981). The prevalence of gender-role bias in mental health services. In E. Howell & M. Bayes (Eds.), *Women and mental health*. New York: Basic Books.

BEATTY, W. W., WONDERLICH, S. A., STATON, R. D., & TERNES, L. A. (1990). Cognitive functioning in bulimia: Comparison with depression. *Bulletin of the Psychosomatic Society, 28*, 289–292.

BEBBINGTON, P. (1993). Transcultural aspects of affective disorders. *International Review of Psychiatry, 5*, 145–156.

BEERE, D. (1995). Loss of "background": A perceptual theory of dissociation. *Dissociation, 8*, 165–174.

BEHERE, P. B., & NATRAJ, G. S. (1984). *Dhat* syndrome: The phenomenology of a culture-bound sex neurosis of the orient. *Indian Journal of Psychiatry, 26*, 76–78.

BENNETT, L. A., JANCA, A., GRANT, B. F., & SARTORIUS, N. (1993). Boundaries between normal and pathological drinking: A cross-cultural comparison. *Alcohol, Health and Research World, 17*, 190–196.

BERREMAN, G. D. (1963). *Hindus of the Himalayas*. Berkeley: University of California Press.

BESNIER, N. (1994). Polynesian gender liminality through time and space. In G. Herdt (Ed.), *Third sex, third gender: Beyond sexual dimorphism in culture and history* (pp. 285–328). New York: Zone Books.

BIRLEY, J., & BROWN, G. W. (1970). Crisis and life changes preceding the onset or relapse of acute schizophrenia: Clinical aspects. *British Journal of Psychiatry, 16,* 327–333.

BLEULER, E. (1908). Die prognose der dementia praecox (schizophreniegruppe). *Allgemeine Zeitschrift fur Psychiatrie, 65,* 436–464.

BLEULER, E. (1924). *Textbook of psychiatry.* A. A. Brill (Trans.). New York: Macmillan.

BLISS, E. L. (1986). *Multiple personality, allied disorders, and hypnosis.* New York: Oxford University Press.

BLISS, E. L. (1988). Professional skepticism about multiple personality. *Journal of Nervous and Mental Disease, 176,* 533–534.

BLUM, K., NOBLE, E. P., SHERIDAN, P. J., MONTGOMERY, A., RITCHIE, T., JAGADEESWARAN, P., NOGAMI, H., BRIGGS, A. H., & COHEN, J. B. (1990). Allelic association of human dopamine D2 receptor gene in alcoholism. *Journal of the American Medical Association, 263* (15), 2055–2060.

BOCK, P. K. (1994). Social structure and personality. In P. K. Bock (Ed.), *Psychological anthropology* (pp. 41–59). Westport, CT: Praeger.

BOEHNLEIN, J. K., & KINZIE, J. D. (1995). Refugee trauma. *Transcultural Psychiatric Research Review, 32,* 223–252.

BOLOS, A. M., DEAN, M., LUCAS-DERSE, A., RAMSBURG, M., BROWN, G. L., & GOLDMAN, D. (1991). Population and pedigree studies reveal a lack of association between the dopamine D2 receptor gene and alcoholism. *Journal of the American Medical Association, 264,* 3156–3160.

BOLTON, R. (1981). *Susto,* hostility, and hypoglycemia. *Ethnology, 20,* 261–276.

BOURGUIGNON, E. (1972). Dreams and altered states of consciousness in anthropological research. In F. K. L. Hsu (Ed.), *Psychological anthropology* (2nd ed.) Homewood, IL: Dorsey Press.

BOURGUIGNON, E. (1973). Introduction: A framework for the comparative study of altered states of consciousness. In E. Bourguignon (Ed.), *Religion, altered states of consciousness, and social change* (pp. 3–35). Columbus: Ohio State University Press.

BOURGUIGNON, E. (1976). *Possession.* San Francisco: Chandler & Sharp.

BOURGUIGNON, E. (1994). Trance and meditation. In P. K. Bock (Ed.), *Psychological anthropology* (pp. 297–314). Westport, CT: Praeger.

BOYER, L. B. (1964). Folk psychiatry of the Apaches of the Mescalero Indian reservation. In A. Kiev (Ed.), *Magic, faith and healing* (pp. 385–419). New York: Free Press.

BRADBURY, R. E. (1966). Fathers, elders, and ghosts in Edo religion. In M. Banton (Ed.), *Anthropological approaches to the supernatural* (pp. 127–153). London: Tavistock Publications.

BRADSHAW, J. (1988). Compulsivity: The black plague of our day. *Lear's Magazine, 42,* 89–90.

BREMNER, J. D., DAVIS, M., SOUTHWICK, S. M., KRYSTAL, J. H., & CHARNEY, D. S. (1994). Neurobiology of posttraumatic stress disorder. In R. S. Pynoos (Ed.), *Posttraumatic stress disorder: A clinical review* (pp. 43–64). Lutherville, MD: Sidran Press. Originally published in J. M. Oldham, M. Riba, & A. Tasman (Eds.), *Review of Psychiatry,* Vol. 12, 1993. Washington, DC: American Psychiatric Press.

BRIQUET, P. (1859). *Traite de l'hysterie.* Paris: Bailliere.

BRODY, E. B. (1995). The humanity of psychotic persons and their rights [Editorial]. *Journal of Nervous and Mental Disease, 183,* 193–194.

BROVERMAN, I., BROVERMAN, D., CLARKSON, F., ROSENKRANTZ, P., & VOGEL, R. (1981). Sex-role stereotypes and clinical judgments of mental health. In E. Howell & M. Bayes (Eds.), *Women and mental health* (pp. 86–97). New York: Basic Books.

BROWN, G. E., MONCK, E., CARSTAIRS, G., ET AL. (1962). Influence of family life on the course of schizophrenic illness. *British Journal of Prevention and Social Medicine, 16,* 55–68.

BROWNELL, K. D., & O'NEIL, P. M. (1993). Obesity. In D. H. Barlow (Ed.), *Clinical handbook of psychological disorders: A step-by-step treatment manual* (2nd ed.) (pp. 318–361). New York: Guilford.

BURROWS, G. D., & DENNERSTEIN, L. (1980). *Handbook of hypnosis and psychosomatic medicine.* New York: Elsevier North-Holland Biomedical Press.

BURTON-BRADLEY, B. G. (1968). The *amok* syndrome in Papua and New Guinea. *Medical Journal of Australia, 1,* 252–256.

CALLENDER, C., & KOCHEMS, L. M. (1993). The North American *berdache.* In D. N. Suggs & A. W. Miracle (Eds.), *Culture and human sexuality* (pp. 367–397). Pacific Grove, CA: Brooks/Cole.

CANINO, G., BURNAM, A., & CAETANO, R. (1992). The prevalence of alcohol abuse/dependence in two Hispanic communities. In J. Helzer & G. Canino (Eds.), *Alcoholism in North America, Europe and Asia* (pp. 131–155). New York: Oxford University Press.

CARLSON, E. T. (1986). The history of dissociation until 1980. In J. M. Quen (Ed.), *Split minds/split brains: Historical and current perspectives* (pp. 7–30). New York: New York University Press.

CARR, J. E. (1985). Ethno-behaviorism and the culture-bound syndromes: The case of *amok.* In R. C. Simons & C. C. Hughes (Eds.), *The culture-bound syndromes: Folk illnesses of psychiatric and anthropological interest* (pp. 199–223). Dordrecht: D. Reidel.

CARR, J. E., & TAN, E. K. (1976). In search of the true *amok: Amok* as viewed within the Malay culture. *American Journal of Psychiatry, 133,* 1295–1299.

CARR, J. E., & VITALIANO, P. P. (1985). Theoretical implications of converging research on depression and culture-bound syndromes. In A. Kleinman & B. Good (Eds.), *Culture and depression* (pp. 244–266). Berkeley: University of California Press.

CARSTAIRS, G. M., & KAPUR, R. L. (1976). *The great universe of Kota: Stress, change and mental disorder in an Indian village.* Berkeley: University of California Press.

CASTILLO, R. J. (1985). The transpersonal psychology of Patañjali's *Yoga-Sûtra* (book 1: *samâdhi*): A translation and interpretation. *Journal of Mind and Behavior, 6,* 391–417.

CASTILLO, R. J. (1990). Depersonalization and meditation. *Psychiatry, 53,* 158–168.

CASTILLO, R. J. (1991a). *Culture, trance and mental illness: Divided consciousness in South Asia.* Unpublished doctoral dissertation, Harvard University, Cambridge, Massachusetts.

CASTILLO, R. J. (1991b). Divided consciousness and enlightenment in Hindu yogis. *Anthropology of Consciousness, 2* (3–4), 1–6.

CASTILLO, R. J. (1992). Cultural considerations for trance and possession disorder in DSM-IV. *Transcultural Psychiatric Research Review, 29,* 333–337.

CASTILLO, R. J. (1994a). Spirit possession in South Asia, dissociation or hysteria? Part 1: Theoretical background. *Cultural Medicine and Psychiatry, 18,* 1–21.

CASTILLO, R. J. (1994b). Spirit possession in South Asia, dissociation or hysteria? Part 2: Case histories. *Culture, Medicine and Psychiatry, 18,* 141–162.

CASTILLO, R. J. (1994c). *Toward a holistic model of mental illness and treatment.* Paper presented at the annual meeting of the Society for the Anthropology of Consciousness, Tempe, Arizona.

CASTILLO, R. J. (1995). Culture, trance, and the mind-brain. *Anthropology of Consciousness, 6,* 17–34.

CHANDRASENA, R. (1983). Culture and clinical psychiatry. *Reveu de Psychiatrie de l' Université d'Ottawa, 8,* 16–19.

CHANDRASHEKAR, C. R. (1989). Possession syndrome in India. In C. A. Ward (Ed.), *Altered states of consciousness and mental health* (pp. 79–95). Newbury Park: Sage.

CHEETHAM, R. W. S., & CHEETHAM, R. J. (1976). Concepts of mental illness amongst the rural Xhosa people in South Africa. *Australian and New Zealand Journal of Psychiatry, 10,* 39–45.

CHO, Y. I., & FAULKNER, W. R. (1993). Conceptions of alcoholism among Koreans and Americans. *International Journal of Addictions, 28*(8), 681–694.

CHOUINARD, G., ANNABLE, L., & ROSS-CHOUINARD, A. (1986). Supersensitivity psychosis and tardive dyskinesia: A survey in schizophrenic outpatients. *Psychopharmacology Bulletin, 22,* 891–896.

CHOUINARD, G., & JONES, B. D. (1980). Neuroleptic-induced supersensitivity psychosis: Clinical and pharmacologic characteristics. *American Journal of Psychiatry, 137,* 16–21.

CHUA, S. E., & McKENNA, P. J. (1995). Schizophrenia—a brain disease? A critical review of structural and functional cerebral abnormality in the disorder. *British Journal of Psychiatry, 166,* 563–582.

CLARK, D. M. (1986). A cognitive approach to panic. *Behaviour Research and Therapy, 24,* 461–470.

CLARK, D. M. (1988). A cognitive model of panic attacks. In S. Rachman & J. D. Maser (Eds.), *Panic: Psychological perspectives* (pp. 71–89). Hillsdale, NJ: Lawrence Erlbaum.

CLARK, M. (1959). *Health in the Mexican-American Community.* Berkeley: University of California Press.

CLAUS, P. J. (1979). Spirit possession and spirit mediumship from the perspective of Tulu oral traditions. *Culture, Medicine and Psychiatry, 3,* 29–52.

CLAUS, P. J. (1983). Medical anthropology and the ethnography of spirit possession. *Contributions to Asian Studies, 18,* 60–72.

CLEMENTZ, B. A., & SWEENEY, J. A. (1990). Is eye movement dysfunction a biological marker for schizophrenia? A methodological review. *Psychological Bulletin, 108,* 77–92.

CLIFFORD, J., & MARCUS, G. (1986). *Writing culture.* Berkeley: University of California Press.

CLONINGER, C. R., GOHMAN, M., & SIGVARDSSON, S. (1981). Inheritance of alcohol abuse: Cross fostering analysis of adopted men. *Archives of General Psychiatry, 38,* 861–868.

COLEMAN, E. (1988a). Chemical dependency and intimacy dysfunction: Inextricably bound. In E. Coleman (Ed.), *Chemical dependency and intimacy dysfunction* (pp. 13–26). New York: Haworth Press.

COLEMAN, E. (1988b). Child physical and sexual abuse among chemically dependent individuals. In E. Coleman (Ed.), *Chemical dependency and intimacy dysfunction* (pp. 27–38). New York: Haworth Press.

CONNOR, L. (1979). Corpse abuse and trance in Bali: The cultural mediation of aggression. *Mankind, 12,* 104–118.

COONS, P. M. (1988). Schneiderian first-rank symptoms in schizophrenia and multiple personality disorder. *Acta Psychiatrica Scandinavica, 77,* 235.

Coons, P. M. (1994). Confirmation of childhood abuse in child and adolescent cases of multiple personality disorder and dissociative disorder not otherwise specified. *Journal of Nervous and Mental Disease, 182,* 461–464.

Coons, P. M., Bowman, E. S., & Milstein, V. (1988). Multiple personality disorder: A clinical investigation of 50 cases. *Journal of Nervous and Mental Disease, 176,* 519–527.

Corin, E., & Bibeau, G. (1980). Psychiatric perspectives in Africa; part II: the traditional viewpoint. *Transcultural Psychiatric Research Review, 17,* 205–223.

Cotman, C. W., & Lynch, G. S. (1989). The neurobiology of learning and memory. *Cognition, 33,* 201–241.

Crapanzano, V., & Garrison, V. (Eds.). (1977). *Case studies in spirit possession.* New York: Wiley.

Critchlow, B. (1986). The powers of John Barleycorn: Beliefs about the effects of alcohol on social behavior. *American Psychologist, 41,* 751–764.

Crittenden, K. S., Fugita, S. S., Bae, H., Lamug, C. B., et al. (1992). A cross-cultural study of self-report depressive symptoms among college students. *Journal of Cross-Cultural Psychology, 23,* 163–178.

Cross-National Collaborative Group. (1992). The changing rate of major depression: Cross-national comparisons. *Journal of the American Medical Association, 268,* 3089–3105.

Csikszentmihalyi, M. (1988). The flow experience and its significance for human psychology. In M. Csikszentmihalyi & I. S. Csikszentmihalyi (Eds.), *Optimal experience: Psychological studies of flow in consciousness* (pp. 15–35). Cambridge: Cambridge University Press.

Csordas, T. J. (1983). The rhetoric of transformation in ritual healing. *Culture, Medicine and Psychiatry, 7,* 333–375.

D'Andrade, R. G. (1984). Cultural meaning systems. In R. A. Shweder & R. A. LeVine (Eds.), *Culture theory: Essays on mind, self, and emotion* (pp. 88–119). Cambridge: Cambridge University Press.

Daniel, E. V. (1984). *Fluid signs: Being a person the Tamil way.* Berkeley: University of California Press.

Day, R., Nielsen, J. A., Korten, A., Ernberg, G., Dube, K. C., Gebhart, J., Jablensky, A., Leon, C., Marsella, A., Olatawura, M., Sartorius, N., Stromgren, E., Takahashi, R., Wig, N., & Wynne, L. C. (1987). Stressful life events preceding the acute onset of schizophrenia: A cross-national study from the World Health Organization. *Culture, Medicine and Psychiatry, 11,* 123–205.

Dennis, P. A. (1985). *Grisi siknis* in Miskito culture. In R. C. Simons & C. C. Hughes (Eds.), *The culture-bound syndromes: Folk illnesses of psychiatric and anthropological interest* (pp. 289–306). Dordrecht: D. Reidel.

Desjarlais, R., Eisenberg, L., Good, B., & Kleinman, A. (1995). *World mental health: Problems and priorities in low-income countries.* New York: Oxford University Press.

DeVos, G. (1984). *Heritage of endurance.* Berkeley: University of California Press.

de Waal, F. B. M. (1987). Tension regulation and nonreproductive functions in captive bonobos (Pan paniscus). *National Geographic Research, 3,* 318–335.

de Waal, F. B. M. (1995, March). Bonobo sex and society. *Scientific American, 272,* 82–88.

DiNardo, P. A., & Barlow, D. H. (1990). Syndrome and symptom comorbidity in the anxiety disorders. In J. D. Maser & C. R. Cloninger (Eds.), *Comorbidity of mood and anxiety disorders* (pp. 205–230). Washington, DC: American Psychiatric Press.

Doi, T. (1981). *The anatomy of dependence.* New York: Kodansha International.

DONOVAN, D. M. (1988). Assessment of addictive behaviors: Implications of an emerging biopsychosocial model. In D. M. Donovan & G. A. Marlatt (Eds.), *Assessment of addictive behaviors*. New York: Guilford Press.

DOW, J. (1986). Universal aspects of symbolic healing: A theoretical synthesis. *American Anthropologist, 88,* 56–69.

DOWEIKO, H. E. (1996). *Concepts of chemical dependency* (3rd ed.). Pacific Grove, CA: Brooks/Cole.

DRESP, C. S. W. (1985). *Nervios* as a culture-bound syndrome among Puerto Rican women. *Smith College Studies in Social Work, 55,* 115–136.

DRISCOLL, J. P. (1971, Mar.-Apr.). Transsexuals. *Transaction,* 28–31.

DUMONT, L. (1980). *Homo hierarchicus: The caste system and its implications.* Chicago: University of Chicago Press.

EBERT, D., & MARTUS, P. (1994). Somatization as a core symptom of melancholic type depression: Evidence from a cross-cultural study. *Journal of Affective Disorders, 32,* 253–256.

EBIGBO, P. O. (1982). Development of a cultural specific (Nigeria) screening scale of somatic complaints indicating psychiatric disturbance. *Culture, Medicine and Psychiatry, 6,* 29–43.

EBIGBO, P. O. (1986). A cross-sectional study of somatic complaints of Nigerian females using Enugu Somatization Scale. *Culture, Medicine and Psychiatry, 10,* 167–186.

EBOMAYI, E. (1987). Prevalence of female circumcision in two Nigerian communities. *Sex Roles, 17,* 130–152.

EDGERTON, R. B. (1971). A traditional African psychiatrist. *Southwestern Journal of Anthropology, 27,* 259–278.

EDWARDS, J. W. (1985). Indigenous *koro,* a genital retraction syndrome of insular Southeast Asia: A critical review. In R. C. Simons & C. C. Hughes (Eds.), *The culture-bound syndromes: Folk illnesses of psychiatric and anthropological interest* (pp. 169–191). Dordrecht: D. Reidel.

EKMAN, P. (1980). *The face of man: Expressions of universal emotions in a New Guinea village.* New York: Garland STPM Press.

EL ISLAM, M. F. (1979). A better outlook for schizophrenics living in extended families. *British Journal of Psychiatry, 135,* 343–347.

EL ISLAM, M. F. (1982). Arabic cultural psychiatry. *Transcultural Psychiatric Research Review, 19,* 5–24.

ELLASON, J. W., & ROSS, C. A. (1995). Positive and negative symptoms in dissociative identity disorder and schizophrenia: A comparative analysis. *Journal of Nervous and Mental Disease, 183,* 236–241.

ESCOBAR, J. I. (1995). Transcultural aspects of dissociative and somatoform disorders. *Psychiatric Clinics of North America, 18,* 555–569.

ESTROFF, S. E. (1981). *Making it crazy: An ethnography of psychiatric clients in an American community.* Berkeley: University of California Press.

FABREGA, H. (1989a). Cultural relativism and psychiatric illness. *Journal of Nervous and Mental Disease, 177,* 415–425.

FABREGA, H. (1989b). On the significance of an anthropological approach to schizophrenia. *Psychiatry, 52,* 45–65.

FABREGA, H. (1992). The role of culture in a theory of psychiatric illness. *Social Science and Medicine, 35,* 91–103.

FABREGA, H. (1993a). Toward a social theory of psychiatric phenomena. *Behavioral Science, 38,* 75–100.

FABREGA, H. (1993b). A cultural analysis of human behavioral breakdowns: An approach to the ontology and epistemology of psychiatric phenomena. *Culture, Medicine and Psychiatry, 17*, 99–132.

FABREGA, H. (1994a). International systems of diagnosis in psychiatry. *Journal of Nervous and Mental Disease, 182*, 256–263.

FABREGA, H. (1994b). Personality disorders as medical entities: A cultural interpretation. *Journal of Personality Disorders, 8*, 149–167.

FENWICK, C. R. (1996). Law and order in contemporary Japan: Commitment, sanctions and the quality of life. In C. B. Fields & R. H. Moore (Eds.), *Comparative criminal justice* (pp. 97–114). Propspect Heights, IL: Waveland Press.

FINK, D., & GOLINKOFF, M. (1990). Multiple personality disorder, borderline personality disorder, and schizophrenia: A comparative study of clinical features. *Dissociation, 3*, 127–134.

FINKELHOR, D. (1984). *Child sexual abuse: New theory and research.* New York: Free Press.

FLECK, S. (1995). Dehumanizing developments in American psychiatry in recent decades. *Journal of Nervous and Mental Disease, 183*, 195–203.

FOSSUM, M. A., & MASON, M. J. (1986). *Facing shame: Families in recovery.* New York: Norton.

FOULKS, E. F. (1985). The transformation of arctic hysteria. In R. C. Simons & C. C. Hughes (Eds.), *The culture-bound syndromes: Folk illnesses of psychiatric and anthropological interest* (pp. 307–324). Dordrecht: D. Reidel.

FRANKEL, F. H., & ZAMANSKY, H. S. (1978). *Hypnosis at its bicentennial.* New York: Plenum Press.

FRANKLIN, J. (1987). *Molecules of the mind.* New York: Dell.

FREED, R. S., & FREED, S. A. (1990). Ghost illness in a north Indian village. *Social Science and Medicine, 30*, 617–623.

FREED, S. A., & FREED, R. S. (1964). Spirit possession as illness in a north Indian village. *Ethnology, 3*, 152–171.

FROMM, E., & SHOR, R. E. (EDS.). (1979). *Hypnosis: Developments in research and new perspectives* (2nd ed.). New York: Aldine.

FURNHAM, A., & MALIK, R. (1994). Cross-cultural beliefs about "depression." *International Journal of Social Psychiatry, 40*, 106–123.

GAINES, A. D. (1992a). From DSM-I to III-R; voices of self, mastery and the other: A cultural constructivist reading of U.S. psychiatric classification. *Social Science and Medicine, 35*, 3–24.

GAINES, A. D. (ED.). (1992b). *Ethnopsychiatry: The cultural construction of professional and folk psychiatries.* Albany: State University of New York Press.

GALANTI, G. (1991). *Caring for patients from different cultures: Case studies from American hospitals.* Philadelphia: University of Pennsylvania Press.

GANDHY, S. (1988, July 31). Crimes against women. *Illustrated Weekly of India*, pp. 8–17.

GANG-MING, M., GUO-QIAN, C., LI-XUN, L., & TSENG, W. S. (1995). *Koro* epidemic in southern China. In T. Y. Lin, W. S. Tseng, & E. K. Yeh (Eds.), *Chinese societies and mental health* (pp. 231–243). New York: Oxford University Press.

GARNER, D. M., GARFINKEL, P. E., SCHWARTZ, D., & THOMPSON, M. (1980). Cultural expectations of thinness in women. *Psychological Reports, 47*, 483–491.

GARRISON, V. (1977). The Puerto Rican syndrome in *espiritismo* and psychiatry. In V. Crapanzano & V. Garrison (Eds.), *Case studies in spirit possession.* New York: Wiley Interscience.

GAW, A. C. (ED.). (1993).*Culture, ethnicity, and mental illness.* Washington, DC: American Psychiatric Press.

GEBHARD, P. H., GAGNON, J. H., POMEROY, W. B., & CHRISTENSON, C. V. (1965). *Sex offenders: An analysis of types.* New York: Harper & Row.

GEERTZ, H. (1968). Latah in Java: A theoretical paradox. *Indonesia, 3,* 93–104.

GELLHORN, E. (1969). Further studies on the physiology and pathophysiology of the tuning of the central nervous system. *Psychosomatics, 10,* 94–104.

GLASSMAN, A. H., & PLATMAN, S. R. (1969). Potentiation of a monoamine oxidase inhibitor by tryptophan. *Journal of Psychiatric Research, 7,* 83–88.

GOFFMAN, E. (1959). *The presentation of self in everyday life.* Garden City: Doubleday.

GOFFMAN, E. (1963). *Stigma.* Englewood Cliffs, NJ: Prentice-Hall.

GOLD, A. N. (1988). Spirit possession perceived and performed in rural Rajasthan. *Contributions to Indian Sociology, 22,* 35–63.

GOLDBERG, D. P., & BRIDGES, K. (1988). Somatic presentations of psychiatric illness in a primary care setting. *Journal of Psychosomatic Research, 32,* 137–144.

GOLDMAN, S. J., D'ANGELO, E. J., DeMASO, D. R., & MEZZACAPPA, E. (1992). Physical and sexual abuse histories among children with borderline personality disorder. *American Journal of Psychiatry, 149,* 1723–1726.

GONZALEZ, C. A., GRIFFITH, E. E. H., LEWIS-FERNÁNDEZ, R., LITTLEWOOD, R., & CASTILLO, R. J. (1992). Cultural considerations for the dissociative disorders (DSM-IV). In J. E. Mezzich, A. Kleinman, H. Fabrega, B. Good, G. Johnson-Powell, K. M. Lin, S. Manson, & D. Parron (Eds.), *Cultural proposals for DSM-IV* (pp. 138–143). Submitted to the DSM-IV Task Force by the Steering Committee, NIMH Group on Culture and Diagnosis. Pittsburgh: University of Pittsburgh.

GOOD, B. J. (1992). Culture and psychopathology: Directions for psychiatric anthropology. In T. Schwartz, G. M. White, & C. A. Lutz (Eds.), *New directions in psychological anthropology* (pp. 181–205). Cambridge: Cambridge University Press.

GOOD, B. J., & KLEINMAN, A. (1985). Epilogue: Culture and depression. In A. Kleinman & B. Good (Eds.), *Culture and depression: Studies in the anthropology and cross-cultural psychiatry of affect and disorder* (pp. 491–505). Berkeley: University of California Press.

GOSSELIN, C., & WILSON, G. (1980). *Sexual variations: Fetishism, sadomasochism, transvestism.* New York: Simon & Schuster.

GOTTESMAN, I. I. (1991). *Schizophrenia genesis: The origins of madness.* New York: W. H. Freeman.

GRAY, J. J., FORD, K., & KELLY, L. M. (1987). The prevalence of bulimia in a black college population. *International Journal of Eating Disorders, 6* (6), 733–740.

GREAVES, G. B. (1992). Alternative hypotheses regarding claims of satanic cult activity: A critical analysis. In D. K. Sakheim & S. E. Devine (Eds.), *Out of darkness: Exploring satanism and ritual abuse* (pp. 45–72). New York: Lexington Books.

GREEN, R. (1975). Adults who want to change sex; adolescents who cross-dress; and children called "sissy" and "tomboy." In R. Green (Ed.), *Human sexuality: A health practitioner's text.* Baltimore: Williams & Wilkins.

GREGERSON, E. (1983). *Sexual practices: The story of human sexuality.* New York: Franklin Watts.

GREGOR, T. (1990). Male dominance and sexual coercion. In J. W. Stigler, R. A. Shweder, & G. Herdt (Eds.), *Cultural psychology: Essays on comparative human development* (pp. 477–495). New York: Cambridge University Press.

GROSSI, V., & VIOLATO, C. (1992). Attempted suicide among adolescents: A stepwise discriminant analysis. *Canadian Journal of Behavioural Science, 24,* 410–412.

GUARNACCIA, P. J., DE LA CANCELA, V., & CARRILLO, E. (1989). The multiple meanings of *ataques de nervios* in the Latino community. *Medical Anthropology, 11,* 47–62.

GUARNACCIA, P. J., & FARIAS, P. (1988). The social meanings of *nervios:* A case study of a Central American woman. *Social Science and Medicine, 26,* 1223–1231.

GUARNACCIA, P. J., GOOD, B. J., & KLEINMAN, A. (1990). A critical review of epidemiological studies of Puerto Rican mental health. *American Journal of Psychiatry, 147,* 1449–1456.

GULLICK, J. M. (1958). *Indigenous political systems of western Malaya.* London School of Economics monographs on social anthropology, No. 21. London: Athlone Press.

GUR, R. C., MOZLEY, L. H., MOZLEY, P. D., RESNICK, S. M., KARP, J. S., ALAVI, A., ARNOLD, S., & GUR, R. E. (1995). Sex differences in regional cerebral glucose metabolism during a resting state. *Science, 267,* 528–531.

GUSSLER, J. (1973). Social change, ecology, and spirit possession among the South African Nguni. In E. Bourguignon (Ed.), *Religion, altered states of consciousness, and social change* (pp. 88–126). Columbus: Ohio State University Press.

GUSSOW, Z. (1985). *Pibliktog* (hysteria) among the Polar Eskimo: An ethnopsychiatric study. In R. C. Simons & C. C. Hughes (Eds.), *The culture-bound syndromes: Folk illnesses of psychiatric and anthropological interest* (pp. 271–287). Dordrecht: D. Reidel.

GUTTMACHER, L. B. (1994). *Concise guide to psychopharmacology and electroconvulsive therapy.* Washington, DC: American Psychiatric Press.

GUZE, S. B. (1970). The role of follow-up studies: Their contribution to diagnostic classification as applied to hysteria. *Seminar Psychiatry, 2,* 392–402.

HAANSTRA, B. (Producer, Director). (1991). *Family of Chimps* [Film]. New York: Filmakers Library.

HALL, R. (1986). Alcohol treatment in American Indian populations: An indigenous treatment modality compared with traditional approaches. *Annals of the New York Academy of Science, 472,* 168–178.

HALPERN, D. (1993). Minorities and mental health. *Social Science and Medicine, 36*(5), 597–607.

HARDING, C. M., BROOKS, G. W., ASHIKAGA, T., ET AL. (1987). The Vermont longitudinal study of persons with severe mental illness. II. Long-term outcome of patients who retrospectively met DSM-III criteria for schizophrenia. *American Journal of Psychiatry, 144,* 727–735.

HARDING, T. W. (1975). Traditional healing methods for mental disorders. *World Health Organization Chronicle, 31,* 436–440.

HARPER, E. B. (1963). Spirit possession and social structure. In B. Ratnam (Ed.), *Anthropology on the march: Recent studies of Indian beliefs, attitudes and social institutions.* Madras: The Book Centre.

HART, E. E., & WILLIAMS, C. L. (1987). Suicidal behavior and interpersonal network. *Crisis, 8,* 112–124.

HARTSUIKER, D. (1993). *Sadhus: India's mystic holy men.* Rochester, VT: Inner Traditions International.

HARVEY, Y. K. (1976). The Korean *Mudang* as a household therapist. In W. Lebra (Ed.), *Culture-bound syndromes: Ethnopsychiatry and alternate therapies* (pp. 189–198). Honolulu: University of Hawaii Press.

HARWOOD, A. (1987). *Rx: Spiritist as needed: A study of a Puerto Rican community mental health resource* (2nd ed.). Ithaca: Cornell University Press.

HAWTON, K. (1986). *Suicide and attempted suicide among children and adolescents.* Newbury Park, CA: Sage.

HEATH, D. B. (1981). The sociocultural model of alcohol use: Problems and prospects. *Journal of Operational Psychiatry, 9,* 55–66.

HEATH, D. B. (1983). Alcohol use among North American Indians: A cross-cultural survey of patterns and problems. In R. G. Smart, F. B. Glaser, Y. Israel, H. Kalant, R. E. Popham, & W. Schmidt (Eds.), *Research advances in alcohol and drug problems* (Vol. 7) (pp. 343–396). New York: Plenum Press.

HEATH, D. B. (1987). A decade of development in the anthropological study of alcohol use, 1970–1980. In M. Douglas (Ed.), *Constructive drinking*. Cambridge: Cambridge University Press.

HEINZE, R. I. (1988). *Trance and healing in Southeast Asia today*. Bangkok: White Lotus.

HELZER, J. E., & CANINO, G. (1992). Comparative analyses of alcoholism in 10 cultural regions. In J. E. Helzer & G. Canino (Eds.), *Alcoholism in North America, Europe and Asia* (pp. 289–308). New York: Oxford University Press.

HENDRY, J. (1994). Drinking and gender in Japan. In M. McDonald (Ed.), *Gender, drink and drugs* (pp. 175–190). Providence, RI: Berg.

HERDT, G. H. (1980). Semen depletion and the sense of maleness. *Ethnopsychiatrica, 3*, 79–116.

HERDT, G. H. (1981). *Guardians of the flutes: Idioms of masculinity*. New York: McGraw-Hill.

HERDT, G. H. (1990). Sambia nosebleeding rites and male proximity to women. In J. W. Stigler, R. A. Shweder, & G. Herdt (Eds.), *Cultural psychology: Essays on comparative human development* (pp. 366–400). New York: Cambridge University Press.

HERDT, G. (ED.) (1994). *Third sex, third gender: Beyond sexual dimorphism in culture and history*. New York: Zone Books.

HIEBERT, K. A., FELICE, M. E., WINGARD, D. L., MUNOZ, R., & FERGUSON, J. M. (1988). Comparison of outcome in Hispanic and Caucasian patients with anorexia nervosa. *International Journal of Eating Disorders, 7* (5), 693–696.

HILGARD, E. R. (1971). Hypnotic phenomena: The struggle for scientific acceptance. *American Scientist, 59*, 567–577.

HILGARD, E. R. (1977). *Divided consciousness: Multiple controls in human thought and action*. New York: Wiley.

HINTON, L., & KLEINMAN, A. (1993). Cultural issues and international psychiatric diagnosis. In J. Costa de Silva & C. Nadelson (Eds.), *International review of psychiatry* (pp. 111–129). Washington, DC: American Psychiatric Press.

HOBSON, J. A. (1988). Introduction. In J. A. Hobson (Ed.), *Readings from the encyclopedia of neuroscience: States of brain and mind* (pp. xi–xii). Boston: Birkhauser.

HOLZMAN, P. S., & LEVY, D. L. (1977). Smooth pursuit eye movements and functional psychoses: A review. *Schizophrenia Bulletin, 3*, 15–27.

HOOPER, A. (1985). Tahitian healing. In C. Parsons (Ed.), *Healing practices in the South Pacific* (pp. 158–189). Honolulu: University of Hawaii Press.

HORNEY, K. (1964). *The neurotic personality of our time*. New York: Norton.

HORNSTEIN, N. L. (1993). Recognition and differential diagnosis of dissociative disorders in children and adolescents. *Dissociation, 6*, 136–144.

HORNSTEIN, N. L., & TYSON, S. (1991). Inpatient treatment of children with multiple personality/dissociative disorders and their families. *Psychiatric Clinics of North America, 14*, 631–638.

HSU, L. K. G. (1987). Are eating disorders becoming more common in blacks. *International Journal of Eating Disorders, 6*(1), 113–124.

HUSSERL, E. (1962). *Ideas: General introduction to pure phenomenology*. New York: Collier Books.

HYDE, J. S. (1994). *Understanding human sexuality* (5th ed.). New York: McGraw-Hill.

IACONO, W. G. (1988). Eye movement abnormalities in schizophrenic and affective disorders. In C. W. Johnson & F. J. Pirozzolo (Eds.), *Neuropsychology of eye movements* (pp. 115–145). Hillsdale, NJ: Lawrence Erlbaum.

INKELES, A., & SMITH, D. H. (1974). *Becoming modern: Individual change in six developing countries.* Cambridge, MA: Harvard University Press.

IVEY, A. E. (1994). *International interviewing and counseling: Facilitating client development in a multicultural society.* Pacific Grove, CA: Brooks/Cole.

JABLENSKY, A., & SARTORIUS, N. (1988). Is schizophrenia universal? *Acta Psychiatrica Scandinavica, 78,* 65–70.

JABLENSKY, A., SARTORIUS, N., ERNBERG, G., ANKER, M., ET AL. (1992). Schizophrenia: Manifestations, incidence and course in different cultures: A World Health Organization ten-country study. *Psychological Medicine* (Monograph Supplement Vol. 20).

JABLENSKY, A., SARTORIUS, N., GULBINAT, W., & ERNBERG, G. (1981). Characteristics of depressive patients contacting psychiatric services in four cultures. *Acta Psychitrica Scandinavica, 63,* 367–383.

JACOB, K. A. (1981). The Mosher report. *American Heritage, 57–64.*

JANCA, A., ISAAC, M., BENNETT, L. A., & TACCHINI, G. (1995). Somatoform disorders in different cultures: A mail questionnaire survey. *Social Psychiatry and Psychiatric Epidemiology, 30,* 44–48.

JEFFERSON, J. W., & GREIST, J. H . (1989). Lithium in psychiatric therapy. In J. A. Hobson (Ed.), *Readings from the encyclopedia of neuroscience: Abnormal states of brain and mind* (pp. 63–64). Boston: Birkhauser.

JELLINEK, E. M. (1952). Phases of alcohol addiction. *Quarterly Journal of Studies on Alcohol, 13,* 673–674.

JELLINEK, E. M. (1960). *The disease concept of alcoholism.* New Haven, CT: College and University Press.

JENKINS, J. H. (1991). Anthropology, expressed emotion, and schizophrenia. *Ethos, 19,* 387–431.

JENKINS, J. H. (1992). Too close for comfort: Schizophrenia and emotional overinvolvement among Mexicano families. In A. D. Gaines (Ed.), *Ethnopsychiatry: The cultural construction of professional and folk psychiatries* (pp. 203–221). Albany: State University of New York Press.

JENKINS, J. H., KLEINMAN, A., & GOOD, B. J. (1990). Cross-cultural studies of depression. In J. Becker & A. Kleinman (Eds.), *Advances in mood disorders: Theory and research, vol. 1, psychosocial aspects* (pp. 67–99). Los Angeles: Erlbaum.

JILEK, W. G. (1993). Traditional medicine relevant to psychiatry. In N. Sartorius, G. de Girolamo, G. Andrews, G. A. German, & L. Eisenberg (Eds.), *Treatment of mental disorders: A review of effectiveness* (pp. 341–383). Washington, DC: American Psychiatric Press (published on behalf of the World Health Organization).

JILEK, W. G. (1994). Tradiitonal healing in the prevention and treatment of alcohol and drug abuse. *Transcultural Psychiatric Research Review, 31,* 219–258.

JILEK, W. G., & JILEK-AALL, L. (1970). Transient psychosis in Africans. *Psychiatric Clinics, 3,* 337–364.

JONES, B. E., & GRAY, B. A. (1986). Problems in diagnosing schizophrenia and affective disorders in blacks. *Hospital and Community Psychiatry, 37,* 61–65.

KAKAR, S. (1982). *Shamans, mystics and doctors: A psychological inquiry into India and its healing traditions.* New York: Alfred A. Knopf.

KANDEL, D. B., & RAVEIS, V. H. (1989). Cessation of illicit drug use in young adulthood. *Archives of General Psychiatry, 46,* 109–116.

KANDEL, E. R. (1989). Genes, nerve cells, and the remembrance of things past. *Journal of Neuropsychiatry & Clinical Neurosciences, 1,* 103–125.

KANDEL, E. R., & HAWKINS, R. D. (1992). The biological basis of learning and individuality. *Scientific American, 262,* (3), 78–86.

KAPLAN, H. S. (1979). *Disorders of sexual desire.* New York: Brunner/Mazel.

KARNO, M., & JENKINS, J. H. (1993). Cross-cultural issues in the course and treatment of schizophrenia. *Psychiatric Clinics of North America, 16,* 339–350.

KARNO, M., JENKINS, J. H., DE LA SELVA, A., ET AL. (1987). Expressed emotion and schizophrenic outcome among Mexican-American families. *Journal of Nervous and Mental Disease, 175,* 143–151.

KAUFMAN, G. (1989). *The psychology of shame.* New York: Springer.

KENDALL, L. (1987). *Shamans, housewives, and other restless spirits: Women in Korean ritual life.* Honolulu: University of Hawaii Press.

KENNY, M. G. (1978). *Latah:* The symbolism of a putative mental disorder. *Culture, Medicine and Psychiatry, 2,* 209–231.

KETTER, T. (1983). Cultural stylization and mental illness in Bali. *Transcultural Psychiatric Research Review, 20,* 87–106.

KHALSA, A., SHANER, A., ANGLIN, M., & WANG, J. (1991). Prevalence of substance abuse in a psychiatric evaluation unit. *Drug and Alcohol Dependence, 28,* 215–223.

KHANDELWAL, S. K., SHARAN, P., & SAXENA, S. (1995). Eating disorders: An Indian perspective. *International Journal of Social Psychiatry, 41,* 132–146.

KHANNA, B. C., WIG, N. N., & VARMA, V. K. (1974). General hospital psychiatric clinic: An epidemiological study. *Indian Journal of Psychiatry, 16,* 211–218.

KHANTZIAN, E. J. (1985). The self-medication hypothesis of addictive disorders: Focus on heroin and cocaine dependence. *American Journal of Psychiatry, 142,* 1259–1264.

KIHLSTROM, J. F. (1979). Hypnosis and psychopathology. *Journal of Abnormal Psychology, 88,* 459–603.

KIM, K., LI, D., JIANG, Z., CUI, X., ET AL. (1993). Schizophrenic delusions among Koreans, Korean-Chinese, and Chinese: A transcultural study. *International Journal of Social Psychiatry, 39,* 190–199.

KIMURA, D. (1992, March). Sex differences in the brain. *Scientific American, 267,* 118–125.

KINSEY, A. C., POMEROY, W. B ., & MARTIN, C. E. (1948). *Sexual behavior in the human male.* Philadelphia: Saunders.

KINSEY, A. C., POMEROY, W. B., MARTIN, C. E., & GEBHARD, P. H. (1953). *Sexual behavior in the human female.* Philadelphia: Saunders.

KINZIE, D., TEOH, J. I., & TAN, E. S. (1976). Native healers in Malaysia. In W. Lebra (Ed.), *Culture-bound syndromes: Ethnopsychiatry and alternate therapies* (pp. 130–146). Honolulu: University of Hawaii Press.

KINZIE, J. D., BOEHNLEIN, J. K., LEUNG, P. K., MOORE L. J., RILEY, C., & SMITH, D. (1990). The prevalence of posttraumatic stress disorder and its clinical significance among Southeast Asian refugees. *American Journal of Psychiatry, 147,* 913–917.

KIRMAYER, L. J. (1984). Culture, affect and somatization. *Transcultural Psychiatric Research Review, 21,* 159–188, 237–262.

KIRMAYER, L. J. (1991). The place of culture in psychiatric nosology: *Taijin kyofusho* and DSM-III-R. *Journal of Nervous and Mental Disease, 179,* 19–28.

KIRMAYER, L. J. (1994). Suicide among Canadian aboriginal peoples. *Transcultural Psychiatric Research Review, 31,* 3–58.

KIRMAYER, L. J., & ROBINS, J. M. (1991). Three forms of somatization in primary care: Prevalence, co-occurrence and sociodemographic characteristics. *Journal of Nervous and Mental Disease, 179,* 647–655.

KIRMAYER, L. J., & WEISS, M. (1994). On cultural considerations for somatoform disorders. In J. E. Mezzich, A Kleinman, H. Fabrega, D. Perron, B. J. Good, K. M. Lin, & S. Manson (Eds.), *Cultural issues and DSM-IV: Support papers,* (pp. 137–147). Submitted for the DSM-IV Sourcebook by the NIMH Group on Culture and Diagnosis. Pittsburgh: University of Pittsburgh.

KIRMAYER, L. J., YOUNG, A., & HAYTON, B. C. (1995). The cultural context of anxiety disorders. *Psychiatric Clinics of North America, 18,* 503–521.

KISHLINE, A. (1996). A toast to moderation. *Psychology Today, 29* (1), 53–56.

KLEINMAN, A. (1980). *Patients and healers in the context of culture: An exploration of the borderland between anthropology, medicine, and psychiatry.* Berkeley: University of California Press.

KLEINMAN, A. (1982). Depression and neurasthenia in the People's Republic of China. *Culture, Medicine and Psychiatry, 6,* 1–80.

KLEINMAN, A. (1986). *Social origins of distress and disease: Depression, neurasthenia, and pain in modern China.* New Haven: Yale University Press.

KLEINMAN, A. (1988a). *The illness narratives: Suffering, healing and the human condition.* New York: Basic Books.

KLEINMAN, A. (1988b). *Rethinking psychiatry: From cultural category to personal experience.* New York: Free Press.

KLEINMAN, A. (1992). How culture is important for DSM-IV. In J. E. Mezzich, A. Kleinman, H. Fabrega, B. Good, G. Johnson-Powell, K. M. Lin, S. Manson, & D. Parron (Eds.), *Cultural proposals for DSM-IV* (pp. 7–28). Submitted to the DSM-IV Task Force by the Steering Committee, NIMH Group on Culture and Diagnosis. Pittsburgh: University of Pittsburgh.

KLEINMAN, A., EISENBERG, L., & GOOD, B. (1978). Culture, illness, and care: Clinical lessons from anthropologic and cross-cultural research. *Annals of Internal Medicine, 88,* 251–258.

KLEINMAN, A., & GOOD, B. (EDS.). (1985). *Culture and depression: Studies in the anthropology and cross-cultural psychiatry of affect and disorder.* Berkeley, CA: University of California Press.

KLEINMAN, A., & KLEINMAN, J. (1995). Remembering the cultural revolution: Alienating pains and the pain of alienation/transformation. In T. Y. Lin, W. S. Tseng, & E. K. Yeh (Eds.), *Chinese societies and mental health* (pp. 141–155). New York: Oxford University Press.

KLUFT, R. P. (1985). The natural history of multiple personality disorder. In R. P. Kluft (Ed.), *Childhood antecedents of multiple personality* (pp. 197–238). Washington, DC: Psychiatric Press.

KLUFT, R. P. (1987). First-rank symptoms as a diagnostic clue to multiple personality disorder. *American Journal of Psychiatry, 144,* 293–298.

KORTMANN, F. (1987). Popular, traditional and professional mental health care in Ethiopia. *Transcultural Psychiatric Research Review, 24,* 255–274.

KRAMER, P. D. (1993). *Listening to Prozac.* New York: Viking.

KUHN, T. S. (1970). *The structure of scientific revolutions* (2nd ed.). Chicago: University of Chicago Press.

KUTCHER, S., KACHUR, E., MARTON, P., SZALAI, J., ET AL. (1992). Substance abuse among adolescents with chronic mental illnesses: A pilot study of descriptive and differentiating features. *Canadian Journal of Psychiatry, 37,* 428–431.

LEBRA, W. (1982). Shaman-client interchange in Okinawa: Performative stages in shamanic therapy. In A. J. Marsella & G. M. White (Eds.), *Cultural conceptions of mental health and therapy* (pp. 303–315). Dordrecht, Holland: D. Reidel.

LEDOUX, S., CHOQUET, M., & MANFREDI, R. (1993). Associated factors for self-reported binge eating among male and female adolescents. *Journal of Adolescence, 16*, 75–91.

LEE, S., HO, T. P., & HSU, L. K. G. (1993). Fat phobic and non-fat phobic anorexia nervosa: A comparative study of 70 Chinese patients in Hong Kong. *Psychologial Medicine, 23*, 999-1017.

LEE, S., & HSU, G. (1995). Eating disorders in Hong Kong. In T. Y. Lin, W. S. Tseng, & E. K. Yeh (Eds.), *Chinese societies and mental health* (pp. 197–208). New York: Oxford University Press.

LEFF, J. (1989). Family factors in schizophrenia. *Psychiatric Annals, 19*, 542–547.

LEFF, J., SARTORIUS, N., JABLENSKY, A., KORTEN, A., ET AL. (1992). The international pilot study of schizophrenia: Five-year follow-up findings. *Psychological Medicine, 22*, 131–145.

LEFF, J., & VAUGHN, C. (EDS.). (1985). *Expressed emotion in families.* New York: Guilford Press.

LEHMANN, A. C., & MYERS, J. E. (1993). Ghosts, souls, and ancestors: Power of the dead. In A. C. Lehmann & J. E. Myers (Eds.), *Magic, witchcraft, and religion: An anthropological study of the supernatural* (pp. 283–286). Mountain View, CA: Mayfield.

LEIGHTON, A., LAMBO, T., HUGHES, C., LEIGHTON, D., MURPHY, J., & MACKLIN, D. (1963). *Psychiatric disorder among the Yoruba.* Ithaca: Cornell University Press.

LENG, G. H. (1985). *Koro: A cultural disease.* In R. C. Simons & C. C. Hughes (Eds.), *The culture-bound syndromes: Folk illnesses of psychiatric and anthropological interest* (pp. 155–159). Boston: D. Reidel.

LEON, M. (1992). The neurobiology of filial learning. *Annual Review of Psychology, 43*, 377–398.

LESHNER, A. (1991). *Treatment. National conference on drug abuse research and practice conference highlights.* Rockville, MD: NIDA.

LEVINE, R. E., & GAW, A. C. (1995). Culture-bound syndromes. *Psychiatric Clinics of North America, 18*, 523–535.

LEVY, M. J., JR. (1967). Social patterns (structures) and problems of modernization. In W. Moore & R. M. Cook (Eds.), *Readings on social change* (pp. 189–208). Englewood Cliffs, NJ: Prentice-Hall.

LEVY, R. I. (1971). The community function of Tahitian male transvestism: A hypothesis. *Anthropology Quarterly, 44*, 12–21.

LEVY, R. I. (1984). Emotion, knowing, and culture. In R. A. Shweder & R. A. LeVine (Eds.), *Culture theory: Essays on mind, self, and emotion* (pp. 214–237). Cambridge: Cambridge University Press.

LEWIS, G., CROFT-JEFFRIES, C., & ANTHONY, D. (1990). Are British psychiatrists racist? *British Journal of Psychiatry, 157*, 410–415.

LEWIS, G., DAVID, A., ANDREASSON, S., & ALLSBECK, P. (1992). Schizophrenia and city life. *Lancet, 340*, 137–140.

LEWIS, I. M. (1989). *Ecstatic religion: A study of shamanism and spirit possession* (2nd ed.). London: Routledge.

LEWIS-FERNÁNDEZ, R. (1992). The proposed DSM-IV trance and possession disorder category: Potential benefits and risks. *Transcultural Psychiatric Research Review, 29*, 301–317.

LEWIS-FERNÁNDEZ, R. (1994). Culture and dissociation: A comparison of *ataque de nervios* among Puerto Ricans and possession syndrome in India. In D. Spiegel (Ed.), *Dissociation: Culture, mind, and body* (pp. 123–167). Washington, DC: American Psychiatric Press.

LEWIS-FERNÁNDEZ, R., GONZALEZ, C. A., GRIFFITH, E. E. H., LITTLEWOOD, R., & CASTILLO, R. J. (1993). Comments on DSM-IV drafts of the dissociative disorders. In J. E.

Mezzich, A. Kleinman, H. Fabrega, D. Parron, B. J. Good, G. Johnson-Powell, K. M. Lin, & S. Manson (Eds.), *Revised cultural proposals for DSM-IV* (pp. 90–104). Submitted to the DSM-IV Task Force by the Steering Committee, NIMH Group on Culture and Diagnosis. Pittsburgh: University of Pittsburgh.

LEWIS-FERNÁNDEZ, R., & KLEINMAN, A. (1994). Culture, personality, and psychopathology. *Journal of Abnormal Psychology, 103,* 67–71.

LEX, B. (1979). The neurobiology of ritual trance. In E. Aquili, C. Laughlin, & J. McManus (Eds.), *The spectrum of ritual: A biogenetic structural analysis.* New York: Columbia University Press.

LIDZ, T. (1994). Genetic and psychosocial evolution and the future of psychiatry [Editorial]. *Journal of Nervous and Mental Disease, 182,* 601–603.

LIGHTFOOT-KLEIN, H. (1989). *Prisoners of ritual: An odyssey into female genital circumcision in Africa.* New York: Haworth.

LIN, K. M., LAU, J. K. C., YAMAMOTO, J., ZHENG, Y. P., KIM, H. S., CHO, K. H., & NAKASAKI, G. (1992). *Hwa-byung:* A community study of Korean Americans. *Journal of Nervous and Mental Disease, 180,* 386–391.

LINDHOLM, C. (1997). The Swat Pukhtun family as a political training ground. In R. J. Castillo (Ed.), *The meanings of madness: Readings on culture and mental illness.* Pacific Grove, CA: Brooks/Cole.

LINGSWILER, V. M., CROWTHER, J. H., & STEPHENS, N. A. (1989). Affective and cognitive antecedents to eating episodes in bulimia and binge eating. *International Journal of Eating Disorders, 8* (5), 533–539.

LITTLEWOOD, R. (1991). From categories to contexts: A decade of the "new cross-cultural psychiatry." *British Journal of Psychiatry, 156,* 308–327.

LOCK, M. (1989). Words of fear, words of power: Nerves and the awakening of political consciousness. *Medical Anthropology, 11,* 79–90.

LORANGER, A. W., SARTORI, N., ANDREOLI, A., BERGER, P., BUCHEIM, P., CHANNABASAVANNA, S. M., COID, B., DAHL, A., DEIKSTRA, R. F. W., FERGUSON, B., JACOBSBERG, L. B., MOMBOUR, W., PULL, C., ONO, Y., & REGIER, D. A. (1994). The International Personality Disorder Examination. *Archives of General Psychiatry, 51,* 215–224.

LOW, S. M. (1989). Health, culture and the nature of nerves: A critique. *Medical Anthropology, 11,* 91–95.

LOWENSTEIN, R. J., & PUTNAM, F. W. (1990). The clinical phenomenology of males with multiple personality disorder: A report of 21 cases. *Dissociation, 3,* 135–143.

LU, F. G., LIM, R. F., & MEZZICH, J. E. (1995). Issues in the assessment and diagnosis of culturally diverse individuals. In J. M. Oldham & M. B. Riba (Eds.), *Review of psychiatry* (Vol. 14) (pp. 477–510). Washington, DC: American Psychiatric Press.

LUDWIG, A. M. (1983). The psychobiological functions of dissociation. *American Journal of Clinical Hypnosis, 26,* 93–99.

LUTZ, C. A. (1985). Depression and translation of emotional worlds. In A. Kleinman & B. Good (Eds.), *Culture and depression: Studies in the anthropology and cross-cultural psychiatry of affect and disorder* (pp. 63–100). Berkeley: University of California Press.

LUTZ, C. A. (1988). *Unnatural emotions: Everyday sentiments on a Micronesian atoll and their challenge to western theory.* Chicago: University of Chicago Press.

MACLACHLAN, M., NYIRENDA, T., & NYANDO, C. (1995). Attributions for admission to Zomba Mental Hospital: Implications for the development of mental health services in Malawi. *International Journal of Social Psychiatry, 41,* 79–87.

MAGLEBY, K. L. (1987). Synaptic transmission, facilitation, augmentation, potentiation, depression. In G. Adelman (Ed.), *The encyclopedia of neuroscience* (pp. 1170–1174). Boston: Birkhauser.

MAGNE-INGVAR, U., OJEHAGEN, A., & TRASKMAN-BENDZ, L. (1992). The social network of people who attempt suicide. *Acta Psychiatrica Scandinavica, 86,* 153–158.

MAKANJUOLA, R. O. A. (1987). *"Ode Ori"*: A culture-bound disorder with prominent somatic features in Yoruba Nigerian patients. *Acta Psychiatrica Scandinavica, 75,* 231–236.

MALEFIJT, A. D. (1968). *Religion and culture: An introduction to anthropology of religion.* New York: Macmillan.

MANDELBAUM, D. G. (1970). *Society in India.* Berkeley: University of California Press.

MANSON, S. M. (1995). Culture and major depression: Current challenges in the diagnosis of mood disorders. *Psychiatric Clinics of North America, 18,* 487–501.

MANSON, S. M., & GOOD, B. J. (1992). Cultural considerations in the diagnosis of DSM-IV mood disorders. In J. E. Mezzich, A. Kleinman, H. Fabrega, B. Good, G. Johnson-Powell, K. M. Lin, S. Manson, & D. Parron. (Eds.), *Cultural proposals for DSM-IV* (pp. 87–103). Submitted to the DSM-IV Task Force by the Steering Committee, NIMH Group on Culture and Diagnosis. Pittsburgh: University of Pittsburgh.

MANSON, S. M., SHORE, J. H., BARON, A. E., ACKERSON, L., & NELIGH, G. (1992). Alcohol abuse and dependence among American Indians. In J. E. Helzer & G. Canino (Eds.), *Alcoholism in North America, Europe and Asia* (pp. 113–130). New York: Oxford University Press.

MARRIOTT, M. (1976). Hindu transactions: Diversity without dualism. In B. Kapferer (Ed.), *Transaction and meaning, directions in the anthropology of exchange and symbolic behavior* (pp. 109–142). Philadelphia: ISHI Publishing.

MARSELLA, A. J. (1979). Depressive experience and disorder across cultures. In H. C. Triandis & J. G. Draguns (Eds.), *Handbook of cross-cultural psychology: Psychopathology* (Vol. 6, pp. 237–289). Boston: Allyn and Bacon.

MARSELLA, A. J. (1989). Ethnocultural issues in the assessment of psychopathology. In S. Wetler (Ed.), *Measuring mental illness: Psychometric assessment for clinicians* (pp. 231–256). Washington, DC: American Psychiatric Press.

MARSELLA, A. J. (1993). Sociocultural foundations of psychopathology: An historical overview of concepts, events and pioneers prior to 1970. *Transcultural Psychiatric Research Review, 30,* 97–142.

MARSELLA, A. J., SARTORIUS, N., JABLENSKY, A., & FENTON, F. R. (1985). Cross-cultural studies of depressive disorders: An overview. In A. Kleinman & B. Good (Eds.), *Culture and depression: Studies in the anthropology and cross-cultural psychiatry of affect and disorder* (pp. 299–324). Berkeley: University of California Press.

MARSHALL, D. S. (1993). Sexual aspects of the life cycle. In A. W. Miracle & D. N. Suggs (Eds.), *Culture and human sexuality* (pp. 91–102). Pacific Grove, CA: Brooks/Cole.

MARTINS, C., DE LEMOS, A., & BEBBINGTON, P. E. (1992). A Portuguese/Brazilian study of expressed emotion. *Social Psychiatry and Psychiatric Epidemiology, 27,* 22–27.

MAYFIELD, D. (1976). Alcoholism, alcohol, intoxication and assaultive behavior. *Diseases of the Nervous System, 37,* 288–291.

MBITI, J. S. (1970). *African religions and philosophies.* Garden City, NY: Doubleday.

MCDANIEL, J. (1989). *The madness of the saints: Ecstatic religion in Bengal.* Chicago: Chicago University Press.

MCGIBBON, L., HANDY, S., BALLARD, C. G., & SILVEIRA, W. R. (1991). "Anorexia nervosa in adolescents of Asian extraction": Comment. *British Journal of Psychiatry, 158,* 285.

MCGLASHAN, T. H. (1988). A selective review of recent North American long-term follow-up studies of schizophrenia. *Schizophrenia Bulletin, 14,* 515–542.

McGuire, M. B. (1988). *Ritual healing in suburban America.* New Brunswick: Rutgers University Press.

Mendis, N. (1986). The outcome of schizophrenia in Sri Lanka—A ten-year follow-up study. *Ceylon Medical Journal, 31,* 119–134.

Menon, R. (1989, April 15). Child prostitutes: Nobody's children. *India Today,* pp. 124–127.

Merskey, H. (1994). The artifactual nature of multiple personality disorder: Comments on Charles Barton's "Backstage in psychiatry: The multiple personality disorder controversy." *Dissociation, 7,* 173–175.

Messenger, J. C. (1993). Sex and repression in an Irish folk community. In D. N. Suggs & A. W. Miracle (Eds.), *Culture and human sexuality* (pp. 240–261). Pacific Grove, CA: Brooks/Cole.

Mezzich, J. E. (1995). Cultural formulation and comprehensive diagnosis: Clinical and research perspectives. *Psychiatric Clinics of North America, 18,* 649–657.

Mezzich, J. E., Honda, Y., & Kastrup, M. C. (Eds.). (1994). *Psychiatric diagnosis: A world perspective.* New York: Springer-Verlag.

Mezzich, J. E., Kleinman, A., Fabrega, H., Good, B., Johnson-Powell, G., Lin, K. M., Manson, S., & Parron, D. (Eds.). (1992). *Cultural proposals for DSM-IV.* Submitted to the DSM-IV Task Force by the Steering Committee, NIMH Group on Culture and Diagnosis. Pittsburgh: University of Pittsburgh.

Mezzich, J. E., Kleinman, A., Fabrega, H., Parron, D., Good, B. J., Lin, K. M., & Manson, S. (Eds.). (1994). *Cultural issues and DSM-IV: Support papers.* Submitted for the DSM-IV Sourcebook by the Steering Committee, NIMH Group on Culture and Diagnosis. Pittsburgh: University of Pittsburgh.

Mezzich, J. E., Kleinman, A., Fabrega, H., et al. (1996). *Culture and psychiatric diagnosis.* Washington, DC: American Psychiatric Press.

Miller, I. W., & Norman, W. H. (1979). Learned helplessness in humans: A review and attribution-theory model. *Psychological Bulletin, 86,* 93–118.

Miller, W. R. (1980). The addictive behaviors. In W. R. Miller (Ed.), *The addictive behaviors* (pp. 3–10). New York: Pergamon Press.

Miller, W. R., & Hester, R. K. (1989). Treating alcohol problems: Toward an informed eclecticism. In R. K. Hester & W. R. Miller (Eds.), *Handbook of alcoholism treatment approaches* (pp. 3–13). New York: Pergamon Press.

Millman, R. (1991). *Indentification of dual diagnosis in drug abusers. National conference on drug abuse research and practice: Conference highlights.* Rockville, MD: NIDA.

Millon, T. (1981). *Disorders of personality.* New York: Wiley.

Mineka, S. (1985a). Animal models of anxiety based disorders: Their usefulness and limitations. In A. H. Tuma & J. D. Maser (Eds.), *Anxiety and the anxiety disorders* (pp. 199–244). Hillsdale, NJ: Lawrence Erlbaum.

Mineka, S. (1985b). The frightful complexity of the origins of fears. In F. R. Bruch & J. B. Overmier (Eds.), *Affect, conditioning, and cognition: Essays on the determinants of behavior* (pp. 55–74). Hillsdale, NJ: Lawrence Erlbaum.

Mineka, S., & Kelly, K. A. (1989). The relationship between anxiety, lack of control and loss of control. In A. Steptoe & A. Appels (Eds.), *Stress, personal control and worker health* (pp. 163–191). New York: Wiley.

Mizes, J. S., & Arbitell, M. R. (1991). Bulimics' perceptions of emotional responding during binge-purge episodes. *Psychological Reports, 69* (2), 527–532.

Moore, M. (1995, April 16). Dowry deaths multiply in India. *Honolulu Advertiser,* p. A8.

MORIYA, N., MIYAKE, Y., MINAKAWA, K., IKUTA, N., & NISHIZONO-MAHER, A. (1993). Diagnosis and clinical features of borderline personality disorder in the East and West: A preliminary report. *Comprehensive Psychiatry, 34,* 418–423.

MOSER, C., & LEVITT, E. E. (1987). An exploratory-descriptive study of a sadomasochistically oriented sample. *Journal of Sex Research, 23,* 322–337.

MOSHER, L. R., VALLONE, R., & MENN, A. (1995). The treatment of acute psychosis without neuroleptics: Six-week psychopathology outcome data from the Soteria Project. *International Journal of Social Psychiatry, 41,* 157–173.

MUMFORD, D. B., WHITEHOUSE, A. M., & CHOUDRY, I. Y. (1992). Survey of eating disorders in English-medium schools in Lahore, Pakistan. *International Journal of Eating Disorders, 11,* 173–184.

MURPHY, H. B. M., & RAMAN, A. C. (1971). The chronicity of schizophrenia in indigenous tropical peoples: Results of a twelve-year follow-up survey in Mauritius. *British Journal of Psychiatry, 118,* 489–497.

MURPHY, J. M. (1992). Contributions of anthropology and sociology to alcohol epidemiology. In J. E. Helzer & G. J. Canino (Eds.), *Alcoholism in North America, Europe, and Asia* (pp. 21–32). New York: Oxford University Press.

MURRAY, R. M., CLIFFORD, C. A., & GURLING, H. M. D. (1983). Twin and adoption studies: How good is the evidence for a genetic role? In M. Galanter (Ed.), *Recent developments in alcoholism* (pp. 25–48). New York: Plenum.

NANDA, S. (1993). The *hijras* of India: Cultural and individual dimensions of an institutionalized third gender role. In D. N. Suggs & A. W. Miracle (Eds.), *Culture and human sexuality* (pp. 279–293). Pacific Grove, CA: Brooks/Cole.

NASSER, M. (1986). Comparative study of the prevalence of abnormal eating attitudes among Arab female students of both London and Cairo universities. *Psychological Medicine, 16,* 621–625.

NDETEI, D. M., & MUHANGI, J. (1979). The prevalence and clinical presentation of psychiatric illness in a rural setting in Kenya. *British Journal of Psychiatry, 135,* 269–272.

NEISSER, U. (1976). *Cognition and reality: Principles and implications of cognitive psychology.* New York: W. H. Freeman.

NIETO-SAMPEDRO, M., & COTMAN, C. W. (1987). Synaptic plasticity. In G. Adelman (Ed.), *The encyclopedia of neuroscience* (pp. 1166–1167). Boston: Birkhauser.

NOBLE, E. P., BLUM, K., RITCHIE, T., MONTGOMERY, A., & SHERIDAN, P. J. (1991). Allelic association of the D2 dopamine receptor gene with receptor-binding characteristics in alcoholism. *Archives of General Psychiatry, 48,* 648–654.

NOLEN-HOEKSEMA, S. (1987). Sex differences in unipolar depression: Evidence and theory. *Psychological Bulletin, 101,* 259–282.

NOLEN-HOEKSEMA, S., GIRGUS, J. S., & SELIGMAN, M. E. P. (1992). Predictors and consequences of childhood depressive symptoms: A 5-year longitudinal study. *Journal of Abnormal Psychology, 101,* 405–422.

NORTH, C. S., RYALL, J. M., RICCI, D. A., & WETZEL, R. D. (1993). *Multiple personalities, multiple disorders: Psychiatric classification and media influence.* New York: Oxford University Press.

OBEYESEKERE, G. (1970). The idiom of demonic possession: A case study. *Social Science and Medicine, 4,* 97–111.

OBEYESEKERE, G. (1977). Psychocultural exegesis of a case of spirit possession in Sri Lanka. In V. Crapanzano & V. Garrison (Eds.), *Case studies in spirit possession* (pp. 235–294). New York: Wiley.

OBEYESEKERE, G. (1981). *Medusa's hair: An essay on personal symbols and religious experience.* Chicago: University of Chicago Press.

OBEYESEKERE, G. (1985). Depression, Buddhism, and the work of culture in Sri Lanka. In A. Kleinman & B. Good (Eds.), *Culture and depression: Studies in the anthropology and cross-cultural psychiatry of affect and disorder* (pp. 134–152). Berkeley: University of California Press.

O'FLAHERTY, W. D. (1973). *Siva: The erotic ascetic.* Oxford: Oxford University Press.

OGATA, S. N., SILK, K. R., GOODRICH, S., LOHR, N. E., WESTEN, D., & HILL, E. M. (1990). Childhood sexual and physical abuse in adult patients with borderline personality disorder. *American Journal of Psychiatry, 147,* 1008–1013.

OHARA, K. (1973). The socio-cultural approach for the manic depressive psychosis. *Psychiatrica et Neurologica Japonica, 75,* 263–273.

O'HARE, T. (1992). The substance-abusing chronically mentally ill client: Prevalence, assessment, treatment and policy concerns. *Social Work, 37,* 185–187.

OKASHA, A., SAAD, A., KHALIL, A. H., SEIF EL DAWLA, A., & YEHIA, N. (1994). Phenomenology of obsessive-compulsive disorder: A transcultural study. *Comprehensive Psychiatry, 35,* 191–197.

O'NELL, T. D. (1993). "Feeling worthless": An ethnographic investigation of depression and problem drinking at the Flathead Reservation. *Culture, Medicine and Psychiatry, 16,* 447–469.

OPLER, M. E. (1958). Spirit possession in a rural area of northern India. In W. A. Lessa & E. Z. Vogt (Eds.), *Reader in comparative religion: An anthropological approach* (pp. 553–566). Evanston, IL: Row, Peterson, & Co.

PACHAURI, P. (1988, October 31). Rajasthan: A murderous tradition. *India Today,* pp. 36–39.

PAGE, G. (EXECUTIVE PRODUCER). (1990). Monkey island. In *Nature.* New York: WNET.

PARDO, J. V., PARDO, P. J., & RAICHLE, M. E. (1993). Neural correlates of self-induced dysphoria. *American Journal of Psychiatry, 150,* 713–719.

PARIS, J. (1991). Personality disorders, parasuicide, and culture. *Transcultural Psychiatric Research Review, 28,* 189–197.

PARIS, J. (1996). Cultural factors in the emergence of borderline pathology. *Psychiatry, 59,* 185–192.

PARKER, S. (1962). Eskimo psychopathology. *American Anthropologist, 64,* 76–96.

PARSIAN, A., & CLONINGER, C. R. (1991). Genetics of high-risk populations. *Addiction & Recovery, 11* (6), 9–11.

PATEL, V., & WINSTON, M. (1994). "Universality of mental illness" revisited: Assumptions, artefacts and new directions. *British Journal of Psychiatry, 165,* 437–440.

PATTISON, E. M. (1977). Psychosocial interpretations of exorcism. *Journal of Operational Psychiatry, 8,* 5–19.

PEIRCE, C. S. (1962). *The collected papers of Charles Sanders Peirce.* Cambridge, MA: Harvard University Press.

PERLEY, M. J., & GUZE, S. B. (1962). Hysteria—the stability and usefulness of clinical criteria: A quantitative study based on a follow-up period of six to eight years in 39 patients. *New England Journal of Medicine, 266,* 421–426.

PETERS, L. G. (1978). Psychotherapy in Tamang shamanism. *Ethos, 6,* 63–91.

PETERS, L. G. (1994). Rites of passage and the borderline syndrome: Perspectives in transpersonal anthropology. *Anthropology of Consciousness, 5* (1), 1–15.

PETERSON, G. (1991). Children coping with trauma: Diagnosis of "dissociation identity disorder." *Dissociation, 3,* 152–164.

PFEIFFER, W. (1968). The symptomatology of depression viewed transculturally. *Transcultural Psychiatric Research Review, 5*, 121–123.

PHILIPPE, J., & ROMAIN, J. B. (1979). *Indisposition* in Haiti. *Social Science and Medicine, 13B*, 129–133.

PICKENS, R. W., SVIKIS, D. S., MCGUE, M., LYKKEN, D. T., HESTON, L. L., & CLAYTON, P. J. (1991). Heterogeneity in the inheritance of alcoholism: A study of male and female twins. *Archives of General Psychiatry, 48*, 19–28.

PIKER, S. (1994). Classical culture and personality. In P. K. Bock (Ed.), *Psychological anthropology* (pp. 1–17). Westport, CT: Praeger.

POLCIN, D. (1992). Issues in the treatment of dual diagnosis clients who have chronic mental illness. *Professional Psychology: Research and Practice, 23*, 30–37.

POST, R. M. (1990). Sensitization and kindling perspectives for the course of carbamazepine. *Pharmacopsychiatry, 23*, 3–17.

POST, R. M. (1992). Transduction of psychosocial stress into the neurobiology of recurrent affective disorder. *American Journal of Psychiatry, 149*, 999–1010.

POST, R. M., RUBINOW, D. R., UHDE, T. W., ROY-BYRNE, P. P., LINNOILA, M., ROSOFF, A., & COWDRY, R. (1989). Dysphoric mania: Clinical and biological correlates. *Archives of General Psychiatry, 46*, 353–358.

PRICE, R. (1987). Dissociative disorders of the self: A continuum extending into multiple personality. *Psychotherapy, 24*, 387–391.

PRICE-WILLIAMS, D., & HUGHES, D. J. (1994). Shamanism and altered states of consciousness. *Anthropology of Consciousness, 5* (2), 1–15.

PRINCE, R. (1979–80). Religious experience and psychosis. *Journal of Altered States of Consciousness, 5*, 167–181.

PUTNAM, F. W. (1989). *The diagnosis and treatment of multiple personality disorder.* New York: Guilford.

PUTNAM, F. W. (1991). Dissociative disorders in children and adolescents: Developmental perspective. *Psychiatric Clinics of North America, 14*, 519–532.

PUTMAN, F. W. (1993). Diagnosis and clinical phenomenology of multiple personality disorder: A North American perspective. *Dissociation, 6*, 80–86.

RACHMAN, S., & HODGSON, R. (1968). Experimentally induced "sexual fetishism": Replication and development. *Psychological Record, 18*, 25–27.

RADA, R. T. (1975). Alcoholism and forcible rape. *American Journal of Psychiatry, 121*, 776–783.

RAO, A. (1973). Depression: A psychiatric analysis of thirty cases. *Indian Journal of Psychiatry, 15*, 231–236.

RATNER, C. (1989). A social constructionist critique of the naturalistic theory of emotion. *Journal of Mind and Behavior, 10*, 211–230.

RAWLINS, R. G., & KESSLER, M. J. (1986). *The Cayo Santiago macaques: History, behavior, and biology.* Albany: State University of New York Press.

REISS, I. L. (1986). *Journey into sexuality: An exploratory voyage.* Englewood Cliffs, NJ: Prentice-Hall.

RESNER, G., & HARTOG, J. (1970). Concepts and terminology of mental disorders among Malays. *Journal of Cross-Cultural Psychology, 1*, 369–381.

RIN, H. (1965). A study of the aetiology of *koro* in respect to the Chinese concept of illness. *International Journal of Social Psychiatry, 11*, 7–13.

RIN, H., & LIN, T. (1962). Mental illness among Formosan aborigines as compared with Chinese in Taiwan. *Journal of Mental Science, 108*, 134–146.

RITENBAUGH, C., SHISSLAK, C., & PRINCE, R. (1992). Eating disorders: A cross-cultural review in regard to DSM-IV. In J. E. Mezzich, A. Kleinman, H. Fabrega, B. Good,

G. Johnson-Powell, K. M. Lin, S. Manson, & D. Parron (Eds.), *Cultural Proposals for DSM-IV* (pp. 158–165). Submitted to the DSM-IV Task Force by the NIMH Group on Culture and Diagnosis. Pittsburgh: University of Pittsburgh.

ROBERTSON, E. (1992). The challenge of dual diagnosis. *Journal of Health Care for the Poor and Underserved, 3*, 198–207.

ROBERTSON, H. A., MARTIN, I. L., & CANDY, J. M. (1978). Differences in benzodiazepine receptor binding in Maudsley reactive and nonreactive rats. *European Journal of Pharmacology, 50*, 455–457.

ROHRER, J., & EDMONSON, M. (1960). *The eighth generation grows up.* New York: Harper and Row.

ROLAND, A. (1988). *In search of self in India and Japan.* Princeton: Princeton University Press.

ROSALDO, M. Z. (1984). Toward an anthropology of self and feeling. In R. A. Shweder & R. A. LeVine (Eds.), *Culture theory: Essays on mind, self, and emotion* (pp. 137–157). Cambridge: Cambridge University Press.

ROSEMAN, M. (1990). Head, heart, odor, and shadow: The structure of the self, the emotional world, and ritual performance among the Senoi Temiar. *Ethos, 18*, 227–250.

ROSEN, L. W., SHAFER, C. L., DUMMER, G. M., CROSS, L. K., DEUMAN, G. W., & MALMBERG, S. R. (1988). Prevalence of pathogenic weight-control behaviors among Native American women and girls. *International Journal of Eating Disorders, 7* (6), 807–811.

ROSS, C. A. (1989). *Multiple personality disorder: Diagnosis, clinical features, and treatment.* New York: Wiley.

ROSS, C. A., & ANDERSON, G. (1988). Phenomenological overlap of multiple personality disorder and obsessive-compulsive disorder. *Journal of Nervous and Mental Disease, 176*, 295–299.

ROSS, C. A., & GAHAN, P. (1988). Techniques in the treatment of multiple personality disorder. *American Journal of Psychotherapy, 42*, 40–52.

ROSS, C. A., HEBER, S., NORTON, G. R., & ANDERSON, G. (1989). Differences between multiple personality disorder and other diagnostic groups on structured interview. *Journal of Nervous and Mental Disease, 177*, 487–491.

ROSS, C. A., NORTON, G. R., & WOZNEY, K. (1989). Multiple personality disorder: An analysis of 236 cases. *Canadian Journal of Psychiatry, 34*, 413–418.

RUBEL, A. J., O'NELL, C. W., & COLLADO, R. (1985). The folk illness called *susto.* In R. C. Simons & C. C. Hughes (Eds.), *The culture-bound syndromes: Folk illnesses of psychiatric and anthropological interest* (pp. 333–350). Dordrecht: D. Reidel.

RUSSELL, G. (1981). The current treatment of anorexia nervosa. *British Journal of Psychiatry, 138*, 164–166.

RUSSELL, J. G. (1989). Anxiety disorders in Japan: A review of the Japanese literature on *shinkeishitsu* and *taijinkyofusho. Culture, Medicine and Psychiatry, 13*, 391–403.

SALAN, R., & MARETSKI, T. (1983). Mental health services and traditional healing in Indonesia: Are the roles compatible? *Culture, Medicine and Psychiatry, 7*, 377–412.

SALISBURY, R. F. (1968). Possession in the New Guinea highlands. *International Journal of Social Psychiatry, 23*, 264–274.

SANDERSON, W. C., DiNARDO, P. A., RAPEE, R. M., & BARLOW, D. H. (1990). Syndrome comorbidity in patients diagnosed with a DSM-III anxiety disorder. *Journal of Abnormal Psychology, 99*, 308–312.

SANUA, V. (1979). Psychological intervention in the Arab world: A review of folk treatment. *Transcultural Psychiatric Research Review, 16*, 205–208.

SARTORIUS, N., JABLENSKY, A., GULBINAT, W., & ERNBERG, G. (1980). WHO collaborative study: Assessment of depressive disorders. *Psychological Medicine, 10*, 743–749.

SARTORIUS, N., JABLENSKY, A., KORTEN, A., ERNBERG, G., ET AL. (1986). Early manifestations and first-contact incidence of schizophrenia in different cultures: A preliminary report on the initial evaluation phase of the WHO collaborative study on determinants of outcome of severe mental disorders. *Psychological Medicine, 16,* 909–928.

SARTORIUS, N., JABLENSKY, A., & SHAPIRO, R. (1977). Two-year follow-up of the patients included in the WHO international pilot study of schizophrenia. *Psychological Medicine, 7,* 529–541.

SAXENA, S., & PRASAD, K. V. S. R. (1989). DSM-III subclassification of dissociative disorders applied to psychiatric outpatients in India. *American Journal of Psychiatry, 146,* 261–262.

SCHEPER-HUGHES, N. (1979). *Saints, scholars, and schizophrenics: Mental illness in rural Ireland.* Berkeley: University of California Press.

SCHEPER-HUGHES, N. (1987). "Mental" in "Southie": Individual, family, and community responses to psychosis in south Boston. *Culture, Medicine and Psychiatry, 11,* 53–78.

SCHIEFFELIN, E. L. (1985). The cultural analysis of depressive affect: An example from New Guinea. In A. Kleinman & B. Good (Eds.), *Culture and depression: Studies in the anthropology and cross-cultural psychiatry of affect and disorder* (pp. 101–133). Berkeley: University of California Press.

SCHILDKRAUT, J. J. (1965). The catecholamine hypothesis of affective disorders: A review of supporting evidence. *American Journal of Psychiatry, 122,* 509–522.

SCHMITZ, J., DEJONG, J., ROY, A., GARNETT, D., MOORE, V., LAMPARSKI, D., WAXMAN, R., & LINNOILA, M. (1991). Substance abuse among subjects seeking treatment for alcoholism. *Archives of General Psychiatry, 48,* 182–183.

SCHNEIDER, D. M. (1980). *American kinship: A cultural account* (2nd ed.) Chicago: University of Chicago Press.

SCHNEIDER, K. (1959). *Clinical psychopathology.* New York: Grune and Stratton.

SCHUCKIT, M. A. (1987). Biological vulnerability to alcoholism. *Journal of Consulting and Clinical Psychology, 55,* 301–309.

SCHWARTZ, J. M., STOESSEL, P. W., BAXTER, L. R., MARTIN, K. M., & PHELPS, M. E. (1996). Systematic changes in cerebral glucose metabolic rate after successful behavior modification treatment of obsessive-compulsive disorder. *Archives of General Psychiatry, 53,* 109–113.

SELIGMAN, M. E. P. (1975). *Helplessness: On depression, development and death.* San Francisco: W. H. Freeman.

SELIGMANN, J., ROGERS, P., & ANNIN, P. (1994, May 2). The pressure to lose. *Newsweek,* pp. 60–61.

SETHI, B., & GUPTA, S. (1970). An epidemiological and cultural study of depression. *Indian Journal of Psychiatry, 12,* 13–22.

SHAFFER, D., GARLAND, A., GOULD, M., FISHER, P., & TRAUTMAN, P. (1988). Preventing teenage suicide: A critical review. *Journal of the American Academy of Child and Adolescent Psychiatry, 27,* 675–687.

SHARP, C. W., & FREEMAN, C. P. L. (1993). The medical complications of anorexia nervosa. *British Journal of Psychiatry, 162,* 452–462.

SHEDLER, J., & BLOCK, J. (1990). Adolescent drug use and psychological health. *American Psychologist, 45,* 612–630.

SHINFUKU, N., KARASAWA, A., YAMADA, O., TUASAKI, S., KANAI, A., & KAWASHIMA, K. (1973). Changing clinical pictures of depression. *Psychological Medicine, 15,* 955–965.

SHWEDER, R. A. (1985). Menstrual pollution, soul loss, and the comparative study of emotions. In A. Kleinman & B. Good (Eds.), *Culture and depression: Studies in the anthropology and cross-cultural psychiatry of affect and disorder* (pp. 182–215). Berkeley: University of California Press.

SHWEDER, R. A. (1990). Cultural psychology—What is it? In J. W. Stigler, R. A. Shweder, & G. Herdt (Eds.), *Cultural psychology: Essays on comparative human development* (pp. 1–43). Cambridge: Cambridge University Press.

SHWEDER, R. A., & BOURNE, E. J. (1984). Does the concept of person vary cross-culturally? In R. A. Shweder & R. A LeVine (Eds.), *Culture theory: Essays on mind, self, and emotion* (pp. 158–199). Cambridge: Cambridge University Press.

SHWEDER, R. A., MAHAPATRA, M., & MILLER, J. G. (1990). Culture and moral development. In J. W. Stigler, R. A. Shweder, & G. Herdt (Eds.), *Cultural psychology: Essays on comparative human development* (pp. 130–204). Cambridge: Cambridge University Press.

SILBER, T. J. (1986). Anorexia nervosa in blacks and Hispanics. *International Journal of Eating Disorders, 5* (1), 121–128.

SIMONS, R. C. (1985). The resolution of the *latah* paradox. In R. C. Simons & C. C. Hughes (Eds.), *The culture-bound syndromes: Folk illnesses of psychiatric and anthropological interest* (pp. 43–62). Dordrecht: D. Reidel.

SINGH, G. (1985). *Dhat* syndrome revisited. *Indian Journal of Psychiatry, 27,* 119–121.

SMALL, M. F. (1992). What's love got to do with it? *Discover, 13,* 46–51.

SMALL, M. F. (1993). *Female choices: Sexual behavior of female primates.* Ithaca: Cornell University Press.

SNOW, J. R., & HARRIS, M. B. (1989). Brief report: Disordered eating in Southwestern Pueblo Indians and Hispanics. *Journal of Adolescence, 12,* 329–336.

SO, A. Y. (1990). *Social change and development: Modernization, dependency, and world-system theories.* Newbury Park, CA: Sage.

SOLOMON, R. C. (1984). The Jamesian theory of emotion in anthropology. In R. A. Shweder & R. A. LeVine (Eds.), *Culture theory: Essays on mind, self, and emotion* (pp. 238–254). Cambridge: Cambridge University Press.

SPARKS, L. (1962). *Self-hypnosis: A conditioned response technique.* New York: Grune & Stratton.

SPERRY, R. W. (1987). Structure and significance of the consciousness revolution. *Journal of Mind and Behavior, 8,* 37–65.

SPIEGEL, D. (1991). Dissociation and trauma. In A. Tasman & S. M. Goldfinger (Eds.), *American psychiatric press annual press review of psychiatry* (Vol. 10, pp. 261–275). Washington, DC: American Psychiatric Press.

SPIEGEL, H., & SPIEGEL, D. (1980). Induction techniques. In G. D. Burrows & L. Dennerstein (Eds.), *Handbook of hypnosis and psychosomatic medicine.* New York: Elsevier/North-Holland.

SPITZER, R. L. (1991). An outsider-insider's views about revising the DSMs. *Journal of Abnormal Psychology, 100,* 294–296.

SPITZER, R. L., GIBBON, M., SKODOL, A. E., WILLIAMS, J. B. W., & FIRST, M. B. (EDS.). (1994). *DSM-IV Casebook.* Washington, DC: American Psychiatric Press.

STALEY, D., & WAND, R. R. (1995). Obsessive-compulsive disorder: A review of the cross-cultural epidemiological literature. *Transcultural Psychiatric Research Review, 32,* 103–136.

STEINBERG, M., CICCHETTI, D., BUCHANAN, J., RAKFELDT, J., & ROUNSAVILLE, B. (1994). Distinguishing between multiple personality disorder (dissociative identity disorder) and schizophrenia using the Structured Clinical Interview for DSM-IV Dissociative Disorders. *Journal of Nervous and Mental Disease, 182,* 495–502.

STEWART, K. J., & HARCOURT, A. H. (1987). Gorillas: Variation in female relationships. In B. B. Smuts, D. L. Cheney, R. M. Seyfarth, R. Wrangham, & T. T. Strusaker (Eds.), *Primate societies* (pp. 155–164). Chicago: University of Chicago Press.

STOLLER, P. (1989). *Fusion of the worlds: An ethnography of possession among the Songhay of Niger.* Chicago: University of Chicago Press.

STROMGREN, E. (1994). Scandinavian contributions to psychiatric nosology. In J. E. Mezzich, Y. Honda, & M. C. Kastrup (Eds.), *Psychiatric diagnosis: A world perspective* (pp. 33–38). New York: Springer-Verlag.

SUGGS, D. N., & MIRACLE, A. W. (1993). *Culture and human sexuality.* Pacific Grove, CA: Brooks/Cole.

SUOMI, J. (1991). Uptight and laid-back monkeys: Individual differences in the response to social challenges. In S. Branch, W. Hall, & E. Dooling (Eds.), *Plasticity of development* (pp. 27–55). Cambridge, MA: MIT Press.

SURYANI, L. K. (1984). Culture and mental disorder: The case of *bebainan* in Bali. *Culture, Medicine and Psychiatry, 8,* 95–113.

SURYANI, L. K., & JENSEN, G. D. (1993). *Trance and possession in Bali: A window on western multiple personality, possession disorder, and suicide.* New York: Oxford University Press.

SUSSER, E., & WANDERLING, J. (1994). Epidemiology of nonaffective acute remitting psychosis vs schizophrenia: Sex and sociocultural setting. *Archives of General Psychiatry, 51,* 294–301.

SUWANLERT, S. (1976). Neurotic and psychotic states attributed to Thai "*Phi Pob*" spirit possession. *Australian and New Zealand Journal of Psychiatry, 10,* 119–123.

SWANSON, G. A. (1964). *The birth of the gods.* Ann Arbor: University of Michigan Press.

SWANSON, L. W., TEYLER, T. J., & THOMPSON, R. F. (1982). Hippocampal long-term potentiation: Mechanisms and implications for memory. *Neuroscience Research Bulletin, 20,* 613–769.

SYMONS, D. (1979). *The evolution of human sexuality.* New York: Oxford University Press.

SYMONS, D. (1987). An evolutionary approach: Can Darwin's view of life shed light on human sexuality? In J. H. Geer & W. T. O'Donohue (Eds.), *Theories of human sexuality* (pp. 91–126). New York: Plenum.

TANAKA-MATSUMI, J., & MARSELLA, A. J. (1976). Cross-cultural variations in the phenomenological experience of depression: Word association. *Journal of Cross-Cultural Psychology, 7,* 379–396.

TATEYAMA, M., ASAI, M., KAMISADA, M., HASHIMOTO, M., ET AL. (1993). Comparison of schizophrenic delusions between Japan and Germany. *Psychopathology, 26,* 151–158.

TEJA, J. S., KHANNA, B. S., & SUBRAHMANYAM, T. B. (1970). "Possession states" in Indian patients. *Indian Journal of Psychiatry, 28,* 71–87.

TEJA, J. S., & NARANG, R. (1970). Pattern of incidence of depression in India. *Indian Journal of Psychiatry, 12,* 33–39.

TERMINSEN, J., & RYAN, J. (1970). Health and disease in a British Columbia community. *Canadian Psychiatric Association Journal, 15,* 121–127.

TEYLER, T. J. (1987). Long-term potentiation and memory. In G. Adelman (Ed.), *The encyclopedia of neuroscience* (p. 598). Boston: Birkhauser.

THOMPSON, R. F. (1987). Learning and memory, neural mechanisms. In G. Adelman (Ed.), *The encyclopedia of neuroscience* (pp. 574–576). Boston: Birkhauser.

THOMPSON, R. F., DONEGAN, N. H., & LAVOND, D. G. (1986). The psychobiology of learning and memory. In R. C. Atkinson, R. J. Herrnstein, G. Lindzey, & R. D. Luce

(Eds.), *Steven's handbook of experimental psychology* (2nd ed.) (pp. 245–347). New York: Wiley.

THONG, D. (1993). *A psychiatrist in paradise: Treating mental illness in Bali.* Bangkok: White Lotus.

THORNICROFT, G., & SARTORIUS, N. (1993). The course and outcome of depression in different cultures: 10-year follow-up of the WHO collaborative study on the assessment of depressive disorders. *Psychological Medicine, 23,* 1023–1032.

TONEATTO, T., SOBELL, L. C., SOBELL, M. B., & LEO, G. I. (1991). Psychoactive substance use disorder (alcohol). In M. Hersen & S. M. Turner (Eds.), *Adult psychopathology & diagnosis* (2nd ed.). New York: Wiley.

TORO, J., SALAMERO, M., & MARTINEZ, E. (1994). Assessment of sociocultural influences on the aesthetic body shape model in anorexia nervosa. *Acta Psychiatrica Scandinavica, 89,* 147–151.

TRIANDIS, H. C. (1995). *Individualism and collectivism.* Boulder, CO: Westview Press.

TSENG, W. S., & HSU, J. (1969). Chinese culture, personality formation and mental illness. *International Journal of Social Psychiatry, 16,* 5–14.

TSENG, W. S., MASAHIRO, A., KITANISHI, K., MCLAUGHLIN, D. G., & KYOMEN, H. (1992). Diagnostic patterns of social phobia: Comparison in Tokyo and Hawaii. *Journal of Nervous and Mental Disease, 180,* 380–385.

TSENG, W. S., MO, K. M., LI, L. S., CHEN, G. Q., OU, L. W., & ZHENG, H. B. (1992). *Koro* epidemics in Guangdong, China: A questionnaire survey. *Journal of Nervous and Mental Disease, 180,* 117–123.

TSENG, W. S., QIU-YUN, L., & YIN, P. Y. (1995). Psychotherapy for the Chinese: Cultural considerations. In T. Y. Lin, W. S. Tseng, & E. K. Yeh (Eds.), *Chinese societies and mental health* (pp. 281–294). New York: Oxford University Press.

TURNER, V. W. (1962). Three symbols of passage in Ndembu circumcision ritual: An interpretation. In M. Gluckman (Ed.), *Essays on the ritual of social relations.* Manchester: Manchester University Press.

ULUSAHIN, A., BASOGLU, M., & PAYKEL, E. S. (1994). A cross-cultural comparative study of depressive symptoms in British and Turkish clinical samples. *Social Psychiatry and Psychiatric Epidemiology, 29,* 31–39.

USHERWOOD, P. N. (1993). Memories are made of this. *Trends in Neurosciences, 16,* 427–429.

UTTAL, W. R. (1988). The psychobiology of mind. In J. A. Hobson (Ed.), *Readings from the encyclopedia of neuroscience: States of brain and mind.* (pp. 56–58). Boston: Birkhauser.

UZZELL, D. (1974). *Susto* revisited: Illness as strategic role. *American Ethnologist, 1,* 359–378.

VAGO, S. (1989). *Social change* (2nd ed.). Englewood Cliffs, NJ: Prentice-Hall.

VAN DER KOLK, B. A., & VAN DER HART, O. (1989). Pierre Janet and the breakdown of adaptation in psychological trauma. *American Journal of Psychiatry, 146,* 1530–1540.

VARMA, L. P., SRIVASTAVA, D. K., & SAHAY, R. N. (1970). Possession syndrome. *Indian Journal of Psychiatry, 28,* 58–70.

VARMA, V. K., BOURI, M., & WIG, N. N. (1981). Multiple personality in India: Comparison with hysterical possession state. *American Journal of Psychotherapy, 35,* 113–120.

VAUGHN, C., DOYLE, M., MCCONAGHY, N., ET AL. (1992). The relationship between relatives' expressed emotion and schizophrenia relapse: An Australian replication. *Social Psychiatry and Psychiatric Epidemiology, 27,* 10–15.

VAUGHN, C., & LEFF, J. (1976). The influence of family and social factors on the course of psychiatric illness: A comparison of schizophrenic and depressed neurotic patients. *British Journal of Psychiatry, 129,* 125–137.

VAUGHN, C., SNYDER, K., JONES, S., ET AL. (1984). Family factors in schizophrenic relapse. Replication in California of British research on expressed emotion. *Archives of General Psychiatry, 41,* 1169–1177.

VON KRAFFT-EBING, R. (1965). *Psychopathia sexualis.* New York: Putnam. (Original work published 1886)

WADLEY, S. S. (1976). The spirit "rides" or the spirit "comes": Possession in a north Indian village. In A Bharati (Ed.), *The realm of the extra-human: Agents and audiences* (pp. 233–252). The Hague: Mouton Publishers.

WAGNER, A. W., & LINEHAN, M. M. (1994). Relationship between childhood sexual abuse and topography of parasuicide among women with borderline personality disorder. *Journal of Personality Disorders, 8,* 1–9.

WALKER, S. S. (1972). *Ceremonial spirit possession in Africa and Afro-America: Forms, meanings, and functional significance for individuals and social groups.* Leiden: Brill.

WALLERSTEIN, I. (1987). World-system analysis. In A. Giddens & J. H. Turner (Eds.), *Social theory today* (pp. 309–324). Stanford: Stanford University Press.

WARD, D. A. (1985). Conceptions of the nature and treatment of alcoholism. *Journal of Drug Issues, 15,* 3–16.

WARNER, R. (1985). *Recovery for schizophrenia: Psychiatry and political economy.* New York: Routledge & Kegan Paul.

WATTS, D. P. (1991). Mountain gorilla reproduction and sexual behavior. *American Journal of Primatology, 24,* 211–255.

WAXLER, N. E. (1974). Culture and mental illness: A social labeling perspective. *Journal of Nervous and Mental Disease, 159,* 379–395.

WAXLER, N. E. (1979). Is outcome for schizophrenia better in nonindustrialized societies? The case of Sri Lanka. *Journal of Nervous and Mental Disease, 167,* 144–158.

WEIDMAN, H. H. (1979). Falling-out: A diagnostic and treatment problem viewed from a transcultural perspective. *Social Science and Medicine, 13,* 95–112.

WEISS, M. G. (1995). Eating disorders and disordered eating in different cultures. *Psychiatric Clinics of North America, 18,* 537–553.

WEISSMAN, M. M., BRUCE, M. L., LEAF, P. J., FLORIO, L. P., & HOLZER, C. (1991). Affective disorders. In L. N. Robins, & D. A. Regier (Eds.), *Psychiatric disorders of America: The epidemiologic catchment area study* (pp. 53–80). New York: Free Press.

WESTERMEYER, J. (1995). Cultural aspects of substance abuse and alcoholism. *Psychiatric Clinics of North America, 18,* 589–605.

WESTERMEYER, J., & CANINO, G. (1992). Culture and substance related disorders. In J. E. Mezzich, A. Kleinman, H. Fabrega, B. Good, G. Johnson-Powell, K. M. Lin, S. Manson, & D. Parron (Eds.), *Cultural proposals for DSM-IV* (pp. 63–75). Submitted to the DSM-IV Task Force by the Steering Committee, NIMH Group on Culture and Diagnosis. Pittsburgh: University of Pittsburgh.

WHO. (1948). *International classification of diseases, sixth edition (ICD-6).* Geneva: World Health Organization.

WHO. (1973). *International pilot study of schizophrenia.* Geneva: World Health Organization.

WHO. (1979). *Schizophrenia: An international follow-up study.* Chichester, NY: Wiley.

WHO. (1983). *Depressive disorders in different cultures.* Geneva: World Health Organization.

WHO. (1989). *International Classification of Diseases, tenth edition (ICD-10)*. Geneva: World Health Organization.

WIG, N. N., MENON, D. K., BEDI, H., ET AL. (1987a). Expressed emotion and schizophrenia in North India, 1: Cross-cultural transfer of ratings of relatives' expressed emotion. *British Journal of Psychiatry, 151*, 156–160.

WIG, N. N., MENON, D. K., BEDI, H., ET AL. (1987b). Expressed emotion and schizophrenia in North India, 2: Distribution of expressed emotion components among relatives of schizophrenic patients in Aarhus and Chandigarth. *British Journal of Psychiatry, 151*, 160–165.

WILLNER, A. R. (1984). *The spellbinders: Charismatic political leadership*. New Haven: Yale University Press.

WILSON, E. O. (1975). *Sociobiology: The new synthesis*. Cambridge: Harvard University Press.

WILSON, M. (1993). DSM-III and the transformation of American psychiatry: A history. *American Journal of Psychiatry, 150*, 399–410.

WINICK, C. (1986). The alcohol offender. In H. Toch (Ed.), *Psychology of crime and criminal justice* (pp. 347–372). Prospect Heights, IL: Waveland Press.

WINKELMAN, M. (1986). Trance states: A theoretical model and cross-cultural analysis. *Ethos, 14*, 174–203.

WISEMAN, C. V., GRAY, J. J., MOSIMANN, J. E., & AHRENS, A. H. (1992). Cultural expectations of thinness in women: An update. *International Journal of Eating Disorders, 11*, 85–89.

WITZTUM, E., & VAN DER HART, O. (1993). Possession and persecution by demons: Janet's use of hypnotic techniques in treating hysterical psychosis. In J. M. Goodwin (Ed.), *Rediscovering childhood trauma: Historical casebook and clinical applications* (pp. 65–88). Washington, DC: American Psychiatric Press.

WOLF, M. (1990). The woman who didn't become a shaman. *American Ethnologist, 17*, 419–430.

WOODRUFF-PAK, D. S., LOGAN, C. G., & THOMPSON, R. F. (1990). Neurobiological substrates of classical conditioning across the life span. *Annals of the New York Academy of Sciences, 608*, 150–178.

YAP, P. M. (1960). The possession syndrome: A comparison of Hong Kong and French findings. *Journal of Mental Science, 106*, 114–137.

YAP, P. M. (1965). *Koro*—a culture-bound depersonalization syndrome. *British Journal of Psychiatry, 111*, 43–50.

ZIMMERMAN, F. (1980). *Rtu-sâtmya:* The seasonal cycle and the principle of appropriateness. *Social Science and Medicine, 14*, 99–106.

Abrams, K. K., 153
Abramson, E. E., 151
Abramson, L. Y., 172
Adityanjee, 228
Ahrens, A. H., 152
Akhtar, S., 238, 264
Allen, L. A., 153
Allsbeck, P., 249
Amarasingham, L. R., 228
American Psychiatric Association (APA), 3,
    7–8, 10–11, 15, 16, 28, 89, 95, 96, 97, 98, 99,
    100, 101, 102, 103, 105, 106, 107, 108, 114,
    124, 130, 132, 134, 140, 141, 142, 143, 144,
    145, 150, 151, 157, 158, 161, 162, 165, 166,
    167, 178, 181, 183, 196, 197, 203, 208, 209,
    210, 211, 214, 215, 216, 224, 225, 226, 227,
    235, 237, 242, 247, 251, 253, 256, 257, 262,
    271, 274–275, 279
Anderson, A. E., 154
Anderson, G., 225, 265
Andreasen, N. C., 13, 26
Andreasson, S., 249
Anglin, M., 166
Angst, J., 4, 248
Annable, L., 279
Annin, P., 153
Anthony, D., 72
Antonovsky, Aaron, 78
Aoki, C., 269, 270
Arbitell, M. R., 149
Asuni, T., 82
Awanbor, D., 82
Awaritefe, A., 179

Babb, L. A., 228
Babor, T. F., 161
Baddeley, J., 82
Ballard, C. G., 151
Bancroft, J., 126

Barlow, D. H., 23, 126, 129, 143, 172, 173, 174,
    177, 201, 211
Bartels, S., 166
Bartol, C. R., 163
Basoglu, M., 204
Bayes, M., 72
Beatty, W. W., 149
Bebbington, P., 204
Bebbington, P. E., 250
Beere, D., 19
Behere, P. B., 28
Bennett, L. A., 161, 191
Berreman, G. D., 227, 228
Besnier, N., 137
Bibeau, G., 82
Birley, J., 5, 279
Bleuler, E., 246
Bliss, E. L., 219, 223, 234, 265
Block, J., 166
Blum, A. M., 159, 160
Bock, P. K., 40
Boehnlein, J. K., 182
Bolos, A. M., 159, 160
Bolton, R., 184
Bourguignon, E., 219, 228, 238
Bouri, M., 264
Bourne, E. J., 39
Bowman, E. S., 234
Boyer, L. B., 82
Bradbury, R. E., 74
Bradshaw, J., 166
Bremner, J. D., 266
Bridges, K., 189
Briquet, P., 190
Brody, E. B., 3
Broverman, I., 72
Brown, G. E., 250
Brown, G. W., 5, 279
Brown, T. A., 174

Brownell, K. D., 152
Burnam, A., 162
Burrows, G. D., 223
Burton–Bradley, B. G., 60, 230

Caetano, R., 162
Callender, C., 135
Candy, J. M., 267
Canino, G., 160, 162, 165
Carlson, G. T., 273
Carr, J. E., 60, 61, 168, 230
Carrillo, E., 229
Carstairs, G. M., 228, 264
Castillo, R. J., 4, 205, 211, 219, 221, 222, 223,
    230, 237, 263, 270, 272, 273, 278
Chaitanya, Krishna, 243
Chandrasena, R., 72
Chandrashekar, C. R., 238
Cheetham, R. J., 82
Cheetham, R. W. S., 82
Cho, Y. I., 162
Choquet, M., 149
Choudry, I. Y., 154
Chouinard, G., 279
Christenson, C. V., 133
Chua, S. E., 10
Clark, D. M., 176
Clark, M., 184
Claus, P. J., 227, 228, 244
Clementz, B. A., 265
Clifford, C. A., 159
Clifford, J., 262
Cloninger, C. R., 159, 160
Coleman, E., 166, 167
Collado, R., 184
Connor, L., 65
Coons, P. M., 234, 265
Corin, E., 82
Cotman, C. W., 269
Crapanzo, V., 238
Craske, M. G., 174
Critchlow, B., 163
Crittenden, K. S., 204
Croft-Jeffries, C., 72
Cross-National Collaborative Group, 211, 213
Crowther, J. H., 149
Csikszentmihalyi, M., 216
Csordas, T., 87

D'Andrade, R. G., 6, 20, 262
D'Angelo, E. J., 103
Daniel, E. V., 276
David, A., 249
Day, R., 251, 263
De La Cancela, V., 228–229
de Lemos, A., 250
DeMaso, D. R., 103
Dennerstein, L., 223
Dennis, P. A., 225, 238
Desjarlais, R., 4, 86, 206
DeVos, G., 164

de Waal, F. B. M., 118, 119
DiNardo, P. A., 172, 201
Doi, T., 52
Donegan, N. H., 268, 269
Donovan, D. M., 165
Dow, J., 82, 83
Doweiko, H. E., 158, 165–166
Doyle, M., 250
Dresp, C. S. W., 183
Driscoll, J. P., 136
Dumont, L., 49
Durand, V. M., 23, 126, 129, 172, 173, 177, 211

Ebert, D., 204
Ebigbo, P. O., 179, 204
Ebomayi, E., 116
Edgerton, R. B., 82
Edmonson, M., 42
Edwards, J. W., 185
Ehrenwald, 83
Eisenberg, L., 4, 31
Ekman, P., 56
El Islam, M. F., 82, 250
Ellason, J. W., 248
Escobar, J. I., 193, 265
Estroff, S. E., 274

Fabrega, H., 4, 9, 97, 241
Farias, P., 183
Faulkner, W. R., 162
Fenton, F. R., 73
Fenwick, C. R., 52
Fink, D., 225
Finkelhor, D., 129
Fleck, S., 3, 4, 9, 31
Ford, K., 153
Fossum, M. A., 167
Foulks, E. F., 230
Frankel, F. H., 223
Franklin, J., 165
Freed, R. S., 67, 83, 227, 228, 264
Freed, S. A., 67, 83, 227, 228, 264
Freemen, C. P. L., 150
Fromm, E., 223
Furnham, A., 203, 208

Gagnon, J. H., 133
Gahan, P., 225
Gaines, A. D., 4
Galanti, G., 64, 70, 108, 176, 196
Gandhy, S., 264
Gang-Ming, M., 185
Garfinkel, 152
Garner, D. M., 152
Garrison, V., 228, 238
Gaw, A. C., 4, 37, 226
Gebhard, P. H., 133
Geertz, H., 229
Gellhorn, E., 213, 270
Girgus, J. S., 173, 264
Glassman, A. H., 172

Goffman, E., 42, 276
Gohman, M., 159
Gold, A. N., 83
Goldberg, D. P., 189
Goldman, S. J., 103
Golinkoff, M., 225
Good, B., 4, 31
Good, B. J., 56, 73, 207
Gosselin, C., 130
Gottesman, I. I., 267
Grant, B. F., 161
Gray, B. A., 72
Gray, J. J., 152, 153
Greaves, G. B., 234
Green, R., 136
Gregerson, E., 120
Gregor, T., 125
Greist, J. H., 80
Grossi, V., 206
Guarnaccia, P. J., 73, 183, 228
Gullick, J. M., 61
Guo-Qian, C., 185
Gupta, S., 204
Gur, R. C., 6
Gurling, H. M. D., 159
Gussler, J., 238
Gussow, Z., 225, 230
Guttmacher, L. B., 3, 5, 90, 261, 279
Guze, S. B., 190

Haanstra, B., 125
Hall, R., 87
Halpern, D., 173
Handy, S., 151
Harcourt, A. H., 114
Harding, T. W., 4, 82, 248
Harper, E. B., 83, 227, 228, 263, 264, 274
Harris, M. B., 154
Hart, E. E., 206
Hartog, J., 203
Hartsuiker, D., 245
Harvey, Y. K., 82
Harwood, A., 229
Hawkins, R. D., 5, 6
Hawton, K., 206
Hay, A., 154
Hayton, B. C., 171, 174
Heath, D. B., 87, 161
Heber, S., 225, 265
Heinze, R. I., 82
Helzer, J. E., 160, 165
Hendry, J., 162
Herdt, G. H., 123, 130, 135
Hester, R. K., 160
Hiebert, K. A., 154
Hilgard, E. R., 223
Hinton, L., 4, 69
Ho, T. P., 152
Hobson, J. A., 268
Hodgson, R., 126
Holzman, P. S., 265

Honda, Y., 4
Hooper, A., 82
Horney, K., 166
Hornstein, N. L., 234
Hsu, J., 203
Hsu, L. K. G., 152, 154
Hughes, D. J., 219
Husserl, E., 17, 18
Hyde, J. S., 125, 128, 129, 130

Iacono, W. G., 265
Inkeles, A., 44
Isaac, M., 191
Ivey, A. E., 70

Jablensky, A., 4, 73, 204
Jacob, K. A., 117
Janca, A, 161, 191, 277
Jefferson, J. W., 80
Jellinek, E. M., 158–159
Jenkins, J. H., 4, 56, 250
Jensen, G. D., 66, 226, 238
Jilek, W. G., 4, 82, 87
Jones, B. D., 279
Jones, B. E., 72

Kakar, S., 83, 228
Kandel, D. B., 166
Kandel, E. R., 5, 6, 82, 269
Kaplan, H. S., 143
Kapur, R. L., 228, 264
Karno, M., 4, 250
Kastrup, M. C., 4
Kaufman, G., 166, 167
Kelly, K. A., 173
Kelly, L. M., 153
Kendall, L., 186
Kenny, M. G., 229
Kessler, M. J., 118
Ketter, T., 82
Khalsa, A., 166
Khandelwal, S. K., 152
Khandelwol, S. K., 228
Khanna, B. S., 227, 264
Khantzian, E. J., 166
Kihlstrom, J. F., 223
Kilek-Aall, L., 4
Kim, K., 244
Kimura, D., 6
Kinsey, A. C., 134
Kinzie, D., 82
Kinzie, J. D., 182
Kirmayer, L. J., 171, 174, 185, 189, 207, 277
Kishline, A., 164
Kleinman, A., 4, 7, 12, 31, 32, 33, 40, 56, 60, 63,
    64, 66, 69, 73, 82, 201, 204, 238, 264, 265, 277
Kleinman, J., 201, 264, 265
Kluft, R. P., 225, 265
Kochems, L. M., 135
Kortmann, F., 82
Kramer, P. D., 34, 167

Kuhn, T. S., 12, 15
Kutcher, S., 166

Lavond, D. G., 268, 269
Lebra, W., 82
Ledoux, S., 149
Lee, S., 152
Leff, J., 4, 250
Lehmann, A. C., 74
Leighton, A., 203
Leng, G. H., 179
Leo, G. I., 159
Leon, M., 269
Leshner, A., 166
Levine, R. E., 37, 226
Levitt, E. E., 131
Levy, D. L., 265
Levy, M. J., Jr., 44
Levy, R. I., 56–58, 60, 135, 137
Lewis, G., 72, 238, 249, 263
Lewis, I. M., 68, 273–274
Lewis-Fernández, R., 40, 64, 229, 230, 253
Lex, B., 213, 270
Lidz, T., 4
Lightfoot-Klein, H., 116
Lim, R. F., 4, 64, 69
Lin, K. M., 186
Lin, T., 4
Lindholm, C., 51, 102, 276
Linehan, M. M., 103
Lingswiler, V. M., 149
Littlewood, R., 4
Li-Xun, L., 185
Lock, M., 183
Logan, C. G., 269
Loranger, A. W., 103
Low, S. M., 183
Lowenstein, R. J., 265
Lu, F. G., 4, 64, 69
Ludwig, A. M., 219, 220
Lutz, C. A., 56, 205, 207
Lynch, G. S., 269

McDaniel, J., 83, 238, 243–244, 245, 246, 278
McGibbon, L., 151
McGlashan, T. H., 4, 248
McGuire, M., 87
McKenna, P. J., 10
Maclachlan, M., 77
Magne-Igvar, U., 206
Mahapatra, M., 49
Makanjuola, R. O. A., 179
Malefijt, A. D., 74
Malik, R., 203, 208
Mandelbaum, D. G., 49
Manfredi, R., 149
Manson, S. M., 160, 207
Marcus, G., 262
Maretski, T., 82
Marriott, M., 276
Marsella, A. J., 4, 5, 73, 203

Marshall, D. S., 121, 127
Martin, C. E., 134
Martin, I. L., 267
Martinez, E., 152
Martins, C., 250
Martus, P., 204
Mason, M. J., 167
Mayfield, D., 163
Mbiti, J. S., 74
Mendis, N., 249
Menn, A., 90
Messenger, J. C., 120
Meyer, A., 8
Mezzacappa, E., 103
Mezzich, J. E., 4, 64, 69
Miller, I. W., 172
Miller, J. G., 49
Miller, W. R., 160, 165
Millman, R., 166
Millon, T., 98
Milstein, V., 234
Mineka, S., 173, 174
Miracle, A. W., 120
Mizes, J. S., 149
Mo, K. M., 185
Moore, M., 264
Moriya, N., 103
Moser, C., 131
Mosher, L. R., 90
Mosimann, J. E., 152
Muhangi, J., 73
Mumford, D. B., 154
Murphy, H. B. M., 249
Murphy, J. M., 161
Murray, R. M., 159
Myers, J. E., 74

Nanda, S., 135
Narang, R., 204
Nasser, M., 154
Natraj, G. S., 28
Ndetei, D. M., 73
Neisser, U., 6
Nieto-Sampedro, M., 269
Noble, E. P., 159, 160
Nolen-Hoeksema, S., 173, 202, 264
Norman, W. H., 172
North, C. S., 103, 264, 265
Norton, G. R., 225, 265
Nyando, C., 77
Nyirenda, T., 77

Obeyesekere, G., 82, 83, 205, 207, 221, 227, 228, 238, 244
O'Flaherty, W. D., 30
Ogata, S. N., 103
Ohara, K., 204
O'Hare, T., 166
Ojehagen, A., 206
Okasha, A., 180
O'Neil, P. M., 152

O'Nell, C. W., 184
O'Nell, T. D., 160, 207–208
Opler, M. E., 83

Pachauri, P., 264
Page, G., 118
Pardo, J. V., 11
Pardo, P. J., 11
Paris, J., 48, 104
Parker, S., 230
Parsian, A., 159, 160
Patel, V., 73
Pattison, E. M., 82
Paykel, E. S., 204
Peirce, C. S., 21
Perley, M. J., 190
Peters, L. G., 48, 82, 104
Peterson, G., 234
Pfeiffer, W., 204
Philippe, J., 238
Pickens, R. W., 159, 160
Platman, S. R., 172
Polcin, D., 166
Pomoroy, W. B., 133, 134
Post, R. M., 213, 264, 266
Prasad, K. V. S. R., 227
Price, R., 265
Price-Williams, D., 219
Prince, R., 151, 220–221
Putnam, F. W., 234, 265

Qui-Yun, L., 77

Rachman, S., 126
Rada, R. T., 163
Raichle, M. E., 11
Raju, G. S. P., 228
Raman, A. C., 249
Rao, A., 73, 204
Rapee, R. M., 172
Ratner, C., 56
Raveis, V. H., 166
Rawlins, R. G., 118
Reiss, I. L., 123
Resner, G., 203
Ricci, D. A., 103
Rin, H., 4, 185
Ritenbaugh, C., 151, 154
Robertson, E., 166
Robertson, H. A., 267
Robins, J. M., 189
Rogers, P., 153
Rohrer, J., 42
Roland, A., 52
Romain, J. B., 238
Rosaldo, M. Z., 56
Roseman, M., 50
Rosen, L. W., 154
Ross, C. A., 225, 248, 265
Ross-Chouinard, A., 279
Rubel, A. J., 184

Russell, G., 150
Russell, J. G., 185
Ryall, J. M., 103
Ryan, J., 203

Sahay, R. N., 227
Salamero, M., 152
Salan, R., 82
Salisbury, R. F., 238
Sanderson, W. C., 172, 201
Sanua, V., 82
Sartorius, N., 4, 73, 161, 204, 248, 249
Saxena, S., 152, 227
Scheper-Hughes, N., 72, 162
Schieffelin, E. L., 203, 204
Schildkraut, J. J., 172
Schmitz, J., 165
Schneider, D. M., 57
Schneider, K., 225, 247
Schuckit, M. A., 159, 160
Schwartz, 152
Schwartz, J. M., 82, 261
Seligman, M. E. P., 172, 173, 264
Seligmann, J., 153
Sethi, B., 204
Shaffer, D., 206
Shaner, A., 166
Shapiro, R., 4
Sharan, P., 152
Sharp, C. W., 150
Shedler, J., 166
Shinfuku, N., 204
Shisslak, C., 151
Shor, R. E., 223
Shweder, R. A., 39, 49, 56, 58–60, 61, 262
Siekevitz, P., 269, 270
Sigvardsson, S., 159
Silber, T. J., 154
Silveira, W. R., 151
Simons, R. C., 229
Singh, G., 28, 32–33, 197
Small, M. F., 118, 119, 120, 126
Smith, D. H., 44
Snow, J. R., 154
Snyder, K., 250
So, A. Y., 44, 45
Sobell, L. C., 159
Sobell, M. B., 159
Solomon, R. C., 56
Sparks, L., 220
Sperry, R. W., 268
Spiegel, D., 223, 265
Spiegel, H., 223
Spitzer, R. L., 8–9, 22, 128, 132, 133, 134, 140,
    143, 191, 194, 195, 208, 229, 231, 232, 235,
    236, 251, 252, 254, 256
Srivastava, D. K., 227
Staley, D., 180
Staton, R. D., 149
Steinberg, M., 225
Stephens, N. A., 149

Stewart, K. J., 114
Stoller, P., 238
Stromgren, E., 248
Subrahmanyam, T. B., 227
Suggs, D. N., 120
Suomi, J., 166, 167, 267
Suryani, L. K., 66, 226, 238
Susser, E., 249
Suwanlert, S., 238
Swanson, G. A., 74
Swanson, L. W., 270
Sweeney, J. A., 265
Symons, D., 117

Tacchini, G., 191
Tan, E. K., 60, 230
Tan, E. S., 82
Tanaka-Matsumi, J., 203
Tateyama, M., 244
Teasdale, J. D., 172
Teja, J. S., 204, 227
Teoh, J. I., 82
Terminsen, J., 203
Ternes, L. A., 149
Teyler, T. J., 270
Thompson, 152
Thompson, R. F., 268, 269, 270
Thong, D., 64–65, 77, 80, 82, 226
Thornicroft, G., 204
Toneatto, T., 159
Toro, J., 152
Traskman-Bendz, L., 206
Triandis, H. C., 39
Tseng, W. S., 77, 185, 203
Turner, V. W., 47
Tyson, S., 234

Ulusahin, A., 204
Usherwood, P. N., 269
Uttal, W. R., 270–271
Uzzell, D., 184

Vago, S., 44, 45
Valene, P., 151
Vallone, R., 90
van der Hart, O., 77, 265
van der Kolk, B. A., 265
Varma, L. P., 227, 228

Varma, V. K., 264, 275–276
Vaughn, C., 250
Violato, C., 206
Vitaliano, P. P., 168
Von Krafft-Ebing, R., 127

Wadley, S. S., 83, 228
Wagner, A. W., 103
Walker, S. S., 238
Wallerstein, I., 45
Wand, R. R., 180
Wanderling, J., 249
Wang, J., 166
Ward, D. A., 166
Warner, R., 249, 263
Watts, D. P., 114
Waxler, N. E., 4, 251, 277
Weidman, H. H., 237
Weiss, M., 189
Weiss, M. G., 152
Weissman, M. M., 173, 202
Westermeyer, J., 160, 161, 165
Wetzel, R. D., 103
Whitehouse, A. M., 154
Wig, N. N., 250, 264
Williams, C. L., 206
Willner, A. R., 30
Wilson, E. O., 117
Wilson, G., 130
Wilson, M., 8–9
Winick, C., 163
Winkelman, M., 213, 223, 270
Winston, M., 73
Wiseman, C. V., 152
Witztum, E., 77
Wolf, M., 72
Wonderlich, S. A., 149
Woodruff-Pak, D. S., 269
World Health Organization (WHO), 7, 161, 193, 204, 242, 243, 248, 251
Wozney, K., 265

Yap, P. M., 185, 238
Yin, P. Y., 77
Young, A., 171, 174

Zamansky, H. S., 223
Zimmerman, F., 276

Acute stress disorder (ASD), 182–183
Adaptation, neurobiology of, 4–5
Addictive personality, 165–166
Adolescence, 46–49, 103–104
  and dependent personality disorder,
    107–108
  and paraphilias, 126, 127, 128, 129, 130, 133,
    134
Affective flattening, 242, 245–246
African Americans, 72, 153–154, 215, 237
Age, 211, 213, 215. *See also* Adolescence
Agoraphobia, 175–176
Alcohol abuse, 87, 153, 158–159. *See also*
    Substance-related disorders
  cultural differences, 16–162, 163–164, 165
Alcoholics Anonymous (AA), 87, 164
Alogia, 242, 245–246
American Disease Model of addiction,
    158–159, 160, 164
Amnesia, 224
Amok, 60–62, 63, 65, 230
Anger, 50–51
Anomalies, 13–15
Anorexia nervosa, 150, 152
Anthropology, 5–6, 11
Antisocial personality disorder, 43, 52, 102,
    166, 167
Anxiety disorders, 171–188. *See also* Dhat
    syndrome
  acute stress disorder, 182–183
  agoraphobia, 175–176
  clinical guidelines, 186–188
  defined, 174
  and depression, 172–173, 177, 181, 203, 204
  generalized, 178–179
  hwa-bung, 185–186
  koro, 79, 184–185
  nervios, 183–184
  obsessive-compulsive disorder, 179–181
  panic attacks, 175

panic disorder, 176–177
phobias, 177–178
posttraumatic stress disorder, 99, 181–182
and somatoform disorders, 171–172, 174,
    181, 189
and substance-related disorders, 167
susto, 184
taijin kyofusho, 178, 185
ASD. *See* Acute stress disorder
Asian cultures, 70, 196. *See also specific cultures*
Assessment. *See* Cultural assessment
Ataques de nervios, 183, 228–229, 253
Atypical dissociative disorder, 227
Auditory hallucinations, 74–75, 225
Autism, 246, 250
Avatars, 243–244
Avoidant personality disorder, 42, 106–107,
    150, 178, 276–277
Avolition, 242, 245–246

Bali, 64–66
Balian, 66
Banjar, 65
Bebainan, 66
Behavior. *See* Idioms of distress
Bengong, 65
Bias. *See* Stereotypes
Biopsychosocial paradigm, 8, 96–97
Bipolar disorders, 72, 202, 208, 210, 211, 214,
    215–216
Bizarre delusions, 244–245
Body dysmorphic disorder, 150, 197–198
Borderline personality disorder, 43, 103–105,
    166, 167
  and adolescence, 48–49, 103–104
Brain abnormalities, 3, 9, 10. *See also* Brain
    plasticity; Disease-centered psychiatry
Brain plasticity, 4–5, 10–11, 268–272
  and coherence, 82
  and culture, 268–269

Brain plasticity (*continued*)
  and disease-centered psychiatry, 6, 9
  and psychotropic medications, 90
  and reification, 19, 20
  and stress, 213–214, 265–267
  synaptic modifications, 269–270
  tuning effects, 213–214, 270–272
Brief clinical ethnography, 63
Brief psychotic disorder, 182
Briquet's syndrome, 103, 190–191
British culture, 70
Buddhism, 205
Buduh, 65
Bulimia nervosa, 151

Capitalism, 41, 52–53
Case studies, 25–26
Caste system, 23, 42, 43, 44, 49
Catatonic schizophrenia, 242, 243
Categories of experience, 20
Category fallacy, 73
Charismatic Christianity, 87–89, 230, 234
Child sexual abuse, 128–130, 234–235
Chinese culture, 12, 73, 152, 205
  and anxiety disorders, 179, 184–185
Christianity, 87–89, 116–117, 230, 234
Churchill, Winston, 163
Class hierarchies, 41, 52–53, 165. *See also*
    Dominance hierarchies
Client-centered psychiatry, 5, 9, 96–97,
    261–280. *See also specific topics*
  and brain plasticity, 268–272
  and clinical reality, 261, 275–277
  and health-illness boundaries, 272–275
  and outcomes, 30–31, 280
  and stress, 262–268
  and treatment, 30, 277–280
Clinical guidelines
  anxiety disorders, 186–188
  dissociative disorders, 238–240
  eating disorders, 154–156
  mood disorders, 217–218
  personality disorders, 109–111
  psychotic disorders, 257–259
  sexuality, 145–147
  somatoform disorders, 198–200
  substance-related disorders, 168–170
  treatment, 90–91
Clinical reality, 25–38
  case study, 25–26
  and client-centered psychiatry, 261, 275–277
  cultural effects on, 27–31
  curing vs. healing, 31–33
  evolution of, 36–38
  mental disorder meanings, 33–36
Clinician-client relationship, 69–70, 72
Clitorectomy, 116
Cognition. *See also* Cognitive schemas;
    Cultural schemas
  and emotion, 56–58, 172–173, 174, 179–180
  vs. perception, 17–18

Cognitive schemas, 6, 176. *See also* Cognition;
    Cultural schemas
Coherence, 78–82
Collectivism. *See* Sociocentrism
Communication question, 59, 62
Comorbidity, 171, 184, 203
Competitive male dominance, 114
Comprehensibility, 79–80
Conduct disorder, 166
Constitutive rules, 22
Constructive function of cultural meaning
    systems, 22–23
Conversion disorder, 192–195
Cooperative egalitarianism, 119–120
Cooperative female dominance, 118–119
Cooperative male dominance, 115–116, 130.
    See also Gender hierarchies
Coprophilia, 134
Corporal punishment, 130
Crime rates, 41, 53. *See also* Violence
Cultural assessment, 55–75
  clinician-client relationship, 69–70, 72
  cultural identity, 63–64
  diagnostic interview schedules, 73
  and emotion, 55–62
  illness vs. disease, 64–67
  overall, 71–73
  psychosocial environment, 67–69, 71–72
Cultural congruency, 235
Cultural constructionist view of emotion, 56
Cultural entities, 22, 36
Cultural identity, 63–64
Cultural learning, 5, 6
Cultural meaning systems, 20–24, 37, 44–46,
    64. *See also* Cultural schemas; *specific top-
    ics*
Cultural schemas, 6, 276–277. *See also specific
    topics*
  and anxiety disorders, 177, 180
  assessment of, 64
  and symbolic healing, 88–89
Cultural significance, 34
Culture-based behavioral response stage of
    emotion, 58, 61
Culture-based subjective experience, 27–28
Culture-bound syndromes, 37–38
  and anxiety disorders, 179
  and dissociative disorders, 226, 275–276
  and gender identity disorder, 138
  and paraphilias, 131, 134
  and personality disorders, 104
  and psychotic disorders, 253
  and sexual dysfunctions, 142
Culture, defined, 20
Curing vs. healing, 31–33
Cyclothymic disorder, 210, 216–217

Death, 74
Dehumanization, 3
Deliverance, 87–88
Delusional disorder, 256

Delusions
  and dissociative disorders, 235–237
  and mood disorders, 208, 214, 215
  and psychotic disorders, 244–245, 256
Dependent personality disorder, 42, 107–108,
    276–277
Depersonalization, 100, 103, 226
Depression
  and anxiety disorders, 172–173, 177, 181,
    203, 204
  and assessment, 69
  and brain abnormalities, 10–11
  and bulimia nervosa, 151
  case study, 25–26, 30, 31
  and category fallacy, 73
  cultural differences, 203–208
  cultural significance, 34
  curing vs. healing, 31–33
  and *dhat* syndrome, 28
  as explanatory model, 35–36
  major depressive episode, 202–208
  outcomes, 30
  symptom meanings, 33–34
Derealization, 103
Detachment, 100
Detoxification, 164
Dhat syndrome, 28–29, 30, 35, 69
  and anxiety disorders, 180, 183
  curing vs. healing, 31–33
  and somatoform disorders, 197
Diagnosis, culture-based, 29
*Diagnostic and Statistical Manual of Mental
    Disorders* (DSM). *See also specifi
    disorders*
  DSM-I, 7–8, 95
  DSM-II, 8, 15, 16, 95
  DSM-III, 8–10, 15, 16, 96, 97
  DSM-III-R, 10
  DSM-IV, 3, 4, 28.
  history of, 7–12, 15, 16
  modernism in, 45
  Outline for Cultural Formation, 62–63, 64,
    67, 69, 71
Diagnostic ethnocentrism, 69, 72
Diagnostic interview schedules, 73
DID. *See* Dissociative identity disorder
Directive function of cultural meaning
    systems, 23–24
Disease-centered psychiatry, 3–4, 8–10, 31. *See
    also specific topics*
  as cause of depression, 177
  and coherence, 79, 80–81
  and illness vs. disease, 7
  and medieval Europe, 36–37
  as paradigm, 13, 16
  and psychic unity theory, 6
  and treatment, 78
Disorganized schizophrenia, 242
Dissociation, 60, 219–223. *See also* Dissociative
    disorders; Trance
  and borderline personality disorder, 103

and posttraumatic stress disorder, 181
and somatoform disorders, 193
and trance as adaptation, 219–221
and trance as focused attention, 221–223
Dissociative amnesia, 224
Dissociative disorders, 224–240. *See also*
    Dissociation; Trance
  atypical dissociative disorder, 227
  clinical guidelines, 238–240
  cultural differences, 226–228
  depersonalization disorder, 226
  dissociative amnesia, 224
  dissociative fugue, 224–225
  dissociative identity disorder, 103, 225–226,
    237, 265
  dissociative trance disorder, 182, 183, 193,
    225, 228–233, 237
  and gender hierarchies, 264
  not otherwise specified, 233–235
  and psychotic disorders, 225, 232, 235–237,
    246–248, 255–256
  and tuning effects, 272
Dissociative fugue, 224–225
Dissociative identity disorder (DID), 103,
    225–226, 237, 265, 275–276
Dissociative trance disorder, 228–233, 237
  and anxiety disorders, 182, 183
  case studies, 231–233
  and dissociative fugue, 225
  and somatoform disorders, 193
Domestic violence, 53. *See also* Gender
    hierarchies
Dominance hierarchies, 40–44, 49–50
  and anxiety disorders, 178, 182
  and emotion, 59–60, 61
  examples, 49–50, 51, 52
  and mood disorders, 201–202
  and personality disorders, 43, 52, 98–99,
    105, 106–107, 109
  and sexuality, 114–124, 125, 142
  and stress, 173–174, 263–264
  and substance-related disorders, 167
Downregulation, 90
Downward causation, 268
Dowry deaths, 264
Drishi-matra, 221
DSM-IV. *See Diagnostic and Statistical Manual
    of Mental Disorders*
Dyspareunia, 143
Dysthymic disorder, 151, 215

East Indian culture, 73. *See also Dhat*
    syndrome
  cultural meaning systems, 23
  and dissociative disorders, 227, 275–276
  dominance hierarchies in, 42, 43, 44, 50,
    263–264
  and eating disorders, 152
  exorcism, 278–279
  and illness duration, 273–274
  and mood disorders, 210–211

East Indian culture (*continued*)
  and personality development, 49–50
  and personality disorders, 100, 107
  psychosocial environment in, 67–68
  and psychotic disorders, 243, 245, 252
  and somatoform disorders, 193–195
  and substance-related disorders, 162–163
Eating disorders, 149–156
  anorexia nervosa, 150, 152
  and body dysmorphic disorder, 150
  bulimia nervosa, 151
  clinical guidelines, 154–156
  and mood alteration, 149, 153
Ecological question, 58–59, 61
Economic development, 262–263. *See also*
    Industrialized societies; Westernization
EE. *See* Expressed emotion
Egalitarianism, 40–44, 50–51, 115, 119–120
Egocentrism, 39–40, 51–52, 53, 207, 250. *See*
    also Sociocentrism
Egyptian culture, 180–181
Emic categories of experience, 20
Emotion, 55–62
  cognitive model, 56–58, 172–173, 174,
    179–180
  and cultural assessment, 58–60, 72
  cultural constructionist view of, 56
  example, 60–62
  and treatment, 77–78
Emotional feeling stage of emotion, 57–58, 61
Environmental stress. *See* Stress
Ethnic hierarchies. *See* Racial/ethnic
  hierarchies
Etic categories of experience, 20
Evocative function of cultural meaning
  systems, 24
Exhibitionism, 125–127
Existential shift, 83
Exorcism, 278–279
Explanatory models, 35–36, 66–67
Expressed emotion (EE), 250, 274
Extraordinary science, 15–16
Eye contact, 70

Fago, 205
Falling out, 237
False memory syndrome, 234
Female dominance, 114
Female orgasmic disorder, 142–143
Female sexual arousal disorder, 141–142
Fetishism, 127–128, 131
Final common pathways, 168
First-rank symptoms of schizophrenia,
  247–248
Flow experiences, 216
Folk healers, 37–38, 66
  and coherence, 79, 80, 81
  and dissociative disorders, 228, 231, 233
  and psychotic disorders, 245, 253–254
  and somatoform disorders, 194
  symbolic healing, 81, 82–89

Frotteurism, 128
Fundamentalist Christianity, 116–117

GAD. *See* Generalized anxiety disorder
Gender differences, 6. *See also* Gender hierarchies
Gender hierarchies, 53, 72
  and anxiety disorders, 185–186
  and eating disorders, 153
  and emotion, 173
  and mood disorders, 202
  and paraphilias, 125
  and personality disorders, 105, 106, 107, 109
  and sexuality, 114–120, 142
  and stress, 263–264
  and substance-related disorders, 165
Gender identity, 136
Gender identity disorder (GID), 113, 134–138
Gender reassignment surgery, 134, 137
Gender role behavior, 136
Gender status, 135
Generalized anxiety disorder (GAD), 178–179
Genetic factors
  stress, 174, 181, 267–268
  substance-related disorders, 159–160, 167
Genital mutilation, 116
Ghosts. *See* Hearing voices; Spirit possession
GID. *See* Gender identity disorder
Grandiose delusions, 208, 215
Grisi siknis, 224–225, 238
Guilt, 52, 58, 204

Haitian culture, 238
Hallucinations, 103. *See also* Psychotic
  disorders
  auditory, 74–75, 225
  and dissociative disorders, 225, 235–237
  and mood disorders, 208, 214, 215
Harangue, 50–51
Healing of memories, 87, 88
Healing vs. curing, 31–33
Hearing voices, 74–75, 225
Hierarchical societies. *See* Dominance
  hierarchies
Hinduism, 50, 100, 205, 210–211, 216
  and psychotic disorders, 245, 246
Hispanic cultures, 70, 154
  and anxiety disorders, 176–177, 183–184
  and dissociative disorders, 228–229, 231
  and psychotic disorders, 253, 254–255
Histrionic personality disorder, 105
Homosexuality, 119, 123–124, 137–138
Honor, 61
Hope, therapeutic use of, 78
Hwa-bung, 185–186
Hypnosis, 223
Hypoactive sexual desire disorder, 138–140
Hypochondriasis, 196–197
Hypomanic episode, 210–211, 216
Hypotheses, 13
Hysteria, 193–195. *See also* Briquet's syndrome

Icons, 21
Idioms of distress, 29, 59, 164, 277
Illness vs. disease, 6, 7, 31–32, 37–38
    assessment of, 64–67
Immigrants, 63, 68–69
Indexes, 21
India. *See* East Indian culture
Indisposition, 238
Individualism. *See* Egocentrism
Individual rights, 49
Indonesian culture, 229
Industrialized societies, 41, 151, 262–263. *See
    also* U.S. society
Infibulation, 116
Inguh, 65
Inis Beag culture, 120–121, 139, 141–142, 144
Initial appraisal stage of emotion, 57, 61, 88
Initiation ceremonies, 4–48, 104
Intentionality, 17–18
International Classification of Diseases (ICD-6)
    (WHO), 7, 193
International Pilot Study of Schizophrenia, 242
Interpreters, 69–70
Interviewing techniques, 70
Irish culture, 120–121, 162
Islamic societies, 116, 180–181

Japanese culture, 42–43, 52, 107
    and anxiety disorders, 178, 185
    and substance-related disorders, 162, 164
Jewish culture, 108–109, 196, 198

Karma, 50
Kenya, 73
Kindling effects, 213–214, 267
Klismaphilia, 134
Korean culture, 162, 185–186
Koro, 179, 184–185

Lalomweiu, 205
Latah, 229
Learned helplessness, 172–173
Learning, neurobiology of, 4–5
Legal systems, 115–116
Lengeh, 65
Liminality, 47, 104
Lithium, 80–81
Liyemam, 205
Long-term potentiation (LTP), 269–270

Made feelings, 225
Made impulses, 225
Made volitional acts, 225
Magical thinking, 100–102
Mahus, 137, 138
Major depressive disorder, 202, 211–214
Major depressive disorder with psychotic
    features, 214
Major depressive episode, 202–208
Malaysian culture, 59, 179, 184–185, 229, 230
Male erectile disorder, 143–144

Male orgasmic disorder, 144
Malumbar, 65
Manageability, 80–81
Management question, 60, 62
Mangaian culture, 121–122, 127, 129, 141, 142,
    145
Mania, 80–81
Manic episode, 208–209
Marijuana, 165
Marriage, 115, 117
Marxist theory, 40
Masochism. *See* Sexual masochism
Masturbation, 125. *See also* Paraphilias;
    Sexuality
Masturbatory conditioning, 126, 127, 131
Meaningfulness, 81–82, 88
Medical industry, 160
Medications, 4, 90, 145, 203
    neuroleptic, 5, 89, 279–280
Medieval Europe, 36
Medusa's Hair (Obeyesekere), 244
Mehinaku culture, 125
Mental disorders. *See also specific disorders and
    topics*
    anthropological approaches, 5–6
    biopsychosocial paradigm, 8
    defined, 3
    holistic conceptions of, 4
    meanings, 33–36
Micronesian culture, 58–59, 205–206
Middle Eastern cultures, 70
Mind-brain, 268
Minnesota Multiphasic Personality Inventory
    (MMPI), 103, 104
Miskito Indian culture, 224–225, 238
Mixed episode, 209
MMPI. *See* Minnesota Multiphasic Personality
    Inventory
Models, 13
Modernism, 45, 97
Modern societies, 44. *See also* U.S. society
    and eating disorders, 151
    and personality disorders, 48–49, 103–104
Moksha, 222
Mood disorders, 201–218
    and anxiety disorders, 171–172
    bipolar disorders, 72, 202, 208, 210, 211, 214,
        215–216
    clinical guidelines, 217–218
    cyclothymic disorder, 210, 216–217
    and dominance hierarchies, 201–202
    dysthymic disorder, 151, 215
    hypomanic episode, 210–211
    major depressive disorder, 202, 211–214
    major depressive episode, 20–208
    manic episode, 208–209
    mixed episode, 209
    and substance-related disorders, 166
        167
Moral career, 42, 106–107, 173, 201
Movement disorders, 5

Multiple personality disorder. *See* Dissociative identity disorder

Narcissistic personality disorder, 43, 52, 105–106
Native American cultures, 70, 87, 154, 184
  and dissociative disorders, 224–225, 229–230, 238
  and mood disorders, 207–208
  and substance-related disorders, 161, 162
Natural attitude, 20
Natural law, 49
Navaho Nation, 161
Necrophilia, 133
Nepal, 86
Nervios, 183–184
Neurasthenia, 12, 191–192
Neuroleptic medications, 5, 89, 279–280
Neuroses, 95, 96
New Guinean cultures, 122–124
Ngamuk, 65
Ngumbang, 65
Ngumikmik, 65
Nigerian culture, 179
Noetic poles, 18
Nonindustrial societies. *See* Nonwestern societies; Premodern societies
Nonwestern societies, 63, 79–80, 107, 129, 152, 182. *See also* Folk healers; Noninindustrial societies; Premodern societies; *specific societies*
Normal science, 12
Nyeh, 65

Object-in-itself, 18
Object intrusion, 65
Obsessive-compulsive disorder (OCD), 179–181
Obsessive-compulsive personality disorder, 43, 108–109
OCD. *See* Obsessive-compulsive disorder
Old age, 213
Orgasmic reconditioning, 128
Outcomes, culture-based, 30–31, 280
Outline for Cultural Formation (DSM-IV), 62–63, 64, 67, 69, 71

Pain disorder, 195–196
Pak, 205
Paling, 65
Panic attacks, 175
Panic disorder, 176–177
Pansexuality, 119
Paradigms, 12–17. *See also specific paradigms*
  and anomalies, 13–15
  crisis in, 15–16
  shifts, 16
Paranoid personality disorder, 98–99
Paranoid schizophrenia, 242
Paraphilias, 113, 124–134
  exhibitionism, 125–127

fetishism, 127–128, 131
frotteurism, 128
and male orgasmic disorder, 144
pedophilia, 128–130
sexual masochism, 130–131, 133, 134
sexual sadism, 131–132, 133, 134
transvestic fetishism, 132, 137
voyeurism, 132–133
Partialism, 13–134
Passing, 42–43
Pedophilia, 128–130
Perception, 17–18
Performance anxiety, 143
Persecutory delusions, 215
Personality development, 39–54
  and adolescence, 46–49
  and anxiety disorders, 178
  cross-cultural overview, 49–54
  and depression, 173
  and dominance hierarchies vs. egalitarianism, 40–44
  and modern vs. premodern meaning systems, 44–45
  and postmodernism, 45–46
  and sociocentrism vs. egocentrism, 39–40
  and substance-related disorders, 165–168
Personality disorders, 53, 95–111
  antisocial, 43, 52, 102, 166, 167
  and anxiety disorders, 178
  avoidant, 42, 106–107, 150, 178, 276–277
  and biopsychosocial paradigm, 96–97
  borderline, 43, 48–49, 103–105, 166, 167
  clinical guidelines, 109–111
  dependent, 42, 107–108, 276–277
  and dominance hierarchies, 42, 43, 50
  histrionic, 105
  narcissistic, 43, 52, 105–106
  obsessive-compulsive, 43, 108–109
  paranoid, 98–99
  schizoid, 99–100
  schizotypal, 100–102
Personal/social meanings, 34–35
Personal space, 70
Peyote, 162
Phenomenology, 16–20
Phobias, 177–178
Pibloktoq, 224–225, 229
Polygyny, 115
Polynesian cultures, 121–122, 137, 138, 141
Positivism, 73
Possession trance, 67–68, 74, 209
  and dissociative disorders, 221, 226, 227–228, 230, 238, 275–276
  exorcism, 278–279
  and illness duration, 273–274
Postmodernism, 11, 45–46
Posttraumatic stress disorder (PTSD), 99, 181–182
Premature ejaculation, 144–145

Premodern societies, 44–45, 50, 51. *See also* Nonwestern societies
  adolescence in, 47–48
  and anxiety disorders, 182–183
  and dissociative disorders, 226, 231–232, 237
  and mood disorders, 209, 216
  and personality disorders, 101, 109
  and psychotic disorders, 4, 248–251
  and somatoform disorders, 191
Primary role identification, 41–42
Primate cultures
  dominance hierarchies, 114, 115, 117–119
  and paraphilias, 126, 129, 133
Psychic unity theory, 5–6
Psychoses, 95
Psychosocial environment, 67–69
Psychotic disorders, 10, 241–259, 263
  anomalies, 14
  brief, 253–256
  clinical guidelines, 257–259
  cultural differences, 242–246, 248–251, 274–275
  and cultural meaning systems, 23
  delusional disorder, 256
  and dissociative disorders, 225, 232, 235–237, 246–248, 255–256
  and mood disorders, 214, 215
  neuroleptic medications, 5, 89, 279–280
  schizoaffective disorder, 214, 251–252
  schizophreniform disorder, 253–256
  shared, 256–257
  and stereotypes, 72
  and substance-related disorders, 166
Psychotropic medications, 4, 90
PTSD. See Posttraumatic stress disorder
Puerto Rican society, 162
Pusing, 65

Race/ethnicity. *See also specific ethnic groups*
  and eating disorders, 153–154
  hierarchies, 41, 43–44, 52, 53, 197–198
Rape, 118
Reaction, 8
Reality testing, loss of, 95–96, 241
Refugees, 182
Reification, 19–20
Reliability, 9–10
Religion, 65, 87–89, 220. *See also* Folk healers; *specific topics and cultures*
  and anxiety disorders, 180
  and dissociative disorders, 232–233
  and dominance hierarchies, 115, 116–117, 124
  and eating disorders, 152
  and mood disorders, 209
  and obsessive-compulsive personality disorder, 108–109
  and psychotic disorders, 245–246, 254
  and sexuality, 120, 121, 124, 180

Representational function of cultural meaning systems, 21–22
Role-playing, 276

Sadism. *See* Sexual sadism
Sambian culture, 122–124, 129, 130
Samun, 65
Satanic ritual abuse syndrome, 233–234
Saudi culture, 161–162
Scandinavian cultures, 248
Schemas. *See* Cognitive schemas; Cultural schemas
Schizoaffective disorder, 214, 251–252
Schizoid personality disorder, 99–100
Schizophrenia, 4, 5, 10, 23, 242–251
  anomalies, 14
  and bipolar disorders, 215
  cultural differences, 242–246, 248–251, 274–275
  and dissociative disorders, 225, 235, 236–237, 246–248
  and stereotypes, 72
  and substance-related disorders, 166
  subtypes, 242
Schizophrenia: An International Follow-up Study (WHO), 242
Schizophreniform disorder, 253–256
Schizotypal personality disorder, 100–102
Self-esteem, 42, 150, 152
  and personality disorders, 103, 106
Semantic question, 59, 62
Semicooperative male dominance, 115
Senoi Temiar, 50–51, 59, 106
Sexual abuse, 140, 143, 167, 181
  and dissociative disorders, 231–232, 234–235
  and psychotic disorders, 255
Sexual aversion disorder, 140–141
Sexual dysfunctions, 113, 138–145
  dyspareunia, 143
  female orgasmic disorder, 142–143
  female sexual arousal disorder, 141–142
  hypoactive sexual desire disorder, 138–140
  male erectile disorder, 143–144
  male orgasmic disorder, 144
  premature ejaculation, 144–145
  sexual aversion disorder, 140–141
  vaginismus, 143
Sexuality, 48, 70. *See also* Paraphilias; Sexual dysfunctions
  and anxiety disorders, 180
  clinical guidelines, 145–147
  cultural variations, 120–124
  dhat syndrome, 28–29, 30, 31–33, 35
  and dominance hierarchies, 114–124, 125, 142
  and psychosocial environment, 67–68
Sexual masochism, 130–131, 133, 134
Sexual preference, 136
Sexual sadism, 131–132, 133, 134
Shamans. *See* Folk healers
Shared psychotic disorder, 256–257

Social phobia, 177–178
Social regulation question, 59–60, 62
Sociobiology, 117–118, 125
Sociocentrism, 39–40
    and emotion, 58–59, 205
    examples, 49–51, 52
    and personality disorders, 101, 109
    and psychotic disorders, 250
Soma, 162–163
Somatization, 60, 203–204, 205, 277. *See also*
        Somatoform disorders
Somatization disorder, 103, 190–191
Somatoform disorders, 12, 189–200
    and anxiety disorders, 171–172, 174, 181,
        189
    body dysmorphic disorder, 150, 197–198
    clinical guidelines, 198–200
    conversion disorder, 192–195
    hypochondriasis, 196–197
    pain disorder, 195–196
    somatization disorder, 103, 190–191
    undifferentiated, 191–192
South African cultures, 256
South Asian cultures, 83–86, 205, 208, 227-228.
    See also East Indian culture
Southeast Asian cultures, 60–62, 63, 65, 182,
    230
Specific phobias, 177
Spirit possession. *See* Possession trance
Spiritual healing, 87
State dependent brain alterations, 11
Stereotypes, 63–64, 72
Stigmatization. *See* Dominance hierarchies;
    Moral career
Stress, 262–268
    and anxiety disorders, 174–175, 181–182
    and brain plasticity, 213–214, 265–267
    and dissociative disorders, 224, 225,
        226–227, 234–235
    and economic development, 262–263
    and gender hierarchies, 263–264
    genetic factors, 267–268
    and highly focused attention, 264
    and mood disorders, 173, 213–214
    and personality disorders, 99, 103
    posttraumatic stress disorder, 99, 181–182
    and psychotic disorders, 251, 263
    and substance-related disorders, 166–167
    and trauma spectrum disorders, 265
Structured diagnostic interview schedules, 73
Subjective experience, culture-based, 27–28
Substance abuse, 157–158
Substance dependence, 158, 164–165
Substance intoxication, 157
Substance-related disorders, 157–170
    American Disease Model, 158–159, 160
    classification of, 157–161
    clinical guidelines, 168–170
    cultural differences, 161–165
    and personality development, 165–168

Substance withdrawal, 158
Suicide, 206–207, 213, 264
Susto, 184
Swat Pukhtun culture, 51–52, 58, 59, 276
    and personality disorders, 52, 99, 102, 106
Sweat Lodge ceremony, 87
Symbolic healing, 81, 82–89, 176–177, 232, 255
Symbols, 21, 82–83
Symptoms as symptoms, 33–34

Taijin kyofusho, 178, 185
Taiwanese culture, 72, 230
Tang lanal, 205
Tardive dyskinesia, 5
Taxonomic question, 58, 61
Telephone scatologia, 133
Theories, 13
Thinking behaviors, 271
Trance. *See also* Dissociation
    as adaptation, 219–221
    as focused attention, 221–223
    and mood disorders, 209, 21–211, 216
    and sexual abuse, 141
    and somatoform disorders, 193
    and symbolic healing, 84–85
Transformational symbols, 82–83
Transvestic fetishism, 132, 137
Trauma. *See* Stress
Trauma spectrum disorders, 265
Treatment, 77–91
    clinical guidelines, 90–91
    coherence, 78–82
    culture-based, 30, 277–280
    of culture-bound syndromes, 37–38
    and emotion, 77–78, 88
    side effects, 5, 89–90
    symbolic healing, 81, 82–89
Tuning effects, 213–214, 270–272

Undifferentiated schizophrenia, 242, 243
Undifferentiated somatoform disorder,
    191–192
United States. *See* U.S. society
U.S. society, 52–53, 70
    American Disease Model of addiction,
        158–159, 160, 164
    and anxiety disorders, 178
    and dissociative disorders, 230, 233–235,
        237, 276
    dominance hierarchies in, 41, 43–44, 116–117
    and mood disorders, 207
    and personality disorders, 99, 102, 107–
        108
    psychosocial environment, 72
    and psychotic disorders, 251
    and sexual dysfunctions, 142, 143, 144, 145
    and substance-related disorders, 161–162,
        163
Upregulation, 5, 89
Urophilia, 134

Vaginismus, 143
Validity, 11–12
Veterinary clinical style, 31
Violence, 41, 50, 51
   amok, 60–62, 63, 65
   and class hierarchies, 53
   and dominance hierarchies, 123, 124
   and paraphilias, 130–132
   and substance-related disorders, 163
Voyeurism, 132–133

West African cultures, 179, 232–233, 253–254, 257
Westernization, 63, 137, 154
   and mood disorders, 206–207, 208, 211

Yoga meditation, 221–223
Yoga-Sutra, 221, 222
Yolmo Sherpa culture, 86

Zoophilia, 134

Meanings of Madness

by RICHARD J. CASTILLO, University of Hawaii—West Oahu

Approximately 280 pages. Paperback. ISBN: 0-534-34560-3. 1997. Available Fall 1996.

An ideal companion for Castillo's *Culture and Mental Illness: A Client-Centered Approach*

This book of readings explores the variety of meanings that mental illness or "madness" can possess and takes into account the current move to expand the traditional medical paradigm to include social and cultural factors in the diagnosis of mental disorders.

This text can serve as a companion volume for *Culture and Mental Illness: A Client-Centered Approach* (also by Richard J. Castillo) or in conjunction with other works on the subject. The 29 articles include illustrations, examples, and case studies that augment the topics discussed in Castillo's main text. Most of the articles are based on ethnographic research or case studies and have appeared in journals of psychiatry, neuroscience, anthropology, and psychology.

Features

- *Meanings of Madness* provides a brief but comprehensive introduction to the study of culture and mental illness.
- In addition to the text's many recent articles, a few "classics" in the field are included.
- Authors of the articles are some of the most influential authorities in the fields of anthropology, psychiatry, psychology, sociology, and neuroscience, including: Arthur Kleinman, Horacio Fabrega, Juan E. Mezzich, Byron Good, Marvin Karno, Nancy Scheper-Hughes, Laurence J. Kirmayer, Spero M. Manson, Joseph Westermeyer, Allan Young, Wolfgang G. Jilek, Wen-Shing Tseng, Theresa D. O'Nell, J. David Kinzie, Thomas J. Csordas, Roger W. Sperry, Janice Hunter Jenkins, Theodore Lidz, L.A. Rebhun, and Marina Roseman.
- Each chapter begins with an introduction that highlights the central points made by each author.

Contents

1. Culture and Psychiatry
2. Culture and Clinical Reality
3. Culture and Personality Development
4. Sociocultural Assessment of Mental Illness
5. Culture and Psychotherapy
6. Culture and Personality Disorders
7. Culture, Social Organization, and Sexuality
8. Culture and Eating Disorders
9. Culture and Alcoholism
10. Culture and Anxiety
11. Culture and Somatization
12. Culture and Depression
13. Culture and Dissociation
14. Culture and Schizophrenia
15. Culture, Mind-Brain, and Mental Illness

(For U.S. college customers only, a discount bundle of Castillo's *Culture and Mental Illness: A Client Centered Approach* with *Meanings of Madness* is available. Bundle ISBN: 0-534-86304-3)

Use form on next page to purchase this book or to obtain a review copy!

Order Form

___ Yes! I want to order Meanings of Madness, by Richard J. Castillo, ISBN: 0-534-34560-3 for $19.00 net*.

___ Yes! Please send me a complimentary review copy of *Meanings of Madness,* by Richard J. Castillo for adoption consideration as a _____ required _____ recommended text

for my course: _____
                    (course number) (course title)

that I teach at: _____
                    (school name)

Residents of: AL, AZ, CA, CT, CO, FL, GA, IL, IN, KS, KY, LA,   **Copies Ordered** _____

MA, MD, MI, MN, MO, NC, NJ, NY, OH, PA, RI,   **Subtotal** _____

SC, TN, TX, UT, VA, WA, WI must add appropriate   **Tax** _____

state sales tax.   **Handling** $4.00

   Total Due _____

Payment options:

_____ Check or money order enclosed or bill my

_____ VISA

_____ MasterCard   **Mail to:**

_____ American Express   **Brooks/Cole Publishing Company**

   Dept. 7BCPY Offer

Card Number: _____   511 Forest Lodge Road

   Pacific Grove, California 93950

Expiration Date: _____   Phone: (408) 373-0728

   Fax: (408) 375-6414

Signature: _____

Please ship my order or review copy to: (please print)

Name _____

Institution_____

Street Address _____

City _____ State _____ Zip+4 _____+_____

Telephone (___)_____

Your credit card will not be billed until your order is shipped. We will refund payment for unshipped out-of-stock titles after 120 days and for not-yet-published titles after 180 days unless an earlier date is requested in writing from you.

*Prices are subject to change.   9/96